P. Kramer
G. John
D. Schenzle

**Group Theory and
the Interaction of
Composite Nucleon
Systems**

Clustering Phenomena in Nuclei

Edited by
K.Wildermuth
P. Kramer

Volume 2

Volume 2
Kramer/John/Schenzle
Group Theory and the Interaction
of Composite Nucleon Systems

P. Kramer

G. John

D. Schenzle

Group Theory and the Interaction of Composite Nucleon Systems

With 40 Figures

Vieweg

CIP-Kurztitelaufnahme der Deutschen Bibliothek

Kramer, Peter:
Group theory and the interaction of composite
nucleon systems/P. Kramer; G. John; D. Schenzle.
− Braunschweig, Wiesbaden: Vieweg, 1980.
  (Clustering phenomena in nuclei; Vol. 2)
  ISBN 3-528-08449-9

NE: John, Gero; Schenzle, Dieter

1981

Set by Vieweg, Braunschweig
Printed by Lengericher Handelsdruckerei, Lengerich
Bookbinder: W. Langelüddecke, Braunschweig
Cover design: Peter Morys, Salzhemmendorf
Printed in Germany-West

ISBN 3-528-08449-9

Preface

The study which forms the second volume of this series deals with the interplay of groups and composite particle theory in nuclei. Three main branches of ideas are developed and linked with composite particle theory: the permutational structure of the nuclear fermion system, the classification scheme based on the orbital partition and the associated supermultiplets, and the representation in state space of geometric transformations in classical phase space.

One of the authors (P. K.) had the opportunity to present some of the ideas underlying this work at the 15th Solvay Conference on Symmetry Properties of Nuclei in 1970. Since this time, the authors continued their joint effort to decipher the conceptual structure of composite particle theory in terms of groups and their representations. The pattern of connections is fully developed in the present study. The applications are carried to the points where the impact of group theory may be recognized. The range of applications in our opinion goes far beyond these points.

We appreciate the criticism, suggestions and contributions with respect to this work offered by the members of our institute. In particular, we would like to mention here K. Wildermuth, M. Brunet and W. Sünkel. Our work was shaped in many respects through presentations and discussions at other institutions. We are indebted in particular to M. Moshinsky and to A. Grossmann for their criticism. It is a pleasure to acknowledge Mrs. S. El Sheikh, Mrs. I. Roser and Mrs. R. Adler for their assistance in preparing the manuscript. Finally we thank the Verlag Vieweg for its excellent cooperation and for the get-up of this book.

Peter Kramer
Gero John
Dieter Schenzle

Tübingen, Germany
August 1980

Contents

1 Introduction

In composite particle theories of nuclear structure and reactions one tries to understand those aspects of the nuclear many-body system which originate from the internal structure and the interaction of subsystems of the full system. These subsystems or clusters will be called composite particles. The full system with a specified subdivision will be called a composite nucleon system. If the internal states of the subsystems are assumed to be given, it is possible to study the interaction of the composite particles which arises from the two-body interaction of their constituents.

The introduction of such subsystems is indespensable for the theory of nuclear reactions since the specification of a reaction channel necessarily presupposes a splitting of the full system into at least two separate subsystems. In the analysis of nuclear structure, the composite particle theories compete with other theories as for example the nuclear shell model. In the nuclear shell theory, the nucleons occupy states of a single nucleon. For the lowest excitations in the harmonic oscillator model it is well-known that the shell and composite particle theories yield the same states. The difference of the theories appears with increasing excitation and in the reaction theory. If the excitations are chosen from the composite particle configurations, they involve selective and non-spurious states which are not easily recognized in the shell theory. With respect to the transition from the reaction region to the reaction channels, the composite particle theories provide a smooth and analytic connection up to the full separation of the system. A description of the separated states in a single-center shell theory would be of no physical interest.

The development of the composite particle theory into a unified theory of the nucleus is treated in the first volume of this series by Wildermuth and Tang [WI 77]. For the interplay between theory and experiment we refer to the proceedings of the three conferences on Clustering Phenomena held at Bochum in 1969, at Maryland in 1975 and at Winnipeg in 1977 [IA 69, GO 75, OE 78].

The subdivision of the system of A nucleons implied by composite particle theories may be conceived in a geometric setting. The 3 A coordinates of the system fix a point in configuration space, and the (orbital) state of the system may be taken as a complex-valued function defined on this configuration space. The introduction of geometric transformation groups in configuration space and their representations by operators in state space is the starting point of the present investigation. The analysis to be presented follows three branches whose common origin is found in the composite particle theory.

The first branch of ideas arises in relation to permutational structure. When we spoke of the subdivision of the system of A nucleons, we did not mention the correlations in the system implied by the fermion nature of the nucleons. The permutations act as geometric transformations with respect to coordinates or to spin-isospin variables. They are the elements of the symmetric group. The fermion nature of the nucleons requires the full state to be antisymmetric under the application of permutations. A first notion of composite particle theory that comes into play is the set of occupation numbers for the chosen composite particle configuration. Associated with this set of occupation numbers is the subgroup of the symmetric group which comprises all internal permutations. For the interaction of two possibly different composite particle configurations, there appear two such groups of internal permutations. The attempt to extract from any permutation to the right and to the left all factors which belong to these two subgroups leads to the concept of exchange. In terms of group theory, the remaining part of the general permutation generates a double coset of the symmetric group with respect to the two subgroups mentioned. These double cosets are abstractly characterized by a set of integers. In terms of physics, they describe the transfer of particles under a permutation within the limits given by the occupation numbers.

The second branch of ideas is centered around the separation of the orbital and the spin-isospin part of the system, the supermultiplet scheme, and the specific properties of orbital states. In the orbital state space, the permutations act as unitary operators. By the application of projection or Young operators, the orbital state space may be broken into the smallest or invariant subspaces with respect to the application of orbital permutations. These irreducible subspaces are characterized by partitions or Young diagrams. With certain restrictions on the partitions, the basis of any such orbital subspace may be coupled in a uniquely defined way with a set of spin-isospin states into an antisymmetric state. The set of spin-isospin states comprises various pairs of the total spin and isospin and is called a supermultiplet. Thus, there are many different and in fact orthogonal states which provide overall antisymmetry. The relation of composite particle theory to this supermultiplet scheme arises as a selection rule among the supermultiplets. The set of occupation numbers of the composite particle configuration restricts the orbital partitions and hence the supermultiplets. It is found that this restriction is fully in line with the structure of low-lying states at least of the light nuclei. Expressed differently, the degrees of freedom associated with the relative motion of composite particles support a supermultiplet model space of physical content.

The next branch of ideas stems from the geometry of classical phase space. The classical canonical description of the A-body system would employ the 6 A-dimensional phase space. The geometry of classical phase space admits translations of position and momentum and linear canonical transformations. The linear canonical transformations are called symplectic since they preserve the symplectic form associated with the Poisson bracket. Whereas the classical phase space does not support the states of quantum mechanics, at least in its standard version, the geometric transformations of classical phase space are represented as unitary operators in state space. These representations allow us to implement new types of geometric transformations or to find a geometric origin for operators encountered in state space.

Associated with phase space is a second aspect of interest. Instead of the real position and momentum variables ξ and π, we are free to use an equivalent pair of complex conjugate numbers $\sqrt{\frac{1}{2}}(\xi \mp i\pi)$ as coordinates of phase space. In quantum mechanics, these combinations yield the oscillator creation and annihilation operators. The abstract commutation and adjoint properties of these operators have been employed by Bargmann to introduce, instead of the familiar Schrödinger representation, a concrete Hilbert space of analytic functions which is unitarily equivalent to the one used by Schrödinger. By construction, this Hilbert space admits an extremely simple description of oscillator states which resembles the standard formalism of creation operators. We work entirely in the Bargmann representation since it provides very transparent analytic expressions when working with oscillator states.

The geometric transformations of phase space play an important role in our analysis of composite particle interaction. We adopt a description of the internal states of composite particles by non-spurious oscillator shell configurations, and we show that the interaction of the composite particles is obtained from configurations where each oscillator shell configuration has been translated with respect to both position and momentum. The symplectic transformations of phase space appear in the form of transformations of coordinates from the single-particle to the composite particle picture, in the dilatation of states and in the interpretation of operators acting in state space.

The first two branches of ideas related to permutational structure, the supermultiplet scheme and the orbital partition are treated in sections 2 and 3. The third branch associated with the geometry of phase space and the harmonic oscillator is exposed in sections 4 and 5.

In section 6, we consider the basic equations of the composite particle theory. These equations are obtained as a set of coupled complex integral equations for the states associated with the relative motion of composite particles. In these integral equations there appear two types of kernels. The first type called normalization kernel reflects the properties of the fermion system and of the chosen internal states on the level of the composite particle system. Considerable insight into the structure of composite particle configurations may already be obtained from these kernels. The second type of kernel called interaction kernel represents the composite particle interaction obtained from the microscopic hamiltonian. We prove a key result on these kernels which allows us to interpret them as matrix elements of the identity or hamiltonian operator in a many-body configuration based on single-particle states whose centers are subject to translations in phase space. This result may be considered as the branching point of the ideas mentioned earlier.

With this framework of concepts, techniques and explicit results we study the structure and interaction of specific composite particle configurations. In section 7 we consider configurations of several simple composite particles. The term simple refers to the assumption of an internally unexcited oscillator state. In section 8 we restrict the consideration to at most two composite particles but admit more general internal states ranging from closed to open-shell states. In section 9 we apply the dilatation operators to achieve a change of radius for the internal state. Section 10 contains a very detailed study of configurations of three simple clusters applied to the states of the lightest nuclei.

Our presentation presupposes from the part of nuclear physics a knowledge of the basic equations of composite particle theory as it may be obtained from the first part of the monograph by Wildermuth and Tang [WI 77]. From the part of group theory we require a knowledge of some basic concepts which are best known from the example of the rotation group. For a condensed account of these concepts we refer to a recent book by Dal Cin and one of the authors of this volume, [KR 80]. The applications to composite particle theory require the introduction of new concepts in the representation theory of the groups under consideration. These new concepts and techniques are fully developed in the present contribution up to the explicit numerical calculation. To make these techniques accessible we give a number of illustrative examples in each section. Most sections contain an introduction on the concepts and motivation underlying the exposition. Additional notes and references are collected at the end of the sections.

2 Permutational Structure of Nuclear States

2.1 Concepts and Motivation

One of the fundamental properties of nuclear systems is that they are composed out of fermions. The variety of nuclear phenomena related to this property can hardly be overestimated. In the present section we elaborate some tools for a more detailed analysis of this property.

In non-relativistic quantum mechanics the fermion property of the state $|\psi\rangle$ of n nucleons requires that the application of a permutation, represented in the Hilbert space of the n-body system by a unitary operator $U(p)$, to the state $|\psi\rangle$ yields

$$U(p)\,|\psi\rangle = |\psi\rangle\,(-1)^p,$$

where $(-1)^p$ is the sign of the permutation (i.e. plus one for even, minus one for odd permutations). The sign clearly obeys the composition law

$$(-1)^{pp'} = (-1)^p\,(-1)^{p'}.$$

If now to an arbitrary state one applies the antisymmetrizer defined as

$$A = [n!]^{-1/2} \sum_{p'} (-1)^{p'}\,U(p'),$$

the new state is automatically a fermion state since by purely algebraic properties of A one finds

$$U(p)\circ A = [n!]^{-1/2} \sum_{p'} (-1)^{p'}\,U(p)\circ U(p') = [n!]^{-1/2} \sum_{p''} (-1)^p\,(-1)^{p''}\,U(p'') = A\,(-1)^p.$$

In these equations, $U(p)$, $U(p')$ and $U(p'') = U(pp')$ stand for permutation operators acting in the Hilbert space of the n-body system.

The more detailed study of permutational properties which will be discussed in the following sections arises by considering separately the degrees of freedom associated with coordinates, spins and isospins, We call the part of the n-body state depending on coordinates the orbital state and the part depending on spins and isospins the spin-isospin state.

If any orbital state $|\psi\rangle$ of n nucleons is given, the application of n! orbital permutations p provides altogether n! states $U(p)|\psi\rangle$. Clearly the application of any additional permutation p' will carry $U(p)|\psi\rangle$ into

$$U(p')\circ U(p)\,|\psi\rangle = U(p'p)\,|\psi\rangle,$$

which is already contained in the original set of n! states. It follows that the n! states $U(p) \, |\psi\rangle$ span a linear subspace which is invariant with respect to the application of permutations. With respect to a basis the operators $U(p)$ then form what is called a finite-dimensional representation of the permutation group $S(n)$. The whole point of the concept of irreducible representation is the search for smaller invariant subspaces which cannot be further decomposed and show characteristic transformation properties under permutations. The simplest invariant irreducible subspaces of this type are those which are generated by the symmetrizer or by the antisymmetrizer. More general spaces will be characterized in section 2.3 and constructed by use of Young operators in section 2.4. For the moment is suffices to state that each characteristic transformation property is labeled by a partition $f = [f_1 f_2 \ldots f_j]$ of n into integers in decreasing order. To each partition f there belongs a set of basis or partner states labeled by an additional index r. Basis states which differ in the orbital partition f or in the index r are orthogonal to each other. It should be noted that this orthogonality can be proved from properties of the representation without invoking eigenvalues of a set of hermitian operators.

A similar construction may be carried out for the states depending on spin and isospin. There is a partition which characterizes the spin-isospin state, and gives rise to a number of pairs ST of the total spin S and the total isospin T, which together form a spin-isospin supermultiplet [WI 37]. This construction will be considered in section 2.6.

To construct antisymmetric states from orbital and spin-isospin states one applies a coupling procedure. It turns out that for a given orbital partition f there is precisely one partition $\hat{f}$ of the spin-isospin state which allows coupling to an overall antisymmetric state. The coupling is achieved by summing over the indices r and $\hat{r}$ associated with f and $\hat{f}$ with appropriate simple coupling coefficients.

The physically allowed orbital partitions may be ordered on the basis of the supermultiplet scheme. For a given orbital partition $f = [f_1 f_2 \ldots f_j]$ one may compute the eigenvalue of the operator

$$\sum_{s < t} \frac{1}{2} (1 + U(p_{s,t}))$$

to obtain the eigenvalue

$$q^f = \frac{1}{4} n(n-1) + \frac{1}{4} [f_1(f_1 - 1) + f_2(f_2 - 3) + \ldots + f_j(f_j - 2j + 1)],$$

which is largest for a low number j of components and increases with j. The operator counts the number of symmetric orbital pairs. For spin-isospin independent central interactions the orbital partition is a rigorous quantum number and it turns out that the orbital partitions in light nuclei appear in energetical order with increasing values of q^f. This property, which essentially arises from the fact that the central interactions favour symmetric orbital pairs, is the basis of the supermultiplet approximation for light nuclei. Franzini and Radicati [FR 63] discussed a mass formula which mainly uses the eigenvalues q^f, expressed through the four components of the associate partition $\hat{f}$. For the p-shell nuclei the validity and refinement of this scheme was discussed in [JO 73]. We shall treat these results in section 2.8.

The approximate validity of the supermultiplet scheme clearly shows that for low-lying nuclear states there are leading orbital partitions f characterized by large values of q^f. It is natural then to look for a construction procedure which provides these partitions from the outset. A procedure of this type is implicit in all of the composite particle methods for nuclear systems. In these methods one always chooses orbital configurations which are invariant under orbital permutations belonging to subsets of $w_1 w_2 \ldots w_j$ nucleons. We briefly sketch here the steps which will be implemented in the following sections in order to cast this intuitive approach into an explicit method within the framework of the super-multiplet classification. Given a state $|\psi)$ which is invariant under permutations of a sub-group

$$S(w) = S(w_1) \times S(w_2) \times \ldots \times S(w_j)$$

of the symmetric group $S(n)$, we must modify the reasoning given at the beginning of this section. The number of possible states which can be reached by the application of permuta-tion operators $U(p)$ is clearly

$$\nu(w) = n! \left[\prod_{i=1}^{j} w_i! \right]^{-1}.$$

A subset of permutations c_i which generates these $\nu(w)$ states in the form

$$U(c_i) |\psi)$$

is given in terms of the left coset generators of the subgroup $S(w)$ in $S(n)$. These left coset generators will be described in section 2.2. In the next step we must reduce the linear subspace spanned by the basis of these $\nu(w)$ states into its parts irreducible under $S(n)$ and characterized by orbital partitions f. We mention one important feature of this con-struction which will be given in sections 2.3 and 2.4: The irreducible subspaces belong to partitions of at most j components and therefore a small number of sets w_i automatically leads to orbital partitions f with large values of q^f. One difference should be noted: The labels $w_1 w_2 \ldots w_j$ do not lead to an orthogonal characterization of the states, but the "induced" partitions f of course provide orthogonal quantum numbers.

Another important physical idea related to the orbital permutations is the concept of exchange. Consider the collision of two composite nuclear systems. One would like to classify the outgoing amplitudes according to the number of particles exchanged. More precisely, one may ask how the nucleons comprising the first fragment before collision are distributed among the fragments after collision. The concept of double cosets of the sym-metric group is the appropriate tool to deal with this situation, and we shall develop this concept in the following sections. In particular it is necessary to link the double coset con-cept with the representation theory of the symmetric group in order to discuss exchange properties for the nuclear fermion system.

The following examples illustrate some considerations of this introductory section:

Example 2.1: States of six nucleons

Mathematically there are the 11 orbital partitions [6] [51] [42] [411] [33] [321] [3111] [222] [2211] [21111] [111111]. The first two of these are not admissible for nuclear states since the corresponding partitions $\hat{f}$ have more than four rows. The remaining partitions are grouped by the eigenvalues q^f in their natural order. Among the states of six nucleons, only the partitions [42] [411] [33] [321] play a role. For these we list the eigenvalues of q^f, the associate partition $\hat{f}$ and the ST-content in the following table:

f	[42]	[411]	[33]	[321]
q^f	10	9	9	7,5
$\hat{f}$	[2211]	[3111]	[222]	[321]
ST	10,01	00,11	00,11	10,20,11,21,01,02,12.

In the standard nuclear shell model, only the first two orbital partitions are accomodated by the $s^4 p^2$ configuration. The other partitions appear in cluster configurations describing, for example, negative parity states of ^{6}Li as shown in section 10.

Example 2.2: Exchange in the six-nucleon system

In the collision of a deuteron and a ^{4}He nucleus with ^{3}H and ^{3}He as outgoing fragments there are three types of exchange: The nucleons comprising the deuteron may both join the ^{3}He, or may separately join the ^{3}He and ^{3}H respectively, or may both join the ^{3}H. It is convenient to set up a square symbol which describes the redistribution of the nucleons. In this square symbol, the column sums give the numbers of nucleons for the ingoing fragments while the row sums give the numbers of nucleons in the outgoing fragments. The three cases have the following square symbols:

$$\begin{Bmatrix} 3 & 0 \\ 1 & 2 \end{Bmatrix} \begin{Bmatrix} 2 & 1 \\ 2 & 1 \end{Bmatrix} \begin{Bmatrix} 1 & 2 \\ 3 & 0 \end{Bmatrix}.$$

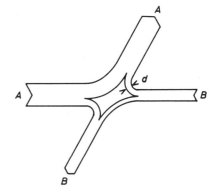

Fig. 2.1

Exchange in the elastic reaction
A + B → A + B. The distance d is a
measure for the number of nucleons
transferred from B to A and hence
a measure of the exchange type.

2.2 The Symmetric Group S (n)

Consider a set Ω of n elements which we denote as 1 2 ... n. The set of all bijections $\Omega \to \Omega$ is the symmetric group S (n) of order

$$|S(n)| = n!.$$

Its elements, the permutations of n elements, we denote by small letters p, h, z ... We discuss now various ways of specifying a given bijection $p \in S(n)$.

First we consider the graph of the bijection p: $\Omega \to \Omega$. If two copies of the set Ω are used to label the columns and rows of an n × n square lattice, the lattice positions may be used to denote the elements of the cartesian product $\Omega \times \Omega$. Each element of $\Omega \times \Omega$ is characterized by its column and row number which serve as a pair of discrete cartesian coordinates. The graph of the bijection p is the subset of elements of $\Omega \times \Omega$ which correlates $l \in \Omega$ with its image $p(l) \in \Omega$. We choose to display the original points l horizontally along the columns and the image points $p(l)$ vertically along the rows of the square $\Omega \times \Omega$ and mark the graph of p by the points in column l and row $p(l)$ for $l = 1\ 2\ldots n$. Clearly the graph of the bijection p^{-1} inverse to p is obtained from the graph of p by reflection with respect to the main diagonal of the square representing $\Omega \times \Omega$.

From this form of the graph of p it is simple to pass to a representation of S(n) by $n \times n$ permutation matrices. To find d(p) we associate the positions of the square representing $\Omega \times \Omega$ with the positions in an $n \times n$ matrix. Into this matrix we insert the entry "1" at all positions belonging to the graph of p and the entry "0" at all other positions. The resulting matrix d(p) has elements

$$d_{il}(p) = \delta_{i, p(l)} \qquad i, l = 1\ 2\ldots n,$$

and it is easy to verify that d is a representation of S(n), that is,

$$d(e) = I_n, d(p'p'') = d(p')\, d(p''), d(p^{-1}) = d^{-1}(p).$$

Moreover, the representation is orthogonal since the inverse p^{-1} of p by construction is represented by the matrix which is the transposed of d(p).

A third condensed way of representing the graph of the bijection p: $\Omega \to \Omega$ is obtained by giving a list of the elements of $\Omega \times \Omega$ belonging to the graph of p. For typographical reasons, we write such a list as a two-row symbol

$$p: \begin{bmatrix} p(s) \\ s \end{bmatrix} = \begin{bmatrix} p(1)\, p(2)\ldots p(n) \\ 1 \quad\ 2 \ \ldots\ n \end{bmatrix} = \begin{bmatrix} 1 \qquad 2 \quad\ \ldots \quad\ n \\ p^{-1}(1)\, p^{-1}(2)\ldots p^{-1}(n) \end{bmatrix}.$$

The graph of p is easily reconstructed from this list by marking in the square representing $\Omega \times \Omega$ the n positions with column numbers l and row numbers $p(l)$ respectively for $l = 1\ 2\ldots n$. Alternatively, the graph is obtained by marking the positions with row number i and column number $p^{-1}(i)$ for $i = 1\ 2\ldots n$. The constructions are illustrated by fig. 2.2 and by the following example.

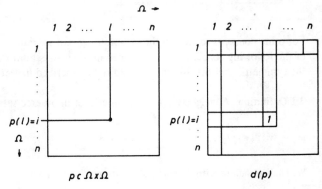

Fig. 2.2

Correspondence between the graph of the permutation p as a subset of the direct product $\Omega \times \Omega$ and the permutation matrix d(p).

Example 2.3: Representation of some elements of S(3)

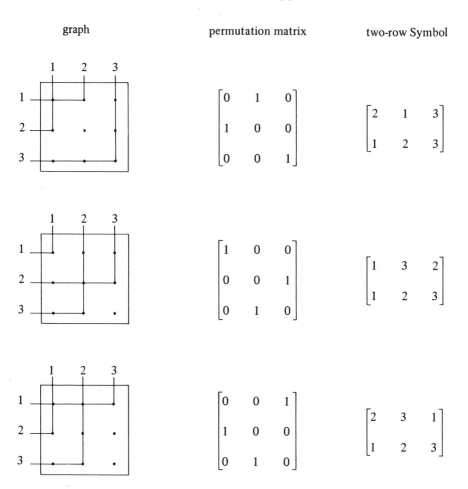

graph   permutation matrix   two-row Symbol

For other concepts related to the symmetric group we refer to Hamermesh [HA 62]. Some of the following concepts are introduced in order to exhibit the correspondence between the symmetric and the full linear group to be described in section 3.

2.1 Definition: A weight **w** of the number n is an ordered set of j non-negative integers

$$w = (w_1 w_2 \ldots w_j), \quad \sum_{i=1}^{j} w_i = n.$$

We shall associate with a weight a partition of the set Ω.

2.2 Definition: A σ-partition $P(\Omega)$ of the set Ω is a collection of j disjoint subsets $\Sigma_1 \Sigma_2 \ldots \Sigma_j$ of Ω such that

$$\Omega = \Sigma_1 \dot{+} \Sigma_2 \dot{+} \ldots \dot{+} \Sigma_j.$$

The stability group $S(P)$ of the σ-partition $P(\Omega)$ is the subgroup of all bijections which transform any subset Σ_i of $P(\Omega)$ into itself.

We add a few simple but important remarks on σ-partitions. The term σ-partition is used to distinguish this concept of set theory from an ordered weight of the number n which we shall call a partition. Clearly a σ-partition is characterized by the number of elements selected for each subset and by the specification of the subset elements. If two partitions $P(\Omega), P'(\Omega)$ coincide up to order in the number of elements for their subsets, there exists a bijection p of Ω such that $P'(\Omega) = pP(\Omega)$ where

$$pP(\Omega) = p\Sigma_1 \dot{+} p\Sigma_2 \dot{+} \ldots \dot{+} p\Sigma_j$$

and $p\Sigma_i$ is the image of the subset Σ_i under p. The stability groups of the two partitions are then related by conjugation,

$$S(P') = pS(P)p^{-1}.$$

From two σ-partitions

$$P' = \Sigma_1' \dot{+} \Sigma_2' \dot{+} \ldots \quad P'' = \Sigma_1'' \dot{+} \Sigma_2'' \dot{+} \ldots$$

one may construct a new σ-partition

$$(P' \cap P'')(\Omega) = \sum_{i,\,l} \Sigma_i' \cap \Sigma_l''.$$

The stability group of this new σ-partition is clearly

$$S(P' \cap P'') = S(P') \cap S(P'').$$

2.3 Definition: Given a weight $w = (w_1 w_2 \ldots w_j)$ of n, the standard σ-partition P_w is defined as

$$P_w(\Omega) = \Sigma_1 \dot{+} \Sigma_2 \dot{+} \ldots \dot{+} \Sigma_j,$$

where the subset Σ_i consists of the w_i elements $w_1 + \ldots + w_{i-1} + 1, w_1 + \ldots + w_{i-1} + 2, \ldots,$ $w_1 + \ldots + w_{i-1} + w_i$ of Ω. The stability group of the standard σ-partition P_w is called the group of the weight w,

$$S(w) = S(w_1) \times S(w_2) \times \ldots \times S(w_j),$$

its order is

$$|S(w)| = w! = \prod_{i=1}^{j} (w_j!).$$

The permutation matrix $d(h)$ for elements h of $S(w)$ clearly breaks into diagonal blocks of dimension equal to the components of the weight w.

We shall now consider a weight w and a weight w^q whose components take the same values but appear in different order.

2.4 Definition: Let w be a weight of j components and q a permutation of $S(j)$. Then the weight w^q obtained from $w = (w_1 w_2 \ldots w_j)$ as

$$w^q = (w_{q^{-1}(1)} \, w_{q^{-1}(2)} \cdots w_{q^{-1}(j)})$$

is called the permuted weight $\tilde{w}$.

From the weight w, the permutation q of $S(j)$ and the permuted weight $\tilde{w} = w^q$ we construct now the graph of a permutation $p(q, w)$ of $S(n)$. Since the weights w and $\tilde{w}$ partition the number n, they may be used to subdivide the n columns and rows respectively of the square lattice representing $\Omega \times \Omega$ into j sets of columns and j sets of rows. To these subdivisions there corresponds a subdivision of the square lattice into $j \cdot j$ in general non-square blocks. The index pair l and i associated with the weight components w_l and $\tilde{w}_i$ of w and $\tilde{w} = w^q$ may be used to label the position of the corresponding $\tilde{w}_i \times w_l$ block. The block positions are in one-to-one correspondence to the positions within the $j \times j$ square lattice which describes the graph of the permutation q. For $i = q(l)$ the corresponding block of $\Omega \times \Omega$ is a square of dimension $\tilde{w}_{q(l)} \times w_l$. Now we define a graph as the subset of points of $\Omega \times \Omega$ on the diagonal positions within these square blocks for $l = 1 \, 2 \ldots j$. In this construction we allow formally for weight components $w_r = 0$ which do not contribute to the graph of $p(q, w)$. It is easy to see that the graph constructed in this way describes a bijection $\Omega \to \Omega$.

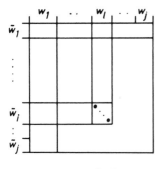
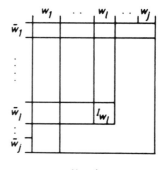

$$p(q,w) \subset \Omega \times \Omega \qquad\qquad d(q,w)$$

Fig. 2.3 Correspondence between the graph of the permutation $p(q, w)$ and its permutation matrix $d(q, w)$. The columns and rows of the direct product $\Omega \times \Omega$ and of the matrix d are partitioned according to the weight $w = (w_1 w_2 \ldots w_j)$ and the permuted weight

$$\tilde{w} = (\tilde{w}_1 \tilde{w}_2 \ldots \tilde{w}_j) = (w_{q^{-1}(1)} \, w_{q^{-1}(2)} \cdots w_{q^{-1}(j)}).$$

2.5 Definition: The permutation p constructed from the weight w, the permutation q and the permuted weight $\tilde{w} = w^q$ will be denoted as $p(q, w)$ and its permutation matrix by

$$d(q, w) = d(p(q, w)).$$

We construct now a two-row symbol for the permutation $p(q, w)$.

2.6 Definition: Given a weight w of n, we denote by $n_1, n_2, \ldots, n_j$ the ordered sets

$$n_1 = 1\ 2 \ldots w_1$$
$$n_2 = w_1 + 1\ \ w_1 + 2 \ldots w_1 + w_2$$
$$\cdot$$
$$\cdot$$
$$\cdot$$
$$n_j = n - w_j + 1\ \ n - w_j + 2 \ldots n.$$

2.7 Proposition: Consider the ordered sets according to definition 2.6 for the weight w and the permuted weight $w^q = \tilde{w} = (\tilde{w}_1 \tilde{w}_2 \ldots \tilde{w}_j)$. Then the two-row symbol of the permutation $p(q, w)$ is given by

$$\begin{bmatrix} p(s) \\ s \end{bmatrix} = \begin{bmatrix} \tilde{n}_{q(1)} & \tilde{n}_{q(2)} & \cdots & \tilde{n}_{q(j)} \\ \tilde{n}_1 & \tilde{n}_2 & \cdots & \tilde{n}_j \end{bmatrix}.$$

Proof: Consider again the n × n square lattice which was used to define the graph of the permutation $p(q, w)$. By construction, the image of the ordered set n_l under p is the ordered set $\tilde{n}_{q(l)}$ belonging to the weight component $\tilde{w}_{q(l)}$ of the weight $\tilde{w} = w^q$. Writing this relation as

$$\tilde{n}_{q(l)} = p n_l$$

and using the sets to write a two-row symbol we find for $p(q, w)$

$$\begin{bmatrix} p(1)\ p(2) \ldots\ p(n) \\ 1 \quad 2 \ \ldots\ \ n \end{bmatrix} = \begin{bmatrix} \tilde{n}_{q(1)}\ \tilde{n}_{q(2)} \cdots \tilde{n}_{q(j)} \\ \tilde{n}_1 \quad \tilde{n}_2 \ \ldots\ \tilde{n}_j \end{bmatrix}. \qquad \square$$

2.8 Proposition: The permutation inverse to $p(q, w)$ has the two-row symbol

$$\begin{bmatrix} p^{-1}(s) \\ s \end{bmatrix} = \begin{bmatrix} n_{q^{-1}(1)}\ n_{q^{-1}(2)} \cdots n_{q^{-1}(j)} \\ n_1 \quad n_2 \quad \ldots \quad n_j \end{bmatrix}.$$

Proof: The inverse permutation is obtained by reflection of the graph of p in the main diagonal. Clearly this reflection is equivalent to the interchange of the weights w and $\tilde{w} = w^q$ and to replacing the permutation q by its inverse q^{-1}. $\qquad \square$

Note that proposition 2.8 may also be used to write

$$\begin{bmatrix} s \\ p^{-1}(s) \end{bmatrix} = \begin{bmatrix} n_1 \quad n_2 \quad \ldots n_j \\ n_{q^{-1}(1)}\ n_{q^{-1}(2)} \cdots n_{q^{-1}(j)} \end{bmatrix}.$$

This type of expressions will be given in the following examples.

2.9 Proposition: For q and r elements of $S(j)$ and a given weight w, the permutations $p'(r, w^q)$ and $p''(q, w)$ obey the multiplication rule

$$p = p'p'' = p'(r, w^q) p''(q, w) = p(rq, w).$$

Proof: Consider the graphs of $p'(r, w^q)$ and $p''(q, w)$. Note that the column division for the graph of $p'(r, w^q)$ matches the row division for the graph of $p''(q, w)$. From this observation it is easy to show that the composition $p'p''$ corresponds to the composition rq of the permutations of weight components. The column and row partitioning of p is associated with the weights w and $(w^q)^r$ and inherited from p' and p'' respectively. Since $(w^q)^r = w^{rq}$, the graph of $p = p'p''$ is associated with the weight w, the permutation rq of $S(j)$ and the permuted weight w^{rq}.   □

2.10 Proposition: The stability groups of the σ-partitions P_w and P_{wq} associated with the weights w and w^q are conjugate subgroups of $S(n)$ related by $p = p(q, w)$,

$$S(w^q) = p\, S(w)\, p^{-1}.$$

Proof: The σ-partitions P_w and P_{wq} have subsets of equal order. By construction, the permutation p^{-1} for $p = p(q, w)$ maps the subsets of P_{wq} into the subsets of P_w. Hence the permutation p transforms by conjugation the stability group $S(w)$ into the stability group $S(w^q)$.   □

Example 2.4: Permutation of weights in a system of n = 6 objects

Consider the weight $w = (3\ 2\ 1)$ of $n = 6$. As r and q choose the permutations of example 2.1. Then $w^q = (3\ 1\ 2)$ and $(w^q)^r = (1\ 3\ 2)$. We display the permutation matrices for the permutations of $S(3)$ and $S(6)$ and their products.

$$d(q) = \begin{bmatrix} 1 & 0 & 0 \\ 0 & 0 & 1 \\ 0 & 1 & 0 \end{bmatrix} \qquad d(q, w) = \begin{bmatrix} I_3 & 0 & 0 \\ 0 & 0 & I_1 \\ 0 & I_2 & 0 \end{bmatrix}$$

$$d(r) = \begin{bmatrix} 0 & 1 & 0 \\ 1 & 0 & 0 \\ 0 & 0 & 1 \end{bmatrix} \qquad d(r, w^q) = \begin{bmatrix} 0 & I_1 & 0 \\ I_3 & 0 & 0 \\ 0 & 0 & I_2 \end{bmatrix}$$

$$d(q^{-1}) = \begin{bmatrix} 1 & 0 & 0 \\ 0 & 0 & 1 \\ 0 & 1 & 0 \end{bmatrix} \qquad d^{-1}(q, w) = \begin{bmatrix} I_3 & 0 & 0 \\ 0 & 0 & I_2 \\ 0 & I_1 & 0 \end{bmatrix}$$

$$d(rq) = \begin{bmatrix} 0 & 0 & 1 \\ 1 & 0 & 0 \\ 0 & 1 & 0 \end{bmatrix} \qquad d(rq, w) = \begin{bmatrix} 0 & 0 & I_1 \\ I_3 & 0 & 0 \\ 0 & I_2 & 0 \end{bmatrix}$$

The two-row form of these permutations is indicated in the following lines. We write the two-row symbol in the form explained after proposition 2.8. The ordered sets n_i are separated by vertical bars.

$$d(q, w) : \begin{bmatrix} 1 & 2 & 3 & | & 4 & 5 & | & 6 \\ 1 & 2 & 3 & | & 6 & 4 & | & 5 \end{bmatrix}$$

$$d(r, w^q) : \begin{bmatrix} 1 & 2 & 3 & | & 4 & 5 & 6 \\ 4 & | & 1 & 2 & 3 & | & 5 & 6 \end{bmatrix}$$

$$d^{-1}(q, w) : \begin{bmatrix} 1 & 2 & 3 & | & 4 & | & 5 & 6 \\ 1 & 2 & 3 & | & 5 & 6 & | & 4 \end{bmatrix}$$

$$d(rq, w) : \begin{bmatrix} 1 & 2 & 3 & | & 4 & 5 & | & 6 \\ 6 & | & 1 & 2 & 3 & | & 4 & 5 \end{bmatrix}.$$

The following concepts deal with pairs of subgroups associated with two different weights of n.

2.11 Definition: A double coset of a group G with subgroups $\widetilde{H}$, H is a set of group elements of the form

$$\widetilde{H}gH = \{\widetilde{h}gh | \widetilde{h} \in \widetilde{H}, h \in H\}.$$

Note that for $\widetilde{H}$ or H being the identity subgroup the double cosets become the left and right cosets respectively for the non-trivial subgroup. For the concept compare [HA 59].

2.12 Proposition: The double cosets of a group G with subgroups $\widetilde{H}$, H yield a partition of G, taken as a set. The number of different pairs $\widetilde{h}$, h for which

$$g = \widetilde{h}gh$$

is given by

$$m(g) = |\widetilde{H} \cap gHg^{-1}| = |g^{-1}\widetilde{H}g \cap H|$$

that is, by the order of the subgroups of G appearing in these equations.

Proof: The relation of two elements of G which are in the same double coset is easily seen to be an equivalence relation. Then it follows [RO 75, vol. 1, p. 15] that the double cosets yield a partition of G. Consider now the equation $g = \widetilde{h}gh$ in G which may be written as

$$\widetilde{h}(ghg^{-1}) = e.$$

From this equation it follows that $\widetilde{h}$ and h are related by the equations

$$\widetilde{h}^{-1} = ghg^{-1}, \quad \widetilde{h} = gh^{-1}g^{-1}.$$

These equations are solved by all elements $\tilde{h}$ which belong both to the subgroups $\tilde{H}$ and gHg^{-1} of G. The elements with this property are simply the elements of the subgroup $\tilde{H} \cap gHg^{-1}$ of G and their number is given by the order of this subgroup. Noting that the order of a subgroup is unchanged under conjugation, we get finally for the number of different elements $\tilde{h}$

$$m(g) = |\tilde{H} \cap gHg^{-1}| = |g^{-1}\tilde{H}g \cap H|. \qquad\qquad\qquad\qquad \square$$

The following concepts describe the double cosets of the symmetric group with respect to subgroups related to weights [KR 69, KR 69a, KR 72].

2.13 Definition: Consider two weights $\tilde{w} = (\tilde{w}_1 \tilde{w}_2 \ldots \tilde{w}_{\tilde{\jmath}})$ and $w = (w_1 w_2 \ldots w_j)$ of n. A double coset symbol is a $\tilde{\jmath} \times j$ matrix k with non-negative integer elements $k_{i l}$ such that

$$\sum_{l=1}^{j} k_{i l} = \tilde{w}_i, \quad \sum_{i=1}^{\tilde{\jmath}} k_{i l} = w_l.$$

We shall denote the matrices k by numbers in curly brackets. The following two propositions relate the double coset symbols to the double cosets. For the proofs we refer to [KR 72].

2.14 Proposition: Consider the subgroups $S(\tilde{w})$ and $S(w)$ of the group $S(n)$ associated with the weights $\tilde{w}$ and w. The double cosets of these two subgroups are in one-to-one correspondence to the different double coset symbols for the weights $\tilde{w}$ and w.

2.15 Proposition: For a given permutation p with permutation matrix $d(p)$, partition the columns according to the weight w and the rows according to the weight $\tilde{w}$ and label the corresponding blocks as $b_{i l}$ where i and l are the component indices of the weights $\tilde{w}$ and w respectively. The double coset symbol k for the double coset generated by p has entries $k_{i l}$ equal to the sum of all matrix elements of $d(p)$ within the block $b_{i l}$.

2.16 Definition: For the weights $\tilde{w}$ and w and for a given double coset $k = (k_{i l})$, the refined weights $w(k)$ and $\tilde{w}(k)$ are defined as

$$w(k) = (k_{11}k_{21} \ldots k_{\tilde{\jmath}1} k_{12}k_{22} \ldots k_{\tilde{\jmath}2} \ldots k_{1j}k_{2j} \ldots k_{\tilde{\jmath}j}),$$
$$\tilde{w}(k) = (k_{11}k_{12} \ldots k_{1j}k_{21}k_{22} \ldots k_{2j} \ldots k_{\tilde{\jmath}1} k_{\tilde{\jmath}2} \ldots k_{\tilde{\jmath}j}).$$

These weights contain the same $\tilde{\jmath} \cdot j$ components in different order. We define a permutation $q(k)$ of $S(\tilde{\jmath} \cdot j)$ which rearranges the order of the components of $w(k)$ into the order of $\tilde{w}(k)$. This permutation $q(k)$ acts on the weights according to definition 2.4,

$$\tilde{w}(k) = (w(k))^{q(k)}.$$

The refined weights may be read off the double coset symbol k in the following manner: To get the components of $w(k)$, we follow the entries in the first, second ... up to the jth column of the matrix k. To get the components of $\tilde{w}(k)$, we follow the entries in the rows of k from the first to the $\tilde{\jmath}^{th}$ row.

2.17 Proposition: For two subgroups $S(\tilde{w})$ and $S(w)$ of $S(n)$, the double coset with symbol k is generated by the permutation z_k defined as

$$z_k = p(q(k), w(k))$$

according to definition 2.5.

Proof: The situation differs from the one considered in the construction of definition 2.5 since the weights w and $\tilde{w}$ are no longer assumed to have the same components. Through the introduction of the refined weights $w(k)$ and $\tilde{w}(k)$ we recover two weights with the same components. Associated with the refined weights are refined standard σ-partitions of the form

$$P_{w(k)} = \Sigma_{11} \dotplus \Sigma_{21} \dotplus \ldots \dotplus \Sigma_{\tilde{j}1} \dotplus \Sigma_{12} \dotplus \Sigma_{22} \dotplus \ldots \dotplus \Sigma_{\tilde{j}2} \dotplus \ldots \dotplus \Sigma_{1j} \dotplus \Sigma_{2j} \dotplus \ldots \dotplus \Sigma_{\tilde{j}j},$$

$$P_{\tilde{w}(k)} = \Sigma_{11} \dotplus \Sigma_{12} \dotplus \ldots \dotplus \Sigma_{1j} \dotplus \Sigma_{21} \dotplus \Sigma_{22} \dotplus \ldots \dotplus \Sigma_{2j} \dotplus \ldots \dotplus \Sigma_{\tilde{j}1} \dotplus \Sigma_{\tilde{j}2} \dotplus \ldots \dotplus \Sigma_{\tilde{j}j}.$$

As explained in the proof of proposition 2.7, the ordered sets associated with the refined weights are related by $\tilde{n}_{q(il)} = z_k n_{il}$. Note that the permutation q now acts on objects labelled by two indices. In terms of the graph of z_k we deduce that there are precisely k_{il} elements belonging to the subset Σ_l of P_w whose images under z_k belong to the subset $\tilde{\Sigma}_i$ of $P_{\tilde{w}}$. Hence the graph of z_k contains k_{il} points in the block b_{il} introduced in proposition 2.15. From this proposition it follows that the permutation z_k belongs to the double coset (symbol) k.   □

Note that with the help of proposition 2.7 we could write down the two-row symbol of the generator z_k in terms of ordered sets associated with the refined weights $w(k)$ or $\tilde{w}(k)$. For an explicit computation compare example 2.5.

2.18 Proposition: For the subgroups $S(\tilde{w})$ and $S(w)$ of $S(n)$, the multiplicity $m(k)$ introduced in proposition 2.12 for the double coset k generated by z_k is given by

$$m(k) = k! = \prod_{i=1}^{\tilde{j}} \prod_{l=1}^{j} (k_{il}!).$$

Proof: From the remarks on σ-partitions following definition 2.2 one concludes that the group $S(\tilde{w}) \cap z_k S(w) z_k^{-1}$ is the stability group of the σ-partition

$$P_{\tilde{w}} \cap z_k P_w = \sum_{i=1}^{\tilde{j}} \sum_{l=1}^{j} \tilde{\Sigma}_i \cap z_k \Sigma_l.$$

As part of the refined σ-partition $P_{w(k)}$, the subset Σ_l has the decomposition

$$\Sigma_l = \Sigma_{1l} \dotplus \Sigma_{2l} \dotplus \ldots \dotplus \Sigma_{\tilde{j}l}.$$

Under z_k, the only elements whose images are in the subset $\tilde{\Sigma}_i$ are the ones belonging to Σ_{il} and hence

$$\tilde{\Sigma}_i \cap z_k \Sigma_l = \tilde{\Sigma}_i \cap z_k \Sigma_{il} = \tilde{\Sigma}_{il}.$$

It follows that we may identify

$$P_{\widetilde{w}} \cap z_k P_w = P_{\widetilde{w}(k)}$$

where $P_{\widetilde{w}(k)}$ is the standard σ-partition associated with $\widetilde{w}(k)$, and hence the stability group associated with this σ-partition is the group of the refined weight $\widetilde{w}(k)$. Its order yields the multiplicity $m(z_k) = m(k)$ in the form

$$m(k) = |S(k_{11}) \times S(k_{12}) \times \ldots \times S(k_{1j}) \times S(k_{21}) \times \ldots \times S(k_{\widetilde{j}j})|$$

$$= \prod_{i=1}^{\widetilde{j}} \prod_{l=1}^{j} (k_{il}!). \qquad\qquad \square$$

If one of the two weights $\widetilde{w}$ or w has all its components equal to one, the associated group of the weight is the identity subgroup. Then the double cosets reduce to cosets. For later application it proves useful to introduce a special notation for a coset. For $S(\widetilde{w})$ being the subgroup consisting of the identity element we introduce a special notation and write the generators of the left cosets of the subgroup $S(w)$ as c_i. Note that now the multiplicity associated with representing a given element p as

$$p = c_i h$$

is $m(i) = 1$ for all left cosets which means that the element h is fixed by p.

Example 2.5: Double cosets and their generators for the subgroup $S(6)$ and the weights $\widetilde{w} = (4 \ 2)$ and $w = (3 \ 3)$.

The double coset symbols are given by the three 2×2 matrices

$$\begin{Bmatrix} 3 & 1 \\ 0 & 2 \end{Bmatrix}, \quad \begin{Bmatrix} 2 & 2 \\ 1 & 1 \end{Bmatrix}, \quad \begin{Bmatrix} 1 & 3 \\ 2 & 0 \end{Bmatrix}.$$

The refined weights $\widetilde{w}(k)$ and $w(k)$ have four components. For the second double coset we have

$$w(k) = (2 \quad 1 \quad 2 \quad 1)$$
$$\widetilde{w}(k) = (2 \quad 2 \quad 1 \quad 1).$$

In all three cases the permutation $q(k)$ associated with the relation $\widetilde{w}(k) = (w(k))^{q(k)}$ belongs to $S(4)$ and is given by

$$q: \begin{bmatrix} 1 & 3 & 2 & 4 \\ 1 & 2 & 3 & 4 \end{bmatrix}.$$

For the three double cosets we write down the generators in terms of ordered sets of numbers separated by bars. We find

$$z_1 = \begin{bmatrix} 1 & 2 & 3 \ | \ 4 \ | \ 5 & 6 \\ 1 & 2 & 3 \ | \ 4 \ | \ 5 & 6 \end{bmatrix}$$

$$z_2 = \begin{bmatrix} 1 & 2 \ | \ 3 \ | \ 4 & 5 \ | \ 6 \\ 1 & 2 \ | \ 4 & 5 \ | \ 3 \ | \ 6 \end{bmatrix}$$

$$z_3 = \begin{bmatrix} 1 \ | \ 2 & 3 \ | \ 4 & 5 & 6 \\ 1 \ | \ 4 & 5 & 6 \ | \ 2 & 3 \end{bmatrix}.$$

Note that both in z_1 and z_3 there appear components of the refined weights of value 0 so that the effective number of ordered sets is reduced from four to three.

2.3 Irreducible Representations of the Symmetric Group S(n)

In this section we survey the irreducible representations of the symmetric group. We shall start from general concepts and propositions valid for any finite group, then treat the standard representation theory of the symmetric group and finally develop those aspects of the representation theory which are of particular importance for many-body states.

2.19 Definition: A linear representation of a group G with elements g is a homomorphism of G into the group of linear operators on a complex linear space. An irreducible representation is a representation which has no proper invariant subspace.

We denote the linear operators of a representation by

$$g \to d(g).$$

The homomorphism properties read

$$d(g'g'') = d(g') d(g'') \qquad \text{for all } g', g'' \in G$$
$$d(e) = I \qquad \text{for the unit element}$$
$$d(g^{-1}) = d^{-1}(g) \qquad \text{for all } g \in G.$$

2.20 Definition: For a finite group G we denote by $|G|$ the order of G and for an irreducible representation d^f by $|f|$ the dimension of the representation.

2.21 Theorem: All irreducible representations of a finite group G have finite dimension. Let $d^{\tilde{f}}$ and d^f denote a pair of irreducible representations of G in bases labeled by $\tilde{s}\tilde{t}$ or st respectively. Then the matrices of $d^{\tilde{f}}$ and d^f obey the orthogonality relations

$$\sum_{g \in G} |f| \, |G|^{-1} \, d^{\tilde{f}}_{\tilde{s}\tilde{t}}(g) \, d^f_{ts}(g^{-1}) = \delta(\tilde{f}, f) \, \delta(\tilde{s}, s) \, \delta(\tilde{t}, t) \, ,$$

$$\sum_{fst} |f| \, |G|^{-1} \, d^f_{st}(g') \, d^f_{ts}(g^{-1}) = \delta(g', g) = \begin{cases} 1 & \text{if } g' = g \\ 0 & \text{otherwise} \end{cases} .$$

In the second relation the sum runs over all irreducible representations of G.

For the proof see Hamermesh [HA 62, p. 101] and [BA 77a, p. 172].

2.22 Theorem: The irreducible representations of a finite group G can be chosen to be unitary, that is

$$(d^f)^{-1}(g) = (d^f)^+(g).$$

Proof: Hamermesh [HA 62, p. 92].

For the representation theory of the symmetric group S(n) we shall refer to the books of Hamermesh [HA 62] and Robinson [RO 61].

2.23 Definition: A partition f of n is a weight, the components of which are arranged in non-increasing order $f = [f_1 f_2 \ldots f_j]$

$$f_1 \geqslant f_2 \geqslant \ldots \geqslant f_j > 0, \quad \sum_{i=1}^{j} f_i = n.$$

The index j denotes the last non-vanishing component of f.

2.24 Definition: A Young diagram f is an arrangement of square boxes in rows of length $f_1 f_2 \ldots f_j$. The letter f will be used for both partitions and corresponding Young diagrams.

Example 2.6: Partitions and Young diagrams for n = 6

The Young diagrams corresponding to the partitions discussed in example 2.1 are given in the following fig. 2.4.

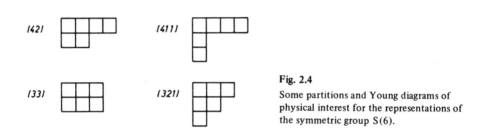

Fig. 2.4
Some partitions and Young diagrams of physical interest for the representations of the symmetric group S(6).

2.25 Theorem: The irreducible representations of the group S(n) are in one-to-one correspondence to the different partitions of n.

For the proof see Hamermesh [HA 62].

2.26 Definition: The irreducible representation corresponding to the partition f will be denoted by d^f, its matrix for a given permutation by $d^f(p)$ and its dimension by $|f|$.

Consider now the weight $w = (w_1 w_2)$ of n and the corresponding group $S(w_1) \times S(w_2)$. As the groups act on different sets Σ_{w_1} and Σ_{w_2}, their operations with respect to Σ_n commute and one has a direct product of two subgroups. From the general theory of representations it is well-known that the irreducible representations of direct product groups are given by the direct product of the irreducible representations of the direct factors [HA 62]. Therefore one has

2.27 Proposition: The irreducible representations of the group $S(w_1) \times S(w_2)$ are direct product matrices $d^{f_1} \times d^{f_2}$ characterized by a partition

$$f_1 = [f_{11} f_{21} \ldots f_{j_1 1}] \qquad \text{of } w_1 \text{ and a partition}$$

$$f_2 = [f_{12} f_{22} \ldots f_{j_2 2}] \qquad \text{of } w_2.$$

The next proposition deals with the reduction of the representation d^f of $S(n)$ when this representation is restricted or subduced to its subgroup $S(w_1) \times S(w_2)$.

2.28 Proposition: The irreducible representation d^f of $S(n)$ for $f = [f_1 f_2 \ldots f_j]$ under subduction to its subgroup $S(w_1) \times S(w_2)$ reduces into the irreducible representation $d^{f_1} \times d^{[w_2]}$ if and only if $f_1 = [f_{11} f_{21} \ldots f_{j_1 1}]$ is a solution of the inequalities

$$f_1 \geqslant f_{11} \geqslant f_2 \geqslant f_{21} \geqslant \ldots \geqslant f_{j-11} \geqslant f_{j1}.$$

Proof: This proposition is a special case of a general reduction theorem given by Robinson [RO 61, p. 61].

Proposition 2.28 gives only part of the reduction of d^f with respect to the subgroup since d^{f_2} of $S(w_2)$ was restricted to $f_2 = [w_2]$. We shall see that this special case is the most important one for the present purpose.

The inequalities appearing in proposition 2.28 are easily visualized by writing the numbers f_{i1} in a second row at a position between its boundary values f_i and f_{i+1}. The generalization of this type of pattern leads to

2.29 Definition: A Gelfand pattern q is a triangular arrangement of non-negative integers f_{il}, $l = 1\, 2 \ldots j - 1$ and $i = 1\, 2 \ldots l$ of the type

$$
\begin{array}{ccccccc}
f_{2j-1} & & f_{2j-1} & \cdots & & f_{j-2j-1} & f_{j-1j-1} \\
& f_{1j-2} & & f_{2j-2} & \cdots & f_{j-3j-2} & f_{j-2j-2} \\
& & f_{1j-3} & & \cdots & & f_{j-3j-3} \\
& & & \ddots & & \ddots & \\
& & & f_{12} & & f_{22} & \\
& & & & f_{11} & &
\end{array}
$$

with

$$f_{il} \geqslant f_{il-1} \geqslant f_{i+1l}, \quad 1 \leqslant i \leqslant l \leqslant j - 1.$$

2.30 Proposition: The irreducible representation d^f of $S(n)$ under subduction to $S(w) = S(w_1) \times S(w_2) \times \ldots \times S(w_j)$ contains the identity representation once for each Gelfand pattern q that fulfills the requirements

$$f_1 \geqslant f_{1j-1} \geqslant f_2 \geqslant f_{2j-1} \geqslant \ldots \geqslant f_{j-1j-1} \geqslant f_j$$

and $w_1 = f_{11}$,

$$\sum_{i=1}^{l} f_{il} - \sum_{i=1}^{l-1} f_{il-1} = w_l, \quad l = 2 \ldots j.$$

Proof: The proposition arises by repeated application of proposition 2.28. Starting first from the group $S(n)$ with representation d^f, subduction to the representation $d^{f_{j-1}} \times d^{[w_j]}$ of the subgroup $S(n - w_j) \times S(w_j)$ yields inequalities between the partitions f and f_{j-1}. Now consider the irreducible representation $d^{f_{j-1}}$ of $S(n - w_j)$ and its subduction to the irreducible representation

$$d^{f_{j-2}} \times d^{[w_{j-1}]} \quad \text{of} \quad S(n - w_j - w_{j-1}) \times S(w_{j-1}).$$

Iteration of this procedure gives a series of inequalities which finally involve the representation f_1 of the group $S(w_1)$. We are interested only in the representation $[w_1]$ of $S(w_1)$. If this choice is implemented in the inequalities considered so far, it yields $f_{i+1\,i} = 0$ for $i = 2\,3\ldots j - 1$. The remaining conditions are the inequalities implied by the Gelfand pattern q and by the inequalities between f and f_{j-1}. $\qquad\qquad\qquad\qquad\qquad\qquad\quad\Box$

If the representation d^f of $S(n)$ subduced with respect to $S(w_1) \times S(w_2)$ yields the representation $d^{f_1} \times d^{[w_2]}$, the Young diagram f_1 is, according to proposition 2.28, a subdiagram of the Young diagram f.

2.31 Definition: The skew diagram $f - f_1$ is the arrangement of boxes belonging to f but not to f_1. (Compare [RO 61, p. 48])

2.32 Definition: Let f be a partition of n and q a Gelfand pattern corresponding to f. A generalized Young tableau is defined by drawing all subdiagrams f_i of the diagram f and labeling each box of $f_i - f_{i-1}$ by the number i, each box of $f - f_{j-1}$ by the number j. For a Gelfand pattern belonging to the weight $w = (1\ 1\ \ldots 1)$, the generalized Young tableau is called a standard Young tableau.

We shall collect all explicit numerical results on the irreducible representations of $S(n)$ in section 2.5 and continue here in the derivation of general properties.

Our interest lies in the irreducible representations d^f of $S(n)$ reduced with respect to subgroups $S(\widetilde{w})$ and $S(w)$ belonging to weights $\widetilde{w}$ and w respectively.

2.33 Definition: A matrix element of the irreducible representation d^f of $S(n)$ is called left- and right-invariant with respect to the subgroups $S(\widetilde{w})$ and $S(w)$ if

$$d^f_{st}(\widetilde{h}ph) = d^f_{st}(p)$$

for all

$$\widetilde{h} \in S(\widetilde{w}), h \in S(w), p \in S(n).$$

2.34 Proposition: The left- and right-invariant matrix elements of $S(n)$ with respect to $S(\widetilde{w})$ and $S(w)$ are functions on the double cosets of $S(n)$. For given partition f these matrix elements are completely labeled by the pairs $\widetilde{q}q$ of Gelfand patterns belonging to the partition f and the weights $\widetilde{w}$ and w.

Proof: The first part is obvious from definition 2.33 and definition 2.11 of double cosets. The left-invariance of the matrix element implies that the row label S of d_{st}^f describes a scheme including the identity representation of the subgroup $S(\tilde{w})$. By proposition 2.30 the Gelfand pattern q for the weight $\tilde{w}$ gives an exhaustive description of this situation. The same reasoning applies to the right-invariance.　　　　　　□

Let $g \rightarrow a(g)$ be a complex-valued function on a group and

$$b = |G|^{-1} \sum_g a(g)$$

be the mean value of a on G. Given a double coset decomposition of G with respect to subgroups $\tilde{H}$ and H we get for this average

2.35 Proposition: The average of a on G under the double coset decomposition is given by

$$b = |G|^{-1} \sum_{\tilde{h} \in \tilde{H}} \sum_{h \in H} \sum_k m^{-1}(k)\, a(\tilde{h}\, z_k\, h).$$

Proof: In the average every group element g contributes the value $a(g)$. Since in the double coset decomposition

$$g = \tilde{h}\, z_k\, h$$

there are $m(k)$ pairs $\tilde{h}, h$ which yield the same element g, one must replace $a(g)$ by $m^{-1}(k)\, a(\tilde{h}\, z_k\, h)$ to get the same mean value under the change of the summation to double cosets and subgroup elements.　　　　　　□

2.36 Proposition: Consider subgroups $S(\tilde{w})$ and $S(w)$ of $S(n)$ for fixed weights $\tilde{w}$ and w and the set of left- and right-invariant matrix elements of the irreducible representations d^f of $S(n)$ labelled by Gelfand patterns $\tilde{q}$ and q according to proposition 2.34. These matrix elements obey the orthogonality relations

$$\sum_k \lambda_f^{-2}\, \tilde{w}!\, w!\, (k!)^{-1}\, d_{\tilde{q}q}^{\tilde{f}}(z_k)\, d_{q'\tilde{q}'}^{f}(z_k^{-1}) = \delta(\tilde{f}, f)\, \delta(\tilde{q}, \tilde{q}')\, \delta(q, q')$$

$$\sum_{f\tilde{q}q} \lambda_f^{-2}\, \tilde{w}!\, w!\, (k!)^{-1}\, d_{\tilde{q}q}^{f}(z_{k'})\, d_{q\tilde{q}}^{f}(z_k^{-1})$$

$$= \delta(k', k) = \begin{cases} 1 & \text{if the double cosets } k' \text{ and } k \text{ coincide} \\ 0 & \text{otherwise} \end{cases}$$

where

$$\lambda_f = \left[\frac{n!}{|f|}\right]^{1/2}.$$

Proof: According to proposition 2.17 we choose the permutations z_k as the generators of the double coset k. The first orthogonality relation of Theorem 2.21 applies to the group $S(n)$ for any choice of the row and column labels, and we choose these labels as Gelfand patterns $s = \tilde{q}$ $t = q$ $t' = q'$ $s' = \tilde{q}'$. Next we introduce the double coset decomposition for each element p of $S(n)$ and replace the sum over elements of $S(n)$ according to proposition 2.35. Because of the left- and right-invariance of the matrix elements, the sums over elements of the subgroups $S(\tilde{w})$ and $S(w)$ contribute as factors the orders $\tilde{w}!$ and $w!$ respectively of these groups. The second orthogonality relation is derived from the second general orthogonality relation for irreducible representations. After introduction of the double coset decompositions

$$p = \tilde{h} z_k h \quad p' = \tilde{h}' z_{k'} h'$$

one performs a sum over the elements $\tilde{h}, \tilde{h}'$ of $S(\tilde{w})$ and the elements h, h' of $S(w)$. Now

$$a(fst) = \sum_{\tilde{h} \in S(\tilde{w})}{}' \sum_{h \in S(w)}{}' d_{st}^f(\tilde{h} z_k h)$$

yields, from the orthogonality of the irreducible representations of $S(\tilde{w})$ and $S(w)$, zero except in case the matrix element is left- and right-invariant. In this case one may replace s and t by Gelfand patterns $\tilde{q}$ and q to obtain

$$a(f\tilde{q}q) = \sum_{\tilde{h} \in S(\tilde{w})}{}' \sum_{h \in S(w)}{}' d_{\tilde{q}q}^f(\tilde{h} z_k h) = \tilde{w}! \; w! \; d_{\tilde{q}q}^f(z_k).$$

Summing the right-hand side of the second general orthogonality relation yields after double coset decomposition

$$\sum_{\tilde{h}, \tilde{h}' \in S(\tilde{w})}{}' \sum_{h, h' \in S(w)}{}' \delta(\tilde{h} z_k h, \tilde{h}' z_{k'} h') = \tilde{w}! \; w! \; k! \; \delta(z_k, z_{k'}).$$

The combination of these expressions gives the second orthogonality relation.   □

Proposition 2.36 may be reformulated in terms of square symbols defined by

$$\begin{bmatrix} f & q \\ \tilde{q} & k \end{bmatrix} = \lambda_f^{-1} [\tilde{w}! \; w!]^{1/2} (k!)^{-1/2} d_{\tilde{q}q}^f(z_k).$$

2.36′ Proposition: The square symbols form an orthogonal and complete set of functions on the double cosets of $S(n)$ with respect to the subgroups $S(\tilde{w})$ and $S(w)$. The orthogonality and completeness relations read

$$\sum_k{}' \begin{bmatrix} f' & q' \\ \tilde{q}' & k \end{bmatrix} \begin{bmatrix} f & q \\ \tilde{q} & k \end{bmatrix} = \delta(f', f) \, \delta(\tilde{q}', \tilde{q}) \, \delta(q', q)$$

$$\sum_{f\tilde{q}q}{}' \begin{bmatrix} f & q \\ \tilde{q} & k' \end{bmatrix} \begin{bmatrix} f & q \\ \tilde{q} & k \end{bmatrix} = \delta(k', k).$$

Proof: We use the unitarity and reality of the representations in the form

$$d_{q'\tilde{q}'}^f(z_k^{-1}) = \overline{d_{\tilde{q}'q'}^f(z_k)}$$

$$d_{\tilde{q}'q'}^f(z_k) = \overline{d_{\tilde{q}'q'}^f(z_k)}$$

and rewrite proposition 2.36 in terms of the square symbols.

If the weight $\tilde{w}$ is taken in the form $w = (1\ 1\ \ldots\ 1)$, one gets the left coset decomposition as a special case of the double coset decomposition. As mentioned at the end of section 2.2, we shall replace k by i and z_k by c_i to indicate this special case. The Gelfand pattern $\tilde{q}$ reduces to a Young tableau which we denote as r. The numbers $\tilde{w}!$ and $m(k)$ are equal to one and we obtain

2.37 Proposition: The special square symbols defined as

$$\begin{bmatrix} f & q \\ r & i \end{bmatrix} = \lambda_f^{-1}\,[w!]^{1/2}\,d_{rq}^f(c_i)$$

form an orthogonal and complete set of functions on the left cosets of $S(w)$ with respect to $S(n)$. The orthogonality and completeness relations read

$$\sum_i{}' \begin{bmatrix} f' & q' \\ r' & i \end{bmatrix} \begin{bmatrix} f & q \\ r & i \end{bmatrix} = \delta(f',f)\,\delta(r',r)\,\delta(q',q),$$

$$\sum_{frq}{}' \begin{bmatrix} f & q \\ r & i' \end{bmatrix} \begin{bmatrix} f & q \\ r & i \end{bmatrix} = \delta(i',i).$$

2.4 Construction of States of Orbital Symmetry, Young Operators

Having completed the description of the irreducible representations of the symmetric group we turn now to the construction of orbital states which transform according to these representations.

In the orbital n-body Hilbert space, the permutation p is represented by a unitary operator which we denote as $U(p)$.

The linear combinations of these operators with complex coefficients depending on the group element form an operator algebra with a multiplication law defined by the representation condition for the operators $U(p)$. This algebra is called the group algebra of the symmetric group $S(n)$.

2.38 Definition: A Young operator is an element of the group algebra given in terms of the irreducible representation d^f of $S(n)$ by

$$c_{rs}^f = |f|\,[n!]^{-1} \sum_{p \in S(n)} d_{rs}^f(p)\,U(p).$$

2.39 Proposition: The Young operators have the multiplication rules

$$U(p) \circ c_{rs}^f = \sum_{r'} c_{r's}^f d_{r'r}^f(p)$$

$$c_{rs}^f \circ U(p) = \sum_{s'} c_{rs'}^f d_{ss'}^f(p)$$

$$c_{\tilde{s}\,\tilde{r}}^{\tilde{f}} \circ c_{rs}^f = \delta(\tilde{f}, f)\, \delta(\tilde{r}, r)\, c_{\tilde{s}s}^f$$

and the adjoint property

$$(c_{rs}^f)^+ = c_{sr}^f.$$

Proof: The multiplication rules are a straightforward application of the representation properties of d^f and of the, operators $U(p)$. The adjoint property follows from the unitarity of both representations. $\square$

Application of the first multiplication law to a state shows that the states

$$c_{rs}^f |\psi)$$

for r ranging over the rows of the irreducible representation d^f, are the partners of a basis for this representation. With respect to the second index s in this expression we now show

2.40 Proposition: Consider a state $|\psi_w)$ which transforms according to the identity representation of the subgroup $S(w)$ of $S(n)$. All linearly independent bases for irreducible representations can be constructed by means of the possible Gelfand patterns q corresponding to the weight w and the partition f as

$$c_{rq}^f |\psi_w).$$

Proof: The assumption means that for all $h \in S(w)$ we have

$$U(h) |\psi_w) = |\psi_w).$$

By the orthogonality between the identity representation of $S(w)$ and all other irreducible representations of this group it is easy to show that the only non-vanishing images of $|\psi_w)$ under c_{rs}^f arise from right-invariant irreducible representation matrix elements d_{rs}^f. These right-invariant matrix elements were shown in proposition 2.30 to be in one-to-one relation to the possible Gelfand patterns q. $\square$

The application to nuclear composite particle systems will lean to a large extent on the content of proposition 2.40. States characterized by a weight appear in two different ways in these systems: In a configuration of simple composite particles we shall assume that the orbital states be stable under all internal permutations. These permutations are the elements of the group of the weight if the components of the weight are identified with the occupation numbers of the composite particles. The Gelfand patterns for given weight provide an exhaustive building-up principle for the orbital partitions. A second application of the same concept arises in shell configurations. Here the weight characterizes the occupation number of the various single-particle states belonging to a given shell. Again the state is stable under the group of the weight and the Gelfand patterns provide a building-up principle of states with fixed orbital partition.

Let us now turn to the evaluation of scalar products of orbital n-body states involving Young operators.

2.41 Definition: Normalized Young operators are defined by

$$c(rfq) = \lambda_f [w!]^{-1/2} c_{rq}^f$$

where q is a Gelfand pattern for the weight w and w! is short-hand for $\Pi w_i!$.

2.42 Proposition: The normalized Young operators may be expressed in terms of the coset generators c_i of $S(w)$ as

$$c(rfq) = \sum_i \lambda_f^{-1} [w!]^{1/2} d_{rq}^f(c_i) U(c_i) \circ c^w$$

with c^w being the Young operator for the identity representation of $S(w)$.

Proof: The coset decomposition is a special double coset decomposition with respect to subgroups $S(\widetilde{w})$ and $S(w)$ where $\widetilde{w} = (1\,1\,\ldots\,1)$. According to the remarks following proposition 2.18 we denote the coset generators by c_i. Since d_{rq}^f is right-invariant with respect to $S(w)$, the Young operator c^w may be split off to the right after multiplication with the factor w!. Note that the factors in front of $U(c_i)$ in the expression for the normalized Young operator are the orthonormal functions on cosets which were discussed in proposition 2.36 for general double cosets.   □

2.43 Proposition: The scalar product of two n-body states $|\psi_{\widetilde{w}})$ and $|\psi_w)$ after application of normalized Young operators is given by

$$(c(\widetilde{r}\widetilde{f}\widetilde{q}) \psi_{\widetilde{w}} | c(rfq) \psi_w) = (\psi_{\widetilde{w}} | c(\widetilde{q}\widetilde{f}\widetilde{r}) c(rfq) | \psi_w)$$
$$= \delta(\widetilde{f}, f) \delta(\widetilde{r}, r) \lambda_f (\psi_{\widetilde{w}} | c(\widetilde{q}fq) | \psi_w)$$

where

$$c(\widetilde{q}fq) = \lambda_f [\widetilde{w}!\,w!]^{-1/2} c_{\widetilde{q}q}^f.$$

Proof: The result follows by application of the adjoint properties and the multiplication rules for Young operators.   □

2.44 Proposition: The Young operator $c(\widetilde{q}fq)$ has the double coset decomposition

$$c(\widetilde{q}fq) = \lambda_f^{-1} [\widetilde{w}!\,w!]^{1/2} \sum_k d_{\widetilde{q}q}^f(z_k)^{-1} c^{\widetilde{w}} \circ U(z_k) \circ c^w.$$

This leads to the double coset form for scalar products given by

$$(c\,(rf\tilde{q})\,\psi_{\tilde{w}}\,|c\,(rfq)\,\psi_w) = [\tilde{w}!\,w!]^{1/2} \sum_k d^f_{\tilde{q}\,q}(z_k)\,(k!)^{-1}\,(\psi_{\tilde{w}}\,|U\,(z_k)|\,\psi_w).$$

The proof follows from proposition 2.43.

The expressions derived in proposition 2.44 yield the interpretation of the normalization or overlap for n-body states of orbital symmetry in terms of a set of basic exchange integrals, each of them being characterized by a double coset of the group $S(n)$. In section 7.2 we shall give an explicit example for this exchange decomposition.

2.5 Computation of Irreducible Representations of the Symmetric Group

In the present section we review some methods which allow us to determine in explicit numerical form all irreducible representations d^f of physical interest of the group $S(n)$. In principle this requires the computation of the corresponding matrices in terms of the matrices of transpositions which are specified in the orthogonal Young and Yamanouchi representation [HA 62, p. 214]. The matrix elements of physical interest are characterized by the identity representation of groups of the type $S(w)$ where w is a weight. This characterization differs from the one used by Young and Yamanouchi by the appearance of generalized instead of standard Young tableaus. We shall show that the use of the so-called axial distance τ and a function μ depending on skew diagrams allows the direct or recursive evaluation of matrix elements defined in terms of generalized Young tableaus or Gelfand patterns [KR 67, 68].

Consider a fixed box in a Young diagram f. Its position is completely specified by the two numbers (α, β) which give the row and column of this box with respect to the diagram f.

2.45 Definition: The axial distance of two fixed boxes i, l in a Young diagram f is defined as

$$\tau_{il} = (\beta_i - \alpha_i) - (\beta_l - \alpha_l)$$

2.46 Definition: Let a, b denote two subsets of boxes of a Young diagram. For $a \cap b = \emptyset$ and $\tau_{il} \neq 0$ if $i \in a$, $l \in b$ define the μ-function

$$\mu\,(a, b) = \prod_{\substack{i \in a \\ l \in b}} \left[\frac{\tau_{il} + 1}{\tau_{il}}\right]^{1/2}.$$

Consider now the special weights $\tilde{w} = (\tilde{w}_1\,\tilde{w}_2)$ and $w = (w_1\,w_2)$ and a double coset belonging to these weights. We shall for the moment introduce a special notation for the double coset by writing

$$\begin{Bmatrix} k_{11} & k_{12} \\ k_{21} & k_{22} \end{Bmatrix} = \begin{Bmatrix} n_a & n_b \\ n_c & n_d \end{Bmatrix}.$$

The letters $abcd$ will be used to indicate partitions of $n_a n_b n_c n_d$ respectively and the letters $eghi$ will denote partitions of the numbers

$$n_e = n_a + n_b = \tilde{w}_1 \qquad n_h = n_a + n_c = w_1$$
$$n_g = n_c + n_d = \tilde{w}_2 \qquad n_i = n_b + n_d = w_2.$$

2.47 Definition: If the irreducible representation d^f of $S(n)$ under subduction to the subgroup $S(w_1) \times S(w_2)$ reduces into the product representation $d^h \times d^i$, we indicate this reduction by the bracket notation $f(hi)$.

We are now prepared to discuss a special representation matrix element depending on nine partitions. This matrix element has been called a 9f symbol because of its close analogy to the well-known 9j recoupling coefficients of $SU(2)$. This 9f symbol plays for the matrix elements d^f characterized by two Gelfand patterns the same role as the transpositions for the matrix elements of the orthogonal Young representation.

2.48 Definition: The 9f symbol is the matrix element of the irreducible representation d^f of $S(n)$ for the double coset z_k and the characterization of rows and columns given by

$$\begin{bmatrix} f & h & i \\ e & a & b \\ g & c & d \end{bmatrix} = d^f_{e(ab)\,g(cd),\,h(ac)\,i(bd)} \begin{Bmatrix} n_a & n_b \\ n_c & n_d \end{Bmatrix}.$$

Here and throughout this section we replace the functional dependence on the permutation z_k by the dependence on the corresponding double coset symbol.

From the reality and unitarity of the representation we get the relation

$$\begin{bmatrix} f & h & i \\ e & a & b \\ g & c & d \end{bmatrix} = \begin{bmatrix} f & e & g \\ h & a & c \\ i & b & d \end{bmatrix}.$$

For other properties we refer to [KR 67]. As the first numerical example of a 9f symbol we consider

$$\begin{bmatrix} f & h & 1 \\ e & a & 1 \\ 1 & 1 & 0 \end{bmatrix} = d^f_{e(a1)\,1,\,h(a1)\,1} \begin{Bmatrix} n-2 & 1 \\ 1 & 0 \end{Bmatrix},$$

where we used the notation $[1] = 1$. The double coset generator z_k for this symbol is given from proposition 2.17 by

$$z_k = \begin{bmatrix} 1\ 2 \ldots n-2 & n-1 & n \\ 1\ 2 \ldots n-2 & n & n-1 \end{bmatrix}.$$

Thus this special $9f$ symbol is the matrix element of a transposition in the orthogonal Young representation [HA 62, p. 214]. Its value may be expressed as

$$\begin{bmatrix} f & h & 1 \\ e & a & 1 \\ 1 & 1 & 0 \end{bmatrix} = \begin{cases} \mu(f-e,e-a)\,\mu(f-h,h-a) & \text{if } (e-a)\cap(h-a) = \emptyset \\ \tau^{-1}_{f-e,h-a} & \text{if } (e-a)\cap(h-a) \neq \emptyset \end{cases}.$$

The next proposition deals with special types of $9f$ symbols for which closed expressions are available.

2.49 Proposition: The following three types of $9f$ symbols are expressible with the help of the axial distance τ and the μ-function.

Type I: $i = [n_i]\; n_i \geqslant 2$

$$\begin{bmatrix} f & h & i \\ e & a & i \\ 1 & 1 & 0 \end{bmatrix} = \begin{cases} \mu(f-e,e-a)\,\mu(f-h,h-a) & \text{if } (e-a)\cap(h-a) = \emptyset \\ \mu(f-e,e-h)\,\mu(e-h,h-a)\,\tau^{-1}_{f-e,h-a} & \text{if } (e-a)\cap(h-a) \neq \emptyset \end{cases}$$

Type II: $i = [n_i]\; g = [n_g]$

$$\begin{bmatrix} f & h & i \\ e & h & b \\ g & 0 & g \end{bmatrix} = [n_b!\,n_g!\,(n_i!)^{-1}]^{1/2}\,\mu(f-e,e-h).$$

Type III: $i = [1^{n_i}]\; g = [1^{n_g}]$

$$\begin{bmatrix} f & h & i \\ e & h & b \\ g & 0 & g \end{bmatrix} = [n_b!\,n_g!\,(n_i!)^{-1}]^{1/2}\,\mu(e-h,f-e)\prod_{\substack{i\in(e-h) \\ l\in(f-e)}} \epsilon_{il}$$

$$\epsilon_{il} = 1 \quad \text{for} \quad \alpha_i \leqslant \alpha_l, \quad \epsilon_{il} = -1 \quad \text{for} \quad \alpha_i > \alpha_l.$$

The expression of type I has been obtained from the recursion relation eq. (A. 3) of [KR 67] by an inductive proof which will not be given here. The expressions of type II and III were derived in eqs. (3.17) and (3.18) of [KR 67]; provided these expressions are rewritten as $9f$ symbols according to eq. (3.31) of [KR 67].

The $9f$ symbols specified in proposition 2.49 are not sufficient to cover all necessary cases, but these cases may be derived by recursion relations.

2.50 Proposition: For $i = [n_i]$, $c = [n_c]$, $g' = [n_{g'}]$ and $g'' = [n_{g''}]$ the $9f$ symbols obey the recursion relation

$$\begin{bmatrix} f & h & i \\ e & a & b \\ g & c & d \end{bmatrix}$$

$$= \sum_{e'a'b'} \begin{bmatrix} g & g' & g'' \\ c & c' & c'' \\ d & d' & d'' \end{bmatrix} \begin{bmatrix} f & e' & g'' \\ e & e & 0 \\ g & g' & g'' \end{bmatrix} \begin{bmatrix} e' & a' & b' \\ e & a & b \\ g' & c' & d' \end{bmatrix} \begin{bmatrix} f & h & i \\ e' & a' & b' \\ g'' & c'' & d'' \end{bmatrix} \begin{bmatrix} h & a & c \\ a' & a & c' \\ c'' & 0 & c'' \end{bmatrix} \begin{bmatrix} i & b & d \\ b' & b & d' \\ d'' & 0 & d'' \end{bmatrix}$$

where the sum runs over all partitions $e'a'b'$ which are compatible with the reductions expressed by the brackets

$$f(e'g''), h(a'c''), i(b'd'').$$

Proof: This is the first one of a number of recursion relations which are proved by factorizing the permutation z_k and using the representation condition. For the present case the expressions described in proposition 2.17 can be factorized according to proposition 2.9 in the form

$$\begin{bmatrix} n_a & n_c & n_b & n_d \\ n_a & n_b & n_c & n_d \end{bmatrix} = \begin{bmatrix} n_a & n_{c'} & n_{c''} & n_b & n_{d'} & n_{d''} \\ n_a & n_b & n_{c'} & n_{c''} & n_{d'} & n_{d''} \end{bmatrix}$$

$$= \begin{bmatrix} n_a & n_b & n_{c'} & n_{d'} & n_{c''} & n_{d''} \\ n_a & n_b & n_{c'} & n_{c''} & n_{d'} & n_{d''} \end{bmatrix} \begin{bmatrix} n_a & n_{c'} & n_b & n_{d'} & n_{c''} & n_{d''} \\ n_a & n_b & n_{c'} & n_{d'} & n_{c''} & n_{d''} \end{bmatrix} \begin{bmatrix} n_a & n_{c'} & n_{c''} & n_b & n_{d'} & n_{d''} \\ n_a & n_{c'} & n_b & n_{d'} & n_{c''} & n_{d''} \end{bmatrix}$$

where $n_g = n_{g'} + n_{g''}$, $n_c = n_{c'} + n_{c''}$, $n_d = n_{d'} + n_{d''}$.

It is now possible to construct the expression given above, starting form the right: Define $n_{b'} = n_b + n_{d'}$ and $n_{a'} = n_a + n_{c'}$, and introduce by two 9f symbols the partitions b' and a'. Note that these two 9f symbols contain the empty partition 0 and that they are matrix elements of the identity element of $S(n)$. Introduce $n_{e'} = n_{a'} + n_{b'}$ and a partition e' to obtain the matrix element of the third factor in the given factorization. Introduce $n_{g'} = n_{c'} + n_{d'}$ and the partition g' to write the second factor as a 9f symbol. The next 9f symbol serves to replace the partitions e' and g' by e and g and the last step allows one to pass from the partitions g' and g'' back to c and d with the help of the first factor. The reduction rules are simply obtained by inspection of the 9f symbols.   □

The recursion relation given in proposition 2.50 allows one to express 9f symbols with given value n_g by other ones with a lower n_g. The second, fifth and sixth 9f symbol in the recursion relation are of the type II given in proposition 2.49. Note that the corresponding permutations are all equal to the identity element of $S(n)$. Since for $n_g = 1$ the values of the 9f symbols are known, this recursion relation suffices to compute recursively all 9f symbols of interest.

Now we proceed to the computation of more complex representations of $S(n)$. Again we shall factorize the double coset generators in a systematic fashion and apply the representation condition to the product of factors. To describe the factorization of double coset generators we shall decompose the double coset symbols into various blocks. For a $\tilde{j} \times j$ double coset symbol we introduce a notation which separates the last row and column from a $(\tilde{j} - 1) \times (j - 1)$ submatrix which we denote as $k_{..}$:

$$\{k\} = \begin{Bmatrix} k_{..} & k_{.j} \\ k_{\tilde{j}.} & k_{\tilde{j}j} \end{Bmatrix}$$

$$\{k_{..}\} = \begin{Bmatrix} k_{11} & k_{12} & \cdots & k_{1j-1} \\ k_{21} & & & \\ \vdots & & & \vdots \\ k_{\tilde{j}-11} & & \cdots & k_{\tilde{j}-1j-1} \end{Bmatrix}.$$

By $k_{.i}$ and $k_{l.}$ we denote the column and row vectors

$$k_{.i} = \begin{Bmatrix} k_{1i} \\ k_{2i} \\ . \\ . \\ . \\ k_{\tilde{j}-1\,i} \end{Bmatrix} \qquad k_{l.} = \{k_{l1}\,k_{l2} \ldots k_{l\,j-1}\}.$$

The additional index s will be used to indicate the following sums:

$$sk_{..} = \sum_{l=1}^{\tilde{j}-1} \sum_{i=1}^{j-1} k_{li}$$

$$sk_{.i} = \sum_{l=1}^{\tilde{j}-1} k_{li} \qquad sk_{l.} = \sum_{i=1}^{j-1} k_{li}.$$

We shall use the explicit form $z\{k\}$ instead of z_k to specify the double coset generators.

2.51 Proposition: For the weights $\tilde{w} = (\tilde{w}_1\,\tilde{w}_2)$ and $w = (w_1 w_2 \ldots w_j)$ the double coset generator can be factorized as

$$z\{k\} = z\begin{Bmatrix} k_{1.} & k_{1j} \\ k_{2.} & k_{2j} \end{Bmatrix} = z\begin{Bmatrix} sk_{1.} & k_{1j} \\ sk_{2.} & k_{2j} \end{Bmatrix} z\begin{Bmatrix} k_{1.} \\ k_{2.} \end{Bmatrix}.$$

The proof is obtained by writing out the permutations in the form given in propositions 2.8 and 2.7, and one obtains the result from the multiplication according to proposition 2.9.

2.52 Proposition: For general weights $\tilde{w} = (\tilde{w}_1\,\tilde{w}_2 \ldots \tilde{w}_{\tilde{j}})$ and $w = (w_1 w_2 \ldots w_j)$ the double coset generators factorize according to

$$z\{k\} = z\begin{Bmatrix} k_{..} & k_{.j} \\ k_{\tilde{j}.} & k_{\tilde{j}j} \end{Bmatrix}$$

$$= z\begin{Bmatrix} sk_{1.} & k_{1j} \\ sk_{2.} & k_{2j} \\ . & . \\ . & . \\ . & . \\ sk_{\tilde{j}-1.} & k_{\tilde{j}-1j} \end{Bmatrix} z\{k_{..}\} z\begin{Bmatrix} sk_{..} & sk_{.j} \\ sk_{\tilde{j}.} & k_{\tilde{j}j} \end{Bmatrix} z\begin{Bmatrix} sk_{.1} & sk_{.2} & \ldots & sk_{.j-1} \\ k_{\tilde{j}1} & k_{\tilde{j}2} & \ldots & k_{\tilde{j}j-1} \end{Bmatrix}.$$

The proof follows the same procedure as in proposition 2.51.

We apply these factorizations to representations of $S(n)$ described by Gelfand schemes. In addition to the bracket notation mentioned earlier, we shall denote a partition f and an associated Gelfand scheme q by $f(q)$. If necessary, we shall partially decompose a Gelfand pattern by use of the partitions appearing in q according to definition 2.29. By a single index of a partition we indicate the corresponding row in the Gelfand pattern, *not* a single component. The same index is used for subpatterns of a Gelfand pattern. Hence we have the identities

$$f(q) = f(f_{j-1}(q_{j-1}) w_j) = f(f_{j-1}(f_{j-2}(q_{j-2}) w_{j-1}) w_j).$$

If necessary we indicate by an additional letter that the Gelfand pattern q_b belongs to the partition b.

2.53 Proposition: For weights and a double coset as in proposition 2.51 the irreducible representation d^f factorizes as

$$d^f_{e(q_{ej})\, g(q_{gj}),\, f_{j-1}(q_{j-1})\, w_j} \begin{Bmatrix} k_1. & k_{1j} \\ k_2. & k_{2j} \end{Bmatrix}$$

$$= d^f_{e(e_{j-1}(q_{ej-1}))\, g(g_{j-1}(q_{gj-1})),\, f_{j-1}(q_{j-1})\, w_j} \begin{Bmatrix} k_1. & k_{1j} \\ k_2. & k_{2j} \end{Bmatrix}$$

$$= d^f_{e(e_{j-1}k_{1j})\, g(g_{j-1}k_{2j}),\, f_{j-1}(e_{j-1}g_{j-1})\, w_j(k_{1j}k_{2j})} \begin{Bmatrix} sk_1. & k_{1j} \\ sk_2. & k_{2j} \end{Bmatrix}$$

$$d^{f_{j-1}}_{e_{j-1}(q_{ej-1})\, g_{j-1}(q_{gj-1}),\, q_{j-1}} \begin{Bmatrix} k_1. \\ k_2. \end{Bmatrix}.$$

The proof uses the decomposition proposition 2.51 and the representation condition. One finds that no intermediate summation appears for the given choice of the intermediate basis.

The result of proposition 2.53 leads to a complete factorization of the matrix element. One easily identifies the first factor as a 9f symbol and obtains by repetition the final result

$$d^f_{e(q_{ej})\, g(q_{gj}),\, f_{j-1}(q_{j-1})\, w_j} \begin{Bmatrix} k_{11} & k_{12} & \cdots & k_{1j} \\ k_{21} & k_{22} & \cdots & k_{2j} \end{Bmatrix}$$

$$\begin{bmatrix} f & f_{j-1} & w_j \\ e & e_{j-1} & k_{1j} \\ g & g_{j-1} & k_{2j} \end{bmatrix}^{j-1} \prod_{i=1} \begin{bmatrix} f_i & f_{i-1} & w_i \\ e_i & e_{i-1} & k_{1i} \\ g_i & g_{i-1} & k_{2i} \end{bmatrix}.$$

All 9f symbols are well-defined if g is a one-row or a one-column diagram.

2.54 Proposition: For weights and a double coset as in proposition 2.52, the irreducible representation d^f decomposes into a sum as

$$d^f_{\widetilde{f}_{j-1}(\widetilde{f}_{j-2}(\widetilde{q}_{j-2})\,\widetilde{w}_{j-1}),\, f_{j-1}(f_{j-2}(q_{j-2})\,w_{j-1})} \{k\}$$

$$= \sum_{a_{j-1}\,\widetilde{q}_{j-1}\,q'_{j-1}}{}' d^{f_{j-1}}_{\widetilde{f}_{j-2}(\widetilde{q}_{j-2})\,\widetilde{w}_{j-1},\, a_{j-1}(\widetilde{q}'_{j-1})\,\widetilde{s}_{j-1}} \begin{Bmatrix} sk_1. & k_{1j} \\ sk_2. & k_{2j} \\ : \\ : \\ sk_{\widetilde{j}-1}. & k_{\widetilde{j}-1j} \end{Bmatrix}$$

$$d^{aj-1}_{\underset{\sim}{q}j-1\,qj-1}\ \{k_{..}\}\ d^{f}_{\widetilde{fj}-1\,(aj-1\,\widetilde{s}j-1),\,fj-1\,(aj-1\,sj-1)} \begin{Bmatrix} sk_{..} & sk_{.j} \\ sk\widetilde{j}. & k\widetilde{j}j \end{Bmatrix}$$

$$d^{fj-1}_{aj-1\,(qj-1)\,sj-1,\,fj-2\,(qj-2)\,wj-1} \begin{Bmatrix} sk_{.1} & sk_{.2} & \ldots & sk_{.j-1} \\ k\widetilde{j}1 & k\widetilde{j}2 & \ldots & k\widetilde{j}j-1 \end{Bmatrix} \Bigg] .$$

The proof is carried out on the basis of proposition 2.52.

We claim that this proposition allows in principle a complete calculation of the matrix element in terms of $9f$ symbols. First of all it can be seen that the last d^{fj-1} is of the type analyzed in proposition 2.53 and hence is a product of $9f$ symbols. Similarly the first $d^{\widetilde{fj}-1}$ is the transposed form of the same type. The third d^f is just equal to a $9f$ symbol, and the remaining d^{aj-1} is a representation of a subgroup of $S(n)$.

The partition a_{j-1} is restricted by the subduction rules

$$\widetilde{f}_{j-1}\,(a_{j-1}\,\widetilde{s}_{j-1}) \qquad f_{j-1}\,(a_{j-1}\,s_{j-1}) \qquad n_{a_{j-1}} = sk_{...}$$

In particular this implies that the partition a_{j-1} has at most $j-1$ components if f has j components.

We shall see in section 3.7 that for two-particle fractional parentage coefficients one needs the $9f$ symbols with $g = [2], [11]$. These symbols may be derived by use of the recursion relation of proposition 2.50 in the two forms

$$c = d = 1 \qquad d' = c'' = 0 \qquad g' = c'$$

$$\begin{bmatrix} f & h & i \\ e & a & b \\ g & 1 & 1 \end{bmatrix} = \sum_{e'} \begin{bmatrix} f & e' & 1 \\ e & e & 0 \\ g & 1 & 1 \end{bmatrix} \begin{bmatrix} e' & h & b \\ e & a & b \\ 1 & 1 & 0 \end{bmatrix} \begin{bmatrix} f & h & i \\ e' & h & b \\ 1 & 0 & 1 \end{bmatrix}$$

$$d = 0 \qquad c' = c'' = 1 \qquad g' = c'$$

$$\begin{bmatrix} f & h & i \\ e & a & i \\ g & g & 0 \end{bmatrix} = \sum_{e'a'} \begin{bmatrix} f & e' & 1 \\ e & e & 0 \\ g & 1 & 1 \end{bmatrix} \begin{bmatrix} e' & a' & i \\ e & a & i \\ 1 & 1 & 0 \end{bmatrix} \begin{bmatrix} f & h & i \\ e' & a' & i \\ 1 & 1 & 0 \end{bmatrix} \begin{bmatrix} h & a & g \\ a' & a & 1 \\ 1 & 0 & 1 \end{bmatrix}$$

which apply both for $g = [2]$ and $g = [11]$, and

$$\begin{bmatrix} f & h & i \\ e & h & b \\ 2 & 0 & 2 \end{bmatrix} = [n_b! \; 2! \; (n_i!)^{-1}]^{1/2} \; \mu\,(f-e,\,e-h).$$

The $9f$ symbols for $g = [11]$ appearing in the two recursion relations are given from proposition 2.49 as

$$\begin{bmatrix} f & e' & 1 \\ e & e & 0 \\ 11 & 1 & 1 \end{bmatrix} = \begin{bmatrix} f & e & 11 \\ e' & e & 1 \\ 1 & 0 & 1 \end{bmatrix} = \left[\frac{1}{2}\right]^{1/2} \mu\,(e'-e,\,f-e')\,\epsilon_{e'-e,\,f-e'}.$$

For later applications our interest is in the representations d^f with $\tilde{w} = (\tilde{w}_1 \tilde{w}_2 \tilde{w}_3)$, $w = (w_1 w_2 w_3)$. With the help of proposition 2.54 the corresponding representations may be expressed as

$$
d^f_{\tilde{f}_2(\tilde{w}_1 \tilde{w}_2), f_2(w_1 w_2)} \left\{ \begin{matrix} k_{11} & k_{12} & k_{13} \\ k_{21} & k_{22} & k_{23} \\ k_{31} & k_{32} & k_{33} \end{matrix} \right\}
$$

$$
= \sum_a \begin{bmatrix} \tilde{f}_2 & a & sk._3 \\ \tilde{w}_1 & sk_1. & k_{13} \\ \tilde{w}_2 & sk_2. & k_{23} \end{bmatrix} \begin{bmatrix} a & sk._1 & sk._2 \\ sk_1. & k_{11} & k_{12} \\ sk_2. & k_{21} & k_{22} \end{bmatrix} \begin{bmatrix} f & f_2 & w_3 \\ \tilde{f}_2 & a & sk._3 \\ \tilde{w}_3 & sk_3. & k_{33} \end{bmatrix} \begin{bmatrix} f_2 & w_1 & w_2 \\ a & sk._1 & sk._2 \\ sk_3. & k_{31} & k_{32} \end{bmatrix} .
$$

The sum runs over all partitions a which are compatible with the reductions $\tilde{f}_2(a\,sk._3)$ and $f_2(a\,sk_3.)$.

Finally we give an expression for the dimension $|f|$ of the irreducible representation d^f of $S(n)$. Consider a box i of f with coordinates (α_i, β_i).

2.55 Definition: The hook h_i of the box i of f is the subset of f consisting of the box i, all boxes to the right of i and all boxes below i. The length $|h_i|$ of a hook is the number of boxes contained in the hook.

2.56 Proposition: The dimension $|f|$ of the irreducible representation d^f of $S(n)$ is given by

$$
|f| = n! \left[\prod_{i \in f} |h_i| \right]^{-1} .
$$

For the proof we refer to [RO 61, p. 44].

The quantity λ_f introduced in proposition 2.36 is given from proposition 2.56 by

$$
\lambda_f = \left[\frac{n!}{|f|} \right]^{1/2} = \left[\prod_{i \in f} |h_i| \right]^{1/2} .
$$

Alternatively the number λ_f may be expressed as a function of the components of the partition f. For $f = [f_1 f_2 \dots f_j]$ we define the integers r_i by

$$
r_i = f_i + j - i + 1, \quad i = 1, 2, \dots, j.
$$

Then λ_f is given by

$$
\lambda_f = \left[\prod_{i=1}^{j} r_i! \Big/ \prod_{i<l} (r_i - r_l) \right]^{1/2} .
$$

Example 2.7: For the partitions given in example 2.1 we write into each box its corresponding hook length and compute the numbers

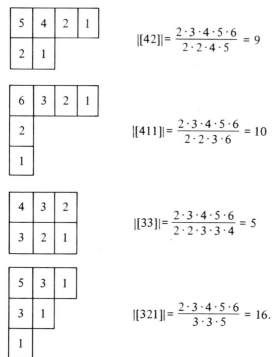

$$|[42]| = \frac{2 \cdot 3 \cdot 4 \cdot 5 \cdot 6}{2 \cdot 2 \cdot 4 \cdot 5} = 9$$

$$|[411]| = \frac{2 \cdot 3 \cdot 4 \cdot 5 \cdot 6}{2 \cdot 2 \cdot 3 \cdot 6} = 10$$

$$|[33]| = \frac{2 \cdot 3 \cdot 4 \cdot 5 \cdot 6}{2 \cdot 2 \cdot 3 \cdot 3 \cdot 4} = 5$$

$$|[321]| = \frac{2 \cdot 3 \cdot 4 \cdot 5 \cdot 6}{3 \cdot 3 \cdot 5} = 16.$$

2.6 Spin, Isospin and the Supermultiplet Scheme

In this section we return to the spin-isospin state of the nuclear system. Each nucleon may be in two possible spin states and in two possible isospin states. We shall give only a brief discussion of the n-nucleon spin-isospin states since these states have been described in many places [JA 51, EL 53]. An n-nucleon spin-isospin state we denote as

$$|\gamma^n \tilde{f} \tilde{r}, \tilde{f} S M_S T M_T).$$

The partition $\tilde{f}$ has at most four rows since there are only four spin-isospin states and yields the transformation properties under permutations. The Young tableau $\tilde{r}$ indicates the partner of this basis. The partition $\tilde{f}$ serves also to describe the transformation properties of the states under the group U(4) of unitary 4×4 matrix transformations acting on the four single-particle spin-isospin states. This group U(4) has a subgroup SU(2) × SU(2) of two unimodular unitary 2×2 matrix transformation groups which act separately on the single-particle spin or isospin states respectively. The irreducible representations and partners of the basis are given by the total spin S and its components M_S and by the total isospin T and its component M_T respectively.

The (ST)-content of an irreducible representation $\tilde{f}$ of U(4) depends only on the representation of the subgroup SU(4). It is customary to denote these representations by the numbers (P P' P'') introduced by Wigner [WI 37]. The relations are given by

$$P = \frac{1}{2}(\hat{f}_1 + \hat{f}_2 - \hat{f}_3 - \hat{f}_4),$$

$$P' = \frac{1}{2}(\hat{f}_1 - \hat{f}_2 + \hat{f}_3 - \hat{f}_4),$$

$$P'' = \frac{1}{2}(\hat{f}_1 - \hat{f}_2 - \hat{f}_3 + \hat{f}_4).$$

Hamermesh [HA 62] gives tables for the ST-content of representations of SU(4).

We now turn to the coupling of orbital and spin-isospin states to antisymmetric n-nucleon states. This coupling is possible only if the corresponding partitions are associate.

2.57 Definition: The Young diagram $\hat{f}$ associate to the Young diagram f is obtained from f by interchange of rows and columns. If r is a standard Young tableau belonging to f with box coordinates

i: (α_i, β_i)

then the standard Young tableau $\hat{r}$ defined by

i: (β_i, α_i)

belongs to $\hat{f}$ and is called the associate tableau.

To determine the coupling of orbital and spin-isospin states we suppress all labels which do not refer to permutational symmetry and write these states simply as

$$|\alpha^n fr), \quad |\gamma^n \tilde{f}\tilde{r}).$$

2.58 Proposition: For any orbital partition $f = [f_1 f_2 \ldots f_j]$ with $f_1 \leqslant 4$ there exist one and only one spin-isospin partition $\tilde{f} = \hat{f}$ and coupling coefficients $\langle fr\hat{f}\hat{r}|[1^n]\rangle$ such that

$$|(\alpha\gamma)^n f[1^n]) = \sum_r |\alpha^n fr) |\gamma^n \hat{f}\hat{r}) \langle fr\hat{f}\hat{r}|[1^n])$$

is an antisymmetric state.

Proof: The coupling is a special case of a Kronecker product of irreducible representations of S(n) [HA 62]. The value of the coupling coefficients depends on the choice of the transformation properties of the spin-isospin states under permutations. If the Young orthogonal representation is adopted, the coupling coefficients become

$$\langle fr\hat{f}\hat{r}|[1^n]\rangle = |f|^{-1/2} (-1)^r$$

where $(-1)^r$ is determined from the Young tableau r. For convenience, we shall follow the procedure of Elliott, Hope and Jahn [EL 53] and incorporate the factor $(-1)^r$ into the spin-isospin states. Then we have simply

$$\langle f r \tilde{f} \tilde{r} | [1^n] \rangle = |f|^{-1/2}.$$ □

2.7 Matrix Elements in the Supermultiplet Scheme

In this subsection we consider matrix elements of operators with respect to states classified by orbital and spin-isospin partitions. For a detailed exposition we refer to [KR 69]. First we treat one-body operators which appear, for example, in the calculation of electromagnetic transitions. Throughout this section we denote by T operators acting on orbital states and by U operators acting on spin-isospin states. We assume for one-body operators the form

$$O(1) = \sum_{s=1}^{n} T(s) U(s) = [(n-1)!]^{-1} \sum_{p} U(p) T(n) U(n) U(p^{-1}).$$

The second expression arises by introducing permutation operators acting both on orbital and spin-isospin states. Now clearly for antisymmetric states we find

$$((\alpha\gamma)^n \tilde{f}[1^n] | O(1) | (\alpha\gamma)^n f[1^n]) = \binom{n}{1} ((\alpha\gamma)^n \tilde{f}[1^n] | T(n) U(n) | (\alpha\gamma)^n f[1^n]).$$

By use of the coupling procedure we may reduce this expression to products of orbital and spin-isospin matrix elements. For the orbital matrix elements we decompose the basis $f(r)$ as

$$f(r) = f(f'(r') 1)$$

to exhibit the representation f' of $S(n-1)$. We claim now for the orbital matrix element

$$(\alpha^n \tilde{f}(\tilde{f}'(\tilde{r}') 1) | T(n) | \alpha^n f(f'(r') 1))$$
$$= \delta(\tilde{f}', f') \delta(\tilde{r}', r') |f'|^{-1/2} (\alpha^n \tilde{f}(f' 1) \| T(n) \| \alpha^n f(f' 1)).$$

For the proof we note that the operator $T(n)$ commutes with all elements of $S(n-1)$. Hence its matrix element can at most depend on the partition f'. The factor $|f'|^{-1/2}$ has been introduced for convenience. Applying the same reasoning to the spin-isospin matrix element and defining the reduced matrix element by

$$(\gamma^n \tilde{f}(\tilde{f}'(\tilde{f}') 1) | U(n) | \gamma^n \hat{f}(\hat{f}'(\hat{f}') 1)) = |\hat{f}'|^{-1/2} (\gamma^n \tilde{f}(\hat{f}' 1) \| U(n) \| \gamma^n \hat{f}(\hat{f}' 1))$$

one obtains.

2.59 Proposition: The matrix element of a one-body operator in the supermultiplet scheme is given by

$$((\alpha\gamma)^n \tilde{f}[1^n]|O(1)|(\alpha\gamma)^n f[1^n]) = \binom{n}{1}(|\tilde{f}| \cdot |f|)^{-1/2}$$

$$\times \sum_{f'} (\alpha^n \tilde{f}(f'1) \| T(n) \| \alpha^n f(f'1)) (\gamma^n \hat{\tilde{f}}(\hat{f}'1) \| U(n) \| \gamma^n \hat{f}(\hat{f}'1)).$$

The diagrams $\tilde{f}$ and f differ at most in the position of one box.

Proof: We use coupled states for both bra and ket configurations and introduce reduced matrix elements for the orbital and for the spin-isospin part. The sum over r' yields a factor $|f'|$ which cancels with $|f'|^{-1}$ from the definition of the reduced matrix elements. The selection rule follows from the reductions $\tilde{f}(f'1)$ and $f(f'1)$ which require that both $\tilde{f}$ and f be obtained from f' by applying a single box. $\square$

Next we consider the matrix elements of two-body operators

$$O(2) = \sum_{s<t} T(s,t) U(s,t) = \frac{1}{(n-2)! \, 2!} \sum_p U(p) T(n-1,n) U(n-1,n) U(p^{-1}).$$

Again we obtain for antisymmetric states the result

$$((\alpha\gamma)^n \tilde{f}[1^n]|O(2)|(\alpha\gamma)^n f[1^n])$$

$$= \binom{n}{2}((\alpha\gamma)^n \tilde{f}[1^n]|T(n-1,n) U(n-1,n)|(\alpha\gamma)^n f[1^n]).$$

To proceed further it proves convenient to pass from the Young orthogonal representation to a representation which is explicitly reduced with respect to the subgroup $S(n-2) \times S(2)$. We denote the corresponding representations as $d^{f'} \times d^{f''}$. The orbital partition f'' takes the values $f'' = [2]$ or $f'' = [11]$ and for the matrix elements leads to the distinction between even and odd contributions. If now we take into account that $T(n-1,n)$ commutes with all elements of $S(n-2) \times S(2)$, we obtain in this basis

$$(\alpha^n \tilde{f}(\tilde{f}'(\tilde{r}')\tilde{f}'') |T(n-1,n)| \alpha^n f(f'(r') f''))$$

$$= \delta(\tilde{f}', f') \, \delta(\tilde{r}', r') \, (\alpha^n \tilde{f}(f'f'') \| T(n-1,n) \| \alpha^n f(f'f'')) \, |f'|^{-1/2}$$

and a corresponding result for the spin-isospin part. With these preparations it is easy to prove as a generalization of proposition 2.59 the following

2.60 Proposition: The matrix element of a two-body operator in the supermultiplet scheme is given by

$$((\alpha\gamma)^n \tilde{f}[1^n]|O(2)|(\alpha\gamma)^n f[1^n]) = \binom{n}{2}(|\tilde{f}| \cdot |f|)^{-1/2}$$

$$\times \sum_{f'f''} (\alpha^n \tilde{f}(f'f'') \| T(n-1,n) \| \alpha^n f(f'f'')) (\gamma^n \hat{\tilde{f}}(\hat{f}'\hat{f}'') \| U(n-1,n) \| \gamma^n \hat{f}(\hat{f}'\hat{f}'')).$$

The diagrams $\tilde{f}$ and f differ at most in the position of two boxes. It is assumed that $T(n-1, n)$ commutes with the orbital permutation of the last two particles.

A special case arises if the operator does not depend on spin and isospin. From the definition of the reduced spin-isospin matrix elements one finds for $U(n) = 1$

$$((\alpha\gamma)^n \tilde{f} [1^n] | O(1) | (\alpha\gamma)^n f[1^n])$$

$$= \binom{n}{1} \delta(\tilde{f}, f) |f|^{-1} \sum_{f'} |f'|^{1/2} (\alpha^n f(f' 1) \| T(n) \| \alpha^n f(f' 1))$$

and for $U(n-1, n) = 1$

$$((\alpha\gamma)^n \tilde{f} [1^n] | O(2) | (\alpha\gamma)^n f[1^n])$$

$$= \binom{n}{2} \delta(\tilde{f}, f) |f|^{-1} \sum_{f' f''} |f'|^{1/2} (\alpha^n f(f' f'') \| T(n-1, n) \| \alpha^n f(f' f'')).$$

We shall combine the expressions for one- and two-body operators by a short-hand notation. For $n'' = 1$ or 2 we write and replace the two expressions by

$$((\alpha\gamma)^n \tilde{f} [1^n] | O(n'') | (\alpha\gamma)^n f[1^n])$$

$$= \binom{n}{n''} (|\tilde{f}| |f|)^{-1/2} \sum_{f' f''} \{(\alpha^n \tilde{f} (f' f'') \| T(n'') \| \alpha^n f(f' f'')) (\gamma^n \tilde{f} (\hat{f}' \hat{f}'') \| U(n'') \| \gamma^n f(\hat{f}' \hat{f}''))\}.$$

Example 2.7: Matrix elements of two-body operators for states of six nucleons.

In the following table we list the possible orbital reduced matrix elements for the lowest partitions $f = [42], [411], [33]$ in the six nucleon system

$\tilde{f}$	f	$f'f''$
[42]	[42]	[4][2], [31][2], [31][11], [22][2]
[42]	[411]	[31][2], [31][11]
[42]	[33]	[31][2]
[411]	[411]	[4][11], [31][2], [31][11], [211][2]
[411]	[33]	[31][2]
[33]	[33]	[31][2], [22][11]

2.8 Supermultiplet Expansion for States of Light Nuclei

In this section we return from the technical analysis of the supermultiplet scheme to its application in nuclear physics.

For interactions independent of spin and isospin, the states of n nucleons are characterized by the supermultiplet quantum numbers $P P' P''$ or, equivalently, by the orbital partition f. This follows from the special cases considered in proposition 2.60 or, more directly, from the observation that these interactions commute with all orbital permutations. The interactions of this type may be grouped into even and odd interactions. An even infinite-range interaction is of the form

$$O(2) = -V_0 \sum_{s<t} \frac{1}{2}(1 + U(p_{s,t}))$$

with V_0 being some positive constant. This schematic interaction is of course diagonal in the supermultiplet scheme. Application of proposition 2.60 to this two-body interaction yields

$$((\alpha\gamma)^n f[1^n] | O(2) | (\alpha\gamma)^n f[1^n]) = -V_0 q^f$$

where

$$q^f = \binom{n}{2} |f|^{-1} \sum_{f'f''} |f'| \delta(f'', [2])$$

and the sum runs over all partitions f' contained in the reduction of the representation d^f of $S(n)$. Alternative expressions for q^f are obtained from the concept of class operators and characters of the symmetric group [KR 66] or from the group $U(4)$ associated with the spin-isospin states. These expressions read

$$q^f = \frac{1}{4}\left\{ n(n-1) + \sum_{i=1}^{j} f_i(f_i - 2i + 1) \right\}$$

$$= \frac{1}{4}\left\{ n(n-1) - \left((P)^2 + (P')^2 + (P'')^2 + 4P + 2P' - \frac{1}{4}n(n-16) \right) \right\} .$$

For given nucleon number, the schematic interaction yields a supermultiplet spectrum which starts with the orbital partition f of the lowest number of rows since this partition provides the maximum number of even pairs. Franzini and Radicati [FR 63] applied this interaction to the binding energy of light nuclei. They assumed an expression for the energy of the form

$$E(A) = a(A) + \frac{1}{2}b(A)\{(P)^2 + (P')^2 + (P'')^2 + 4P + 2P'\}$$

and allowed for a dependence of the quantities a and b on the mass number n = A. The values of b were deduced by comparing ground state energies of neighbouring isobars and the assignment $P = |T_3| = \frac{1}{2}|Z - N|$ along with the minimum numbers P' and P''. Franzini and Radicati found that $b(A)$ is indeed a smooth function of A up to the mass number A = 110. Thus, the schematic interaction gives a reasonable account of average properties of nuclei over a wide range of mass numbers.

The expression for the energy given above yields for fixed mass number a spectrum of degenerate excited states which belong to the same supermultiplet. If a specific choice of the orbital states is made and a general two-body interaction is employed, we expect a splitting of the degenerate states and, moreover, a mixing of supermultiplets. We give now a discussion of the nuclear p-shell configurations for the numbers A = 5 ... 16 from this point of view. For simplicity we omit the filled s-shell. The three single-particle states of the p-shell allow the construction of orbital partitions f with up to three components. We use a basis labeled by the orbital partition f, the orbital angular momentum L, the total spin S and the total angular momentum J. In this basis we diagonalize the effective interaction POT employed by Cohen and Kurath [CO 65]. Whereas these authors work in the jj-coupling scheme, our states after diagonalization are obtained in the supermultiplet scheme and provide a supermultiplet expansion within the p-shell. The single-particle splitting employed by Cohen and Kurath is incorporated as a one-body spin-orbit potential. Typical results for A = 8 and A = 10 are displayed in figs. 2.5 and 2.6 taken from [JO 73]. The figures show the experimental levels, the degenerate supermultiplet levels according to the expression of Franzini and Radicati with b = 8 MeV, and the grouping of the eigenstates of the POT interaction. Dominant partitions are indicated to the right of each level.

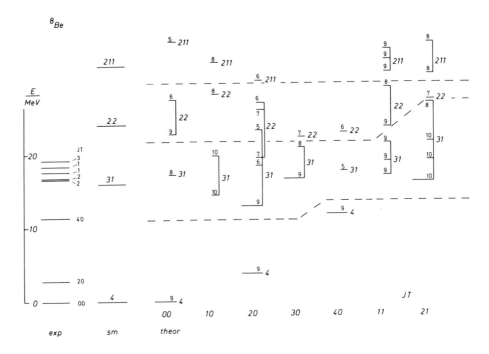

Fig. 2.5 Supermultiplet expansion in the p-shell for nuclei with A = 8. From left to right: Experimental levels taken from [LA 66], energy of supermultiplets according to [FR 63] with b(A) = 8 MeV, and calculated levels E(J T) for the POT interaction of [CO 65]. Dominant orbital partitions are given to the right of the level. Numbers on top of each level indicate the probability of the dominant partition, multiplied by a factor 10.

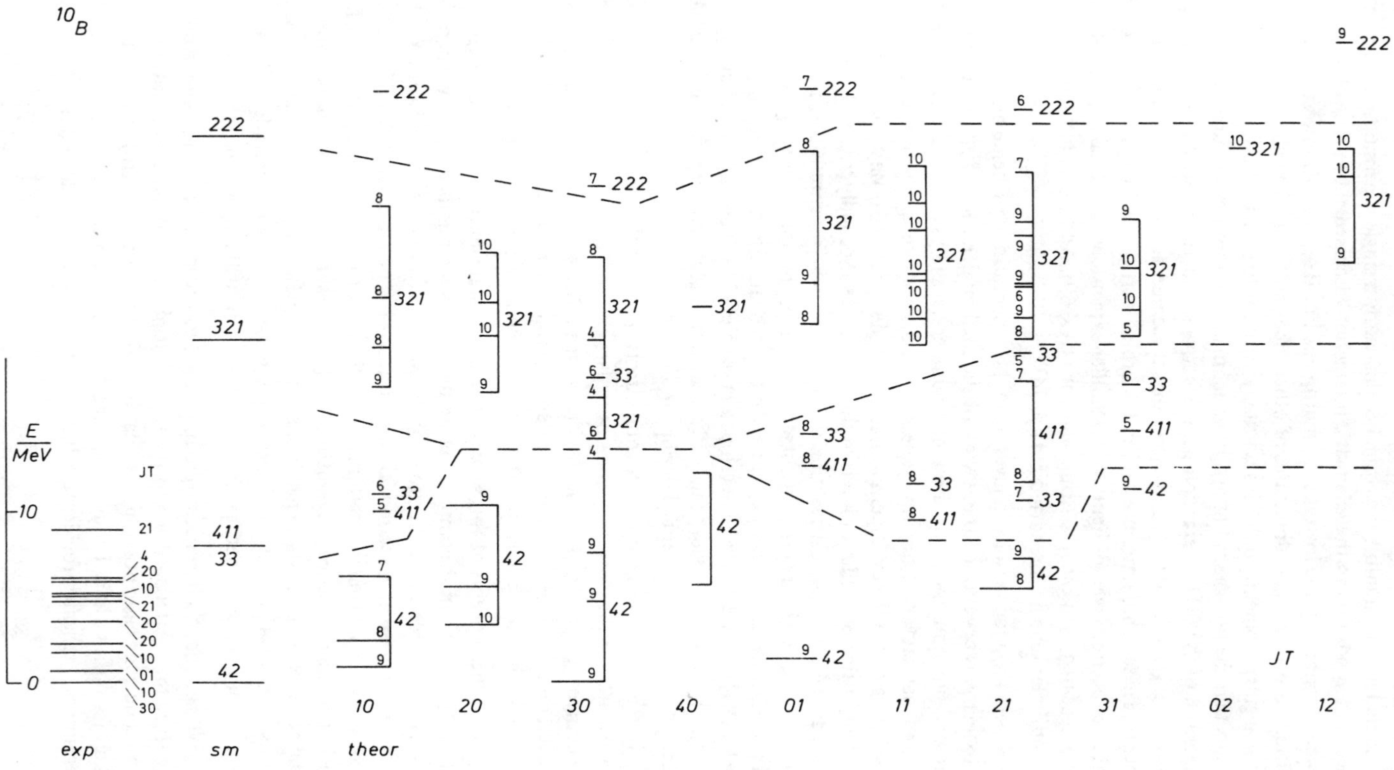

Fig. 2.6 Supermultiplet expansion in the p-shell for nuclei with A = 10. See caption of fig. 2.6 for details.

The excited levels fall into bands each dominated by a single supermultiplet. These bands correspond in position to the schematic interaction discussed above. The observed levels are well described by the lowest supermultiplets. For fixed JT, the lowest levels of a given partition have very small admixtures of other supermultiplets. The mixing of different orbital angular momenta and spins is usually stronger than that of different supermultiplets. It seems that the non-central interactions act mainly within a given supermultiplet. A comparison of the POT interaction with effective interactions derived from nucleon-nucleon-data is given in [JO 73] and shows that these interactions have comparable matrix elements. These computations establish the orbital partition as an approximate quantum number of excited levels of light nuclei. Similar expansions for the sd-configuration have been considered by Akiyama, Arima and Sebe [AK 69]. Additional information on the supermultiplet scheme is reported in [KR 74].

There are good reasons to investigate the supermultiplet scheme and corresponding approximations beyond the framework of the shell model. First of all, it seems that only the lowest supermultiplets for given mass number have physical significance. One should therefore maintain these supermultiplets but at the same time improve the orbital states. The splitting of the lowest supermultiplets is of the order of 30 MeV and hence competes with the splitting of oscillator levels in the shell model. Secondly, the shell model does not provide a scheme for nuclear reaction theory whereas the supermultiplet scheme is applicable to reaction channels as discussed for example by John and Seligman [JO 74]. We shall presently describe the scheme used in the resonating group method introduced by Wheeler [WH 37, WH 37a] and developed in full detail by Wildermuth and other authors [WI 77]. This scheme provides implicitly a supermultiplet model space which can be made explicit by use of the concepts described in this section.

In the resonating group method one starts from a trial state which is the product of internal states for the clusters or composite particles and a state for the relative motion of these composite particles. For simple composite particles or clusters it is usually assumed that the orbital state be stable under internal permutations. In the standard methods this state is multiplied by spin-isospin-states and antisymmetrized.

Using the concepts of this section, the orbital state corresponds to a weight $w = (w_1 w_2 \ldots w_j)$ whose components are the occupation numbers of the clusters. The orbital state is stable under the group of the weight $S(w)$ introduced in section 2.2. From the construction given in section 2.4 we learn that the possible partitions f for given weight may be classified by Gelfand patterns. In particular it follows that the partition f has at most j components. Hence the construction of the resonating group method provides orbital states corresponding to partitions with a restricted number of components, and these partitions are precisely the physically significant low supermultiplets. The choice of the supermultiplet is further restricted by the choice of the total spin.

We said that the resonating group method provides implicitly a supermultiplet model space since the orbital partition or the supermultiplet quantum numbers never appear in this method. Our basic point in this relation is that the orbital partition f should be made explicit for both technical and physical reasons. The technical reasons are as follows: The supermultiplet scheme provides us with a separation of the orbital and spin-isospin matrix elements and with the concept of reduced matrix elements which in turn allows for an exchange decomposition. We refer to [KR 69, 69a and 72] for the corresponding technique. The use of the general linear group to be described in section 3 is fully based on the use of the orbital partition. The physical reasons may be summarized in this way: It is essential in the discussion to separate the concept of a weight w or cluster structure from the concept of the orbital partition f. Both concepts are needed to sharpen the analysis of nuclear structure in terms of composite particle configurations. A discussion of nuclear structure based on the weight or the occupation number is not exhaustive and does not lead to an orthogonal scheme. An exhaustive, orthogonal and physically significant scheme is introduced by building up an orbital partition via a Gelfand pattern. This scheme is close to the physical states and equivalent to the supermultiplet scheme. In contrast to the concept of a weight it explains the qualitative and quantitative differences of levels and transitions in nuclei. In section 10 we shall take up this point of view and discuss in detail states and reactions of the lightest nuclei. At present we give a few simple examples of the reasoning based on the weight and the orbital partition.

Example 2.8: Channels and orbital partitions in the six-nucleon system

Consider the channels ^{3}He + ^{3}H and ^{4}He + ^{2}H in the system of six nucleons. These two channels correspond to the weights w = (3 3) and w = (4 2) respectively. For building up the physically allowed orbital partitions we do not need the concept of a Gelfand state. In terms of partitions we get

$$[3] \times [3] \rightarrow [42] + [33]$$
$$[4] \times [2] \rightarrow [42].$$

Hence, both weights or cluster structures may be used to build the partition f = [42], but only the first one induces the partition f = [33]. For bound state calculations this implies that both weights would contribute to the states with f = [42], and in fact, for the lowest oscillator excitation the two weights lead to the same orbital state. If now a resonance above the threshold of both channels exhibits the orbital partition f = [33], this resonance should not couple directly to the second channel. This selection rule is weakened by the presence of supermultiplet mixing or by indirect coupling via the two-body hamiltonian. Compare section 10.8 for more details on the six nucleon system and on similar selection rules.

Example 2.9: Electromagnetic transitions in the nine-nucleon system

The electromagnetic transitions are induced by a one-body operator. In terms of orbital partitions it follows that states involved in the transition may differ at most in the position of a single box of the Young diagram. Consider now the electromagnetic excitation of ^{9}Be from the ground state which corresponds to a good approximation to the partition f = [441]. Transitions are possible to the partitions f = [441], [432], [4311]. The last supermultiplet may be discarded for low energies. For the desintegration of the excited resonances we have the channels ^{8}Be + n, ^{7}Li + ^{2}H and ^{6}Li + ^{3}H. The last two channels open only above an excitation energy of E = 15 MeV. Only these two channels could be coupled to the orbital partition f = [432]. This follows since w = (441) is not an allowed weight for this partition. Resonances in this reaction below E = 15 MeV must therefore involve exclusively the partition f = [441].

Additional selection rules for electromagnetic transitions and in particular for E1 transitions are discussed for individual nuclei in section 10.8.

2.9 Notes and References

We conclude section 2 by giving some additional comments and references for the concepts and applications covered so far.

For the symmetric group and its standard representation theory we mention the book of Weyl [WE 31] and a review by Coleman [CO 68] as introductory accounts. Advanced treatments are given by Hamermesh [HA 62], Weyl [We 46], and by Robinson [RO 61]. The non-standard representations which employ reductions with respect to more general subgroups than the standard ones were first discussed by Elliott, Hope and Jahn [EL 53], by Kaplan [KA 61 and KA 61a] and by Horie [HO 64]. A systematic analysis was given in [KR 67, 68, 68a and 72]. Basic concepts are the permutation of sets and the 9f symbols. This analysis is summarized, modified and further developed in the present section. The most important modification is a redefinition of the product of permutations compared to [KR 68]. The Gelfand pattern, devised originally for the representation theory of the unitary group, is introduced in section 2.3 as an equivalent of a generalized Young tableau. In section 2.5 we extend the hook algorithm of [KR 67] to more general representations.

Double cosets of the symmetric group, their relation to exchange integrals and to the representations of the symmetric group were introduced in [KR 69a] and [KR 72].

We gave here only a brief account of these concepts since our applications will employ the relation to the general linear group to be developed in section 3. New results are the orthogonality relations of representations on double cosets treated in section 2.3. These orthogonality relations were first considered by Sullivan [SU 73]. The factorizations and decompositions given in propositions 2.51−2.53 are new, but special cases have been considered before in [KR 72]. Double cosets of the symmetric group have by now been applied in other fields of physics and in particular in quantum chemistry. Surveys are given for example by Seligman [SE 74], by Klein [KL 77], by Roël [RO 76] and by Jansen and Roël [JA 80].

The technique of the supermultiplet scheme introduced by Wigner [WI 37] was advanced in the work of Jahn, van Wieringen, Elliott and Hope [JA 51, EL 53]. These authors treated fully the spin-isospin states and the corresponding matrix elements for one- and two-body interactions. Hecht and Pang [HE 69] derived algebraic coefficients for the supermultiplet scheme and its application in nuclear shell models. In relation to the shell model, Jahn and coworkers developed the method of the last pair. The latter method was recognized in [KR 69] as a general concept of reduced matrix elements in the supermultiplet scheme, independent of the specific nuclear model. The alternative method of irreducible tensor operators with respect to the symmetric group was applied by Mahmoud and Cooper [MA 64] and by Vanagas and collaborators [VA 67, VA 71]. The algebraic relation of both methods is given in [KR 69].

The supermultiplet scheme in terms of schematic interactions was applied to nuclear structure by Franzini and Radicati [FR 63], extensions to schematic many-body interactions were considered already by Wheeler [WH 37, WH 37a], and later on by Burdet, Maguin and Partensky [BU 69]. The role of the orbital partition in the shell model was examined by many authors, we mentioned already the work of Akiyama, Arima and Sebe [AK 69] and [JO 73] as typical examples. The importance of the orbital partition for the resonating group method was recognized by Wheeler [WH 37, WH 37a]. Neudatchin and coworkers and Smirnov [NE 65, NE 69, SM 69] applied it to the interpretation of nuclear states and transitions. The interpretation and analysis of the nuclear cluster model as providing a supermultiplet model space was advocated and developed in [KR 69, 69a, 72, 73 and 74].

3 Unitary Structure of Orbital States

3.1 Concepts and Motivation

In principle it is possible to analyse the permutational symmetry of orbital states entirely in terms of the symmetric group, and for the nuclear states this approach has been adopted in [KR 69, 69a, 72]. The use of the unitary and general linear groups for the same purpose can be justified both on physical and mathematical grounds.

In many physical situations one deals with n-particle states built from a single-particle basis $\{\varphi_\alpha\}$. Here the index α denotes single-particle quantum numbers but for the present purpose we shall use it simply to enumerate j different single-particle states. The non-singular basis transformations of the type

$$\varphi'_\beta = \sum_\alpha \varphi''_\alpha c_{\alpha\beta}$$

yield $j \times j$ matrices $\{c_{\alpha\beta}\}$ which with respect to matrix multiplication are the elements of the general linear group in j dimensions denoted by $GL(j, \mathbb{C})$. Given two bases $\{\varphi_\alpha\}$ and $\{\varphi'_\beta\}$, we denote by ϵ the matrix of inner products

$$\epsilon_{\alpha\beta} = (\varphi_\alpha | \varphi'_\beta).$$

If the matrix ϵ is non-singular, it may be used to connect the basis $\{\varphi'_\beta\}$ with the basis $\{\varphi''_\gamma\}$ by use of $c_{\alpha\beta} = \epsilon_{\alpha\beta}$. Then clearly the basis $\{\varphi''_\gamma\}$ is biorthogonal to $\{\varphi_\alpha\}$, that is,

$$(\varphi_\alpha | \varphi''_\beta) = \delta_{\alpha\beta}.$$

If we start with an orthonormal single-particle basis, the linear transformation preserving this property must be elements of the unitary subgroup $U(j)$ of $GL(j, \mathbb{C})$.

The construction of n-particle states may be based on n-fold products of non-orthogonal single-particle states. These n-fold products admit the action both of the permutation group $S(n)$ and of the general linear group $GL(j, \mathbb{C})$. The transformation properties of the product states under $S(n)$ and $GL(j, \mathbb{C})$ gives rise to representations of both groups which we denote as d and D respectively. Mathematically, the analysis deals with the reduction of n-fold tensor products into irreducible parts. This reduction in general is well-known since the work of Weyl [WE 31], but the purpose of the present detailed treatment is the explicit correlation of mathematical concepts stemming from the representation theory of the symmetric and unitary group. In particular we shall examine in sections 3.2–3.6 the finite representations of the groups $S(n)$ and $GL(j, \mathbb{C})$, the Wigner coefficients of the group $GL(j, \mathbb{C})$ and the conjugation relation of representations of the group $GL(j, \mathbb{C})$.

The physical application is taken up in the remaining sections 3.7–3.11. The splitting of orbital states into products with the help of fractional parentage coefficients is discussed in section 3.7 and applied to the decomposition of orbital matrix elements in section 3.10. Orbital states are considered in section 3.9. Their inner products are reduced to basic exchange integral with the help of representations of the group $GL(j, \mathbb{C})$. In section 3.11 we analyse the orbital configuration with partition $f = [4^j]$ which is the basis of nuclear states built from j composite α-particles.

3.2 The General Linear and the Unitary Group and Their Finite-Dimensional Representations

The general linear and the unitary group in j dimensions are denoted as $GL(j, \mathbb{C})$ and $U(j)$ respectively. All representations which we are going to consider will be obtained from the n th Kronecker product of the natural representation

$$g \to D^{[1]}(g) = g.$$

Consider a j-dimensional complex linear space with a basis $\{\varphi_\alpha\}$, $\alpha = 1\ 2 \ldots j$ whose elements we shall call states. To build up tensors we shall employ n such spaces and distinguish their bases by a second index $i = 1\ 2 \ldots n$. Under $GL(j, \mathbb{C})$ we assume the bases $\{\varphi_{\alpha i}\}$, $i = 1\ 2 \ldots n$ to transform according to

$$(g\varphi)_{\beta i} = \sum_{\alpha = 1}^{j} \varphi_{\alpha i}\, D^{[1]}_{\alpha\beta}(g), \quad i = 1\ 2 \ldots n.$$

The n-fold products or product states

$$\prod_{i = 1}^{n} \varphi_{\alpha_i i}$$

for $\alpha_1 \alpha_2 \ldots \alpha_j$ ranging over all possible combinations of indices apparently span a basis of a representation of the group $GL(j, \mathbb{C})$. The corresponding representation is called the n th Kronecker power and we denote it as $(D^{[1]})^n$. A definition of general Kronecker products of representations is given in section 3.3. Consider now the action of permutations $p \in S(n)$ which act on the basis $\{\varphi_{\alpha i}\}$ according to

$$(p\varphi)_{\alpha i} = \sum_{k = 1}^{n} \varphi_{\alpha k}\, d_{ki}(p), \quad \alpha = 1\ 2 \ldots j.$$

3.1 Proposition: The action of the n th Kronecker power of $GL(j, \mathbb{C})$ is bisymmetric, that is, commutes with all permutations of $S(n)$.

Proof: The computation of the action of GL (j, $\mathbb{C}$) and S (n) in different orders yields

$$((p \circ g)\,\varphi)_{\beta i} = \sum_k (g\,\varphi)_{\beta k}\, d_{ki}(p) = \sum_{k\alpha} \varphi_{\alpha k}\, D^{[1]}_{\alpha\beta}(g)\, d_{ki}(p)$$

$$((g \circ p)\,\varphi)_{\beta i} = \sum_\alpha (p\,\varphi)_{\alpha i}\, D^{[1]}_{\alpha\beta}(g) = \sum_{\alpha k} \varphi_{\alpha k}\, d_{ki}(p)\, D^{[1]}_{\alpha\beta}(g)$$

and since both expressions are identical the group actions commute.   □

Proposition 3.1 shows that the product basis of the representation $(D^{[1]})^n$ of GL(j, $\mathbb{C}$) allows for the action of the group S(n), and since both actions commute, the product basis allows for the action of the direct product group GL (j, $\mathbb{C}$) $\times$ S (n). To distinguish the action of both groups on the single-particle states we use Greek and Latin indices respectively. It is well known that the irreducible representations of a direct product group are obtained as products of the irreducible representations of the factors. The peculiar feature of the present product basis is a correlation of the irreducible representations of both factors in such a way that the pairs of irreducible representations of GL (j, $\mathbb{C}$) and S(n) are described by partitions f of n. For the moment, we continue in the analysis of the action of S(n) and pass from the product basis to bases of irreducible representations of S(n). To get an exhaustive classification we first analyse the product basis with respect to the action of subgroups of S(n). In the original product basis, each index α occurs with a multiplicity which we call w_α and which obeys $0 \leqslant w_\alpha \leqslant n$. Apparently the collection

$$w = (w_1\,w_2\,\ldots\,w_j)$$

of these numbers has all properties of a weight as specified in definition 2.1. Products which belong to the same weight may be classified by

3.2 Definition: For all product states belonging to the same weight the reference product state is given by

$$\Pi_{w1} = \prod_{i=1}^{j} \varphi_{\alpha_i i}: \quad \text{if } i < k \text{ then } \alpha_i \leqslant \alpha_k.$$

Apparently this reference state is uniquely determined by the weight and moreover, it spans the identity representation of the group of the weight which was defined in definition 2.3 as the subgroup

$$S(w) = S(w_1) \times S(w_2) \times \ldots \times S(w_j)$$

of S (n). All other product states belonging to the same weight are obtained by the application of the left coset generators c_i of S (w) in S (n) which were defined in section 2.2. Choosing $c_1 = e$ we express this new classification of product states in the form

$$\Pi_{wi} = U(c_i)\,\Pi_{w1}.$$

We shall use the classification by the weight and the coset for all elements of the product basis, keeping in mind that the structure of the coset i is of course dependent on the subgroup S (w) and hence on the weight w, and summarize the construction as

3.3 Theorem: The basis of the n th Kronecker power $(D^{[1]})^n$ of GL (j, $\mathbb{C}$) can be characterized by weights w and corresponding cosets i of the group of the weight S(w). Under S(n), this basis transforms according to the representation induced by the identity representation of S(w).

The reduction of this induced representation can be described by a Gelfand scheme q according to proposition 2.29. Explicitly this reduction may be carried out by the application of Young operators. We choose the normalized Young operators c(rfq) of section 2.4 to define a new basis

$$\Pi_{wrfq} = c(rfq)\,\Pi_{w1} = \sum_i \Pi_{wi}\begin{bmatrix} f & q \\ r & i \end{bmatrix}$$

where the numbers

$$\begin{bmatrix} f & q \\ r & i \end{bmatrix} = \lambda_f^{-1}\,[w!]^{1/2}\,d_{rq}^f(c_i)$$

from proposition 2.37 are known to form the elements of a unitary matrix. We arrange this new basis first according to the partition f and then according to the other labels wrq.

Now we return to the action of the group GL (j, $\mathbb{C}$) on the new basis described so far in terms of the group S(n) and its action.

3.4 Theorem: The representation space of the n th Kronecker power $(D^{[1]})^n$ of GL(j, $\mathbb{C}$) can be decomposed into subspaces characterized by the partitions f of n. These subspaces are invariant under the action of both GL(j, $\mathbb{C}$) and S(n) and carry irreducible representations of GL (j, $\mathbb{C}$) $\times$ S(n).

Proof: With respect to the action of S(n), the basis is characterized by the partition f, the Young tableau r and by the Gelfand label q corresponding to a weight w. Since the action of GL(j, $\mathbb{C}$) commutes with the one of S(n), it cannot intertwine any subspaces which differ in the partition f and must be independent of the tableau r. The action of GL (j, $\mathbb{C}$) does of course affect the Gelfand pattern q and the weight w, whereas these labels do not change under the action of S(n). It follows that the partition f characterizes subspaces invariant under GL (j, $\mathbb{C}$). Weyl [WE 31] has shown that these invariant subspaces carry irreducible representations of GL (j, $\mathbb{C}$). □

We denote the matrix elements of the irreducible representations D^f of GL(j, $\mathbb{C}$) by Gelfand patterns as

$$D_{qq}^f(g).$$

We now turn our attention to the subgroup U (j) of GL (j, $\mathbb{C}$). It is well known that the representations of GL (j, $\mathbb{C}$) remain irreducible under this subduction. What happens actually is that the complex conjugate adjoint representations of GL (j, $\mathbb{C}$) coincide under the subduction [BA 77]. We claim now

3.5 Theorem: The representations D^f of GL (j, $\mathbb{C}$) when subduced to the subgroup U (j) are unitary.

Proof: For the subgroup $U(j)$ of $GL(j, \mathbb{C})$ the representation $D^{[1]}$ is clearly unitary. This property carries over to the n th Kronecker product $(D^{[1]})^n$. As pointed out in the construction, the reduction into irreducible parts was carried out by a *unitary* transformation by use of normalized Young operators. Hence the final irreducible form of the representation is still unitary and fulfills

$$D^f(u) [D^f]^+(u) = I. \qquad \qquad \square$$

The mutual relationship between representations of $GL(j, \mathbb{C})$ and $S(n)$ will now be extended by the introduction of an hermitian inner product in the complex linear space spanned by the basis $\{\varphi_\alpha\}$. For later physical application this inner product may be taken to be the standard inner product of the one-particle Hilbert space. This scalar product will be denoted as $(\ |\ )$. The single-particle scalar product induces in an obvious way an inner product with respect to the product basis states.

3.6 Definition: Two single-particle bases $\{\varphi_\alpha\}$, $\{\varphi_\beta''\}$ of a linear complex space of dimension j are called biorthogonal if

$$(\varphi_\alpha | \varphi_\beta'') = \delta_{\alpha\beta}.$$

If now we pass from the two biorthogonal bases to the respective product bases characterized by weights w, w'' and cosets i, i'', we clearly get

3.7 Proposition: The product states derived from two biorthogonal bases have the inner products

$$(\Pi_{wi} | \Pi_{w''i''}'') = \delta(w, w'') \delta(i, i'').$$

Because of the unitarity of the matrix which we used to pass from this basis to a basis characterized by the labels $wrfq$, we get from proposition 3.7 the corresponding result

3.8 Proposition: The bases of the Kronecker power $(D^{[1]})^n$ characterized by the labels $wrfq$ have the biorthogonal property

$$(\Pi_{wrfq} | \Pi_{w''r''f''q''}'') = \delta(w, w'') \delta(rfq, r''f''q'').$$

We analyse now a similar scalar product for two bases $\{\varphi_\alpha\}$, $\{\varphi_\beta'\}$ which are not orthogonal. Using properties of the normalized Young operators given in section 2.4 we have

$$(\Pi_{wrfq} | \Pi_{w'r'f'q'}') = (c(rfq) \Pi_{w1} | c(r'f'q') \Pi_{w'1}') = (\Pi_{w1} | c(qfr) c(r'f'q') \Pi_{w'1}')$$
$$= \delta(f, f') \delta(r, r') (\Pi_{w1} | \lambda_f c(qfq') \Pi_{w'1}').$$

Using the double coset decomposition of section 2.4 we get

$$\lambda_f (\Pi_{w1} | c(qfq') \Pi_{w'1}')$$

$$= \sum_k [w! \, w'!]^{1/2} d_{qq'}^f(z_k) (k!)^{-1} (\Pi_{w1} | U(z_k) | \Pi_{w'1}').$$

Now defining the matrix ϵ with elements

$$\epsilon_{\alpha\beta} = (\varphi_\alpha | \varphi'_\beta)$$

and applying the double coset generator z_k for the DC-symbol with entries $(k_{\alpha\beta})$ one obtains

$$(\Pi_{w1} | U(z_k) | \Pi'_{w'1}) = \prod_{\alpha,\beta=1}^{j} (\epsilon_{\alpha\beta})^{k_{\alpha\beta}} = \epsilon^k$$

and therefore finally finds

$$(\Pi_{wrfq} | \Pi'_{w'r'f'q'}) = \delta(r, r')\, \delta(f, f') \sum_k [w!\, w'!]^{1/2}\, d^f_{qq'}(z_k)\, (k!)^{-1}\, \epsilon^k.$$

On the other hand, we use now the transformation between the basis $\{\varphi'_\alpha\}$ and the basis $\{\varphi''_\gamma\}$ biorthogonal to $\{\varphi_\alpha\}$ given by

$$\varphi'_\beta = \sum_{\alpha=1}^{j} \varphi''_\alpha\, \epsilon_{\alpha\beta}.$$

For the n-body states we obtain by use of the representation D^f of $GL(j, \mathbb{C})$

$$\Pi'_{w'r'f'q'} = \sum_{q''} \Pi''_{w''r'f'q''}\, D^f_{q''q'}(\epsilon).$$

We can now evaluate the inner product in terms of $D^f(\epsilon)$ and get from proposition 3.8

$$(\Pi_{wrfq} | \Pi'_{w'r'f'q'}) = \delta(r, r')\, \delta(f, f')\, D^f_{qq'}(\epsilon).$$

Comparison of the two expressions for D^f yields

3.9 Theorem: The irreducible representations D^f of $GL(j, \mathbb{C})$ and d^f of $S(n)$ are related by the equation

$$D^f_{qq'}(\epsilon) = \sum_k [w!\, w'!]^{1/2}\, d^f_{qq'}(z_k)\, (k!)^{-1}\, \epsilon^k.$$

Note that the matrix ϵ, although defined originally in terms of single-particle overlaps, is used to describe a general element of the group $GL(j, \mathbb{C})$.

The explicit computation of the representation D^f will be discussed in sections 3.4, 3.5 and 3.6. Here we give only an expression for the dimension of this representation. For this expression we recall the definition 2.55 of the hook length $|h_i|$.

3.10 Proposition: The dimension $\dim(f, j)$ of the irreducible representation D^f of $GL(j, \mathbb{C})$ is given by the quotient

$$\dim(f, j) = \prod_{i \in f} (j + \beta_i - \alpha_i) \Big/ \prod_{i \in f} |h_i|.$$

This expression is given on p. 60 of [RO 61]. Since both products associate factors with each box of the diagram f, the simplest way of applying this expression is to draw two graphs by putting the factors of the two products into the boxes of the diagram f. In a symbolic fashion we determine the dimensions of the irreducible representations D^f of $GL(j, \mathbb{C})$ for $f = [1], [2]$ and $[11]$:

$$\dim([1], j) = \boxed{j} \Big/ \boxed{1} = j/1 = j$$

$$\dim([2], j) = \boxed{j \;\; j+1} \Big/ \boxed{2 \;\; 1} = j(j+1)/2$$

$$\dim([11], j) = \boxed{\begin{array}{c} j \\ j-1 \end{array}} \Big/ \boxed{\begin{array}{c} 2 \\ 1 \end{array}} = j(j-1)/2.$$

3.3 Wigner Coefficients of the Group GL (j, $\mathbb{C}$)

We recall the concept of Wigner coefficients from the familiar group $SU(2)$. These coefficients serve to couple product states of two angular momenta to eigenstates of the total angular momentum. With respect to irreducible representations the same coefficients reduce the Kronecker product of two irreducible representations into the irreducible parts. We summarize the generalization of these concepts to the group $GL(j, \mathbb{C})$.

3.11 Definition: The Kronecker product of two irreducible representations $D^{f'}, D^{f''}$ is the matrix representation $D^{f' \times f''}$ with elements

$$D^{f' \times f''}_{\tilde{q}'\tilde{q}'', q'q''}(\epsilon) = D^{f'}_{\tilde{q}'q'}(\epsilon) \, D^{f''}_{\tilde{q}''q''}(\epsilon)$$

3.12 Proposition: The irreducible representations of the group $GL(j, \mathbb{C})$ contained in $D^{f' \times f''}$ are determined by the Littlewood rules applied to the product $f' \times f''$ of partitions.

For a statement of the Littlewood rules we refer to the reduction theorem given by Robinson [RO 61, p. 61]. The following cases will be of particular interest to us since they are multiplicity-free:

(a) $f'' = [n'']$
(b) $f'' = [1^{n''}] = [1\ 1 \dots 1]$
(c) $f = [a^j] = [a\ a \dots a]$.

Case (a) was treated already in proposition 2.28. Case (b) is very similar to (a) and actually may be obtained from it by considering the associate problem

$$\hat{f}' \times \hat{f}'' = \hat{f}' \times [n''],$$

solving it and returning from $\hat{f}$ to f by association. Case (c) is different since it states a condition on the result of the reduction. In this case f' and f'' must be conjugate to each other, a concept to be explained in section 3.6.

In what follows we shall assume all reductions of Kronecker product representations to be multiplicity-free.

3.13 Definition: The explicit reduction of the Kronecker product representation $D^{f' \times f''}$ of GL (j, ℂ) is given by the Wigner coefficients

$$\langle f'q'f''q'' | fq \rangle = \overline{\langle fq | f'q'f''q'' \rangle}$$

in the forms

$$D^{f'}_{\tilde{q}'q'}(\epsilon) \, D^{f''}_{\tilde{q}''q''}(\epsilon) = \sum_{f\tilde{q}q} \langle f'\tilde{q}'f''\tilde{q}'' | f\tilde{q} \rangle \, D^{f}_{\tilde{q}q}(\epsilon) \, \langle fq | f'q'f''q'' \rangle$$

$$D^{f}_{\tilde{q}q}(\epsilon) = \sum_{\tilde{q}'q'\tilde{q}''q''} \langle f\tilde{q} | f'\tilde{q}'f''\tilde{q}'' \rangle \, D^{f'}_{\tilde{q}'q'}(\epsilon) \, D^{f''}_{\tilde{q}''q''}(\epsilon) \, \langle f'q'f''q'' | fq \rangle .$$

3.14 Proposition: The Wigner coefficients obey the two orthogonality conditions

$$\sum_{q'q''} \langle f'q'f''q'' | \tilde{f}\tilde{q} \rangle \langle fq | f'q'f''q'' \rangle = \delta(\tilde{f}, f) \, \delta(\tilde{q}, q)$$

$$\sum_{fq} \langle f'\tilde{q}'f''\tilde{q}'' | fq \rangle \langle fq | f'q'f''q'' \rangle = \delta(\tilde{q}', q') \, \delta(\tilde{q}'', q'') .$$

Proof: If the unitary subgroup U (j) of GL (j, ℂ) is considered, the relations given in the definition are just the definition of Wigner coefficients. The orthogonality of the Wigner coefficients then expresses the proposition that the reduction of unitary representations can be performed by a unitary matrix [HA 62].   □

3.4 Computation of Irreducible Representations of GL (j, ℂ) from Double Gelfand Polynomials

Consider j^2 complex numbers $z = (z_{il})$, $i, l = 1\,2\ldots j$ and all double coset symbols k according to section 2.2 such that

$$\sum_{i,l} k_{il} = n.$$

We shall construct certain polynomial functions in the variables z related to the irreducible representations of GL (j, ℂ). For complex linear spaces of analytic functions we shall make use of an inner product introduced by Bargmann [BA 68] to prove certain orthonormality properties. First of all, we define monomials $P^k(z)$ of degree n as

$$P^k(z) = (k!)^{-1/2} z^k = \prod_{i,l=1}^{j} [k_{il}!]^{-1/2} (z_{il})^{k_{il}}.$$

3.15 Proposition: The monomials $P^k(z)$ of degree n in the variables $z = (z_{il})$ are an ortho-normal and complete basis of all polynomials of degree n with respect to the Bargmann inner product.

For the proof we refer to section 4 where the Bargmann space is treated in detail. Now we recall from section 2.3 that the square symbols defined by

$$\begin{bmatrix} f & q \\ \tilde{q} & k \end{bmatrix} = \lambda_f^{-1} [\tilde{w}! \, w!]^{1/2} (k!)^{-1/2} \, d^f_{\tilde{q}q}(z_k)$$

obey the two orthonormality relations given in proposition 2.36′. This leads to the

3.16 Definition: The polynomials of degree n given by

$$P^f_{\tilde{q}q}(z) = {\sum_k}' \begin{bmatrix} f & q \\ \tilde{q} & k \end{bmatrix} (k!)^{-1/2} z^k$$

are called double Gelfand polynomials.

3.17 Proposition:

(1) The double Gelfand polynomials of degree n for all partitions of n and all possible pairs $\tilde{q}q$ of Gelfand patterns form a complete basis of all polynomials of degree n. This basis is orthonormal with respect to the inner product of Bargmann.

(2) The polynomials are proportional to the matrix elements of the irreducible representation D^f of $GL(j, \mathbb{C})$ according to

$$P^f_{\tilde{q}q}(z) = \lambda_f^{-1} D^f_{\tilde{q}q}(z).$$

(3) The polynomials are a basis of the irreducible representation D^f both under left and right action of $GL(j, \mathbb{C})$.

Proof:

(1) The orthonormality and completeness follows from the two orthonormality properties of the square symbols which relate the double Gelfand polynomials to the bases considered in proposition 3.15.

(2) The proportionality to matrix elements of the representation D^f follows by rewriting theorem 3.9 in terms of square symbols.

(3) Consider the right action of $GL(j, \mathbb{C})$ on z according to

$$(z\epsilon)_{il} = \sum_{s=1}^{j} {}' z_{is} \epsilon_{sl}.$$

From the representation property of D^f one gets for the double Gelfand polynomials

$$P^f_{\tilde{q}q}(z\epsilon) = {\sum_{q'}}' P^f_{\tilde{q}q'}(z) D^f_{q'q}(\epsilon)$$

which is just the condition that $P^f_{\tilde{q}q}(z)$ be a basis of the irreducible representation D^f. A similar result is obtained for the left action.   □

The relations given in proposition 3.15 are of great importance since powerful methods have been developed to compute explicitly the double Gelfand polynomials. To describe this computation we introduce two important concepts:

3.18 Definition: The weight $w = (w_1 w_2 \ldots w_j)$ is higher than the weight $\tilde{w} = (\tilde{w}_1 \tilde{w}_2 \ldots \tilde{w}_j)$ iff the first non-vanishing number $w_i - \tilde{w}_i$ for $i = 1\ 2 \ldots j$ is positive.

3.19 Proposition: For given partition f of n with $f = [f_1 f_2 \ldots f_j]$, the highest weight is given by $w_{max} = (f_1 f_2 \ldots f_j)$.

Proof: All weights of n can be ordered according to definition 3.18. For given partition f, inspection of the Gelfand patterns according to definition 2.29 shows that the Gelfand pattern of highest weight has the form

$$
\begin{array}{ccccc}
f_1 & f_2 & f_3 & \ldots & f_{j-1} \\
 & f_1 & f_2 & \ldots & f_{j-2} \\
 & & \cdot & & \\
 & & \cdot & \cdot & \\
 & & \cdot & & \\
 & f_1 & f_2 & & \\
 & & f_1 & &
\end{array}
$$

which we denote as q_{max}. The highest weight is determined from this Gelfand pattern in the form given above.

3.20 Proposition: The Gelfand polynomial of highest weight is given by

$$
P^f_{q_{max} q_{max}}(z) = [|f| (n!)^{-1}]^{1/2} (\Delta_1^1)^{f_1 - f_2} (\Delta_{1\,2}^{1\,2})^{f_2 - f_3} \ldots (\Delta_{1\,2\ldots j-1}^{1\,2\ldots j-1})^{f_{j-1} - f_j} (\Delta_{1\,2\ldots j}^{1\,2\ldots j})^{f_j}
$$

where $\Delta_{1\,2\ldots i}^{1\,2\ldots i}$ is the determinant of the submatrix obtained from z by selecting the rows $1\ 2 \ldots i$ and the columns $1\ 2 \ldots i$. All other Gelfand polynomials P^f may be obtained from this polynomial of highest weight by application of lowering operators.

The polynomials of highest weight were constructed by Moshinsky [MO 63], the lowering operators were derived by Nagel and Moshinsky [NA 65].

The construction of the representations D^f through double Gelfand polynomials will be extremely useful for applications to be discussed later. A few examples may serve to get an impression of the power of this method.

Consider first the partition of a closed block,

$$f = [a^j] = [a\ a \ldots a]$$

which for a = 4 would describe the orbital state of a configuration of α-clusters. There is only one possible weight w = (a a ... a) and the representation D^f is given from proposition 3.20 by

$$D^{[a^j]}(\epsilon) = (\Delta^{1\,2\,...\,j}_{1\,2\,...\,j})^a.$$

Another important type of representations is

$$f = [a\,a\,...\,a\,b]$$

for the highest weight. Again from proposition 3.20 one finds

$$D^{[a\,...\,ab]}_{q_{max}\,q_{max}}(\epsilon) = (\Delta^{1\,2\,...\,j-1}_{1\,2\,...\,j-1})^{a-b}(\Delta^{1\,2\,...\,j}_{1\,2\,...\,j})^b.$$

This case will lateron be applied for a = 4, b = 1, 2, 3. In some simple but physically important cases it proves useful to establish a correspondence between the Gelfand pattern and the index or index combination of the matrix ϵ.

Consider first the representation $D^{[1]}$ of GL (j, ℂ). The corresponding Gelfand pattern is completely determined by the weight w, and the weight is of the general form $w = (0^{r-1}\,1^{j-r+1})$ with $1 \leqslant r \leqslant j$. The single index r suffices to specify the weight, and with the correspondences

$$\tilde{q} \leftrightarrow \tilde{w} \leftrightarrow i \qquad q \leftrightarrow w \leftrightarrow r$$

one easily finds the result

$$D^{[1]}(\epsilon): \quad \begin{array}{c|c} & r \\ \hline i & \epsilon_{ir} \end{array}\quad.$$

Of particular interest are the representations f = [2] and f = [11] since they describe two-body states. In both cases the weight is completely sufficient to characterize the Gelfand pattern with respect to GL (j, ℂ).

For the partition f = [2] we specify a weight with components $w_r = 1$ $w_s = 1, r < s$ by the pair of numbers rs and a weight with a single component $w_r = 2$ by the pair rr. Hence the numbers r, s range according to

$$1 \leqslant r \leqslant s \leqslant j.$$

For the partition f = [11] the weight must have two components $w_r = w_s = 1, r < s$ and again we use instead of the Gelfand pattern these numbers with range

$$1 \leqslant r < s \leqslant j.$$

Our notation for these states is then

$$|[2]\,q) = |[2]\,rs)$$
$$|[11]\,q) = |[11]\,rs).$$

From theorem 3.9 it is easy to compute the corresponding matrix elements of the representations D^f. We obtain

$D^{[2]}$:

	r r	r $<$ s
i i	$\epsilon_{ir}\epsilon_{ir}$	$\sqrt{2}\,\epsilon_{ir}\epsilon_{is}$
i $<$ l	$\sqrt{2}\,\epsilon_{ir}\epsilon_{lr}$	$\epsilon_{ir}\epsilon_{ls} + \epsilon_{is}\epsilon_{lr}$

$D^{[11]}$:

	r $<$ s
i $<$ l	$\epsilon_{ir}\epsilon_{ls} - \epsilon_{is}\epsilon_{lr}$

For later use we indicate the correspondence between the Gelfand pattern, the weight and the pair r, s:

$$f = [1] \quad f: \begin{matrix} 1 & 0 \\ q & 1 \end{matrix} \quad . \quad . \quad . \quad \begin{matrix} 0 & 0 - j \\ 0 \end{matrix}$$

$$\begin{matrix} 1 & 0 & . & 0 & - - r \\ 0 & & 0 \end{matrix}$$

$$0$$

$$f = [2] \quad f: \begin{matrix} 2 & 0 \\ q & 2 \end{matrix} \quad \cdot \quad \cdot \quad \cdot \quad \cdot \quad \cdot \quad \cdot \quad \begin{matrix} 0 & 0 \\ 0 \end{matrix}$$

$$\begin{matrix} 2 & . & \cdot & \cdot & \cdot & \cdot & \cdot & 0 & - - s \\ 1 & & & & & & & 0 \end{matrix}$$

$$\begin{matrix} 1 & \cdot & \cdot & 0 & \cdot & - - \cdot - r \\ 0 & & 0 \end{matrix}$$

$$0$$

$$f: \begin{matrix} 2 & 0 \\ q & 2 \end{matrix} \quad \cdot \quad \cdot \quad \cdot \quad \cdot \quad \begin{matrix} 0 & 0 \\ 0 \end{matrix}$$

$$\begin{matrix} 2 \cdot & \cdot & \cdot & 0 & - - - s = r \\ 0 & & 0 \end{matrix}$$

$$0$$

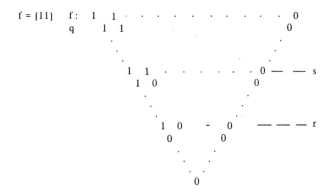

3.5 Computation of Irreducible Representations of GL (j, ℂ) from Representations of the Symmetric Group S (n)

Since the irreducible representation D^f of GL (j, ℂ) is a polynomial with coefficients determined by irreducible representations d^f of the symmetric group, this polynomial may in principle be constructed with the help of the representations d^f. Two simple but important examples will illustrate this possibility.

3.21 Proposition: For f = [n] the irreducible representation of GL(j, ℂ) is given by

$$D_{\tilde{q}q}^{[n]}(\epsilon) = [\tilde{w}!\,w!]^{1/2} \sum_k (k!)^{-1} \epsilon^k$$

with the sum over the double cosets restricted by the weights $\tilde{w}$, w.

Proof: For the partition f = [n] the specification of the weight completely determines the Gelfand pattern. Then the result follows from theorem 3.9 since $d^{[n]}(z_k) = 1$.   □

3.22 Proposition: For f = $[1^n]$, n = j the irreducible representation of GL (j, ℂ) is given by

$$D_{\tilde{q}q}^{[1^n]}(\epsilon) = \sum_k (-1)^{z_k} \epsilon^k = \Delta_{1\,2\,\dots\,n}^{1\,2\,\dots\,n}.$$

Proof: The first line follows from 3.9 with the restriction that the components for the weights $\tilde{w}$ and w be one or zero. The Gelfand patterns and corresponding generalized Young tableaus become the standard Young tableau of $d^{[1^n]}$ and this leads to the determinant given in the second line.   □

3.6 Conjugation Relations of Irreducible Representations of GL (j, ℂ)

Consider a partition [a a ... a] = $[a^j]$ and the corresponding irreducible one-dimensional representation of GL (j, ℂ) given from proposition 3.20 as

$$D^{[aa\dots a]}(\epsilon) = (\Delta_{1\,2\,\dots\,j}^{1\,2\,\dots\,j})^a.$$

3.23 Definition: Let f be a partition of j components, $f = [f_1 f_2 \ldots f_j]$ such that $f_1 \leqslant a$. The partition f^c a-conjugate to f is defined by

$$f^c = [a - f_j, a - f_{j-1}, \ldots, a - f_2, a - f_1].$$

The relation between conjugate representation is expressed by

3.24 Theorem: For a partition f as in definition 3.23, the only partition $\widetilde{f}$ which allows the reduction of the Kronecker product representation of D^f and $D^{\widetilde{f}}$ to $D^{[a\,a\,\cdots\,a]}$ is the conjugate partition f^c and the reduction is given by

$$D^{[aa\cdots a]}(\epsilon) = \sum_{\widetilde{q}q} \langle [a^j] | f^c \widetilde{q}^c f\widetilde{q} \rangle \, D^{f^c}_{\widetilde{q}^c q^c}(\epsilon) \, D^{f}_{\widetilde{q}q}(\epsilon) \, \langle f^c q^c fq | [a^j] \rangle.$$

The Gelfand patterns q^c and q are uniquely related to each other.

Proof: For the group SL $(j, \mathbb{C})$ of unimodular matrices the conjugation relation has been given in full detail by Baird and Biedenharn [BA 64]. These authors obtained explicit results for the Wigner coefficients related to conjugation.   □

The relation between the Gelfand patterns q and q^c may be expressed by saying that the partitions occuring in the row i of the patterns q and q^c respectively are a-conjugate partitions belonging to GL $(i, \mathbb{C})$.

3.25 Proposition: The conjugate representation D^{f^c} may be rewritten in terms of D^f according to

$$\langle [a^j] | f^c \widetilde{q}^c f\widetilde{q} \rangle \, D^{f^c}_{\widetilde{q}^c q^c}(\epsilon) \, \langle f^c q^c fq | [a^j] \rangle = D^{f}_{q\widetilde{q}}(\epsilon^{-1}) \, \dim^{-1}(f, j) \, (\Delta^{1\,2\,\cdots\,j}_{1\,2\,\cdots\,j})^a.$$

Proof: We rewrite the dimension dim (f, j) of the irreducible representation D^f according to

$$\dim(f, j) = \text{trace}(D^f(e)) = \text{trace}(D^f(\epsilon^{-1}\epsilon)) = \sum_{\widetilde{q}q} D^{f}_{q\widetilde{q}}(\epsilon^{-1}) \, D^{f}_{\widetilde{q}q}(\epsilon).$$

Therefore we get

$$D^{[aa\cdots a]}(\epsilon) = \dim^{-1}(f, j) \, (\Delta^{1\,2\,\cdots\,j}_{1\,2\,\cdots\,j})^a \sum_{\widetilde{q}q} D^{f}_{q\widetilde{q}}(\epsilon^{-1}) \, D^{f}_{\widetilde{q}q}(\epsilon).$$

The result follows by comparing this expression with the one given in theorem 3.24.   □

We shall use proposition 3.25 in a modified form by introducing the algebraic complements of ϵ as the matrix

$$\beta = {}^t\epsilon^{-1} \, \Delta^{1\,2\,\cdots\,j}_{1\,2\,\cdots\,j}.$$

Then we find

3.25' Proposition: The conjugate representations D^{f_c} and D^f are related by the equation

$$\langle [a^j] | f^c \widetilde{q}^c f\widetilde{q} \rangle \, D^{f^c}_{\widetilde{q}^c q^c}(\epsilon) \, \langle f^c q^c fq | [a^j] \rangle = \dim^{-1}(f, j) \, (\Delta^{1\,2\,\cdots\,j}_{1\,2\,\cdots\,j})^{a-n} \, D^{f}_{\widetilde{q}q}(\beta).$$

For $\epsilon \in SL(j, \mathbb{C})$ this relation yields the equivalence of the representation D^f with the conjugate or adjoint representation. The special case $\epsilon = e$ shows that

$$|\langle [a^j] | f^c q^c f q \rangle|^2 = \dim^{-1}(f, j)$$

and since the Wigner coefficients may be chosen to be real, they depend on the Gelfand pattern only through a factor ± 1.

As a specific example we consider the partitions $f = [2]$ and $f = [11]$ for the group $GL(j, \mathbb{C})$.

We get for these two cases

$$\langle [a^j] | [a^{j-1} 2] \, \tilde{q}^c [2] \, \tilde{q} \rangle \, D^{[a^{j-1} 2]}_{\tilde{q}^c q^c}(\epsilon) \, \langle [a^{j-1} 2] q^c [2] q | [a^j] \rangle = \frac{2}{j(j+1)} \, (\Delta^{1 2 \ldots j}_{1 2 \ldots j})^{a-2} \, D^{[2]}_{\tilde{q} q}(\beta)$$

$$\langle [a^j] | [a^{j-2} a - 1 a - 1] \, \tilde{q}^c [11] \, \tilde{q} \rangle \, D^{[a^{j-2} a - 1 a - 1]}_{\tilde{q}^c q^c}(\epsilon) \, \langle [a^{j-2} a - 1 a - 1] q^c [11] q | [a^j] \rangle$$

$$= \frac{2}{j(j-1)} \, (\Delta^{1 2 \ldots j}_{1 2 \ldots j})^{a-2} \, D^{[11]}_{\tilde{q} q}(\beta).$$

These matrix elements may easily be rewritten in the notation introduced at the end of section 3.5.

3.7 Fractional Parentage Coefficients and their Computation

The fractional parentage coefficients arise as the coefficients in an expansion of n-body states of permutational symmetry into products of n'-body and n''-body states of similar type. We analyse this expansion first in terms of the symmetric group, then in terms of the linear group and thus derive a new general relation between concepts arising from these groups.

The index $', ''$ refers throughout this section to the two sets of particles, it does not denote components of a partition. Consider the n-body Young operator

$$c(f'r'f''r''fq) = \lambda_f^{-1} [w!]^{-1/2} \sum_p d^f_{f'r'f''r'',q}(p) \, U(p).$$

Introducing the double coset decomposition with respect to $S(\tilde{w}) = S(n') \times S(n'')$ and $S(w)$ and writing

$$p = \tilde{h}\tilde{h}'' z_k h$$

one obtains the decomposition

$$d^f_{f'r'f''r'',q}(p) = \sum_{q'q''} d^{f'}_{r'q'}(\tilde{h}') \, d^{f''}_{r''q''}(\tilde{h}'') \, d^f_{f'q'f''q'',q}(z_k h).$$

The introduction of Gelfand patterns $q'q''$ for the intermediate summation is justified by observing that the double coset symbol determines the weights w', w'' as

$$w' = (k_{11}, k_{12}, \ldots, k_{1j})$$
$$w'' = (k_{21}, k_{22}, \ldots, k_{2j}).$$

The multiplicity $m(k)$ becomes

$$m(k) = k! = w'! \, w''!$$

If d^f is written in the new form and if the three Young operators

$$c(r'f'q') = \left[\frac{|f'|}{n'! \, w'!}\right]^{1/2} \sum_{\tilde{h}'} d^{f'}_{r'q'}(\tilde{h}') \, U(\tilde{h}')$$

$$c(r''f''q'') = \left[\frac{|f''|}{n''! \, w''!}\right]^{1/2} \sum_{\tilde{h}''} d^{f''}_{r''q''}(\tilde{h}'') \, U(\tilde{h}'')$$

$$c^w = \left[\frac{1}{w!}\right] \sum_k d^{[w_1] \times [w_2] \times \ldots \times [w_j]}(h) \, U(h)$$

are introduced, one obtains after a change of the summation the decomposition

$$c(f'r'f''r''fq) = \sum_{kq'q''} c(r'f'q') \, c(r''f''q'') \, U(z_k) \circ c^w$$

$$\lambda_f^{-1} \lambda_{f'} \lambda_{f''} \left[\frac{w!}{w'! \, w''!}\right]^{1/2} d^f_{f'q'f''q'',fq}(z_k).$$

We now apply this operator to the reference n-body product state Π_{w1}.

3.26 Proposition: The double coset generator z_k acts on the reference product state as

$$U(z_k) \, \Pi_{w1} = \Pi_{w'1} \, \Pi_{w''1}$$

Proof: The property is obtained from the explicit form of z_k given in proposition 2.17. The double coset symbol is given by

$$k = \left\{ \begin{array}{cccc} k_{11} & k_{12} \ldots k_{1j} \\ k_{21} & k_{22} \ldots k_{2j} \end{array} \right\}$$

and the corresponding refinements of the weights $w = (w_1 w_2 \ldots w_j)$ and $\tilde{w} = (n'n'')$ are from definition 2.16 given as

$$w(k) = (k_{11} k_{21} k_{12} \ldots k_{1j} k_{2j})$$

$$\tilde{w}(k) = (k_{11} k_{12} \ldots k_{1j} k_{21} k_{22} \ldots k_{2j}).$$

Comparing these refined weights one obtains from $\tilde{w}(k) = (w(k))^q$ the permutation q as

$$q: \begin{bmatrix} 1 & 2 \ldots & j & j+1 & j+2 & \ldots & 2j \\ 1 & 3 \ldots & 2j-1 & 2 & 4 & \ldots & 2j \end{bmatrix}.$$

The permutation matrix and the permutation z_k are now constructed from

$$d(z_k) = d(q, w(k)).$$

The application of z_k to the reference state with respect to the weight w is then found to yield the product of the reference states with respect to the weights w' and w''.   □

3.27 Proposition: The fractional parentage coefficients in the expansion

$$c\,(f'r'f''r''fq)\,\Pi_{w1} = \sum_{q'q''} c\,(r'f'q')\,\Pi_{w'1}\,c\,(r''f''q'')\,\Pi_{w''1}\,\langle f'q'f''q''|fq\rangle$$

are given by

$$\langle f'q'f''q''|fq\rangle = \lambda_f^{-1}\,\lambda_{f'}\lambda_{f''}\left[\frac{w!}{w'!\,w''!}\right]^{1/2} d^f_{f'q'f''q'',\,q}(z_k).$$

Proof: We use proposition 3.26 and $c^w\,\Pi_{w1} = \Pi_{w1}$ along with the double coset decomposition.   □

The alternative derivation of the fractional parentage coefficients is based on the group GL (j, $\mathbb{C}$). We have shown in section 3.2 that the states

$$c\,(r'f'q')\,\Pi_{w'1},\quad c\,(r''f''q'')\,\Pi_{w''1},\quad c\,(rfq)\,\Pi_{w1}$$

transform according to the representations

$$D^{f'},D^{f''},D^f$$

of GL (j, $\mathbb{C}$) respectively. By standard Wigner coefficients of the group GL (j, $\mathbb{C}$), it is possible to couple the bases of the representations $D^{f'}, D^{f''}$ to a basis of the representation D^f. Consider now the coupling

$$\sum_{q'q''} c\,(r'f'q')\,\Pi_{w'1}\,c\,(r''f''q'')\,\Pi_{w''1}\,\langle f'q'f''q''|fq\rangle.$$

Under GL (j, $\mathbb{C}$), this state must transform according to the representation D^f. Under S(n') and S(n'') it clearly transforms according to the representations d^f and $d^{f''}$. But the representation label of S(n) must coincide with the representation label f of GL (j, $\mathbb{C}$) and hence the coupling procedure automatically establishes the representation d^f of S(n), so that alternatively we have

$$c\,(f'r'f''r''fq)\,\Pi_{w1} = \sum_{q'q''} c\,(r'f'q')\,\Pi_{w'1}\,c\,(r''f''q'')\,\Pi_{w''1}\,\langle f'q'f''q''|fq\rangle$$

and we find

3.28 Theorem: The Wigner coefficients of GL (j, $\mathbb{C}$) are explicitly related to irreducible representations of S (n) by

$$\langle f'q'f''q''|fq\rangle = \lambda_f^{-1}\,\lambda_{f'}\lambda_{f''}\left[\frac{w!}{w'!\,w''!}\right]^{1/2} d^f_{f'q'f''q'',\,fq}(z_k).$$

Of course it is implied here that the Kronecker product is multiplicity-free. We shall use this theorem exclusively for one-row or one-column partitions f''. Note also that $|f|$ is always the dimension of the representation d^f of $S(n)$. Note that we anticipated the result of this theorem in the notation of proposition 3.27 in order to avoid additional symbols.

3.29 Theorem: The Wigner coefficients of $GL(j, \mathbb{C})$ are given in terms of $9f$ symbols as

$$\langle f'q'f''q''|fq\rangle = \lambda_f^{-1}\lambda_{f'}\lambda_{f''}\left[\frac{w!}{w'!\,w''!}\right]^{1/2}\begin{bmatrix} f & f_{j-1} & w_j \\ f' & f'_{j-1} & k_{1j} \\ f'' & f''_{j-1} & k_{2j} \end{bmatrix}\prod_{i=2}^{j-1}\begin{bmatrix} f_i & f_{i-1} & w_i \\ f'_i & f'_{i-1} & k_{1i} \\ f''_i & f''_{i-1} & k_{2i} \end{bmatrix},$$

Proof: We employ proposition 2.53 to factorize the representation d^f of $S(n)$. $\square$

The factorization of Wigner coefficients in the representation theory of the unitary group $U(j)$ is expressed through the introduction of reduced Wigner coefficients. We rephrase theorem 3.29 in this formulation:

3.29′ Theorem: The Wigner coefficients of $GL(j, \mathbb{C})$ factorize into a product of reduced Wigner coefficients according to

$$\langle f'q'f''q''|fq\rangle = \left\langle \begin{matrix} f' & f'' \\ f'_{j-1} & f''_{j-1} \end{matrix} \,\middle|\, \begin{matrix} f \\ f_{j-1} \end{matrix} \right\rangle \prod_{i=2}^{j-1} \left\langle \begin{matrix} f'_i & f''_i \\ f'_{i-1} & f''_{i-1} \end{matrix} \,\middle|\, \begin{matrix} f_i \\ f_{i-1} \end{matrix} \right\rangle .$$

where the reduced Wigner coefficients are given by

$$\left\langle \begin{matrix} f' & f'' \\ f'_{j-1} & f''_{j-1} \end{matrix} \,\middle|\, \begin{matrix} f \\ f_{j-1} \end{matrix} \right\rangle = \lambda_f^{-1}\lambda_{f'}\lambda_{f''}\lambda_{f_{j-1}}\,\lambda_{f'_{j-1}}^{-1}\,\lambda_{f''_{j-1}}^{-1}\left[\frac{w_j!}{w'_j!\,w''_j!}\right]^{1/2}\begin{bmatrix} f & f_{j-1} & w_j \\ f' & f'_{j-1} & w'_j \\ f'' & f''_{j-1} & w''_j \end{bmatrix} .$$

3.8 Bordered Decomposition of Irreducible Representations for the Group GL (j, ℂ)

In the present section we treat certain decompositions of finite irreducible representations for the group $GL(j, \mathbb{C})$ which will be used in later applications. Consider the irreducible representations $D^f(\epsilon)$ of $GL(j, \mathbb{C})$. The matrix elements of this representation are polynomials in the elements of the matrix ϵ. By $\epsilon_{..}$ we denote the $(j-1)\times(j-1)$ submatrix of ϵ obtained by omitting the last row and column which we term the border of ϵ. Now we derive a decomposition of the polynomials $D^f(\epsilon)$ into a sum of products of polynomials depending on $\epsilon_{..}$ and on the border of ϵ respectively.

3.30 Proposition: The finite irreducible representations of the group $GL(j, \mathbb{C})$ have the bordered decomposition

$$D^{f}_{\tilde{f}_{j-1}(\tilde{q}_{j-1})\,\tilde{w}_j,\,f_{j-1}(q_{j-1})\,w_j}(\epsilon)$$

$$= [\tilde{w}_j!\,w_j!]^{1/2} \sum_{a_{j-1}\tilde{q}_{j-1}q_{j-1}'\,\tilde{s}_{j-1}\,\tilde{q}_{j-1}''\,s_{j-1}\,q_{j-1}''} \left\{ \langle \tilde{f}_{j-1}\tilde{q}_{j-1} \mid a_{j-1}\tilde{q}_{j-1}'\tilde{s}_{j-1}\tilde{q}_{j-1}'' \rangle\, \lambda_{\tilde{f}_{j-1}}\lambda^{-1}_{a_{j-1}}\lambda^{-1}_{\tilde{s}_{j-1}} \right.$$

$$\langle a_{j-1}q_{j-1}'s_{j-1}q_{j-1}'' \mid f_{j-1}q_{j-1} \rangle\, \lambda_{f_{j-1}}\lambda^{-1}_{a_{j-1}}\lambda^{-1}_{s_{j-1}} \begin{bmatrix} f & f_{j-1} & \tilde{w}_j \\ \tilde{f}_{j-1} & a_{j-1} & \tilde{s}_{j-1} \\ \tilde{w}_j & s_{j-1} & k_{jj} \end{bmatrix}$$

$$\left. D^{a_{j-1}}_{\tilde{q}_{j-1}'\,q_{j-1}'}(\epsilon_{..}) \prod_{i<j}(k_{ij}!)^{-1/2}(\epsilon_{ij})^{k_{ij}} \prod_{j>l}(k_{jl}!)^{-1/2}(\epsilon_{jl})^{k_{jl}}(k_{jj}!)^{-1}(\epsilon_{jj})^{k_{jj}} \right\}.$$

The notation is taken from proposition 2.54 for $\bar{j} = j$ with the following redefinitions: $\tilde{s}_{j-1}$ and s_{j-1} are partitions of a single component with

$$\tilde{s}_{j-1} = sk_{.j} = \sum_{l=1}^{j-1} k_{lj} \qquad s_{j-1} = sk_{j.} = \sum_{i=1}^{j-1} k_{ji}$$

and the corresponding Gelfand patterns $\tilde{q}_{j-1}''$ and q_{j-1}'' are completely determined by the weights

$$\tilde{w}'' = (k_{1j}k_{2j} \ldots k_{j-1j}), \quad w'' = (k_{j1}k_{j2} \ldots k_{jj-1}).$$

The algebraic coefficients are Wigner coefficients of the group $GL(j-1, \mathbb{C})$, a 9f symbol and the factors λ.

Proof: We start from the expression for $D^f(\epsilon)$ given in theorem 3.9,

$$D^{f}_{\tilde{q}\,q}(\epsilon) = [\tilde{w}!\,w!]^{1/2} \sum_k d^{f}_{\tilde{q}\,q}(z_k)\,(k!)^{-1}\,\epsilon^k.$$

To the representation matrix $d^f(z_k)$ of $S(n)$ we apply the decomposition given in proposition 2.54. The representation matrices $d^{\tilde{f}_{j-1}}$ and $d^{f_{j-1}}$ are converted into Wigner coefficients of the group $GL(j-1, \mathbb{C})$ according to theorem 3.28. This conversion introduces the six powers of coefficients λ. The representation matrix d^f yields a 9f symbol according to definition 2.48. Having decomposed the algebraic factors we return to the polynomial in the matrix elements of the matrix ϵ. The sum over the entries of the submatrix $k_{..}$ of k applies to the representation matrix $d^{a_{j-1}}$ and to the corresponding part of ϵ^k which we denote as $(\epsilon_{.})^{k_{..}}$. We combine this part of the polynomial according to

$$D^{a_{j-1}}_{\tilde{q}_{j-1}'\,q_{j-1}'}(\epsilon_{..}) = [\tilde{w}'!\,w'!]^{1/2} \sum_{k_{..}} d^{a_{j-1}}_{\tilde{q}_{j-1}'\,q_{j-1}'}(z_{k_{..}})\,(k_{..}!)^{-1}(\epsilon_{.})^{k_{..}}.$$

The remaining numerical factors arise from the combination of factorials of weight components.   □

Proposition 3.30 may be used in principle to decompose the full representation $D^f(\epsilon)$ in j steps. The basic algebraic coefficient is in all steps a 9f symbol without multiplicity. We display this property by writing the decomposition for the product of one of the Wigner coefficients multiplied by the corresponding factors of the type λ:

$$\langle a_{j-1} q'_{j-1} s_{j-1} q''_{j-1} | f_{j-1} q_{j-1} \rangle \lambda_{f_{j-1}} \lambda^{-1}_{a_{j-1}} \lambda^{-1}_{s_{j-1}}$$

$$= \langle \begin{array}{cc} a_{j-1} & s_{j-1} \\ a_{j-2} & s_{j-2} \end{array} \left| \begin{array}{c} f_{j-1} \\ f_{j-2} \end{array} \right. \rangle \; \lambda_{f_{j-1}} \lambda^{-1}_{a_{j-1}} \lambda^{-1}_{s_{j-1}}$$

$$\langle a_{j-2} q'_{j-2} s_{j-2} q''_{j-2} | f_{j-2} q_{j-2} \rangle$$

$$= \left[\frac{w_{j-1}!}{w'_{j-1}! \, w''_{j-1}!} \right]^{1/2} \begin{bmatrix} f_{j-1} & f_{j-2} & w_{j-1} \\ a_{j-1} & a_{j-2} & w'_{j-1} \\ s_{j-1} & s_{j-2} & w''_{j-1} \end{bmatrix}$$

$$\langle a_{j-2} q'_{j-2} s_{j-2} q''_{j-2} | f_{j-2} q_{j-2} \rangle \lambda_{f_{j-2}} \lambda^{-1}_{a_{j-2}} \lambda^{-1}_{s_{j-2}}.$$

Here we used the reduced Wigner coefficient and its relation to a 9f symbol according to proposition 3.29′.

Example 3.1: Decomposition of a representation for the group $GL(5, \mathbb{C})$.

We study here a specific example for use in section 8. Consider the representation $f = [44b00]$ with weights $\tilde{w} = w = (00b44)$ and with the Gelfand patterns

$$\tilde{q} = q = \begin{array}{cccc} 4 & b & 0 & 0 \\ & b & 0 & 0 \\ & & 0 & 0 \\ & & & 0 \end{array} .$$

Moreover we take the matrix ϵ in the particular form

$$\epsilon = \begin{bmatrix} \epsilon_{11} & 0 & 0 & 0 & \epsilon_{15} \\ 0 & \epsilon_{11} & 0 & 0 & \epsilon_{25} \\ 0 & 0 & \epsilon_{11} & 0 & \epsilon_{35} \\ 0 & 0 & 0 & \epsilon_{11} & \epsilon_{45} \\ \epsilon_{51} & \epsilon_{52} & \epsilon_{53} & \epsilon_{54} & \epsilon_{55} \end{bmatrix} .$$

In this case the 4×4 submatrix $\epsilon_{..}$ is given by

$$\epsilon_{..} = I_4 \epsilon_{11} .$$

Applying proposition 3.30 to this special case we note first of all that

$$D^{a_4}_{q_4 q_4}(\epsilon_{..}) = \delta(\tilde{q}_4, q_4) (\epsilon_{11})^{n_{a_4}}$$

and hence this part does not contribute to an explicit dependence on the partition a_4 except through the number n_{a_4} given by

$$n_{a_4} = n - \widetilde{w}_5 - w_5 + k_{55} = b + k_{55}.$$

From the special form of D^{a_4}, the choice $\widetilde{q} = q$ and the conditions implied by the Wigner coefficients we get that all symbols marked by the sign $\sim$ coincide with the corresponding ones without this sign and that moreover $k_{35} = k_{53}$ and $k_{45} = k_{54}$. Hence the complete decomposition must be of the form

$$D_{qq}^{[44b00]}(\epsilon) = \sum_{k_{35}k_{45}k_{55}} \{C(44b, k_{35}k_{45}k_{55}) \delta_{k_{35}+k_{45}+k_{55},4} \delta_{k_{35},k_{53}} \delta_{k_{45},k_{54}}$$

$$\epsilon_{11}^{b+k_{55}} (k_{35}!)^{-1} \epsilon_{35}^{k_{35}} (k_{45}!)^{-1} \epsilon_{45}^{k_{45}} (k_{53}!)^{-1} \epsilon_{53}^{k_{53}} (k_{54}!)^{-1} \epsilon_{54}^{k_{54}} (k_{55}!)^{-1} \epsilon_{55}^{k_{55}} \}.$$

There is no dependence on $\epsilon_{15}\epsilon_{25}\epsilon_{51}\epsilon_{52}$ because of the chosen weights. Now we claim that this expression can be computed explicitly. To show this we note that the polynomial is not of highest weight but differs from a polynomial of doubly highest weights only by a permutation of weight components. Comparing proposition 3.20 we conclude that

$$D_{qq}^{[44b00]}(\epsilon) = (\Delta_{45}^{45})^{4-b} (\Delta_{345}^{345})^b$$

where for the special form of the matrix ϵ the determinants are

$$\Delta_{45}^{45} = \epsilon_{11}\epsilon_{55} - \epsilon_{45}\epsilon_{54}$$

$$\Delta_{345}^{345} = \epsilon_{11}(\epsilon_{11}\epsilon_{55} - \epsilon_{35}\epsilon_{53} - \epsilon_{45}\epsilon_{54}).$$

A simple multinomial expansion yields

$$D_{qq}^{[44b00]}(\epsilon) = \sum_{k_{55}\,\kappa} \left\{ (-1)^{k_{55}} \frac{(4-\kappa)!\,b!\,\kappa!\,(4-k_{55}-\kappa)!}{(b-\kappa)!} \epsilon_{11}^{b+k_{55}} \right.$$

$$\left. (\kappa!)^{-2} (\epsilon_{35}\epsilon_{53})^{\kappa} ((4-k_{55}-\kappa)!)^{-2} (\epsilon_{45}\epsilon_{54})^{4-k_{55}-\kappa} (k_{55}!)^{-1} \epsilon_{55}^{k_{55}} \right\}.$$

Comparing this explicit expansion with the form given above one obtains with $\kappa = k_{35} = k_{53}$ for the coefficient

$$C(44b, k_{35}k_{45}k_{55}) = (-1)^{k_{55}} \frac{(4-k_{35})!\,b!\,k_{35}!\,(4-k_{35}-k_{55})!}{(b-k_{35})!}.$$

A direct evaluation of this coefficient from proposition 3.30 would have involved a sum over three 9f symbols.

We restricted the discussion to the case where, below the level of the representations of the subgroup GL$(3, \mathbb{C})$, the Gelfand patterns $\widetilde{q}, q$ of $D^f(\epsilon)$ have the form

$$\begin{matrix} \widetilde{f}_3 \\ \\ \widetilde{q}_3 \end{matrix} = \begin{matrix} f_3 \\ \\ q_3 \end{matrix} = \begin{matrix} b & 0 & 0 \\ & 0 & 0 \\ & & 0 \end{matrix} \, .$$

From the remarks following proposition 3.30, it is clear that a change of the labels $\tilde{q}_3 q_3$ would introduce Wigner coefficients below this level. Replacing $k_{35} = k_{53}$ by a label s_3, we must simply substitute instead of the term

$$(s_3!)^{-1} \, (\epsilon_{35})^{s_3} \, (\epsilon_{53})^{s_3}$$

the sum

$$\sum_{q_3' \tilde{q}_3'' q_3''} \langle b \, \tilde{q}_3 \, | \, a_3 q_3' s_3 \tilde{q}_3'' \rangle \, P^{s_3}_{\tilde{q}_3''.} \, (\epsilon_{15} \epsilon_{25} \epsilon_{35}) \, P^{s_3}_{.q_3''} \, (\epsilon_{51} \epsilon_{52} \epsilon_{53}) \, \langle a_3 q_3' s_3 q_3'' \, | \, b \, q_3 \rangle$$

where all partitions have a single component and the polynomials are double Gelfand polynomials of the type

$$P^{s_3}_{\tilde{q}_3''.} \, (\epsilon_{15} \epsilon_{25} \epsilon_{35}) = [\tilde{w}_1''! \, \tilde{w}_2''! \, \tilde{w}_3''!]^{-1/2} \, (\epsilon_{15})^{\tilde{w}_1''} \, (\epsilon_{25})^{\tilde{w}_2''} \, (\epsilon_{35})^{\tilde{w}_3''},$$

$$P^{s_3}_{.q_3''} \, (\epsilon_{51} \epsilon_{52} \epsilon_{53}) = [w_1''! \, w_2''! \, w_3''!]^{-1/2} \, (\epsilon_{51})^{w_1''} \, (\epsilon_{52})^{w_2''} \, (\epsilon_{53})^{w_3''}.$$

The former result is recovered upon choosing

$$\tilde{w}_1'' = \tilde{w}_2'' = w_1'' = w_2'' = 0.$$

3.9 Orbital Configurations of n Particles

In this section we return to the physical problem of adapting n-particle states to orbital partitions and show how the formal developments of sections 2 and 3 intervene in the construction of these states.

The fundamental assumption on the given form of the orbital states is their correspondence to a weight $w = (w_1 w_2 \ldots w_j)$ and to a group $S(w)$ of this weight in such a way that the states are stable under application of elements of this subgroup of $S(n)$. This assumption is a general feature of several composite-particle theories of nuclear structure like the resonating group and generator coordinate method. Composite particles which show a more general behaviour under internal permutations may in many cases be assumed to consist of subsets with this simple property.

Given this general property of the states which we denote as $| \psi_w \rangle$, we conclude that the bases of possible irreducible representations f of $S(n)$ which can be constructed out of the state $| \psi_w \rangle$ and its images under $S(n)$ correspond to all partitions f obtained from the rules specified in propositions 2.30 and 2.40. Moreover, we know how to label repetitions of a given partition f by means of Gelfand patterns q belonging to the weight w and the partition f according to proposition 2.30. In particular, we know that f has at most j components.

The explicit construction of the states proceeds through the application of Young operators and yields the n-particle states

$$c(rfq) | \psi_w \rangle = | \alpha^n frq \rangle.$$

If $|\tilde{\psi}_{\tilde{w}})$ is a second state of this type, we consider the subgroups $S(\tilde{w})$ and $S(w)$ of $S(n)$ and the corresponding double cosets. From the definition of the double cosets and the properties of $|\tilde{\psi}_{\tilde{w}})$ and $|\psi_w)$ under $S(\tilde{w})$ and $S(w)$ respectively, it is clear that the matrix element of any permutation operator $U(p)$ is equal to a corresponding matrix element of a double coset generator.

3.31 Definition: The basic exchange integrals are the matrix elements of the double coset generators z_k between the states $|\tilde{\psi}_{\tilde{w}})$ and $|\psi_w)$, that is, the matrix elements

$$(\tilde{\psi}_{\tilde{w}}|U(z_k)|\psi_w).$$

The contraction and adjoint properties of the Young operators yield from propositions 2.39–2.44

3.32 Proposition: The inner products of the states $c(\tilde{r}\tilde{f}\tilde{q})|\tilde{\psi}_{\tilde{w}})$, $c(rfq)|\psi_w)$ are given by

$$(\alpha^n\tilde{f}\tilde{r}\tilde{q}|\alpha^n frq) = (c(\tilde{r}\tilde{f}\tilde{q})\,\tilde{\psi}_{\tilde{w}}|c(rfq)\,\psi_w)$$

$$= \delta(\tilde{f},f)\,\delta(\tilde{r},r)\,[\tilde{w}!\,w!]^{1/2} \sum_k d^f_{\tilde{q}q}(z_k)\,(k!)^{-1}\,(\tilde{\psi}_{\tilde{w}}|U(z_k)|\psi_w).$$

If the states $|\tilde{\psi}_{\tilde{w}})$ and $|\psi_w)$ are particularized to products of non-orthogonal single-particle states $|\tilde{\varphi}_\alpha)$ and $|\varphi_\beta)$, introduction of the overlap matrix ϵ with elements

$$\epsilon_{\alpha\beta} = (\tilde{\varphi}_\alpha|\varphi_\beta)$$

yields the inner product in the condensed form of theorem 3.9,

$$(\alpha^n\tilde{f}\tilde{r}\tilde{q}|\alpha^n frq) = D^f_{\tilde{q}q}(\epsilon) = [\tilde{w}!\,w!]^{1/2} \sum_k d^f_{\tilde{q}q}(z_k)\,(k!)^{-1}\,\epsilon^k.$$

The computation of the latter expression may be accomplished with the results of sections 3.4 and 3.5.

A specific case of interest in nuclear physics is the configuration with weight $w = (4\ 4\ \dots\ 4)$. In this case one gets $q = q_{max}$ and

$$D^{|4\,4\,\dots\,4|}(\epsilon) = (\Delta^{1\,2\,\dots\,j}_{1\,2\,\dots\,j})^4.$$

Similarly for $\tilde{w} = w = (4\ 4\ \dots\ 4b)$ one gets from section 3.4 the result

$$D^{|4\,4\,\dots\,4b|}_{q_{max}\,q_{max}}(\epsilon) = (\Delta^{1\,2\,\dots\,j-1}_{1\,2\,\dots\,j-1})^{4-b}\,(\Delta^{1\,2\,\dots\,j}_{1\,2\,\dots\,j})^b.$$

3.10 Decomposition of Orbital Matrix Elements

In section 2.7 we introduced the concept of reduced orbital matrix elements for n-particle states. Let us assume for the moment that the orbital states are built from products of single-particle states. Since the reduced orbital matrix elements contain an operator

$T(n'')$ acting on the last n'' particles, we shall employ fractional parentage coefficients to decompose these matrix elements. With the help of the fractional parentage coefficients we introduce the decomposition

$$|\alpha^n f(f'r'f''r'') q) = \sum_{q'q''} |\alpha^{n'} f'r'q') |\alpha^{n''} f''r''q'') \langle f'q'f''q''|fq\rangle.$$

For the operator $T(n'')$ we assume that it commutes with all elements of $S(n'')$. We introduce the matrix elements

$$(\alpha^{n''} f''\tilde{q}'' \| T(n'')\| \alpha^{n''} f''q'') = |f''|^{1/2} (\alpha^{n''} f''r''\tilde{q}''| T(n'')|\alpha^{n''} f''r''q'').$$

Employing now the fractional parentage coefficients for the bra and ket configuration we get

3.33 Proposition: The reduced orbital matrix elements of the operator $T(n'')$ are given in terms of n''-particle matrix elements by

$$(\alpha^n \tilde{f}(f'f'') \tilde{q} \| T(n'')\| \alpha^n f(f'f'') q)$$

$$= |f'|^{1/2} \sum_{\tilde{q}'q'\tilde{q}''q''} \{\langle \tilde{f}\tilde{q}| f'\tilde{q}'f''\tilde{q}''\rangle D^{f'}_{\tilde{q}'q'}(\epsilon) (\alpha^{n''} f''\tilde{q}'' \| T(n'')\| \alpha^{n''} f''q'')$$

$$|f''|^{-1/2} \langle f'q'f''q''|fq\rangle\}.$$

Now we particularize the general expression to the cases of one- and two-body operators. For one-body operators the notation q'' of the one-particle states is simply equivalent to the index of the single-particle state and we express this equivalence by the equation

$$(\alpha[1]\tilde{q}'' \| T(1)\| \alpha[1] q'') = (\alpha i | T(1)|\alpha r).$$

For two-body operators we use the results of section 3.4 to correlate the index q'' for $f'' = [2]$ and $f'' = [11]$ with the single-particle state labels rs. This leads to the following correspondences

$$(\alpha^2 [2] ii \| T(2)\| \alpha^2 [2] rr) = (\alpha^2 ii | T(2)|\alpha^2 rr)$$

$$(\alpha^2 [2] il \| T(2)\| \alpha^2 [2] rr) = \sqrt{\frac{1}{2}} \{(\alpha^2 il | T(2)|\alpha^2 rr) + (\alpha^2 li | T(2)|\alpha^2 rr)\}$$

$$(\alpha^2 [2] ii \| T(2)\| \alpha^2 [2] rs) = \sqrt{\frac{1}{2}} \{\alpha^2 ii| T(2)|\alpha^2 rs) + (\alpha^2 ii| T(2)|\alpha^2 sr)\}$$

$$(\alpha^2 [2] il \| T(2)\| \alpha^2 [2] rs) = \frac{1}{2} \{(\alpha^2 il | T(2)|\alpha^2 rs) + (\alpha^2 li| T(2)|\alpha^2 rs)$$

$$+ (\alpha^2 il | T(2)|\alpha^2 sr) + (\alpha^2 li | T(2)|\alpha^2 sr)\}$$

$$(\alpha^2 [11] il \| T(2)\| \alpha^2 [11] rs) = \frac{1}{2} \{(\alpha^2 il | T(2)|\alpha^2 rs) - (\alpha^2 li | T(2)|\alpha^2 rs)$$

$$- (\alpha^2 il | T(2)|\alpha^2 sr) + (\alpha^2 li | T(2)|\alpha^2 sr)\}.$$

3.34 Proposition: Consider the overlap matrix ϵ of a non-orthogonal n-particle configuration and assume that it may be written as

$$\epsilon = \epsilon_1 \epsilon_2 .$$

Then the reduced orbital matrix elements of an orbital operator $T(n'')$ can be written as

$$(\alpha^n \widetilde{f}(f'f'') \, \widetilde{q} \parallel T(n'') \parallel \alpha^n f(f'f'') \, q) = |f'|^{1/2} \sum_{\substack{\overline{\overline{q}}\overline{q} \ \widetilde{q}''q''}} [D^{\widetilde{f}}_{\overline{q}\widetilde{q}}(\epsilon_1) \langle f\widetilde{q} | f'q'f''\widetilde{q}'' \rangle$$

$$\{\alpha^{n''} f''\widetilde{q}'' \parallel T(n'') \parallel \alpha^{n''} f''q''\} \langle f'q'f''q'' | f\overline{q} \rangle \, D^f_{\overline{q}q}(\epsilon_2)]$$

where

$$\{\alpha^{n''} f''\widetilde{q}'' \parallel T(n'') \parallel \alpha^{n''} f''q''\}$$

$$= \sum_{\overline{\overline{q}}''\overline{q}''} [D^{f''}_{\widetilde{q}''\overline{\overline{q}}''}(\epsilon_1^{-1}) \, (\alpha^{n''} f''\overline{\overline{q}}'' \parallel T(n'') \parallel \alpha^{n''} f''\overline{q}'') \, D^{f''}_{\overline{q}''q''}(\epsilon_2^{-1})]$$

Proof: We start from the expression given in proposition 3.33 in the form

$$(\alpha^n \widetilde{f}(f'f'') \, \widetilde{q} \parallel T(n'') \parallel \alpha^n f(f'f'') \, q)$$

$$= |f'|^{1/2} \sum_{\substack{\widetilde{\overline{q}}' \overline{q}' \ \widetilde{\overline{q}}''\overline{q}''}} [\langle \widetilde{f}\widetilde{q} | f'\overline{\overline{q}}'f''\overline{\overline{q}}'' \rangle \, D^{f'}_{\overline{\overline{q}}'\overline{q}'}(\epsilon) \, (\alpha^{n''} f''\overline{\overline{q}}'' \parallel T(n'') \parallel \alpha^{n''} f''\overline{q}'') \, \langle f'\overline{q}'f''\overline{q}'' | fq \rangle].$$

From the definition of the expression in curly brackets we easily derive the identity

$$(\alpha^{n''} f''\overline{\overline{q}}'' \parallel T(n'') \parallel \alpha^{n''} f''\overline{q}'')$$

$$= \sum_{\widetilde{q}''q''} [D^{f''}_{\overline{\overline{q}}''\widetilde{q}''}(\epsilon_1) \, \{\alpha^{n''} f''\widetilde{q}'' \parallel T(n'') \parallel \alpha^{n''} f''q''\} \, D^{f''}_{q''\overline{q}''}(\epsilon_2)].$$

The representation property gives for $D^{f'}(\epsilon) = D^{f'}(\epsilon_1 \epsilon_2)$ the relation

$$D^{f'}_{\overline{\overline{q}}'\overline{q}'}(\epsilon_1\epsilon_2) = \sum_{q'} D^{f'}_{\overline{\overline{q}}'q'}(\epsilon_1) \, D^{f'}_{q'\overline{q}'}(\epsilon_2).$$

Now we combine the Wigner coefficients with the representations according to

$$\sum_{\overline{\overline{q}}'\widetilde{\overline{q}}''} D^{f'}_{\overline{\overline{q}}'q'}(\epsilon_1) \, D^{f''}_{\overline{\overline{q}}''\widetilde{q}''}(\epsilon_1) \, \langle \widetilde{f}\widetilde{q} | f'\overline{\overline{q}}'f''\overline{\overline{q}}'' \rangle = \sum_{\overline{\overline{q}}} D^{\widetilde{f}}_{\overline{\overline{q}}\widetilde{q}}(\epsilon_1) \, \langle f\overline{\overline{q}} | f'q'f''\widetilde{q}'' \rangle$$

and

$$\sum_{\overline{q}'\overline{q}''} D^{f'}_{q'\overline{q}'}(\epsilon_2) \, D^{f''}_{q''\overline{q}''}(\epsilon_2) \, \langle f'\overline{q}'f''\overline{q}'' | fq \rangle = \sum_{\overline{q}} \langle f'q'f''q'' | f\overline{q} \rangle \, D^f_{\overline{q}q}(\epsilon_2).$$

If these expressions are introduced into the first equation, this equation exhibits the form claimed in the proposition. □

3.11 Orbital Matrix Elements for the Configuration f = [4^j]

The configuration with the partition $f = [4^j]$ covers cases of great interest in nuclear physics. For example, it describes states built from j α-clusters or states of two ^{16}O clusters. We shall employ the conjugation property discussed in section 3.6 to derive simple expressions for the reduced matrix elements.

3.35 Proposition: The reduced orbital matrix element of the operator $T(n'')$ in the configuration $f = [4^j]$ are given by

$$(\alpha^n [4^j] (f'f'') q_{max} \| T(n'') \| \alpha^n [4^j] (f'f'') q_{max})$$

$$= |f'|^{1/2} \dim^{-1} (f,j) (\Delta_{12\ldots j}^{12\ldots j})^{4-n''} \sum_{\tilde{q}''q''} D_{\tilde{q}''q''}^{f''} (\beta) (\alpha^{n''} f'' \tilde{q}'' \| T(n'') \| \alpha^{n''} f'' q'')$$

Proof: The requirement that the representation d^f of $S(n)$ subduces the representation $d^{f'} \times d^{f''}$ of $S(n') \times S(n'')$ means that f' and f'' are conjugate according to definition 3.23 with a = 4. Writing $f' = (f'')^c$ and applying proposition 3.25 to $D^{f'}$ in the expression of proposition 3.33, one obtains the result.   □

The most important cases are one- and two-body operators and we rewrite proposition 3.35 in the notation which was introduced in section 3.4.

We obtain for one-body operators

$$(\alpha^n [4^j] [4^{j-1} 3] [1] \| T(1) \| \alpha^n [4^j] [4^{j-1} 3] [1])$$

$$= |[4^{j-1} 3]|^{1/2} \frac{1}{j} (\Delta_{12\ldots j}^{12\ldots j})^3 \sum_{i,r=1}^{j} \beta_{ir} (\alpha i | T(1) | \alpha r)$$

and for two-body operators

$$(\alpha^n [4^j] [4^{j-1} 2] [2] \| T(2) \| \alpha^n [4^j] [4^{j-1} 2] [2]) = |[4^{j-1} 2]|^{1/2} \frac{2}{j(j+1)} (\Delta_{12\ldots j}^{12\ldots j})^2$$

$$\left\{ \sum_{i,r}^{j} \beta_{ir}\beta_{ir} (\alpha^2 ii | T(2) | \alpha^2 rr) \right.$$

$$+ \sum_{i<l}^{j} \sum_{r}^{j} \beta_{ir}\beta_{lr} [(\alpha^2 il | T(2) | \alpha^2 rr) + (\alpha^2 li | T(2) | \alpha^2 rr)]$$

$$+ \sum_{i}^{j} \sum_{r<s}^{j} \beta_{ir}\beta_{is} [(\alpha^2 ii | T(2) | \alpha^2 rs) + (\alpha^2 ii | T(2) | \alpha^2 sr)]$$

$$+ \sum_{i<l}^{j} \sum_{r<s}^{j} (\beta_{ir}\beta_{ls} + \beta_{is}\beta_{lr}) \frac{1}{2} [(\alpha^2 il | T(2) | \alpha^2 rs) + (\alpha^2 li | T(2) | \alpha^2 rs)$$

$$\left. + (\alpha^2 il | T(2) | \alpha^2 sr) + (\alpha^2 li | T(2) | \alpha^2 sr)] \right\}$$

$$(\alpha^n [4^j] [4^{j-2} 33] [11] \parallel T(2) \parallel \alpha^n [4^j] [4^{j-2} 33] [11]) = |4^{j-2} 33|^{-1/2}$$

$$= |[4^{j-2} 33]|^{1/2} \frac{2}{j(j-1)} (\Delta_{12 \ldots j}^{12 \ldots j})^2$$

$$\left\{ \sum_{i<l}^{j} \sum_{r<s}^{j} (\beta_{ir}\beta_{ls} - \beta_{is}\beta_{lr}) \frac{1}{2} [(\alpha^2 i l | T(2) | \alpha^2 rs) - (\alpha^2 l i | T(2) | \alpha^2 rs) \right.$$

$$\left. - (\alpha^2 i l | T(2) | \alpha^2 sr) + (\alpha^2 l i | T(2) | \alpha^2 sr)] \right\}.$$

3.12 Notes and References

In the following remarks we single out a few references and concepts related to the present section. We start with the concepts of group theory involved. Tensor bases for irreducible representations of the unitary and general linear group were constructed by Weyl [WE 31], an exposition along similar lines is given by Hamermesh [HA 62] and by Bacry [BA 77]. The full technical development of the representation theory for the unitary group as a Lie group stems from the years since 1950. Gelfand and Zetlin [GE 50] gave a characterization of what is now called the canonical representation and introduced the pattern now called Gelfand pattern. Moshinsky [MO 63] constructed bases of highest weight and gave with Nagel [NA 65] the lowering operators which allow one to generate the full basis. Biedenharn and coworkers and Biedenharn and Louck studied in detail the structure of this representation. For their work we quote in particular the reviews [HO 71, LO 70, LO 78] and the series [BI 72, BI 72a and LO 73]. A recent treatment of the representations is given by Barut and Raczka [BA 77a].

The present exposition is fully based on the representation theory of the symmetric group in the spirit of Weyl's treatment. Within this approach we introduce concepts which allow us to reconstruct the unitary representation of Gelfand and Zetlin. The connection is made through the concepts of weights, double cosets, Gelfand patterns and normalized Young operators considered in relation to the symmetric group. It yields a number of identities between algebraic quantities from the representation theory of the symmetric and unitary group. Some of them have been given in earlier work [KR 68, 69b]. We derive and exploit the proportionality between finite representations of the general linear group and double Gelfand states found originally by Louck [LO 70]. Other algebraic relations which follow from this proportionality are given in [KR 77]. The application of the hook algorithm to the general linear group and the bordered decomposition treated in section 3.8 are believed to be new results.

Most applications of the unitary group to many-body systems deal with configurations based on a finite number of orthogonal single-particle states. The general linear group arises whenever non-orthogonal single-particle states are introduced. The Lie-algebraic approach to many-body systems along these lines was introduced by Moshinsky [MO 68], applications to non-orthogonal single-particle state were given by Moshinsky and Seligman [MO 71].

In the present approach we maintain concepts which are meaningful from the viewpoints of both the symmetric and the general linear group. This allows us to combine techniques from both groups. Applications to composite particle systems will be made in later sections since we shall show that interactions of these particles may be analysed in terms of non-orthogonal single-particle states.

4 Geometric Transformations in Classical Phase Space and their Representation in Quantum Mechanics

4.1 Concepts and Motivation

The geometry of classical phase space is determined by the Poisson bracket of functions on phase space. Canonical transformations of the classical coordinates and momenta are defined by the property that the fundamental Poisson brackets be preserved. In this section we shall study in detail the linear canonical transformations in phase space and their representations in quantum mechanics. The reason for developing these concepts is twofold. First of all there are a number of geometric transformations common to classical and quantum mechanics which appear naturally in the analysis of many-body systems. Examples are rotations of the three space coordinates, permutations of single-particle coordinates and transformations to various types of relative vectors. To these we shall add translations of coordinates and momenta and construct the operators which represent these geometric transformations in the Hilbert space of quantum mechanics. The second reason for dealing with these transformations is the fact that certain operators encountered in quantum mechanics may be interpreted as representatives of underlying geometric transformations in classical phase space. This applies in particular to dilatation operators and to Gaussian interactions. Recognition of the underlying geometric transformation allows us to reduce operator multiplication to combination on the geometric level like matrix multiplication.

For the Hilbert space of quantum mechanics we prefer the Bargmann representation instead of the familiar Schrödinger representation. The Bargmann representation and corresponding Hilbert space is related to an explicit solution of the commutation rules of oscillator creation and annihilation operators in a way similar to the relation of the Schrödinger representation to the Heisenberg commutation relations. Our reason for choosing the Bargmann space is that it yields the simplest form of the oscillator states along with analytic expressions for all important kernels of operators.

In the first subsection we develop the geometrical concepts of classical phase space. After giving the basic structure of Bargmann space in section 4.3 we proceed to representations of translations in phase space by Weyl operators in section 4.4 and to the representation of linear canonical transformations in subsection 4.5. In section 4.6 we consider single-particle oscillator states and matrix elements for the most important operators to be used lateron. The application of these concepts to many-particle systems is taken up in section 5.

4.2 Symplectic Geometry of Classical Phase Space

For real and complex vectors a, b $\in$ IR^q or $\mathbb{C}^q$ we use a point to denote the scalar product

$$a \cdot b = \sum_{j=1}^{q} a_j b_j$$

where the range of summation will be clear from the problem in question.

Consider the real linear space IR^{2m} with elements

$$\alpha = (\alpha'\alpha'') = (\alpha'_1 \alpha'_2 \ldots \alpha'_m \alpha''_1 \alpha''_2 \ldots \alpha''_m).$$

4.1 Definition: For real $\alpha, \beta \in$ IR^{2m}, the symplectic form $\{\alpha, \beta\}$ is given by

$$\{\alpha, \beta\} = \alpha \cdot K\beta = \alpha' \cdot \beta'' - \alpha'' \cdot \beta'$$

where K is the matrix

$$K = \begin{bmatrix} 0_m & I_m \\ -I_m & 0_m \end{bmatrix}.$$

The real symplectic group Sp(2m, IR) is the group of real 2m $\times$ 2m matrices g which preserve the form $\{\alpha, \beta\}$, that is,

$$\{g\alpha, g\beta\} = \{\alpha, \beta\}$$

for any pair α, β.

The symplectic group defined in this way may be linked to linear canonical transformations on classical phase space with coordinates

$$\xi = (\xi_1 \xi_2 \ldots \xi_m)$$

and momenta

$$\pi = (\pi_1 \pi_2 \ldots \pi_m).$$

Define for two real vectors α, β the linear expressions

$$\varphi_\alpha(\xi, \pi) = \alpha' \cdot \pi + \alpha'' \cdot \xi$$
$$\varphi_\beta(\xi, \pi) = \beta' \cdot \pi + \beta'' \cdot \xi.$$

Evaluation of the standard Poisson bracket yields

$$\{\varphi_\alpha, \varphi_\beta\}_{PB} = - \{\alpha, \beta\}.$$

Consider now a linear homogeneous transformation that is canonical, that is, preserves the fundamental Poisson brackets.

4.2 Proposition: A necessary and sufficient condition for a 2m $\times$ 2m matrix g to describe a linear canonical transformation is

$$\{g\alpha, g\beta\} = \{\alpha, \beta\}$$

or that g be an element of the real symplectic group

$$Sp(2m, \mathbb{R}).$$

Proof: For a linear transformation to be canonical it is necessary and sufficient that the Poisson bracket

$$\{\varphi_\alpha, \varphi_\beta\}_{PB} = -\{\alpha, \beta\}$$

be preserved for arbitrary real vectors α, β. From definition 4.1 this determines the linear transformation to be an element of the real symplectic group $Sp(2m, \mathbb{R})$. □

Now we consider complex vectors $\alpha, \beta \in \mathbb{C}^{2m}$ and define

$$\alpha_c = (\alpha'_c \alpha''_c)$$
$$\beta_c = (\beta'_c \beta''_c)$$

where

$$\alpha'_c = \sqrt{\frac{1}{2}(\alpha' + i\alpha'')} \qquad \beta'_c = \sqrt{\frac{1}{2}(\beta' + i\beta'')}$$

$$\alpha''_c = \sqrt{\frac{1}{2}(\alpha' - i\alpha'')} \qquad \beta''_c = \sqrt{\frac{1}{2}(\beta' - i\beta'')}.$$

4.3 Definition: The complex symplectic group $Sp(2m, \mathbb{C})$ is the group preserving on $\mathbb{C}^{2m}$ the symplectic form

$$\{\alpha_c, \beta_c\} = \alpha'_c \cdot \beta''_c - \alpha''_c \cdot \beta'_c.$$

4.4 Definition: The unitary group $U(m, m)$ is the group preserving on $\mathbb{C}^{2m}$ the hermitian form

$$(\alpha_c, \beta_c) = \overline{\alpha}'_c \cdot \beta'_c - \overline{\alpha}''_c \cdot \beta''_c.$$

4.5 Proposition: Any element

$$g_c \in Sp(2m, \mathbb{C}) \cap U(m, m)$$

preserving on $\mathbb{C}^{2m}$ both the forms $\{,\}$ and $(,)$ is equivalent to an element $g \in Sp(2m, \mathbb{R})$ of the real symplectic group.

Proof: For complex α, β it is easy to show that

$$\{\alpha, \beta\} = i\{\alpha_c, \beta_c\}$$
$$\{\overline{\alpha}, \beta\} = i(\alpha_c, \beta_c).$$

Suppose first that g_c preserves the forms on the righthand sides. Then, if initially α was real, it follows that

$$0 = \{\alpha - \overline{\alpha}, \beta\}$$

holds true after the transformation. Since $\{,\}$ is non-degenerate this shows that $\alpha - \overline{\alpha} = 0$ and therefore α remains real.

Conversely, suppose that the transformation preserves $\{\alpha, \beta\}$ for real α, β. Then it must preserve both $\{\alpha_c, \beta_c\}$ and (α_c, β_c) and hence g_c must belong to

$$\mathrm{Sp}(2m, \mathbb{C}) \cap \mathrm{U}(m, m). \qquad\qquad \square$$

The relationship between elements $g \in \mathrm{Sp}(2m, \mathbb{R})$ and $g_c \in \mathrm{Sp}(2m, \mathbb{C}) \cap \mathrm{U}(m, m)$ may be expressed in matrix notation by writing column vectors instead of row vectors,

$$\alpha_c = \begin{pmatrix} \alpha'_c \\ \alpha''_c \end{pmatrix} = R \begin{pmatrix} \alpha' \\ \alpha'' \end{pmatrix}, \quad R = \sqrt{\frac{1}{2}} \begin{bmatrix} I_m & i\,I_m \\ I_m & -i\,I_m \end{bmatrix}.$$

Then one finds

$$g_c = R g R^{-1}.$$

The matrix g_c may be written in the $m \times m$ block form

$$g_c = \begin{bmatrix} \lambda & \mu \\ \nu & \rho \end{bmatrix}.$$

To find the properties of these blocks we use the matrix of definition 4.1 associated with the symplectic form $\{,\}$ and the matrix

$$M = \begin{bmatrix} I_m & 0_m \\ 0_m & -I_m \end{bmatrix}$$

associated with the hermitian form $(,)$. Then proposition 4.2 yields the two equations s

$$^t g_c K g_c = K \qquad g_c^+ M g_c = M$$

which with the help of $K^{-1} = -K$, $M^{-1} = M$ may be rewritten as

$$g_c^{-1} = -K\,^t g_c\, K, \qquad g_c^{-1} = M g_c^+ M.$$

When expressed in terms of the blocks $\lambda\mu\nu\rho$, these equations yield

$$g_c^{-1} = \begin{bmatrix} ^t\rho & -\,^t\mu \\ -\,^t\nu & ^t\lambda \end{bmatrix}, \quad g_c^{-1} = \begin{bmatrix} \lambda^+ & -\nu^+ \\ -\mu^+ & \rho^+ \end{bmatrix}.$$

4.6 Proposition: The blocks $\lambda\mu\nu\rho$ of the matrix $g_c \in \mathrm{Sp}(2m, \mathbb{C}) \cap \mathrm{U}(m, m)$ are subject to the two alternative and equivalent sets of equations

$$\lambda\lambda^+ - \mu\mu^+ = I_m \qquad \rho = \bar\lambda \quad \nu = \bar\mu$$
$$-\lambda\,^t\mu + \mu\,^t\lambda = 0_m$$

or

$$\lambda^+\lambda - \,^t\mu\bar\mu = I_m \qquad \rho = \bar\lambda \quad \nu = \bar\mu$$
$$\lambda^+\mu - \,^t\mu\bar\lambda = 0_m$$

Proof: The expressions for ρ and ν are obtained by comparing the two expressions for the inverse of g_c. The first set of conditions for λ and μ is then obtained from the block form of the equation

$$g_c \, M g_c^+ M = I_{2m},$$

while the second set is obtained from

$$M g_c^+ M g_c = I_{2m}. \qquad \square$$

Note that the block λ must be invertible since

$$\lambda \lambda^+ = I_m + \mu \mu^+$$

is positive definite.

4.3 Basic Structure of Bargmann Space

Consider a system of m degrees of freedom with a configuration space $\mathbb{R}^m$, and denote the linear position and momentum operators by Ξ_j and Π_j, $j = 1\,2 \ldots m$, respectively. The basic properties of these operators are given by

4.7 Definition: The position and momentum operators are subject to the fundamental commutator and hermitian relations

$$[\Pi_j, \Xi_k] = \frac{1}{i} \delta_{jk} I$$

$$\Pi_j^+ = \Pi_j, \qquad \Xi_j^+ = \Xi_j$$

where I denotes the unit operator. Note that Planck's constant $\hbar$ has been absorbed into the operators. The well-known construction of a representation of these abstract operators due to Schrödinger may be summarized by

4.8 Definition: On $\mathbb{R}^m$ with real coordinates $\xi = (\xi_1 \xi_2 \ldots \xi_m)$ consider complex-valued functions $\varphi(\xi)$, $\psi(\xi)$. Introduce the inner product

$$\langle \varphi | \psi \rangle = \int \overline{\varphi(\xi)} \, \psi(\xi) \, d\xi,$$

$$d\xi = \prod_{j=1}^m d\xi_i$$

and the Hilbert space *H* associated with these functions and this inner product. Define the position and momentum operators by

$$(\Xi_j \varphi)(\xi) = \xi_j \, \varphi(\xi),$$

$$(\Pi_j \varphi)(\xi) = \frac{1}{i} \frac{\partial}{\partial \xi_j} \, \varphi(\xi).$$

These operators provide the Schrödinger representation of the fundamental commutator and hermitian relations stated in definition 4.7.

In most applications, we shall consider states of harmonic oscillators. Incorporating the mass and frequency of an oscillator into the corresponding position and momentum operators, the creation and annihilation operators of an harmonic oscillator are given by

$$\Gamma_j = \sqrt{\frac{1}{2}}\,(\Xi_j - i\,\Pi_j)$$

$$\Delta_j = \sqrt{\frac{1}{2}}\,(\Xi_j + i\,\Pi_j).$$

4.9 Definition: The oscillator creation and annihilation operators obey the fundamental commutator and hermitian relations

$$[\Delta_j, \Gamma_k] = \delta_{jk}\,I$$

$$\Delta_j^+ = \Gamma_j.$$

Segal [SE 63] and Bargmann [BA 61, 62, 67, 68] constructed a Hilbert space of analytic functions which yields a representation of these operator relations. Obviously, the commutator relations can be solved in a similar fashion as in the Schrödinger case. The hermitian properties impose necessary conditions on the inner product which lead to

4.10 Definition: On $\mathbb{C}^m$ with complex coordinates

$$x = (x_1 x_2 \ldots x_m)$$

consider complex-valued entire analytic functions $f(x), g(x)$. Introduce the inner product

$$(f|g) \;=\; \int \overline{f(x)}\,g(x)\,d\mu(x),$$

$$d\mu(x) = \pi^{-m} \prod_{j=1}^{m} \exp[-\,\bar{x}_j x_j]\,d\,\mathrm{Re}(x_j)\,d\,\mathrm{Im}(x_j)$$

and the Hilbert space B associated with this inner product.

Define the creation and annihilation operators X_j, D_j by

$$(X_j f)\,(x) = x_j f(x)$$

$$(D_j f)\,(x) = \frac{\partial}{\partial x_j}\,f(x).$$

These operators provide the Bargmann representation of the fundamental commutator and hermitian properties for creation and annihilation operators Γ_j and Δ_j respectively, as stated in definition 4.9.

We shall not give the proof of the last property since this was discussed in great detail by Bargmann [BA 61]. Instead we discuss a number of examples.

Throughout this and the following sections we adopt the following notation: For the real variables associated with the Schrödinger representation, we use greek letters, while the complex variables of the Bargmann representation are taken as latin letters. We distinguish the inner products in the Hilbert spaces H and B by $\langle | \rangle$ and $(|)$ respectively.

Example 4.1: Harmonic oscillators in Bargmann space

For m = 1 consider in Bargmann space B the states

$$f_N(x) = [N!]^{-1/2} x^N.$$

Upon putting $x = r \exp i\varphi$ one finds

$$(f_{N'}| f_N) = [N'! N!]^{-1/2} \pi^{-1} \int_0^\infty \int_0^{2\pi} r^{N'+N} \exp[i(N-N')\varphi] \exp[-r^2] r \, dr \, d\varphi$$

$$= \delta_{N'N} [N!]^{-1} 2 \int_0^\infty r^{2N+1} \exp[-r^2] dr$$

$$= \delta_{N'N}.$$

Apparently, these states provide an orthonormal set which actually turns out to be a basis of the Hilbert space B. Noting that

$$(Df_0)(x) = 0$$
$$(Xf_N)(x) = f_{N+1}(x)[N+1]^{1/2}$$
$$(Df_N)(x) = f_{N-1}(x)[N]^{1/2}$$

one finds that these states are the eigenstates of the operator

$$H = X \circ D$$

with eigenvalue $N = 0, 1, 2, \ldots$ and hence the eigenstates of the harmonic oscillator.

For m degrees of freedom, an orthonormal basis is provided by the product states

$$f_{N_1 N_2 \ldots N_m}(x) = [N_1! N_2! \ldots N_m!]^{-1/2} (x_1)^{N_1} (x_2)^{N_2} \ldots (x_m)^{N_m}.$$

Clearly the Bargmann representation is closely related to the expression of states as polynomials in the creation operators applied to the ground state. For a single particle moving in three-dimensional space, the oscillator states of fixed angular momentum L and component M become

$$f_{NLM}(x) = P_{LM}^N(x) = A_{NL}(x \cdot x)^{\frac{1}{2}(N-L)} Y_{LM}(x)$$

where $x \cdot x = x_1^2 + x_2^2 + x_3^2$, $Y_{LM}(x)$ is a solid spherical harmonic and A_{NL} is a constant

$$A_{NL} = (-1)^{\frac{1}{2}(N-L)} \left[\frac{4\pi}{(N+L+1)!! (N-L)!!} \right]^{1/2}$$

derived by Brody and Moshinsky [BR 60] which is given here in the notation of [KR 70].

Since the operator properties (definition 4.7 and 4.9) are related by the linear transformation which connects position and momentum operators with creation and annihilation operators, one expects a map between the Hilbert spaces H and B. The following map via an integral transform is due to Bargmann.

4.11 Proposition: A one-to-one correspondence between pairs φ, f of elements of the Hilbert spaces H and B is provided by the integral transforms

$$A : H \to B$$

$$(A\,\varphi)\,(x) = f(x) = \int A(x, \xi)\,\varphi(\xi)\,d\xi$$

$$A^{-1} : B \to H$$

$$(A^{-1}f)\,(\xi) = \varphi(\xi) = \int \overline{A(x, \xi)}\,f(x)\,d\mu(x) \qquad \text{where}$$

$$A(x, \xi) = \prod_{j=1}^{m} A(x_j, \xi_j)$$

$$A(x_j, \xi_j) = \pi^{-1/4}\,\exp\left[-\frac{1}{2}x_j x_j - \frac{1}{2}\xi_j \xi_j + \sqrt{2}\,x_j \xi_j\right].$$

This map is unitary according to the relations

$$(A\,\varphi|\,A\,\psi) = \langle\varphi|\,\psi\rangle$$

$$\langle A^{-1}f|\,A^{-1}g\rangle = (f|\,g).$$

We refer to Bargmann [BA 61] for the proof. The map A may actually be found up to normalization from the operator relations

$$X_j \circ A = A \circ \Gamma_j \qquad D_j \circ A = A \circ \Delta_j$$

Example 4.2: Transformation of oscillator states

For the states discussed in example 4.1 one finds

$$(A^{-1}f_N)\,(\xi) = \int \overline{A(x, \xi)}\,f_N(x)\,d\mu(x).$$

The integral on the right-hand side may be written as an inner product in Bargmann space,

$$\int \overline{A(x, \xi)}\,f_N(x)\,d\mu(x) = (A(\,, \xi)|\,f_N).$$

Upon expanding $A(x, \xi)$ into a power series with respect to x, the inner product yields a single contribution from the power x^N because of the orthonormal properties of the states $f_N(x)$. A re-interpretation of this equation tells us that the integral kernel $\overline{A(x, \xi)}$ is a generating function of normalized oscillator states $\varphi_N(\xi)$, that is,

$$\overline{A(x, \xi)} = \sum_{N=0}^{\infty} \varphi_N(\xi)\,[N!]^{-1/2}\,\overline{x^N}.$$

For the three-dimensional oscillator in an angular momentum basis, the corresponding expression is

$$\overline{A(x_1 x_2 x_3, \xi_1 \xi_2 \xi_3)} = \sum_{NLM} \psi_{NLM}(\xi_1 \xi_2 \xi_3) \, \overline{P_{LM}^N(x_1 x_2 x_3)}.$$

Example 4.3: Plane wave in Bargmann space

For the state

$$\varphi_k(\xi) = (2\pi)^{-3/2} \exp[ik \cdot \xi], \quad k \cdot \xi = k_1 \xi_1 + k_2 \xi_2 + k_3 \xi_3$$

a straight-forward integration yields in Bargmann space

$$(A\varphi_k)(x) = \pi^{-3/4} \exp\left[i\sqrt{2}\,k \cdot x + \frac{1}{2}x \cdot x - \frac{1}{2}k \cdot k\right].$$

Example 4.4: Coherent state in Bargmann space

For m degrees of freedom define in Bargmann space the states

$$e_a(x) = \exp[\bar{a} \cdot x] = \sum_{N=0}^{\infty} [N!]^{-1}(\bar{a} \cdot x)^N.$$

Use of the series expansion yields for the inner product

$$(e_a | e_b) = \exp[a \cdot \bar{b}]$$

and shows that e_a is square-integrable. Moreover, one finds that

$$(D_k e_a)(x) = \bar{a}_k e_a(x)$$

and hence e_a is an eigenstate of the annihilation operator D_k with eigenvalue $\bar{a}_k$ or a coherent state [GL 63]. Transforming back to the Schrödinger representation one finds

$$(A^{-1} e_a)(\xi) = (A(\,,\xi)|e_a)$$
$$= \overline{A(a, \xi)}.$$

To interpret this expression in the Schrödinger representation, we introduce the real and imaginary part of the complex vector a according to

$$a_j = \sqrt{\frac{1}{2}}(\alpha_j' + i\alpha_j'').$$

Introducing this decomposition into $\overline{A(a, \xi)}$, the coherent state may be rewritten as

$$(A^{-1} e_a)(\xi) = \pi^{-\frac{m}{4}} \exp\left[-i\alpha'' \cdot \left(\xi - \frac{1}{2}\alpha'\right)\right] \exp\left[-\frac{1}{2}(\xi - \alpha') \cdot (\xi - \alpha')\right]$$
$$\exp\left[\frac{1}{4}(\alpha' \cdot \alpha' + \alpha'' \cdot \alpha'')\right].$$

The second exponential shows that we are dealing with an harmonic oscillator whose average position is determined by the vector α'. The first exponential may be interpreted as a shift of the average momentum of the oscillator by the amount α''. The remaining factors determine the phase and the normalization.

This result allows one to interpret the transformation from B to H as an expansion of the elements of H into superpositions of nonorthogonal coherent states, the expansion coefficients being given by the Bargmann states.

We now turn to the analysis of some operators in Bargmann space.

4.12 Proposition: The identity operator I in Bargmann space B may be written as an integral operator with kernel $I(x, x')$ such that

$$(If)(x) = \int I(x, x') f(x') \, d\mu(x') = f(x),$$
$$I(x, x') = \exp[x \cdot \bar{x}'].$$

Proof: Using the orthonormal basis $f_{N_1 N_2 \ldots N_m}(x)$ given in example 4.1, one finds the expansions

$$f(x') = \sum_{N_1 N_2 \ldots N_m} f_{N_1 N_2 \ldots N_m}(x') \, a_{N_1 N_2 \ldots N_m}$$

$$\exp[x \cdot \bar{x}'] = \sum_{N=0}^{\infty} [N!]^{-1} (x \cdot \bar{x}')^N = \sum_{N_1 N_2 \ldots N_m} f_{N_1 N_2 \ldots N_m}(x) \, \overline{f_{N_1 N_2 \ldots N_m}(x')}$$

which immediately give the result.   □

We express the relationship between the kernel of the identity operator I and the coherent state as

$$I(, a) = e_a.$$

4.13 Proposition: For any linear operator K in Bargmann space there exists a kernel $K(x, x')$ such that, for $f \in B$

$$(Kf)(x) = \int K(x, x') f(x') \, d\mu(x')$$

Proof: First we note that

$$(K e_{x'})(x) = (K I(, x'))(x)$$

where $I(, x')$ is considered as a state in B. But then, since $K = K \circ I$, one finds

$$(Kf)(x) = ((K \circ I) f)(x) = (K(If))(x) = \int ((KI)(, x'))(x) f(x') \, d\mu(x')$$

and hence the kernel of the operator K is given by

$$K(x, x') = (K e_{x'})(x).$$ □

An alternative expression for the kernel may be given in terms of inner products:

4.14 Proposition: For any operator K in Bargmann space the kernel $K(x, x')$ is given by

$$K(x, x') = (e_x | K | e_{x'})$$

Proof: It suffices to note that

$$(e_x | f) = \int \exp[x \cdot \bar{x}'] f(x') \, d\mu(x') = f(x). \qquad \square$$

Example 4.5: The kernel for the momentum operator

From the definition of the creation and annihilation operators given with definition 4.8 one finds for the momentum operator in Bargmann space

$$\Pi_j = i \sqrt{\frac{1}{2}} (X_j - D_j).$$

The kernel of this operator becomes

$$\Pi_j(x, x') = (\Pi_j e_{x'})(x) = i \sqrt{\frac{1}{2}} (x_j - \bar{x}'_j) \exp[x \cdot \bar{x}'].$$

A similar computation yields for m = 3 and the operator

$$\Pi^2 = \sum_{j=1}^{3} \Pi_j \circ \Pi_j \qquad \text{the kernel}$$

$$\Pi^2(x, x') = -\frac{1}{2} (x \cdot x - 2x \cdot \bar{x}' + \bar{x}' \cdot \bar{x}' - 3) \exp[x \cdot \bar{x}'].$$

4.4 Representation of Translations in Phase Space by Weyl Operators

The interpretation of the fundamental commutation relations in terms of geometric transformations in phase space and their unitary representations in Hilbert space was given by Weyl in 1928 [WE 31]. For the present purpose we follow the exposition and notation of Bargmann [BA 68]. First we introduce the Weyl operators as the unitary representations of position and momentum translations in phase space. We refer to section 4.2 for the definition of the vectors α, β and the symplectic form $\{\alpha, \beta\}$.

4.15 Definition: In the Hilbert space H corresponding to the Schrödinger representation, the Weyl operator T_α for $\alpha = (\alpha'\alpha'') \in \mathrm{IR}^{2m}$ is defined by

$$(T_\alpha \varphi)(\xi) = \exp\left[-i\alpha'' \cdot \left(\xi - \frac{1}{2}\alpha'\right)\right] \varphi(\xi - \alpha')$$

where

$$\varphi(\xi - \alpha') = \varphi(\xi_1 - \alpha'_1 \, \xi_2 - \alpha'_2 \ldots \xi_m - \alpha'_m).$$

4.16 Proposition: The Weyl operators are unitary with

$$(T_\alpha)^{-1} = (T_\alpha)^+ = T_{-\alpha},$$

they have the multiplication law

$$T_\alpha \circ T_\beta = \exp\left[\frac{i}{2}\{\alpha, \beta\}\right] T_{\alpha + \beta},$$

and obey the Weyl relations

$$T_\alpha \circ T_\beta = \exp\left[i\{\alpha, \beta\}\right] T_\beta \circ T_\alpha.$$

The proofs are straightforward from definition 4.15.

For a geometric interpretation of the Weyl operators we note the operator relations

$$T_\alpha \circ \Xi_j = (\Xi_j - \alpha'_j I) \circ T_\alpha$$
$$T_\alpha \circ \Pi_j = (\Pi_j + \alpha''_j I) \circ T_\alpha$$

which again are easily derived from definition 4.15. These operator relations show that the Weyl operator T_α represents shifts for the jth component of the position and momentum by the amount $-\alpha'_j$ and α''_j respectively.

Now we construct the Weyl operators in Bargmann space. It proves convenient to introduce the complex numbers

$$a_j = \sqrt{\frac{1}{2}}(\alpha'_j + i\,\alpha''_j) \quad \overline{a}_j = \sqrt{\frac{1}{2}}(\alpha'_i - i\,\alpha''_j), \quad j = 1\,2\ldots m$$

along with $\alpha_c \in \mathbb{C}^{2\,m}$ where

$$\alpha_c = (a\,\overline{a}) = (a_1\,a_2\ldots a_m\,\overline{a}_1\overline{a}_2\ldots\overline{a}_m).$$

4.17 Proposition: In Bargmann space B, the Weyl operator W_{α_c} acts according to

$$(W_{\alpha_c} f)(x) = \exp\left[\overline{a}\cdot\left(x - \frac{1}{2}a\right)\right] f(x - a).$$

These operators are unitary with

$$(W_{\alpha_c})^{-1} = (W_{\alpha_c})^+ = W_{-\alpha_c},$$

have the multiplication law

$$W_{\alpha_c} \circ W_{\beta_c} = \exp\left[-\frac{1}{2}\{\alpha_c, \beta_c\}\right] W_{\alpha_c + \beta_c}$$

and obey the Weyl relations

$$W_{\alpha_c} \circ W_{\beta_c} = \exp\left[-\{\alpha_c, \beta_c\}\right] W_{\beta_c} \circ W_{\alpha_c}.$$

Moreover, the Weyl operators W_{α_c} in the Bargmann representation are related to the Weyl operators in the Schrödinger representation by

$$W_{\alpha_c} \circ A = A \circ T_\alpha$$

where A is the integral transform given in proposition 4.11.

The Weyl operators in the Bargmann representation were given by Bargmann [BA 68]. The exponents of the factors appearing in the multiplication and Weyl relations are related to $\{\alpha, \beta\}$ as given in proposition 4.5, $\{\alpha, \beta\} = i \{\alpha_c, \beta_c\}$. The properties of the Weyl operators in Bargmann space may be expressed by the operator relations

$$W_{\alpha_c} \circ X_j = (X_j - a_j I) \circ W_{\alpha_c}$$
$$W_{\alpha_c} \circ D_j = (D_j - \bar{a}_j I) \circ W_{\alpha_c}.$$

The kernel for the Weyl operator is given by straight-forward application of proposition 4.13:

4.18 Proposition: The kernel of the Weyl operator W_{α_c} is

$$W_{\alpha_c}(x, x') = \exp\left[\bar{a} \cdot x + x \cdot \bar{x}' - a \cdot \bar{x}' - \frac{1}{2} a \cdot \bar{a}\right].$$

Example 4.6: Weyl translation of the oscillator ground state

The unexcited oscillator state in Bargmann space is given by

$$f_{0\,0\ldots0}(x) = 1.$$

Application of the Weyl operator W_{α_c} yields

$$(W_{\alpha_c} f_{0\,0\ldots0})(x) = \exp\left[\bar{a} \cdot x - \frac{1}{2} a \cdot \bar{a}\right].$$

This state is the normalized coherent state in Bargmann space B, and its form in H was obtained in example 4.4 except for the normalization factor $\exp\left[-\frac{1}{2} a \cdot \bar{a}\right]$.

In what follows we shall be interested in the application of Weyl operators to general oscillator states. For this purpose it proves convenient to factorize the Weyl operators into pairs of in general unbounded operators Λ_a and V_a.

4.19′ Definition: The (not necessarily bounded) operators V_a and Λ_a are defined by their actions

$$(V_a f)(x) = f(x - a),$$
$$(\Lambda_a f)(x) = ((W_{\alpha_c} \circ V_{-a}) f)(x) \exp\frac{1}{2} a \cdot \bar{a}$$
$$= \exp[x \cdot \bar{a}] f(x).$$

If an operator is unbounded, it is not completely defined unless its domain of definition is given. Though the domains of these operators may be larger, we are only interested in applying them to the linear spaces spanned by oscillator states and to the images of these linear spaces under the action of Weyl operators.

4.19″ Definition: Let P be the linear space consisting of all polynomials in the complex variables $x = (x_1 x_2 \ldots x_m)$. P is a pre-Hilbert space contained in the Hilbert space B. For any Weyl operator $W_{\gamma c}$ we define $P_{\gamma c}$ as the image of P under $W_{\gamma c}$,

$$P_{\gamma c} = W_{\gamma c} P.$$

Certainly $P_{\gamma c}$ is a pre-Hilbert space for any γ_c.

4.20 Proposition: The operators Λ_a, V_a are defined on the spaces $P_{\gamma c}$ for any γ_c. For the operators V_a, V_b we have the multiplication and inversion properties

$$V_a : P_{\gamma c} \to P_{\gamma c} \qquad\qquad V_b : P_{\gamma c} \to P_{\gamma c}$$
$$V_a \circ V_b = V_{a+b} \qquad\qquad V_a \circ V_b : P_{\gamma c} \to P_{\gamma c}$$
$$V_a^{-1} = V_{-a} \qquad\qquad V_a^{-1} : P_{\gamma c} \to P_{\gamma c}$$

and for the operators Λ_a, Λ_b we have

$$\Lambda_a : P_{\gamma c + \beta c} \to P_{\gamma c + \beta c + \alpha c} \qquad\qquad \Lambda_b : P_{\gamma c} \to P_{\gamma c + \beta c}$$
$$\Lambda_a \circ \Lambda_b = \Lambda_{a+b} \qquad\qquad \Lambda_a \circ \Lambda_b : P_{\gamma c} \to P_{\gamma c + \beta c + \alpha c}$$
$$\Lambda_a^{-1} = \Lambda_{-a} \qquad\qquad \Lambda_a^{-1} : P_{\gamma c} \to P_{\gamma c - \alpha c}.$$

Proof: Let $f \in P$ be an arbitrary polynomial. From

$$(V_a f)(x) = f(x - a)$$

it follows that $(V_a f)$ is again a polynomial of the same degree and hence that $(V_a f) \in P$. To any polynomial $f \in P$ there corresponds an element $(W_{\gamma c} f) \in P_{\gamma c}$ where

$$(W_{\gamma c} f)(x) = \exp\left[\overline{c} \cdot \left(x - \frac{1}{2} c\right)\right] f(x - c),$$

and all elements of $P_{\gamma c}$ may be taken in this way. From

$$((V_a \circ W_{\gamma c}) f)(x) = (W_{\gamma c} f)(x - a)$$
$$= \exp\left[\overline{c} \cdot \left(x - \frac{1}{2} c\right)\right] \exp[-\overline{c} \cdot a] f(x - \overline{c} - a)$$

and the observation that the polynomial $f(x - c - a)$ allows for an expansion in terms of polynomials depending on the variables $(x - c)$ it follows that $(V_a \circ W_{\gamma c}) f \in P_{\gamma c}$. The claims on the domains and ranges of the operators Λ_a, Λ_b follow from the definition in terms of the operators V_a, V_b. The multiplication and inversion rules follow directly from the definition of the actions for both operators. $\square$

4.21 Proposition: The operators V and Λ have the multiplication rules

$$V_a \circ \Lambda_b : P_{\gamma_c} \to P_{\gamma_c + \alpha_c}$$

$$V_a \circ \Lambda_b = \Lambda_b \circ V_a \exp\left[-a \cdot \overline{b}\right]$$

$$\Lambda_a \circ V_a = W_{\alpha_c} \exp\left[\frac{1}{2} a \cdot \overline{a}\right]$$

$$\Lambda_a \circ V_b \circ \Lambda_{a'} \circ V_{b'} : P_{\gamma_c} \to P_{\gamma_c + \alpha_c + \alpha_c'}$$

$$\Lambda_a \circ V_b \circ \Lambda_{a'} \circ V_{b'} = \Lambda_{a+a'} \circ V_{b+b'} \exp\left[-b \cdot \overline{a}'\right]$$

and the hermitian properties

$$V_a^+ = \Lambda_{-a} \qquad V_a^+ : P_{\gamma_c} \to P_{\gamma_c - \alpha_c}$$

$$\Lambda_a^+ = V_{-a} \qquad \Lambda_a^+ : P_{\gamma_c} \to P_{\gamma_c}.$$

Proof: The multiplication rules follow again by composition of the action of the operators and by consideration of domains and ranges. To prove the hermitian property of V_a we write

$$(f \mid V_a g) = \int \overline{f(x)} \, (V_a g)(x) \, d\mu(x)$$

$$= \int \overline{f(x)} \left[\int \exp\left[(x - a) \cdot \overline{x}'\right] g(x') \, d\mu(x')\right] d\mu(x)$$

$$= \int \left[\int \overline{f(x)} \exp\left[x \cdot \overline{x}'\right] d\mu(x)\right] \exp\left[-a \cdot \overline{x}'\right] g(x') \, d\mu(x')$$

$$= \int \overline{(\Lambda_{-a} f)(x')} \, g(x') \, d\mu(x') = (\Lambda_{-a} f \mid g).$$

The hermitian properties of Λ_a follow along similar lines. $\square$

Finally, we construct the infinitesimal generators of the Weyl operators. To this end we introduce one-parameter families of Weyl operators $T_{\tau\alpha}$ and $W_{\tau\alpha_c}$ depending on a real parameter τ in the Hilbert spaces H and B respectively. Then one finds from the explicit forms of the Weyl operators given in definitions 4.15 and 4.17 respectively:

4.22 Proposition: The generators L_α, L_{α_c} of the Weyl operators $T_{\tau\alpha}$ and $W_{\tau\alpha_c}$ are given by

$$(L_\alpha \varphi)(\xi) = \lim_{\tau \to 0} \left(\frac{i}{\tau}(T_{\tau\alpha} - I) \varphi\right)(\xi)$$

$$L_\alpha = \sum_j (\alpha_j' \Pi_j + \alpha_j'' \Xi_j) = \alpha' \cdot \Pi + \alpha'' \cdot \Xi$$

$$(L_{\alpha_c} f)(x) = \lim_{\tau \to 0} \left(\frac{i}{\tau}(W_{\tau\alpha_c} - I) f\right)(x)$$

$$L_{\alpha_c} = i \sum_j (\overline{a}_j X_j - a_j D_j) = i(\overline{a} \cdot X - a \cdot D).$$

Proof: The form of the generators is easily derived from propositions 4.15 and 4.17. Their existence is assured by Stone's theorem, see [BA 77a, p. 162].   □

For use in the next section we rewrite the generators L_α, L_{α_c} in the form

$$L_\alpha = -(\alpha', \alpha'') \cdot K \begin{pmatrix} \Xi \\ -\Pi \end{pmatrix}$$

and

$$L_{\alpha_c} = -i(a, \bar{a}) \cdot K \begin{pmatrix} X \\ D \end{pmatrix}$$

where K is the matrix associated with the symplectic form of definition 4.1.

4.5 Representation of Linear Canonical Transformations

It was shown by von Neumann [NE 31] that the unitarity and irreducibility of a set of abstract operators fulfilling the Weyl relations of proposition 4.15 specifies the Schrödinger representation up to a unitary transformation. Consider now an element $g \in Sp(2m, \mathbb{R})$ and any pair of Weyl operators $T_{g\alpha}$, $T_{g\beta}$. Since $\{g\alpha, g\beta\} = \{\alpha, \beta\}$, these operators fulfill the Weyl relations and hence, according to von Neumann, there exists a unitary operator S_g such that

$$T_{g\alpha} = S_g \circ T_\alpha \circ S_g^{-1}.$$

4.23 Proposition: The operators S_g form a projective representation of the group $Sp(2m, \mathbb{R})$.

Proof: For $g', g'' \in Sp(2m, \mathbb{R})$ one easily finds that

$$S_{g'g''} \circ T_\alpha \circ S_{g'g''}^{-1} = S_{g'} \circ S_{g''} \circ T_\alpha \circ S_{g''}^{-1} \circ S_{g'}^{-1}.$$

Hence the operator $S_{g''}^{-1} \circ S_{g'}^{-1} \circ S_{g'g''}$ commutes with the irreducible set of Weyl operators and must, by Schur's lemma [BA 77a, p. 143] be a multiple of the identity, that is

$$S_{g'} \circ S_{g''} = \kappa(g', g'') S_{g'g''}.$$

By the unitarity of the operators S_g, the complex factor κ must obey $\kappa \bar{\kappa} = 1$.

This projective representation is in fact a unitary representation of the universal covering group of the symplectic group $Sp(2m, \mathbb{R})$. This universal covering group was considered by Bargmann [BA 68] and is often called the metaplectic group. When considered as a representation of this group, the representation is called the metaplectic representation, compare Sternberg [ST 78].   □

In the following propositions we shall consider sets of operator relations involving the operators Ξ and Π. We shall arrange these operators into a single column and operate with symplectic matrices on this column vector.

4.24 Proposition: The operators S_g transform the position and momentum operators Ξ and Π according to

$$S_g^{-1} \circ \begin{bmatrix} \Xi \\ -\Pi \end{bmatrix} \circ S_g = \begin{bmatrix} S_g^{-1} \circ \Xi \circ S_g \\ -S_g^{-1} \circ \Pi \circ S_g \end{bmatrix} = g \begin{bmatrix} \Xi \\ -\Pi \end{bmatrix}.$$

Proof: From the relation between the operators Ξ and Π one finds for the one-parameter families of operators $T_{\tau\alpha}, T_{\tau g^{-1}\alpha}$ introduced in proposition 4.22 the relation

$$S_g^{-1} \circ T_{\tau\alpha} \circ S_g = T_{\tau g^{-1}\alpha}.$$

This yields for the generators given in proposition 4.22 the relation

$$S_g^{-1} \circ L_\alpha \circ S_g = L_{g^{-1}\alpha}.$$

Using the symplectic property of the matrix g in the form

$$^tg^{-1} K = Kg$$

and the arbitrariness of the numbers α one obtains

$$S_g^{-1} \circ \begin{bmatrix} \Xi \\ -\Pi \end{bmatrix} \circ S_g = g \begin{bmatrix} \Xi \\ -\Pi \end{bmatrix}.$$

In Bargmann space we denote the operators representing symplectic transformations by S_{g_c}. These operators by definition fulfill the relations

$$W_{g_c\alpha_c} = S_{g_c} \circ W_{\alpha_c} \circ S_{g_c}^{-1}. \qquad \square$$

4.25 Proposition: The operators S_{g_c} transform the creation and annihilation operators X and D according to

$$S_{g_c}^{-1} \circ \begin{bmatrix} X \\ D \end{bmatrix} \circ S_{g_c} = g_c \begin{bmatrix} X \\ D \end{bmatrix}.$$

Proof: Similar as in proposition 4.24 one derives for the generators of the Weyl operators W_{α_c} the relation

$$S_{g_c}^{-1} \circ L_{\alpha_c} \circ S_{g_c} = L_{g_c^{-1}\alpha_c}$$

and, with the help of the matrix K and the symplectic property of the matrix g_c expressed as

$$^tg_c^{-1} K = Kg_c,$$

the transformation law stated above. $\qquad \square$

We shall now derive the kernel of S_{g_c} in Bargmann space.

4.26 Proposition: Under S_{g_c}, the state e_0 transforms as

$$(S_{g_c} e_0)(x) = \nu_{g_c} \exp\left[\frac{1}{2} x \cdot \bar{\mu} \lambda^{-1} x\right].$$

Proof: For the operators D, proposition 4.25 may be rewritten with the help of the blocks λ, μ given in proposition 4.6 as

$$S_{g_c} \circ D = (-\mu^+ X + {}^t\lambda D) \circ S_{g_c}.$$

Applying this equation to the oscillator ground state e_0, the left-hand side yields zero. Using the inverse of ${}^t\lambda$ and ${}^t\lambda^{-1}\mu^+ = \bar{\mu}\lambda^{-1}$ one finds

$$(D_j \circ S_{g_c}) e_0 = \sum_l (\bar{\mu}\lambda^{-1})_{jl} (X_l \circ S_{g_c}) e_0.$$

The solution of these differential equations is clearly

$$(S_{g_c} e_0)(x) = \nu_{g_c} \exp\left[\frac{1}{2} x \cdot \bar{\mu} \lambda^{-1} x\right]. \qquad \qquad \square$$

4.27 Proposition: The kernel of the operator S_{g_c} in B is given by

$$S_{g_c}(a, b) = \nu_{g_c} \exp\left[\frac{1}{2} a \cdot \bar{\mu}\lambda^{-1} a + a \cdot {}^t\lambda^{-1}\bar{b} - \frac{1}{2} \bar{b} \cdot \lambda^{-1}\mu\bar{b}\right]$$

Proof: From proposition 4.14 the kernel of S_{g_c} may be obtained as

$$S_{g_c}(a, b) = (e_a | S_{g_c} | e_b).$$

With the help of the Weyl operators this expression may be transformed into

$$S_{g_c}(a, b) = (e_a | S_{g_c} \circ W_{\beta_c} | e_0) \exp\left[\frac{1}{2} \bar{b} \cdot b\right]$$

$$= (e_a | W_{g_c\beta_c} \circ S_{g_c} | e_0) \exp\left[\frac{1}{2} \bar{b} \cdot b\right]$$

$$= ((W_{g_c\beta_c} \circ S_{g_c}) e_0)(a) \exp\left[\frac{1}{2} \bar{b} \cdot b\right].$$

From proposition 4.17 and the definition of the coherent state in example 4.4, the last expression is given by

$$S_{g_c}(a, b) = \nu_{gc} \exp\left[\frac{1}{2} \bar{b} \cdot b + \bar{q} \cdot \left(a - \frac{1}{2} q\right) + \frac{1}{2}(a - q) \cdot \bar{\mu}\lambda^{-1}(a - q)\right]$$

where we defined $g_c\beta_c = \left(\begin{matrix} q \\ q \end{matrix}\right)$. Using the relation

$$\bar{q} = {}^t\lambda^{-1}\bar{b} + \bar{\mu}\lambda^{-1} q$$

obtained from proposition 4.6 one finds the expression given above. $\qquad \square$

Now we give the form of the so far undetermined factor ν_{g_c} appearing in front of the kernel of the operator S_{g_c}. For an $m \times m$ matrix N whose operator norm fulfills $|N - I| < 1$, the logarithm is well-defined by the power series

$$\log N = \sum_{k=1}^{\infty} k^{-1}(-1)^{k-1}(N-I)^k.$$

Consider two elements g_{1c} and g_{2c} of $Sp\,(2m,\,\mathbb{C}) \cap U(m,m)$ and their product

$$g_c = g_{1c}\,g_{2c}.$$

The operator norms of the $m \times m$ matrices $\lambda_1^{-1}\mu_1$ and $\bar{\mu}_2\lambda_2^{-1}$ may be shown from proposition 4.6 to obey

$$|\lambda_1^{-1}\mu_1| < 1 \qquad |\bar{\mu}_2\lambda_2^{-1}| < 1.$$

If the matrix N is defined as

$$N = \lambda_1^{-1}\lambda\lambda_2^{-1} = \lambda_1^{-1}(\lambda_1\lambda_2 + \mu_1\bar{\mu}_2)\lambda_2^{-1} = I + \lambda_1^{-1}\mu_1\bar{\mu}_2\lambda_2^{-1}$$

one easily finds that $|N - I| < 1$ which allows one to define $\log N$ by the power series given above. We are then in a position to give Bargmann's result on the choice of the operators S_{g_c} and their multiplication rule. Note that the absolute value of ν_{g_c} is determined by the requirement of unitarity.

4.28 Proposition: For $g_c \in Sp\,(2m,\,\mathbb{C}) \cap U(m,m)$ introduce the blocks $\lambda\,\mu$ given in proposition 4.6 and decompose λ as

$$\lambda = \Lambda \exp i\,\Theta, \quad \det \Lambda = |\det \lambda| > 0.$$

Define

$$(\det\lambda)^{-1/2} = |\det\lambda|^{-1/2} \exp\left[-i\frac{m}{2}\,\Theta\right]$$

and choose the kernel of the operator S_{g_c} in the form

$$S_{g_c}(a, b) = \nu_{g_c} \exp\left[\frac{1}{2}\,a\cdot\bar{\mu}\lambda^{-1}\,a + a\cdot{}^t\lambda^{-1}\bar{b} - \frac{1}{2}\,\bar{b}\cdot\lambda^{-1}\mu\bar{b}\right],$$

$$\nu_{g_c} = (\det\lambda)^{-1/2}.$$

Denote by g_{1c}, g_{2c} two matrices parametrized in this way and by g_c their product $g_{1c}g_{2c} = g_c$. Then the representation condition becomes

$$S_{g_{1c}} \circ S_{g_{2c}} = S_{g_c}$$

provided that Θ_1, Θ_2 and Θ are related as

$$\Theta = \Theta_1 + \Theta_2 + \mathrm{Im}\,\rho,$$

$$\rho = \frac{1}{m}\,\mathrm{trace}\,\log[\lambda_1^{-1}\lambda\lambda_2^{-1}].$$

The proof given by Bargmann [BA 68] makes use of the universal covering group of the real symplectic group.

Example 4.7: Representation of orthogonal point transformations

A real orthogonal point transformation has the symplectic matrix description

$$g_1 = \begin{bmatrix} A & 0 \\ 0 & A \end{bmatrix}, \quad g_{1c} = \begin{bmatrix} A & 0 \\ 0 & A \end{bmatrix}, \quad {}^t A A = I_m.$$

Multiplication of the operator $S_{g_{1c}}$ with $S_{g_{2c}}$ for an arbitrary element $g_{2c} \in Sp(2m, \mathbb{C}) \cap U(m, m)$ yields according to proposition 4.28

$$N = \lambda_1^{-1} (\lambda_1 \lambda_2 + \mu_1 \bar{\mu}_2) \lambda_2^{-1} = I_m$$

since $\mu_1 = 0$. Therefore we get for

$$S_{g_c} = S_{g_{1c}} \circ S_{g_{2c}}$$

the simple result

$$\Theta = \Theta_1 + \Theta_2.$$

Finally we consider the combination of phase space translations with symplectic transformations.

4.29 Definition: The inhomogeneous symplectic group $I\,Sp\,(2\,m, \mathbb{R})$ is the group with elements (α, g) where α is a phase space translation and g is an element of $Sp\,(2\,m, \mathbb{R})$. The multiplication law is given by

$$(\alpha_1, g_1)(\alpha_2, g_2) = (\alpha_1 + g_1 \alpha_2, g_1 g_2).$$

The complex form of this group has elements (α_c, g_c) where $\alpha_c = (a\bar{a})$ and $g_c \in Sp\,(2\,m, \mathbb{C}) \cap U(m, m)$ and the multiplication law

$$(\alpha_{1c}, g_{1c})(\alpha_{2c}, g_{2c}) = (\alpha_{1c} + g_{1c} \alpha_{2c}, g_{1c} g_{2c}).$$

Using the action of the operators S_{g_c} on the Weyl operators, the representation property of Weyl operators given in proposition 4.17 and the representation property of the operators S_{g_c} given in proposition 4.28, it is possible to prove

Proposition 4.30: The operators

$$V_{\alpha_c, g_c} = W_{\alpha_c} \circ S_{g_c}$$

form a unitary projective representation of the inhomogeneous symplectic group $I\,Sp(2m, \mathbb{R})$ with the multiplication rule

$$V_{\alpha_{1c}, g_{1c}} \circ V_{\alpha_{2c}, g_{2c}} = \exp\left[-\frac{1}{2} \{\alpha_{1c}, g_{1c} \alpha_{2c}\}\right] V_{\alpha_{1c} + g_{1c} \alpha_{2c}, g_{1c} g_{2c}}$$

Proof: Written out in detail, one finds

$$W_{\alpha_{1c}} \circ S_{g_{1c}} \circ W_{\alpha_{2c}} \circ S_{g_{2c}} = W_{\alpha_{1c}} \circ W_{g_{1c}\alpha_{2c}} \circ S_{g_{1c}} \circ S_{g_{2c}}$$

$$= \exp\left[-\frac{1}{2}\{\alpha_{1c}, g_{1c}\alpha_{2c}\}\right] W_{\alpha_{1c}+g_{1c}\alpha_{2c}} \circ S_{g_{1c}g_{2c}}. \qquad \square$$

4.6 Oscillator States of a Single Particle with Angular Momentum and Matrix Elements of Some Operators

In example 4.1 we introduced the states of a single particle with angular momentum as homogeneous polynomials of degree N which involved solid spherical harmonics in the convention of Edmonds [ED 57]. We first summarize the explicit form of these polynomials along with some simple properties.

4.31 Proposition: The normalized states of a single particle with angular momentum in Bargmann space are given by

$$P_{LM}^N (x) = A_{NL} (x \cdot x)^{\frac{1}{2}(N-L)} Y_{LM}(x).$$

These states are homogeneous polynomials of degree N,

$$P_{LM}^N (\alpha x) = \alpha^N P_{LM}^N (x)$$

and under complex conjugation obey

$$\overline{P_{LM}^N (\overline{x})} = (-1)^M P_{L-M}^N (x).$$

The symmetry group of the oscillator hamiltonian is the group $U(3)$ whose irreducible representations are characterized by partitions $h = [h_1 h_2 h_3]$. The irreducible representations of the subgroup $SU(3)$ are then described by the numbers $h_1 - h_3, h_2 - h_3$ or by the labels λ, μ introduced by Elliott [EL 58, 58a],

$$\lambda = h_1 - h_2, \quad \mu = h_2 - h_3.$$

The states of a single particle carry the representation $h = [N00] = [N]$ and hence we get under elements $u \in U(3)$

$$P_{LM}^N (xu) = \sum_{\tilde{L}\tilde{M}} P_{\tilde{L}\tilde{M}}^N (x) D_{\tilde{L}\tilde{M}, LM}^{[N]}(u).$$

In contrast to expressions given in section 3, the matrix of the representation $D^{[N]}$ is now labeled by the pair of indices LM.

For two particles one may couple the corresponding bases to bases of the irreducible representation

$$[N'] \times [N''] = [N' + N''00] + [N' + N'' - 1\,1\,0] + \ldots$$

Indicating coupling by square brackets we write

4.32 Definition: The two-particle bases of the representation $[h_1 h_2 0]$ of $U(3)$ are given by the coupled polynomials

$$[P^{N'}(x') P^{N''}(x'')]_{\Omega LM}^{[h_1 h_2 0]}$$

$$= \sum_{L'L''} [P_{L'}^{N'}(x') P_{L''}^{N''}(x'')]_{LM} \left\langle \begin{array}{cc} N'N'' \\ L'L'' \end{array} \middle| \begin{array}{c} [h_1 h_2 0] \\ \Omega LM \end{array} \right\rangle$$

where the coefficients in the expansion are the reduced Wigner coefficients of $U(3)$ in the subgroup reduction $U(3) > SO(3, \mathbb{R})$ and Ω is a multiplicity index for repeated values of L.

We shall need mostly the particular coefficient for the partition $h = [N' + N''00]$ which was derived in [KR 70].

4.33 Proposition: For the coupling of two single-particle states to a basis $D^{[N]}$ of $U(3)$ the reduced Wigner-coefficients are given by

$$\left\langle \begin{array}{cc} N' & N'' \\ L' & L'' \end{array} \middle| \begin{array}{c} N \\ L \end{array} \right\rangle = \delta_{N'+N'',N} A_{N'L'} A_{N''L''} A_{NL}^{-1} \left[\frac{N'! N''!}{N!} \right]^{1/2} H(L'L''L)$$

$$H(L'L''L) = \left[\frac{(2L'+1)(2L''+1)}{4\pi(2L+1)} \right]^{1/2} \langle L'0L''0| L0 \rangle.$$

For later use we define the coefficients

$$A(N'L'N''L'', NL) = \delta_{N'+N'',N} \left\langle \begin{array}{cc} N' & N'' \\ L' & L'' \end{array} \middle| \begin{array}{c} N \\ L \end{array} \right\rangle \left[\frac{N!}{N'! N''!} \right]^{1/2}.$$

We now proceed to the determination of matrix elements of operators between oscillator states. Consider first the kernel of the identity operator in Bargmann space which was given in proposition 4.12. The completeness relation for oscillator states yields

4.34 Proposition: The kernel of the identity operator has the expansion

$$\exp[x \cdot \bar{x}'] = \sum_{NLM} P_{LM}^N(x) \overline{P_{LM}^N(x')}$$

in terms of oscillator states. For given degree N this implies

$$\sum_{LM} P_{LM}^N(x) \overline{P_{LM}^N(x')} = (N!)^{-1} (x \cdot \bar{x}')^N.$$

Next we turn to the matrix elements of Weyl operators. From proposition 4.21 one may write

$$W_{\alpha_c} = \Lambda_a \circ V_a \exp\left[-\frac{1}{2} a \cdot \bar{a} \right].$$

To derive the matrix elements of the operator V_a we use from [KR 70] the expansion

$$P_{LM}^N (x' + x'') = \sum_{N'N''} \sum_{L'L''} [[P_{L'}^{N'}(x') P_{L''}^{N''}(x'')]_{LM} \times A(N'L'N''L'', NL)].$$

Application of this expansion yields immediately

$$(V_a P_{LM}^N)(x) = P_{LM}^N (x - a)$$

$$= \sum_{N'N''} \sum_{L'M'L''M''} P_{L'M'}^{N'}(x) P_{L''M''}^{N''}(-a) \langle L'M'L''M''|LM \rangle A(N'L'N''L'', NL)$$

and hence

4.35 Proposition: The matrix elements of the operators V_a and Λ_a are given by

$$(N'L'M'|V_a|NLM) = \sum_{L''_j} P_{L''M''}^{N''}(-a) \langle L'M'L''M''|LM \rangle A(N'L'N''L'', NL)$$

$$(NLM|\Lambda_a|N'L'M') = \overline{(N'L'M'|V_{-a}|NLM)}$$

$$= \sum_{L''} \overline{P_{L''M''}^{N''}(a)} \langle L'M'L''M''|LM \rangle A(N'L'N''L'', NL).$$

The matrix elements of Λ_a were obtained from the hermitian properties given in proposition 4.21. In these expressions the non-vanishing contributions have $N' \leqslant N$. Note the special values

$$(NLM|\Lambda_a|000) \quad = P_{LM}^N(a)$$

$$(NLM|\Lambda_a|NL'M') = \delta_{LL'}\delta_{MM'}.$$

For the Weyl operator one finds

4.36 Proposition: The matrix elements of the Weyl operator W_{α_c} between oscillator states are given by

$$(\tilde{N}\tilde{L}\tilde{M}|W_{\alpha_c}|NLM)$$

$$= \exp\left[-\frac{1}{2}a \cdot \overline{a}\right] \sum_{N'L'M'} (\tilde{N}\tilde{L}\tilde{M}|\Lambda_a|N'L'M')(N'L'M'|V_a|NLM).$$

In particular,

$$(000|W_{\alpha_c}|NLM) = P_{LM}^N(-a) \ \exp\left[-\frac{1}{2}a \cdot \overline{a}\right]$$

$$(\tilde{N}\tilde{L}\tilde{M}|W_{\alpha_c}|000) = \overline{P_{\tilde{L}\tilde{M}}^{\tilde{N}}(a)} \quad \exp\left[-\frac{1}{2}a \cdot \overline{a}\right]$$

a result which is also easily obtained from the coherent state considered in example 4.6. In general note that the matrix of the Weyl operator W_{α_c} between a set of oscillator states up to a fixed excitation appears from proposition 4.36 as a product of a lower and an upper triangular matrix each with entries one along the diagonal, multiplied by the overall factor $\exp\left[-\frac{1}{2}\, a \cdot \bar{a}\right]$.

In a similar fashion we give now the matrix elements of an operator S_{g_c} between single-particle oscillator states. We consider only linear canonical transformations which act in the same way on all three components of a particle coordinate. The kernel of S_{g_c} then reads from proposition 4.27

$$S_{g_c}(x, x') = \nu_{g_c} \exp\left[A x \cdot x + C x \cdot \bar{x}' + B \bar{x}' \cdot \bar{x}'\right]$$

where we used

$$\frac{1}{2}\, \bar{\mu}\lambda^{-1} = I_3 A, \quad {}^t\lambda^{-1} = I_3 C, \quad -\frac{1}{2}\lambda^{-1}\mu = I_3 B.$$

Now we expand the individual terms of the exponential, using properties given in proposition 4.31 and proposition 4.34. We obtain

$$\exp A x \cdot x = \sum_{n_\alpha = 0}^{\infty} \frac{1}{n_\alpha!}\, (A)^{n_\alpha} A_{2n_\alpha 0}^{-1} P_{00}^{2n_\alpha}(x)$$

$$\exp B \bar{x}' \cdot \bar{x}' = \sum_{n_\beta = 0}^{\infty} \frac{1}{n_\beta!}\, (B)^{n_\beta} A_{2n_\beta 0}^{-1} \overline{P_{00}^{2n_\beta}(x')}$$

$$\exp C x \cdot \bar{x}' = \sum_{q = 0}^{\infty} P_{LM}^{q}(x)\, \overline{P_{LM}^{q}(x')}\, (C)^q$$

Combining these expressions one easily derives

4.37 Proposition: The matrix elements of the operator S_{g_c} between single-particle oscillator states are given by

$$(N'L'M'|S_{g_c}|NLM) = \delta_{L'L}\, \delta_{M'M}\, \nu_{g_c}\, A_{N'L'}^{-1} A_{NL}^{-1}$$

$$\times \sum_{q} \left[\left(\tfrac{1}{2}(N' - q)\right)!\, \left(\tfrac{1}{2}(N - q)\right)!\right]^{-1} A_{qL}^2\, (A)^{\frac{1}{2}(N'-q)}\, (B)^{\frac{1}{2}(N-q)}\, (C)^q$$

where the summation over q is restricted by $0 \leqslant N' - q = \text{even}$, $0 \leqslant N - q = \text{even}$, $q \geqslant 0$. This expression appeared in [KR 73].

4.7 Notes and References

A clear exposition of the geometry and group theory underlying the correspondence between classical and quantum mechanics is given by Weyl [WE 31]. More recent treatments are given by Mackey [MA 63] and by Souriau [SO 70]. Segal [SE 63] and Bargmann [BA 61, 62, 67, 68] introduced the Hilbert space of analytic functions associated with the commutation properties of oscillator creation and annihilation operators. For a generalization we refer to Grossmann [GR 78], for a review on the Weyl group to Wolf [WO 75]. The unitary representations in quantum mechanics of real linear canonical transformations in the Schrödinger representation are derived by Moshinsky and Quesne [MO 71a, 74] and in the Bargmann representation by Bargmann [BA 68] and by Itzykson [IT 67]. Recent descriptions of the metaplectic representation are given by Souriau [SO 76] and by Sternberg [ST 78]. A survey of canonical transformations and their applications is given by Kramer, Moshinsky and Seligman [KR 75]. For generalizations of coherent states we refer to the review by Bacry, Grossmann and Zak [BA 75].

The present exposition follows Bargmann [BA 68]. The factorization of Weyl operators given in section 4.4 is new and will be applied in later sections. For the group theory of harmonic oscillators and its application to nuclear structure we refer to Kramer and Moshinsky [KR 68b]. Here we use the Bargmann representation to convert the state description in terms of creation operators into a description in terms of analytic functions. For semigroup extensions of linear canonical transformations we refer to section 5.

5 Linear Canonical Transformations and Interacting n-Particle Systems

5.1 Orthogonal Point Transformations in n-particle Systems and Their Representations

For n particles moving in three-dimensional space, each coordinate should carry an index $i = 1, 2, 3$ denoting the vector component and an index $l = 1, 2, \ldots, n$ denoting the particle number. Among the linear point transformations acting on these coordinates there are two commuting subgroups of transformations. The elements of the first one are given by product matrices $M_3 \times I_n$ where the 3×3 matrix M_3 acts on the vector components. The elements of the second one are of the form $I_3 \times M_n$ where the $n \times n$ matrix M_n acts on the vectors for the different particles. To the first subgroup there belong the rotations giving rise to the rotation group $SO(3, \mathbb{R})$. The second subgroup contains permutations and transformations to various types of relative coordinates. In the present section we shall deal with this second subgroup and hence shall drop the reference to the three vector components. Moreover we shall need at present only orthogonal $n \times n$ transformation matrices.

With respect to single-particle coordinates, any permutation p is represented by its orthogonal permutation matrix $d(p)$ as specified in section 2.2. The representation of a permutation may now be expressed as

$$U(p) = S_{g_c(d(p))}.$$

The systems of relative coordinates are all based on the choice of a weight $w = (w_1 w_2 \ldots w_j)$ of n. In the composite particle theory to be developed, the weight components describe the number of particles belonging to the various composite particles. The corresponding relative coordinates refer to the relative position of composite particles and to the relative position of their constituents respectively. The transformations are described by the well-known Jacobi matrices in orthogonal form. As will be shown, the use of orthogonal transformations has the great advantage that the complex coordinates $x_1 x_2 \ldots x_n$ transform in the same way as the real coordinates $\xi_1 \xi_2 \ldots \xi_n$. Since we prefer to work in the Bargmann representation, all transformations are given with respect to the complex coordinates.

5.1 Definition: A Jacobi matrix J_m of dimension m is an orthogonal matrix with non-vanishing elements

$$l \leqslant i < m: \quad J_{li} = [i(i+1)]^{-1/2}$$

$$l = i + 1: \quad J_{li} = -\left[\frac{i}{i+1}\right]^{1/2}$$

$$1 \leqslant l \leqslant m: \quad J_{lm} = [m]^{-1/2}.$$

For a weight $w = (w_1 w_2 \ldots w_j)$ of n we define the orthogonal $n \times n$ matrix J by

$$J = \begin{bmatrix} J_{w_1} & & & \\ & J_{w_2} & & \\ & & \ddots & \\ & & & J_{w_j} \end{bmatrix} = \oplus \sum_{i=1}^{j} J_{w_i}.$$

Obviously J^{-1} describes a transformation to relative and center-of-mass vectors for each set of $w_1, w_2, \ldots, w_j$ particles. We rearrange the order of these vectors with the help of a permutation matrix.

5.2 Definition: For given weight, the permutation matrix Q is defined as

$$Q = d(r^Q, w^Q) = d(p)$$

according to definition 2.5 with

$$w^Q = (1 \ 1 \ 1 \ldots 1 \ w_1 - 1 \ w_2 - 1 \ldots w_j - 1) \qquad \text{and}$$

$$r^Q = \begin{bmatrix} 2 & 4 \ldots 2j & 1 & \ldots & 2j-1 \\ 1 & 2 \ldots j & j+1 & \ldots & 2j \end{bmatrix}.$$

Example 5.1: The permutation matrix Q for the weight w = (321)

The weight w^Q and the permutation r^Q in this case become

$$w^Q = (1 \ 1 \ 1 \ 2 \ 1 \ 0)$$

$$r^Q = \begin{bmatrix} 2 & 4 & 6 & 1 & 3 & 5 \\ 1 & 2 & 3 & 4 & 5 & 6 \end{bmatrix}.$$

The permuted weight w^Q is given from definition 2.4 as

$$(w^Q)^{r^Q} = (2 \ 1 \ 1 \ 1 \ 0 \ 1).$$

From the definitions and propositions 2.4–2.8, the permutation associated with $d(r^Q, w^Q)$ is found to be

$$p: \begin{bmatrix} 1 & 2 & 3 & 4 & 5 & 6 \\ 4 & 5 & 1 & 6 & 2 & 3 \end{bmatrix} = \begin{bmatrix} 3 & 5 & 6 & 1 & 2 & 4 \\ 1 & 2 & 3 & 4 & 5 & 6 \end{bmatrix}.$$

The permutation matrix Q acts on the coordinates $[\begin{smallmatrix} z \\ y \end{smallmatrix}]$ as

$$Q \begin{bmatrix} z_1 \\ z_2 \\ z_3 \\ y_1 \\ y_2 \\ y_3 \end{bmatrix} = \begin{bmatrix} y_1 \\ y_2 \\ z_1 \\ y_3 \\ z_2 \\ z_3 \end{bmatrix},$$

compare the following definition 5.3.

5.3 Definition: The j center coordinates z_i and $n - j$ internal coordinates y_l are defined by the transformation

$$\begin{pmatrix} z \\ y \end{pmatrix} = (JQ)^{-1} \begin{pmatrix} x_1 \\ x_2 \\ \vdots \\ x_n \end{pmatrix}.$$

We require yet another transformation which leads from the center coordinates to relative coordinates between the centers.

5.4 Definition: For given weight w, define the $j \times j$ matrix w_j^{-1} by the transformation

$$s_i = \left[\frac{w_{i+1}}{q_{i+1} q_i} \right]^{1/2} \sum_{l=1}^{i} [w_l]^{1/2} z_l - \left[\frac{q_i}{q_{i+1}} \right]^{1/2} z_{i+1}$$

$$i = 1 \; 2 \ldots j - 1$$

$$s_j = [n]^{-1/2} \sum_{l=1}^{j} [w_l]^{1/2} z_l$$

$$q_i = \sum_{l=1}^{i} w_l$$

and the $n \times n$ matrix W by

$$W = \begin{bmatrix} W_j & 0 \\ 0 & I_{n-j} \end{bmatrix}.$$

Then the j cluster coordinates $s_1 s_2 \ldots s_j$ are defined by

$$\begin{bmatrix} s \\ y \end{bmatrix} = W^{-1} \begin{bmatrix} z \\ y \end{bmatrix} = (JQW)^{-1} \begin{bmatrix} x_1 \\ x_2 \\ \vdots \\ x_n \end{bmatrix}.$$

Note that the matrices J, Q and W depend explicitly on the chosen weight w.

Example 5.2: Cluster coordinates for two and three composite particles

For $j = 2$, the matrix W_2^{-1} takes the form

$$(W_2)^{-1} = \begin{bmatrix} \left[\dfrac{w_2}{n} \right]^{1/2} & -\left[\dfrac{w_1}{n} \right]^{1/2} \\ \left[\dfrac{w_1}{n} \right]^{1/2} & \left[\dfrac{w_2}{n} \right]^{1/2} \end{bmatrix}$$

and for $j = 3$ we find

$$(W_3)^{-1} = \begin{bmatrix} \left[\dfrac{w_2}{w_1 + w_2}\right]^{1/2} & -\left[\dfrac{w_1}{w_1 + w_2}\right]^{1/2} & 0 \\[3mm] \left[\dfrac{w_3 w_1}{n(w_1 + w_2)}\right]^{1/2} & \left[\dfrac{w_3 w_2}{n(w_1 + w_2)}\right]^{1/2} & -\left[\dfrac{w_1 + w_2}{n}\right]^{1/2} \\[3mm] \left[\dfrac{w_1}{n}\right]^{1/2} & \left[\dfrac{w_2}{n}\right]^{1/2} & \left[\dfrac{w_3}{n}\right]^{1/2} \end{bmatrix}.$$

The orthogonal point transformations are particular cases of symplectic transformations, the symplectic matrix being given by

$$g = \begin{bmatrix} B & 0 \\ 0 & B \end{bmatrix} = g(B), \quad {}^t\!BB = I_n.$$

For these transformations one easily derives

5.5 Proposition: The complex symplectic matrix g_c associated with an orthogonal point transformation is given by

$$g_c(B) = R g(B) R^{-1} = \begin{bmatrix} B & 0 \\ 0 & B \end{bmatrix}$$

where R is the matrix introduced in section 4.2.

Proposition 5.5 implies that, with respect to the complex coordinates $x_1 x_2 \ldots x_n$, an orthogonal point transformation remains a point transformation (that is, does not mix the creation and annihilation operators) with the same orthogonal matrix B.

Now we consider the representation of an orthogonal point transformation $g_c(B)$ by an operator $S_{g_c(B)}$ in Bargmann space. For describing a composite system of nucleons it will be convenient to consider states which are written in Bargmann space as analytic functions of center or cluster and internal coordinates. The relation between functions depending on different but linearly related sets of vectors is expressible by the operators $S_{g_c(B)}$ where B is the linear transformation matrix.

5.6 Proposition: The kernel of the representation $S_{g_c(B)}$ for a linear orthogonal point transformation B is given by

$$S_{g_c(B)} (\tilde{x}, x) = \exp\left[\sum_{i,\, l = 1}^{n} B_{il}\, \tilde{x}_i \cdot \overline{x}_l \right].$$

This operator transforms the states of n particles according to

$$(S_{g_c(B)} f) (\tilde{x}) = f(B^{-1} \tilde{x}).$$

Proof: Note that we consider actually a $3n \times 3n$ matrix $I_3 \times B$ in a phase space of dimension $6n$. The dependence on vector components appears only through the inner products

$\tilde{x}_i \cdot \bar{x}_l$ as explained in proposition 5.8 below. The form of the kernel is obtained from the expression for g_c given above which yields in terms of the blocks λ, μ as defined in proposition 4.6 the relation $\lambda = {}^t\lambda^{-1} = B$, $\mu = 0$. Inserting these values into the expression for the kernel given in proposition 4.28 yields the result given above. Next consider the integral

$$(S_{g_c(B)} f)(\tilde{x}) = \int S_{g_c(B)} (\tilde{x}, x) f(x) \, d\mu(x).$$

From the action of the kernel for the identity operator given in proposition 4.12 one easily deduces for the integral on the right-hand side the value

$$\int S_{g_c(B)} (\tilde{x}_1 \tilde{x}_2 \ldots \tilde{x}_n, x_1 x_2 \ldots x_n) \, f(x_1 x_2 \ldots x_n) \prod_i d\mu(x_i)$$

$$= f \left(\sum_{i=1}^{n} B_{i1} \tilde{x}_i \; \sum_{i=1}^{n} B_{i2} \tilde{x}_i \ldots \sum_{i=1}^{n} B_{in} \tilde{x}_i \right) = f({}^t B \tilde{x}) = f(B^{-1} \tilde{x})$$

where $f(B^{-1} \tilde{x})$ is a short-hand notation,

$$f(B^{-1} \tilde{x}) = f \left(\sum_{i=1}^{n} B_{1i}^{-1} \tilde{x}_i \; \sum_{i=1}^{n} B_{2i}^{-1} \tilde{x}_i \ldots \sum_{i=1}^{n} B_{ni}^{-1} \tilde{x}_i \right). \qquad \square$$

Example 5.3: States of n *particles expressed as functions of single-particle, center or cluster and internal coordinates*

Suppose the state of n particles is given as a function of single-particle coordinates. Then, employing from definition 5.4 the matrices J, Q and W and the coordinates (zy) and (sy), we find the identities

$$f(x) = (S_{g_c((JQ)^{-1})} f) ((JQ)^{-1} x) = (S_{g_c((JQ)^{-1})} f) (zy)$$

$$f(x) = (S_{g_c((JQW)^{-1})} f) ((JQW)^{-1} x) = (S_{g_c((JQW)^{-1})} f) (sy).$$

In turn, if the state is given as some function say of cluster and internal coordinates (sy), then the same state expressed as a function of single-particle coordinates is given by the identity

$$l(sy) = l((JQW)^{-1} x) = (S_{g_c(JQW)} l)(x).$$

Finally we apply the kernel given in proposition 5.6 to the determination of the general transformation bracket [KR 70] for two-particle states. This transformation bracket is the matrix element of the operator $S_{g_c(B)}$ for B being a 2×2 matrix between products of two single-particle oscillator states coupled with respect to angular momentum. The kernel

$$S_{g_c(B)}(\tilde{x}_1 \tilde{x}_2, x_1 x_2) = \exp [B_{11} \tilde{x}_1 \cdot \bar{x}_1 + B_{12} \tilde{x}_1 \cdot \bar{x}_2 + B_{21} \tilde{x}_2 \cdot \bar{x}_1 + B_{22} \tilde{x}_2 \cdot \bar{x}_2]$$

may be expanded with the help of the expressions given in section 4.6. The only additional result required is the identity

$$[P_{L'}^{N'}(x)\, P_{L''}^{N''}(x)]_{LM} = P_{LM}^{N'+N''}(x)\, A(N'L'N''L'',\, N' + N''L)$$

derived in [KR 70]. Then by standard recoupling transformations for angular momenta one finds

5.7 Proposition: The general two-particle transformation bracket is given by

$$(\widetilde{N}_1\widetilde{L}_1\widetilde{N}_2\widetilde{L}_2 L | S_{g_c(B)} | N_1 L_1 N_2 L_2 L) = \sum_{N_{11}N_{12}N_{21}N_{22}} \left\{ \prod_{i,\,l=1}^{2} (B_{il})^{N_{il}} \right.$$

$$\sum_{L_{11}L_{12}L_{21}L_{22}} A(N_{11}L_{11}N_{12}L_{12},\, \widetilde{N}_1\widetilde{L}_1)\, A(N_{21}L_{21}N_{22}L_{22},\, \widetilde{N}_2\widetilde{L}_2)$$

$$A(N_{11}L_{11}N_{21}L_{21},\, N_1 L_1)\, A(N_{12}L_{12}N_{22}L_{22},\, N_2 L_2)$$

$$\left. \langle\langle (L_{11}L_{12})\, \widetilde{L}_1 (L_{21}L_{22})\, \widetilde{L}_2 L | (L_{11}L_{21})\, L_1 (L_{12}L_{22})\, L_2 L\rangle \right\}.$$

5.2 General Linear Canonical Transformations for n-particles and State Dilatation

We shall require more general types of linear canonical transformations than the orthogonal point transformations considered so far. This will allow us to implement dilatations in the present section and Gaussian interactions in the next section.

The geometry of classical phase space of n particles moving in 3 space dimensions is given according to section 4.2 by symplectic forms and the real symplectic group $Sp(6n, \mathbb{R})$ in $6n$ dimensions. If each coordinate is labeled by a vector component and a particle index, we may consider subgroups of this symplectic group with elements acting separately on the vector component and particle indices. Two important subgroups of $Sp(6n, \mathbb{R})$ defined in this way are the direct product

$$SO(3, \mathbb{R}) \times Sp(2n, \mathbb{R}) < Sp(6n, \mathbb{R})$$

and the symplectic subgroup

$$I_3 \times Sp(2n, \mathbb{R}) < Sp(6n, \mathbb{R}).$$

In the present section we are dealing exclusively with the last subgroup whose elements we write again as g or g_c respectively.

For the kernels of the operators S_{g_c} associated with this symplectic group one obtains

5.8 Proposition: In a system of n particles with 3 degrees of freedom, the representation of the subgroup $I_3 \times Sp(2n, \mathbb{R})$ in Bargmann space is given by the operator S_{g_c} with kernel

$$S_{g_c}(\tilde{x}, x) = [\nu_{g_c}]^3 \exp\left[\frac{1}{2}\sum_{i,l=1}^{n} (\bar{\mu}\lambda^{-1})_{il}\tilde{x}_i \cdot \tilde{x}_l + \sum_{i,l=1}^{n} ({}^t\lambda^{-1})_{il}\tilde{x}_i \cdot \bar{x}\right.$$
$$\left. -\frac{1}{2}\sum_{i,l=1}^{n} (\lambda^{-1}\mu)_{il}\bar{x}_i \cdot \bar{x}_l\right].$$

Note that the factor in front of the kernel is affected and that the dependence on the vector components enters only through scalar products.

The geometrical interpretation of a linear canonical transformation whose matrix g is given in terms of $n \times n$ blocks $A B C D$ by

$$g = \begin{bmatrix} A & -B \\ -C & D \end{bmatrix}$$

is easily recovered from the action of the operators S_g in the Schrödinger representation on the position and momentum operators. According to proposition 4.24 one may write

$$S_{g^{-1}} \circ \begin{bmatrix} \Xi \\ -\Pi \end{bmatrix} \circ S_g = g\begin{bmatrix} \Xi \\ -\Pi \end{bmatrix}.$$

The transformation

$$g\begin{bmatrix} \Xi \\ -\Pi \end{bmatrix} = \begin{bmatrix} A & -B \\ -C & D \end{bmatrix}\begin{bmatrix} \Xi \\ -\Pi \end{bmatrix} = \begin{bmatrix} A\Xi + B\Pi \\ -C\Xi - D\Pi \end{bmatrix}$$

yields the geometric transformation of the coordinates and momenta represented by the matrix g and the operator S_g. We choose a negative sign for the off-diagonal $n \times n$ blocks B, C in order to keep in line with the notation of [KR 75] for the transformation of coordinates and momenta. The following property of real symplectic matrices should be noted:

5.9 Proposition: If g is real symplectic and

$$g' = MgM^{-1}$$

with

$$M = \begin{bmatrix} I_n & 0 \\ 0 & -I_n \end{bmatrix}$$

then g' is also real symplectic.

From the block form of the matrix g, one obtains for the complex matrix g_c the expression

$$g_c = \begin{bmatrix} \lambda & \mu \\ \bar{\mu} & \bar{\lambda} \end{bmatrix}, \qquad \begin{aligned} \lambda &= \frac{1}{2}(A + D) + i\frac{1}{2}(B - C) \\ \mu &= \frac{1}{2}(A - D) - i\frac{1}{2}(B + C) \end{aligned}$$

5.10 Definition: A real (not necessarily orthogonal) point transformation is a symplectic transformation $g \in Sp(2n, \mathbb{R})$ with $B = C = 0$, its matrix form is

$$g = \begin{bmatrix} A & 0 \\ 0 & {}^tA^{-1} \end{bmatrix}$$

and the corresponding complex form g_c is given by the real matrix

$$g_c = \frac{1}{2} \begin{bmatrix} A + {}^tA^{-1} & A - {}^tA^{-1} \\ A - {}^tA^{-1} & A + {}^tA^{-1} \end{bmatrix} .$$

Note that in general a point transformation does not lead to a block diagonal matrix g_c. Clearly in the Schrödinger representation we get

5.11 Proposition: A real point transformation transforms the states in the Schrödinger representation according to

$$(S_g \varphi)(\xi) = [\det A]^{3/2} \, \varphi(A^{-1} \xi).$$

The factor in front of this expression is obtained from the requirement of normalization. The case of most physical interest is a real dilatation.

5.12 Definition: A dilatation is a real point transformation such that

$$A = (A_{il}) = (d_i \delta_{il}), \quad d_i > 0 \quad \text{for} \quad i, l = 1 \; 2 \ldots n.$$

From this definition and the action of a real point transformation stated in proposition 5.11 it is obvious that a dilatation changes the scale of the real coordinate ξ_i of particle i by a factor d_i^{-1} for $i = 1 \; 2 \ldots n$. The application of the operator S_{g_c} to a state in Bargmann space describes the transformation of this state under a dilatation. Now to define the Bargmann space we chose some standard oscillator frequency ω. By noting that the position and momentum operators transform according to

$$(g \Xi)_i = d_i \Xi_i$$
$$(g \Pi)_i = d_i^{-1} \Pi_i \qquad i = 1 \; 2 \ldots n$$

one concludes that under application of S_g (or S_{g_c}) to an oscillator state of standard frequency ω this state is transformed into one of frequency

$$\tilde{\omega}_i = d_i^{-2} \, \omega.$$

The kernel of S_{g_c} for a dilatation from proposition 5.8 and definition 5.12 is given by

$$S_{g_c}(\tilde{x}, x) = \left[\prod_{i=1}^{n} \frac{1}{2}(d_i + d_i^{-1}) \right]^{-3/2}$$

$$\exp\left[\frac{1}{2} \sum_{i=1}^{n} \left(\frac{d_i - d_i^{-1}}{d_i + d_i^{-1}} \right) \tilde{x}_i \cdot \tilde{x}_i + \sum_{i=1}^{n} \frac{2}{(d_i + d_i^{-1})} \tilde{x}_i \cdot \bar{x}_i - \frac{1}{2} \sum_{i=1}^{n} \left(\frac{d_i - d_i^{-1}}{d_i + d_i^{-1}} \right) \bar{x}_i \cdot \bar{x}_i \right].$$

5.3 Interactions in n-body Systems and Complex Extension of Linear Canonical Transformations

So far, linear canonical transformations have been used to deal with kinematical aspects of the n-body system. We now show that the class of operators associated with linear canonical transformation can be extended to encompass for example Gaussian operators which have been used extensively in computations of nuclear properties. Before giving the general theorem we discuss two important examples.

Example 5.4: The Gaussian operator

Consider in the Schrödinger representation for m = 3 the unitary operator

$$U(\alpha) = \exp\left[i\frac{1}{2}\alpha \sum_{l=1}^{3} \Xi_l \circ \Xi_l\right].$$

A straight-forward computation yields the operator relations

$$U^{-1}(\alpha) \circ \Xi_l \circ U(\alpha) = \Xi_l$$

$$U^{-1}(\alpha) \circ \Pi_q \circ U(\alpha) = \Pi_q - i\frac{1}{2}\alpha\left[\sum_l \Xi_l \circ \Xi_l, \Pi_q\right] = \Pi_q + \alpha\Xi_q.$$

Writing this in the short-hand form

$$U^{-1}(\alpha) \circ \left[\begin{array}{c} \Xi \\ -\Pi \end{array}\right] \circ U(\alpha) = \left[\begin{array}{c} \Xi \\ -\Pi - \alpha\Xi \end{array}\right]$$

it follows by comparison from proposition 4.24 that $U(\alpha)$ is the representation S_g of the real symplectic transformation

$$g = \left[\begin{array}{cc} 1 & 0 \\ -\alpha & 1 \end{array}\right]$$

which we write as a 2×2 matrix, not as a 6×6 matrix, following the remarks made in section 5.1. If now we extend the values of α to imaginary numbers $i\gamma$ with $\gamma > 0$, the operator $U(i\gamma)$ becomes the Gaussian operator

$$U(i\gamma) = \exp\left[-\frac{1}{2}\gamma \sum_{l=1}^{3} \Xi_l \circ \Xi_l\right]$$

whose kernel in Bargmann space is easily computed to yield

$$U(i\gamma)(\tilde{x}, x) = \left[\frac{2+\gamma}{2}\right]^{-3/2} \exp\left[-\frac{1}{2}\frac{\gamma}{2+\gamma}\tilde{x}\cdot\tilde{x} + \frac{2}{2+\gamma}\tilde{x}\cdot\bar{x} - \frac{1}{2}\frac{\gamma}{2+\gamma}\bar{x}\cdot\bar{x}\right].$$

Comparing this kernel with the expression given in proposition 5.14 for the kernel of a linear canonical transformation associated with an operator S_{g_c} one finds formally

$$g_c = \frac{1}{2}\begin{bmatrix} 2+\gamma & \gamma \\ -\gamma & 2-\gamma \end{bmatrix} = R\begin{bmatrix} 1 & 0 \\ -i\gamma & 1 \end{bmatrix}R^{-1}$$

where the matrix R is given in section 4.2. We stress that this is still a formal result since the matrix g is symplectic but not real, and hence the matrix g_c is not an element of the group $Sp(2, \mathbb{C}) \cap U(1, 1)$. Looking at the operator $U(i\gamma)$ we also notice that it is bounded and self-adjoint but not unitary and in general not invertible. We shall show below what modification of the analysis given in section 4.5 is necessary to include the operators of Gaussian type.

Example 5.5: The complex dilatation

Consider in Bargmann space the operator $S(\delta)$ with kernel

$$S(\delta)(\tilde{x}, x) = \delta^{3/2} \exp[\delta \tilde{x} \cdot \overline{x}], \quad 0 < \delta < 1.$$

Comparing again with the kernels of the operators S_{g_c} given in proposition 5.14 we would associate with this operator the matrix

$$g_c = \begin{bmatrix} \delta^{-1} & 0 \\ 0 & \delta \end{bmatrix}.$$

Notice that this matrix belongs to $Sp(2, \mathbb{C})$ but does not belong to $U(1, 1)$ and hence again does not correspond to a real symplectic matrix. The operator $S(\delta)$ may be shown to be of Hilbert-Schmidt type and certainly is not unitary. We shall encounter operators of this type in the normalization kernels of composite particle systems.

Now we return to the extension of the symplectic group and its representation in Bargmann space. We recall from section 4.2 that the group $U(m, m)$ on $\mathbb{C}^{2m}$ preserves the hermitian inner product

$$(\alpha_c, \beta_c) = \overline{\alpha}'_c \cdot \beta'_c - \overline{\alpha}''_c \cdot \beta''_c$$

that is,

$$(g_c\alpha_c, g_c\alpha_c) - (\alpha_c, \alpha_c) = 0 \quad \text{for} \quad g_c \in U(m, m).$$

5.13 Definition: The length-increasing semigroup $U^{\geqslant}(m, m)$ and the strictly length-increasing semigroup $U^{>}(m, m)$ are defined as the matrix semigroups

$$U^{\geqslant}(m, m): \{g_c | (g_c\alpha_c, g_c\alpha_c) - (\alpha_c, \alpha_c) \geqslant 0\}$$

$$U^{>}(m, m): \{g_c | (g_c\alpha_c, g_c\alpha_c) - (\alpha_c, \alpha_c) > 0\}$$

for all $\alpha_c \in \mathbb{C}^{2m}$.

Note that both sets are indeed semigroups since any product of (strictly) length-increasing transformations is (strictly) length increasing.

In the following theorem we shall need the semigroups whose elements belong both to the complex symplectic group $\mathrm{Sp}(2m, \mathbb{C})$ and one of the length-increasing semigroups. These semigroups we denote as

$$\mathrm{Sp}(2m, \mathbb{C}) \cap U^{\geqslant}(m, m) \quad \text{and} \quad \mathrm{Sp}(2m, \mathbb{C}) \cap U^{>}(m, m)$$

respectively. In the following theorem we write kernels similar to the ones given in proposition 4.28 but with $\bar{\mu}$ replaced by ν as we do not wish to employ the group $U(m, m)$.

5.14 Theorem: For elements g_c of the two semigroups $\mathrm{Sp}(2m, \mathbb{C}) \cap U^{\geqslant}(m, m)$ and $\mathrm{Sp}(2m, \mathbb{C}) \cap U^{>}(m, m)$ with block form

$$g_c = \begin{bmatrix} \lambda & \mu \\ \nu & \rho \end{bmatrix}$$

the operators S_{g_c} with kernel

$$S_{g_c}(\widetilde{x}, x) = (\det \lambda)^{-1/2} \exp\left[\frac{1}{2}\widetilde{x} \cdot \nu \lambda^{-1} \widetilde{x} + \widetilde{x} \cdot {}^t\lambda^{-1} \overline{x} - \frac{1}{2}\overline{x} \cdot \lambda^{-1} \mu \overline{x} \right]$$

form a representation of the corresponding semigroup which is bounded for length-increasing transformations and of Hilbert-Schmidt type for strictly length-increasing transformations.

For the geometry of the semigroups, the proof of this theorem and additional details we refer to [BR 78, 78a].

Example 5.6: Gaussian operators and complex dilatations as representations of semigroup elements

In the examples 5.4 and 5.5 we associated the Gaussian operators and the complex dilatations with 2×2 matrices which are easily seen to be symplectic. To check the semigroup property we write with the help of the matrix M introduced in section 4.2

$$(g_c \alpha_c, g_c \alpha_c) - (\alpha_c, \alpha_c) = (\overline{\alpha}_c', \overline{\alpha}_c'') (g_c^+ M g_c - M) \begin{pmatrix} \alpha_c' \\ \alpha_c'' \end{pmatrix}.$$

Hence we must check if the matrix $g_c^+ M g_c - M$ is positive definite or semi-definite. For the Gaussian operator we obtain

$$g_c^+ M g_c - M = \gamma \begin{bmatrix} 1 & 1 \\ 1 & 1 \end{bmatrix} \geqslant 0$$

and for the complex dilatation

$$g_c^+ M g_c - M = \begin{bmatrix} \delta^{-2} - 1 & 0 \\ 0 & 1 - \delta^2 \end{bmatrix} > 0.$$

It follows from theorem 5.14 that the Gaussian operator and the complex dilatation represent elements of the length increasing and strictly length increasing semigroups respectively.

In [BR 78] it is shown that general elements of the semigroups may be factorized into elements of the group $\mathrm{Sp}(2m, \mathbb{C}) \cap U(m, m)$ and block diagonal matrices which contain at most 2×2 blocks corresponding to Gaussians or complex dilatations. The same factorization is shown in [BR 78a] to be valid for the representations of the semigroup.

To summarize the development of this section we have shown how to extend the class of integral operators described by linear canonical transformations. Among these operators are the Gaussian two-body interactions whose kernel is obtained by applying a simple point transformation to the kernel of the Gaussian operator given above.

5.4 Density Operators

In the computation of the interaction kernel for composite nucleon systems from the various types of two-body interactions it will be convenient to write analytic results without considering all specific types of interactions. To do this we introduce first the general density operator and then its reduced translationally invariant form for the two-nucleon system.

5.15 Definition: Let K be an operator in Bargmann space and f, h be two states. The density operator D for these two states is defined by the condition that, for any operator K,

$$(f|K|h) = \mathrm{trace}\,(K \circ D).$$

The trace may be expressed as a double integral over the complex variables v and $\tilde{v}$ involving the kernel of the operator K,

$$(f|K|h) = \iint K(\tilde{v}, v)\, D(v, \tilde{v})\, d\mu(v)\, d\mu(\tilde{v}).$$

Then clearly we get the kernel of the density operator as

$$D(v, \tilde{v}) = \overline{f(\tilde{v})}\, h(v).$$

The operator D depends on the choice of the states f and h, but we can pass to another operator $d_{v\tilde{v}}$ such that

$$D(v, \tilde{v}) = (f|d_{v\tilde{v}}|h).$$

The kernel of $d_{v\tilde{v}}$ is clearly given by

$$d_{v\tilde{v}}(\tilde{x}, x) = (e_{\tilde{x}}|e_{\tilde{v}})(e_v|e_x) = \exp[\tilde{x} \cdot \tilde{v} + v \cdot \bar{x}]$$

where we used the expansions

$$(f|e_{\tilde{v}}) = \int (f|e_{\tilde{x}})(e_{\tilde{x}}|e_{\tilde{v}})\, d\mu(\tilde{x})$$

$$(e_v|h) = \int (e_v|e_x)(e_x|h)\, d\mu(x)$$

discussed in section 4.3. The operator $d_{v\tilde{v}}$ is the density operator D for f and h taken as coherent states.

Our main interest will be in density operators between states which have been shifted by generalized Weyl operators. These density operators are best computed from the kernel of the product operator

$$(\Lambda_{\tilde{a}} \circ V_{\tilde{b}})^+ \circ d_{v\tilde{v}} \circ (\Lambda_a \circ V_b)$$

which we call a density operator modified by Weyl operators. From the definitions of the operators Λ and V given in section 4.4, we have

$$(\Lambda_a \circ V_b)(v, x) = (e_v | \Lambda_a \circ V_b | e_x)$$

$$= ((\Lambda_a \circ V_b) e_x)(v) = \exp[\overline{x} \cdot (v - b) + v \cdot \overline{a}]$$

$$(\Lambda_{\tilde{a}} \circ V_{\tilde{b}})^+ (\tilde{x}, \tilde{v}) = (e_{\tilde{x}} | (\Lambda_{\tilde{a}} \circ V_{\tilde{b}})^+ | e_{\tilde{v}})$$

$$= (\Lambda_{-\tilde{b}} \circ V_{-\tilde{a}})(\tilde{x}, \tilde{v}) = \exp[\overline{\tilde{v}} \cdot (\tilde{x} + \tilde{a}) + \tilde{x} \cdot (-\overline{\tilde{b}})].$$

Using these expressions and the definition of the operator $d_{v\tilde{v}}$ we find

5.16 Proposition: The kernel of the density operator $d_{v\tilde{v}}$, modified by generalized Weyl operators, is given by

$$((\Lambda_{\tilde{a}} \circ V_{\tilde{b}})^+ \circ d_{v\tilde{v}} \circ (\Lambda_a \circ V_b))(\tilde{x}, x) = (e_{\tilde{x}} | (\Lambda_{\tilde{a}} \circ V_{\tilde{b}})^+ | e_{\tilde{v}})(e_v | \Lambda_a \circ V_b | e_x)$$

$$= \exp[\tilde{x} \cdot (\overline{\tilde{v}} - \overline{\tilde{b}}) + \tilde{a} \cdot \overline{\tilde{v}} + (v - b) \cdot \overline{x} + v \cdot \overline{a}].$$

We pass now to the specific system of 2 particles in 3 space dimensions. The dots between vectors will then be reserved for scalar products of vectors with three components. We denote the single-particle coordinates as x_1, x_2 and introduce the relative and center-of-mass coordinates by

$$s_1 = \sqrt{\frac{1}{2}(x_1 - x_2)}$$

$$s_2 = \sqrt{\frac{1}{2}(x_1 + x_2)}.$$

To transform states from the dependence on the coordinates x_1, x_2 to the dependence on the coordinates s_1, s_2, we write

$$f(x_1, x_2) = f\left(\sqrt{\frac{1}{2}}(s_1 + s_2), \sqrt{\frac{1}{2}}(-s_1 + s_2)\right) = (S_{g_c} f)(s_1, s_2)$$

where g_c is the matrix in four-dimensional phase space given by

$$g_c = g_c(B) = \begin{bmatrix} B & 0 \\ 0 & B \end{bmatrix}, \quad B = \sqrt{\frac{1}{2}} \begin{bmatrix} 1 & -1 \\ 1 & 1 \end{bmatrix}.$$

For translationally invariant two-body operators it now suffices to compute the translationally invariant reduced two-body density operator which has the form of the general density operator but acts non-trivially only with respect to the state associated with coordinate s_1.

5.17 Definition: In the coordinates $s_1 s_2$, the translationally invariant density operator $(S_{g_c} \circ D(2) \circ S_{g_c^{-1}})$ is defined as the matrix element of the kernel

$$(S_{g_c} \circ d_{v\tilde{v}}(2) \circ S_{g_c^{-1}})\,(\tilde{s}_1 \tilde{s}_2, s_1 s_2) = (e_{\tilde{s}_1} \mid e_{\tilde{v}})(e_v \mid e_{s_1})(e_{\tilde{s}_2} \mid e_{s_2}).$$

Again we shall require the matrix elements of this reduced density operator between two-particle states subject to a transformation by generalized Weyl operators. We note that for generalized Weyl operators one finds similarly as in section 4.5 for standard Weyl operators

$$((S_{g_c(B)} \circ \Lambda_a \circ V_b)\, h)\,(s_1 s_2) = ((\Lambda_{Ba} \circ V_{Bb} \circ S_{g_c(B)})\, h)\,(s_1 s_2)$$

where B is the 2×2 matrix given above and where

$$a = \begin{pmatrix} a_1 \\ a_2 \end{pmatrix} \quad b = \begin{pmatrix} b_1 \\ b_2 \end{pmatrix} \quad Ba = \begin{pmatrix} \sqrt{\frac{1}{2}}(a_1 - a_2) \\ \sqrt{\frac{1}{2}}(a_1 + a_2) \end{pmatrix} \quad Bb = \begin{pmatrix} \sqrt{\frac{1}{2}}(b_1 - b_2) \\ \sqrt{\frac{1}{2}}(b_1 + b_2) \end{pmatrix}.$$

It is now possible to compute the kernel of the reduced density operator in the relative coordinates $s_1 s_2$ between states subject to Weyl translation operators. With respect to the coordinates $\tilde{s}_1$, s_1, this kernel has precisely the form given in proposition 5.16 with all vectors $\tilde{a}\,\tilde{b}\,a\,b$ replaced according to

$$\tilde{a} \to \sqrt{\frac{1}{2}}(\tilde{a}_1 - \tilde{a}_2) \quad \tilde{b} \to \sqrt{\frac{1}{2}}(\tilde{b}_1 - \tilde{b}_2) \quad a \to \sqrt{\frac{1}{2}}(a_1 - a_2) \quad b \to \sqrt{\frac{1}{2}}(b_1 - b_2).$$

With respect to the coordinates $\tilde{s}_2$, s_2 we have to compute the kernel of the product

$$(\Lambda_{\tilde{a}} \circ V_{\tilde{b}})^+ \circ \Lambda_a \circ V_b = \Lambda_{-\tilde{b}} \circ V_{-\tilde{a}} \circ \Lambda_a \circ V_b = \Lambda_{a-\tilde{b}} \circ V_{-\tilde{a}+b} \exp[\tilde{a} \cdot \overline{a}]$$

where we used the rules given in proposition 4.21. The kernel of this operator is

$$(e_{\tilde{s}_2} \mid \Lambda_{a-\tilde{b}} \circ V_{-\tilde{a}+b} \mid e_{s_2})\exp[\tilde{a} \cdot \overline{a}] = \exp[\tilde{s}_2 \cdot \overline{s}_2 - (-\tilde{a} + b)\cdot \overline{s}_2 + \tilde{s}_2 \cdot(\overline{a} - \overline{\tilde{b}}) + \tilde{a}\cdot \overline{a}]$$

where now we have to replace the vectors according to

$$\tilde{a} \to \sqrt{\frac{1}{2}}(\tilde{a}_1 + \tilde{a}_2) \quad \tilde{b} \to \sqrt{\frac{1}{2}}(\tilde{b}_1 + \tilde{b}_2) \quad a \to \sqrt{\frac{1}{2}}(a_1 + a_2) \quad b \to \sqrt{\frac{1}{2}}(b_1 + b_2).$$

Combining both expressions we get

5.18 Proposition: The kernel of the translationally invariant reduced density operator $d_{v\tilde{v}}(2)$ with respect to the coordinates $s_1 s_2$ is given by

$$(S_{g_c} \circ (\Lambda_{\tilde{a}} \circ V_{\tilde{b}})^+ \circ d_{v\tilde{v}}(2) \circ (\Lambda_a \circ V_b) \circ S_{g_c^{-1}})\,(\tilde{s}_1 \tilde{s}_2, s_1 s_2)$$

$$= \exp\left[\sqrt{\frac{1}{2}}(\tilde{a}_1 - \tilde{a}_2)\cdot \overline{\tilde{v}} + v \cdot \sqrt{\frac{1}{2}}(\overline{a}_1 - \overline{a}_2) + \frac{1}{2}(\tilde{a}_1 + \tilde{a}_2)\cdot(\overline{a}_1 + \overline{a}_2)\right]$$

$$\exp\left[\tilde{s}_1 \cdot\left(\overline{\tilde{v}} - \sqrt{\frac{1}{2}}(\overline{\tilde{b}}_1 - \overline{\tilde{b}}_2)\right) + \left(v - \sqrt{\frac{1}{2}}(b_1 - b_2)\right)\cdot \overline{s}_1\right]$$

$$\exp\left[\tilde{s}_2 \cdot \sqrt{\frac{1}{2}}(\overline{a}_1 + \overline{a}_2 - \overline{\tilde{b}}_1 - \overline{\tilde{b}}_2) + \tilde{s}_2 \cdot \overline{s}_2 - \sqrt{\frac{1}{2}}(b_1 + b_2 - \tilde{a}_1 - \tilde{a}_2)\cdot \overline{s}_2\right].$$

The kernel in the coordinates $x_1 x_2$ is obtained by expressing the coordinates s_1 and s_2 in terms of x_1 and x_2, it reads

$$((\Lambda_{\tilde{a}} \circ V_{\tilde{b}})^+ \circ d_{v\tilde{v}}(2) \circ (\Lambda_a \circ V_b))\,(\tilde{x}_1 \tilde{x}_2, x_1 x_2)$$

$$= \exp\left[\sqrt{\tfrac{1}{2}}(\bar{a}_1 - \tilde{a}_2)\cdot\tilde{\tilde{v}} + v\cdot\sqrt{\tfrac{1}{2}}(\bar{a}_1 - \tilde{a}_2) + \tfrac{1}{2}(\tilde{a}_1 + \tilde{a}_2)\cdot(\bar{a}_1 + \bar{a}_2)\right]$$

$$\exp\left[\tilde{x}_1\cdot\tilde{\bar{c}}_1 + \tilde{x}_2\cdot\tilde{\bar{c}}_2 + \tfrac{1}{2}(\tilde{x}_1\cdot\bar{x}_1 + \tilde{x}_1\cdot\bar{x}_2 + \tilde{x}_2\cdot\bar{x}_1 + \tilde{x}_2\cdot\bar{x}_2) + c_1\cdot\bar{x}_1 + c_2\cdot\bar{x}_2\right]$$

where

$$\tilde{\bar{c}}_1 = \sqrt{\tfrac{1}{2}}\left(\tilde{\bar{v}} - \sqrt{\tfrac{1}{2}}(2\tilde{\bar{b}}_1 - \bar{a}_1 - \bar{a}_2)\right)$$

$$\tilde{\bar{c}}_2 = \sqrt{\tfrac{1}{2}}\left(-\tilde{\bar{v}} - \sqrt{\tfrac{1}{2}}(2\tilde{\bar{b}}_2 - \bar{a}_1 - \bar{a}_2)\right)$$

$$c_1 = \sqrt{\tfrac{1}{2}}\left(v - \sqrt{\tfrac{1}{2}}(2b_1 - \tilde{a}_1 - \tilde{a}_2)\right)$$

$$c_2 = \sqrt{\tfrac{1}{2}}\left(-v - \sqrt{\tfrac{1}{2}}(2b_2 - \tilde{a}_1 - \tilde{a}_2)\right).$$

The kernel may now be used to derive directly the density operator between oscillator states. To compute the contributions between single-particle oscillator states up to the excitation $N = 1$, it suffices to expand the second exponential up to the corresponding order. This expansion yields

$$\exp\left[\tilde{x}_1\cdot\tilde{\bar{c}}_1 + \tilde{x}_2\cdot\tilde{\bar{c}}_2 + \tfrac{1}{2}(\tilde{x}_1\cdot\bar{x}_1 + \tilde{x}_1\cdot\bar{x}_2 + \tilde{x}_2\cdot\bar{x}_1 + \tilde{x}_2\cdot\bar{x}_2) + c_1\cdot\bar{x}_1 + c_2\cdot\bar{x}_2\right]$$

$$= 1$$

$$+ (\tilde{x}_1\cdot\tilde{\bar{c}}_1) + (\tilde{x}_2\cdot\tilde{\bar{c}}_2) + (c_1\cdot\bar{x}_1) + (c_2\cdot\bar{x}_2)$$

$$+ (\tilde{x}_1\cdot\tilde{\bar{c}}_1)(c_1\bar{x}_1) + \tfrac{1}{2}(\tilde{x}_1\cdot\bar{x}_1) + (\tilde{x}_1\tilde{\bar{c}}_1)(c_2\bar{x}_2) + \tfrac{1}{2}(\tilde{x}_1\bar{x}_2)$$

$$+ (\tilde{x}_2\tilde{\bar{c}}_2)(c_1\bar{x}_1) + \tfrac{1}{2}(\tilde{x}_2\bar{x}_1) + (\tilde{x}_2\tilde{\bar{c}}_2)(c_2\bar{x}_2) + \tfrac{1}{2}(\tilde{x}_2\bar{x}_2)$$

$$+ (\tilde{x}_1\tilde{\bar{c}}_1)(\tilde{x}_2\tilde{\bar{c}}_2) + (c_1\bar{x}_1)(c_2\bar{x}_2)$$

$$+ (\tilde{x}_1\tilde{\bar{c}}_1)(\tilde{x}_2\tilde{\bar{c}}_2)(c_1\bar{x}_1) + \tfrac{1}{2}(\tilde{x}_1\tilde{\bar{c}}_1)(\tilde{x}_2\bar{x}_1) + \tfrac{1}{2}(\tilde{x}_2\tilde{\bar{c}}_2)(\tilde{x}_1\bar{x}_1)$$

$$+ (\tilde{x}_1\tilde{\bar{c}}_1)(\tilde{x}_2\tilde{\bar{c}}_2)(c_2\bar{x}_2) + \tfrac{1}{2}(\tilde{x}_2\tilde{\bar{c}}_2)(\tilde{x}_1\bar{x}_2) + \tfrac{1}{2}(\tilde{x}_1\tilde{\bar{c}}_1)(\tilde{x}_2\bar{x}_2)$$

$$+ (\tilde{x}_1\tilde{\bar{c}}_1)(c_1\bar{x}_1)(c_2\bar{x}_2) + \tfrac{1}{2}(c_2\bar{x}_2)(\tilde{x}_1\bar{x}_1) + \tfrac{1}{2}(c_1\bar{x}_1)(\tilde{x}_1\bar{x}_2)$$

$$+ (\tilde{x}_2\tilde{\bar{c}}_2)(c_1\bar{x}_1)(c_2\bar{x}_2) + \tfrac{1}{2}(c_2\bar{x}_2)(\tilde{x}_2\bar{x}_1) + \tfrac{1}{2}(c_1\bar{x}_1)(\tilde{x}_2\bar{x}_2)$$

$$+ (\tilde{x}_1 \bar{\tilde{c}}_1)(\tilde{x}_2 \bar{\tilde{c}}_2)(c_1 \bar{x}_1)(c_2 \bar{x}_2)$$

$$+ \frac{1}{2}(\tilde{x}_1 \bar{\tilde{c}}_1)(\tilde{x}_2 \bar{x}_1)(c_2 \bar{x}_2)$$

$$+ \frac{1}{2}(\tilde{x}_1 \bar{\tilde{c}}_1)(\tilde{x}_2 \bar{x}_2)(c_1 \bar{x}_1)$$

$$+ \frac{1}{2}(\tilde{x}_2 \bar{\tilde{c}}_2)(\tilde{x}_1 \bar{x}_1)(c_2 \bar{x}_2)$$

$$+ \frac{1}{2}(\tilde{x}_2 \bar{\tilde{c}}_2)(\tilde{x}_1 \bar{x}_2)(c_1 \bar{x}_1)$$

$$+ \frac{1}{4}(\tilde{x}_1 \bar{x}_1)(\tilde{x}_2 \bar{x}_2) + \frac{1}{4}(\tilde{x}_1 \bar{x}_2)(\tilde{x}_2 \bar{x}_1)$$

+ higher powers.

The five groups of terms have been arranged in terms of increasing total degree 0, 1, 2, 3, 4 in the coordinates $\tilde{x}_1 \tilde{x}_2 \bar{x}_1 \bar{x}_2$.

5.5 Notes and References

Applications of linear canonical transformations to n-body systems and in particular to nuclear structure are given in [KR 73] and [KR 75]. Semigroup extensions of linear canonical transformations were introduced in [KR 75] and are fully explored by Brunet and Kramer [BR 75, 78, 78a]. The use of dilatations for a change of frequency in an oscillator state was introduced in [KR 75] and is developed in more detail in section 9. The density operators used in section 5.4 are somewhat different from the usual ones since they yield general matrix elements as well as expectation values.

6 Composite Nucleon Systems and their Interaction

6.1 Concepts and Motivation

The present section is central for thé development of the theory of composite nucleon systems. We start in section 6.2 from an interacting system of n nucleons and introduce a partition of n to specify j occupation numbers $(n_1 n_2 \ldots n_j)$. Using these occupation numbers we pass from the coordinates $x_1 x_2 \ldots x_n$ of the single particles to j center coordinates z and $n - j$ internal coordinates y. Next we specify the orbital state with respect to the internal coordinates, establish the orbital partition through the application of an orbital Young operator and couple the orbital state with the spin-isospin state to an antisymmetric state. In section 6.3 we consider linear superpositions of configurations as described above. From the stationary variational principle

$$(\delta_\psi \, |H - E| \, \psi) = 0$$

we develop by a variation restricted to the state $u(z)$ describing the relative motion of the composite particles, the integral equations which govern this state. These integral equations are characterized by kernels of interaction and normalization operators which depend on the choice of the internal states, on the choice of the orbital partition and on the nucleon-nucleon interaction. The kernels of these operators are expressible as matrix elements between particular orbital states involving, with respect to center coordinates z, the coherent states described in section 4.3. In section 6.4 we develop the concept of a distribution of n particles into j shell configurations which are then subject to translations in phase space. We show that for non-spurious shell configurations the application of Weyl translation operators leads precisely to the coherent states needed for the evaluation of interaction kernels. In section 6.5 we use this interpretation to write the interaction and normalization operators and their kernels as matrix elements between single-particle configurations. This interpretation allows the full use of the concepts and methods developed in sections 2 and 3 in the composite particle dynamics and serves as the starting point for the analysis of specific systems in later sections.

We should mention here that in the present article we do not intend to solve the complex integral equations in general. The variational principle is introduced in a formal way to define the kernels which we study in more detail in the following sections. Approximate solutions of the integral equations in the oscillator representation are considered in section 10.

6.2 Configurations of Composite Nucleon Systems

In this section we specify what we call a configuration of composite nucleon systems within a system of n nucleons. We shall lateron denote a single configuration of this type by a greek letter $\rho\sigma$ .... First of all we choose the occupation numbers of the composite particles which we enumerate as $1\ 2 \ldots j$ and denote as $(n_1 n_2 \ldots n_j)$. The choice of these numbers is motivated by the physical problem in question, in a nuclear reaction they could in simple cases coincide with the occupation numbers of the colliding nuclei. Next we inquire about the permutational structure of each composite particle and of the full system. We speak of a configuration of simple clusters if each composite particle has an internally symmetric orbital state. In this case we call the set of occupation numbers a weight $w = (w_1 w_2 \ldots w_j)$. The n-particle state is stable under the subgroup of internal permutations which we called the group of the weight in section 2,

$$S(w) = S(w_1) \times S(w_2) \times \ldots \times S(w_j).$$

The overall transformation of the n-particle state is then governed by partitions f obtained from the rules specified in section 2.3. For nucleons, both the numbers w_i and the first component of the partition f must be less or equal than four. An exhaustive classification of the different partitions f is given through the construction of the Gelfand patterns q for given weight w. The Gelfand pattern q moreover provides a systematic building-up principle for these configurations. To establish from any orbital state belonging to the fixed weight a new state transforming according to the representation d^f of $S(n)$, we employ the Young operators $c(rfq)$ introduced in section 2.4.

If one of the composite particles is not symmetric under internal permutations, it is reasonable to assume that it be characterized by some fixed representation of the group of internal permutations. Again the internal state could be constructed from the occupation of various single-particle states which would allow its characterization by an internal Gelfand pattern. We shall consider this case for internal closed shell states. For open shells, it would be preferable to characterize the internal orbital state by other quantum numbers like the orbital angular momentum L or the quantum numbers $\lambda\mu$ of the SU(3) scheme. These labels replace the internal Gelfand pattern. In both cases the combination with other simple clusters proceeds as before.

The next step in the specification of a configuration of composite nucleon systems is the choice of appropriate coordinates. For configurations of simple clusters it is appropriate to introduce the center and cluster coordinates along with internal coordinates. The center coordinates which we denoted as $z_1 z_2 \ldots z_j$ determine the positions of the composite particles. The cluster coordinates $s_1 s_2 \ldots s_j$ provide a set of $j - 1$ relative coordinates between the composite particles along with the overall center-of-mass coordinate which should drop out of the dynamics of the system.

To describe a configuration of composite nucleon systems, it is reasonable to specify the orbital state in a representation based on center and internal coordinates. We call this state $h(zy)$ and consider the passage to single-particle coordinates given by the substitutions

$$l(x) = h(zy) = h((JQ)^{-1} x).$$

Using the operator $S_{g_c}(JQ)$ as explained in section 5.1 this transformation may be written as

$$l(x) = (S_{g_c(JQ)} h)(x)$$

and leads to

6.1 Proposition: For a given state $h(zy)$ in center and internal coordinates, the corresponding state $l(x)$ in single-particle coordinates is obtained by the application of the operator $S_{g_c(JQ)}$ to h.

An antisymmetric state is obtained by coupling the orbital state with the spin-isospin state to an antisymmetric state. According to proposition 2.58 this is done by the summation over the index r and leads in bracket notation to the expression

$$|(\alpha_\gamma)^n l f[1^n]) = |f|^{-1/2} \sum_r |\alpha^n l f r) |\gamma^n \hat{f} \hat{r}) (-1)^r$$

where α^n and γ^n indicate orbital and spin-isospin configurations of n nucleons. We shall consider linear combinations of states of this form and distinguish the various configurations by a greek index ρ or σ.

6.3 Projection Equations and Interaction of Composite Nucleon Systems

We shall now introduce a projection which leads from a system of n interacting nucleons to a system of j interacting composite particles. This projection for bound states may be obtained from the variational principle

$$(\delta_\psi |H - E|_\psi) = 0$$

as explained in detail in [WI 77], and for unbound states has at least been successfully extended to the description of nuclear reactions.

Consider a single configuration of composite nucleon systems as described in section 6.2. The first assumption we shall make is that the orbital state, in the representation based on center and internal coordinates, separates before application of the Young operator, that is

$$h(zy) = (uv)(zy) = u(z) v(y).$$

The symbol (uv) is used to describe a product of functions. The state $u(z)$ will become the orbital state of the composite particles in terms of their positions $z_1 z_2 \ldots z_j$ while the state $v(y)$ should be considered as a product of j internal orbital states for the composite particles. The assumption of separability is not restrictive since we are going to consider superpositions of states of this type.

The second and much more restrictive assumption will be that the internal state $v(y)$ be completely fixed. From the point of view of variational principles, this assumption may be expressed as

$$\delta h(zy) = \delta(uv)(zy) = (\delta u)(z) v(y).$$

From the point of view of a projection we could introduce a projection operator P with the kernel

$$P(zy, z'y') = \exp[z \cdot \bar{z}'] v(y) \overline{v(y')}$$

and replace the free variation $\delta h(zy)$ by the restricted variation $\delta(Ph)(zy)$.

We want to write down the interaction of composite particles in terms of operators acting on the orbital states $u(z)$. To extract the state $u(z)$ from the ket configuration we rewrite $u(z)$ in the form

$$u(z) = \int \exp[z \cdot \bar{z}'] u(z') \, d\mu(z')$$

$$= \int e_{z'}(z) u(z') \, d\mu(z')$$

In the first line we use the kernel for the identity operator in the Bargmann space for 3j degrees of freedom. In the second line we interpret this kernel as a coherent state

$$e_{z'}(z) = \exp\left[\sum_{i=1}^{j} z_i \cdot \bar{z}_i'\right]$$

and the integral as a superposition of coherent states characterized by the vectors $z_1' z_2' \ldots z_j'$. For this interpretation we refer to section 4.3. The corresponding reasoning in the Schrödinger representation involves the use of delta functions.

The full orbital state may now be written as

$$h(zy) = (uv)(zy) = u(z) v(y)$$

$$= \int e_{z'}(z) v(y) u(z') \, d\mu(z')$$

$$= \int (e_{z'} v)(zy) u(z') \, d\mu(z').$$

In this expression the state u is replaced by the coherent state $e_{z'}$, and all operators acting previously on the state (uv) now act on the state $(e_{z'} v)$ whereas z' and $u(z')$ could be considered as complex numbers. With the help of proposition 6.1 we now pass to the representation in single-particle coordinates and write the orbital state $l(x)$ as

$$l(x) = (S_{g_c(JQ)} h)(x) = \int l_{z'}(x) u(z') \, d\mu(z')$$

where the orbital state $l_{z'}$ is the image of $(e_{z'} v)$ under $S_{g_c(JQ)}$,

$$l_{z'}(x) = (S_{g_c(JQ)} (e_{z'} v))(x).$$

In section 4.3 it was shown that the matrix elements of an operator between coherent states yield the kernel of this operator. We shall presently show that the matrix elements of the n-body hamiltonian H between configurations based on the orbital states $l_{z'}$ yields the kernel of the interaction operator for the composite particles.

6.2 Definition: A superposition of configurations is an n-particle state given by

$$|\psi\rangle = \sum_{\sigma} |(\alpha\gamma)^n l_\sigma f_\sigma [1^n]\rangle = \sum_{\sigma} |f_\sigma|^{-1/2} \sum_{r} c(rf_\sigma q_\sigma) |\alpha^n l_\sigma\rangle |\gamma^n \hat{f} \hat{r}\rangle (-1)^r.$$

Note that this superposition at first sight looks highly redundant since we are admitting various coordinate dependencies for the same n-particle state. This redundancy is removed by restricting the variation for each configuration to the state $u_\rho(z_\rho)$ for the motion of composite particles.

The normalization and interaction operators for pairs of configurations are introduced by

6.3 Definition: The normalization and interaction kernels between two configurations $\rho\,\sigma$ are the matrix elements of the unit operator and the n-body hamiltonian H between the orbital states $l_{\tilde{z}_\rho}$ and l_{z_σ} respectively,

$$N_{\rho\sigma}(\tilde{z}_\rho, z_\sigma) = ((\alpha\gamma)^n l_{\tilde{z}_\rho} f_\rho [1^n] \, | \, (\alpha\gamma)^n l_{z_\sigma} f_\sigma [1^n])$$

$$H_{\rho\sigma}(\tilde{z}_\rho, z_\sigma) = ((\alpha\gamma)^n l_{\tilde{z}_\rho} f_\rho [1^n] \, |H| \, (\alpha\gamma)^n l_{z_\sigma} f_\sigma [1^n]).$$

From the expansion of the general orbital state l in terms of the special state l_z it is clear that the two kernels given above will enter the interaction of the composite particles associated with the various configurations.

6.4 Proposition: Consider the stationary variational principle

$$(\delta_\psi |H - E| \psi) = 0$$

for $|\psi)$ being a superposition of configurations as specified in definition 6.1. Under the restricted variation of the composite particle state for each configuration, the variational principle yields the integral equations

$$\sum_\sigma \int [H_{\rho\sigma}(\tilde{z}_\rho, z_\sigma) - E\,N_{\rho\sigma}(\tilde{z}_\rho, z_\sigma)]\, u_\sigma(z_\sigma)\, d\mu(z_\sigma) = 0$$

where $H_{\rho\sigma}$ and $N_{\rho\sigma}$ are the interaction operator and normalization operator according to definition 6.3.

Proof: It suffices to note that the states u_σ by the coherent state expansion are removed from the integrals. The variational equation may then be rewritten as

$$(\delta_\psi |H - E| \psi) = \sum_{\rho,\sigma} \int (\delta u_\rho)\,(\tilde{z}_\rho)\,[H_{\rho\sigma}(\tilde{z}_\rho, z_\sigma) - E\,N_{\rho\sigma}(\tilde{z}_\rho, z_\sigma)]\, u_\sigma(z_\sigma)$$

$$\times\, d\mu(\tilde{z}_\rho)\, d\mu(z_\sigma) = 0$$

Since we allow unrestricted variation of all states this yields the integral equations given above.   □

From the construction of the n-particle states it is clear that the interaction and normalization operator may be decomposed into an orbital and a spin-isospin part. The orbital part of the interaction operator is a sum of terms of the general form

$$H_{\rho\sigma}(\tilde{z}_\rho, z_\sigma) = (|f_\rho| \, |f_\sigma|)^{-1/2}\, (\alpha^n l_{\tilde{z}_\rho} |c(q_\rho f_\rho r_\rho) \circ H \circ c(r_\sigma f_\sigma q_\sigma)| \, \alpha^n l_{z_\sigma}).$$

This operator could be treated by the methods described in sections 2 and 3. For the normalization operator the spin-isospin part may be evaluated and yields a non-vanishing result only if the orbital partitions f_ρ and f_σ coincide. The normalization operator becomes

$$N_{\rho\sigma}(\tilde{z}_\rho, z_\sigma) = \delta(f_\rho, f_\sigma)\, |f_\sigma|^{-1} \sum_r (\alpha^n l_{\tilde{z}_\rho} | c(q_\rho\, f_\sigma\, r) \circ c(rf_\sigma\, q_\sigma) | \alpha^n l_{z_\sigma}).$$

Note that, although the interaction and normalization kernel were defined above, it is by no means an easy task to compute these expressions in a general form. The evaluation of the kernels will be taken up on the basis of a new interpretation derived in sections 6.4 and 6.5.

6.4 Phase Space Transformations for Configurations of Oscillator Shells and for Composite Nucleon Systems

In this section we develop the concept of an orbital shell configuration based on single-particle states, consider its transformation under translations in phase space and employ a point transformation to construct the same state in the representation based on center and internal coordinates (zy).

An orbital n-particle shell configuration may be constructed by the application of a Young operator $c(rfq)$ to a product

$$l(x) = \prod_{i=1}^{n} l_i(x_i)$$

of single-particle states. For a single such configuration consider now the translation on 6n-dimensional phase space associated with the 6n component vector

$$\tau_c = \begin{bmatrix} t \\ \overline{t} \end{bmatrix}, \qquad t = \begin{bmatrix} t_1 \\ t_1 \\ \vdots \\ t_1 \end{bmatrix}.$$

This special vector describes a translation of position and momentum independent of the particle number and in Bargmann space is represented by a Weyl operator W_{τ_c}:

We now determine the effect of this operator on an orbital state in the representation based on single-particle and center coordinates. The relation

$$h(zy) = l(x)$$

we write in the form

$$h(zy) = (S_{g_c^{-1}(JQ)}\, l)\, (zy)$$

and consider the mappings corresponding to the diagram

$$
\begin{array}{ccc}
 & W_{\tau_c} & \\
l & \longrightarrow & l' \\
S_{g_c}^{-1}\ \Big\downarrow & & \Big\downarrow\ S_{g_c}^{-1} \\
h & \longrightarrow & h' \\
 & S_{g_c}^{-1} \circ W_{\tau_c} \circ S_{g_c}. &
\end{array}
$$

The diagram shows that under the map

$$l \to l' = W_{\tau_c} l$$

the states in center and internal coordinates transform according to

$$h \to h' = (S_{g_c}^{-1} \circ W_{\tau_c} \circ S_{g_c} h).$$

From the definition 4.24 of the operators S_{g_c} we find the identity

$$S_{g_c}^{-1} \circ W_{\tau_c} \circ S_{g_c} = W_{g_c^{-1} \tau_c}$$

and the computation of the vector $g_c^{-1} \tau_c$ yields for a single center, using the properties of the matrices JQ as given in definitions 5.1, 5.2, and 5.3,

$$g_c^{-1} \tau_c = \begin{bmatrix} (JQ)^{-1} t \\ \overline{(JQ)^{-1} t} \end{bmatrix}$$

$$(JQ)^{-1} t = \begin{bmatrix} [n]^{1/2}\, t_1 \\ 0 \\ \cdot \\ \cdot \\ \cdot \\ 0 \end{bmatrix}.$$

From the action of the Weyl operator according to proposition 4.17 one finds in the center and internal coordinates for a single center

$$h(zy) \to h'(zy) = (W_{g_c^{-1}\tau_c} h)(zy) = h(z - [n]^{1/2} t_1, y) \exp\left[[n]^{1/2}\, z \cdot \overline{t}_1 - \frac{n}{2} t_1 \cdot \overline{t}_1 \right].$$

Obviously the Weyl operator affects only the center vector z which is proportional to the overall complex center-of-mass vector of the n-particle system.

In the next step let us assume that the orbital n-particle shell configuration is chosen non-spurious, that is, without center-of-mass excitation after orbital projection. This implies from the interpretation of Bargmann space that

$$(c(rfq)\, h)(zy) = (c(rfq)\, h)(0y)$$

is independent of the center vector z. Under this assumption one gets the simple result

$$(c(rfq)\, h)(zy) \to (c(rfq)\, h)'(zy)$$

$$(c(rfq)\, h)'(zy) = (c(rfq)\, h)(oy) \exp\left[[n]^{1/2}\, z \cdot \overline{t}_1 - \frac{n}{2} t_1 \cdot \overline{t}_1 \right]$$

which reflects the fact that under the action of the Weyl operator the unexcited state with respect to the center-of-mass vector is transformed into a coherent state. We summarize this results by

6.5 Definition: An orbital single center shell configuration is called non-spurious if, after transforming it to the center coordinate z and internal coordinates y, it is independent of the center vector z.

6.6 Proposition: Under application of the Weyl operator W_{τ_c} to a non-spurious single-center shell configuration, the state in center and internal coordinates becomes the product of a coherent state with respect to the coordinate z and a state depending on the internal coordinates y.

Example 6.1: Non-spurious two-particle states

Consider a state of two particles which occupy the oscillator levels for the excitation $N = 1$ and $N = 0$ respectively. The state is given by

$$l(x_1 x_2) = (x_1)^1 (x_2)^0.$$

The Young operator for the orbital partition $f = [11]$ becomes

$$c(r[11]\, q) = \left[\frac{1}{2}\right]^{1/2} [I - U(1, 2)]$$

and yields

$$(c(r[11]\, q)\, l)(x_1 x_2) = \left[\frac{1}{2}\right]^{1/2} (x_1 - x_2).$$

The center and internal coordinates are

$$z = \left[\frac{1}{2}\right]^{1/2} (x_1 + x_2)$$

$$y = \left[\frac{1}{2}\right]^{1/2} (x_1 - x_2)$$

and the state in these coordinates becomes

$$(c(r[11]\, q)\, h)(zy) = y.$$

Hence application of the Weyl operator yields

$$(W_{\tau_c}\, l)(x) = (x_1 - t_1) \exp\left[(x_1 + x_2) \cdot \bar{t}_1 - t_1 \cdot \bar{t}_1\right]$$

$$(W_{\tau_c} \circ c(r[11]\, q)\, l)(x) = \left[\frac{1}{2}\right]^{1/2} (x_1 - x_2) \exp\left[(x_1 + x_2) \cdot \bar{t}_1 - t_1 \cdot \bar{t}_1\right]$$

$$(W_{g_c^{-1}\, \tau_c} \circ c(r[11]\, q)\, h)(zy) = \exp\left[[2]^{1/2} z \cdot \bar{t}_1 - t_1 \cdot \bar{t}_1\right] y$$

It should be noted that $(c(r[11]\, q)\, l)(x)$, not $l(x)$ is a non-spurious two-particle state. We proceed to a configuration of several centers.

6.7 Definition: Consider a partition $(n_1 n_2 \ldots n_j)$ and j vectors $t_1 t_2 \ldots t_j$ with 3 components. Form a $3n$ dimensional vector t by repeating the vector component t_i n_i times,

$$t: (\underbrace{t_1 \ldots t_1}_{n_1} \underbrace{t_2 \ldots t_2}_{n_2} \ldots \underbrace{t_j \ldots t_j}_{n_j})$$

The translation in $6n$ dimensional phase space associated with

$$\tau_c = \begin{bmatrix} t \\ t \end{bmatrix}$$

will be called the center translation for the partition $(n_1 n_2 \ldots n_j)$.

With the partition $(n_1 n_2 \ldots n_j)$ we associate now a fixed center translation τ_c, a corresponding Weyl operator W_{τ_c}, and a linear point transformation from the n single-particle coordinates $x_1 x_2 \ldots x_n$ to j center coordinates $z_1 z_2 \ldots z_j$ and $n-j$ internal coordinates y obtained from definitions 5.1–5.3. Then, by repeating the analysis given above for each center, we prove

6.8 Proposition: Consider a partition $(n_1 n_2 \ldots n_j)$ of n and a single-particle configuration such that the n_i particles belonging to center $i = 1\ 2 \ldots j$ occupy j non-spurious shell configurations. Application of the Weyl operator W_{τ_c} with τ_c being a center translation for the partition yields in single-particle coordinates

$$l(x) \rightarrow (W_{\tau_c} l)(x)$$

and in center and internal coordinates $(z_1 z_2 \ldots z_j y)$

$$h(zy) \rightarrow (S_{g_c^{-1}} \circ W_{\tau_c} \circ S_{g_c} h)(zy) = (W_{g_c^{-1} \tau_c} h)(zy)$$

$$= h(z_1 - [n_1]^{1/2} t_1, z_2 - [n_2]^{1/2} t_2 \ldots z_j - [n_j]^{1/2} t_j, y)$$

$$\times \exp\left[\sum_{i=1}^{j} [n_i]^{1/2} z_i \cdot \bar{t}_i - \frac{1}{2} \sum_{i=1}^{j} n_i t_i \cdot \bar{t}_i\right].$$

Proof: The derivation generalizes the steps taken for the case of a single center. The transformation of the center translation vector τ_c specified in definition 6.7 under the point transformation

$$g_c^{-1} = \begin{bmatrix} (JQ)^{-1} & 0 \\ 0 & (JQ)^{-1} \end{bmatrix}$$

yields

$$g_c^{-1} \begin{bmatrix} t \\ t \end{bmatrix} = \begin{bmatrix} (JQ)^{-1} t \\ (JQ)^{-1} \bar{t} \end{bmatrix}$$

where

$$(JQ)^{-1} t = \left.\begin{bmatrix} [n_1]^{1/2}\, t_1 \\ [n_2]^{1/2}\, t_2 \\ \vdots \\ [n_j]^{1/2}\, t_j \\ 0 \\ \vdots \\ 0 \end{bmatrix}\right\}\begin{matrix} \\ \\ j \\ \\ \\ \\ n-j. \end{matrix}$$

The result follows from

$$W_{g_c^{-1}\,\tau_c} = S_{g_c}^{-1} \circ W_{\tau_c} \circ S_{g_c}$$

and the action of the Weyl operator according to proposition 4.17. $\qquad\square$

6.9 Proposition: For an orbital single particle configuration of j non-spurious shell configurations, the orbital state h(zy) in center and internal coordinates (zy) after application of a center translation τ_c becomes a product of a coherent state with respect to the center vectors $z_1 z_2 \ldots z_j$ multiplied by a function v of the internal coordinates y

$$h(zy) \rightarrow (W_{g_c^{-1}\,\tau_c} h)\,(z_1 z_2 \ldots z_j y) = \exp\left[\sum_{i=1}^{j} [n_i]^{1/2}\, z_i \cdot \bar{t}_i - \frac{1}{2}\sum_{i=1}^{j} n_i t_i \cdot \bar{t}_i\right] v(y)$$

Proof: From the condition of non-spurious states at each center it follows that the state h(zy) does not depend on the center coordinates $z_1 z_2 \ldots z_j$. Then from proposition 6.8 the application of the Weyl operator $W_{g_c^{-1}\,\tau_c}$ yields for the dependence on $z_1 z_2 \ldots z_j$ only the coherent state. $\qquad\square$

6.5 Interpretation of Composite Particle Interaction in Terms of Single-Particle Configurations

In section 6.3 the interaction and normalization operators were introduced. These operators were given through their kernels which in turn were obtained as matrix elements between states specified in the representation based on center and internal coordinates. It was required that the orbital states should be products (uv) of a function u(z) of the center coordinates, multiplied by a function v(y) of the internal coordinates. Then the state u(z) was replaced by an integral over coherent states to define the interaction and normalization kernels. In section 6.4 we started from the opposite viewpoint of a state description in terms of single-particle coordinates. This state was chosen according to occupation numbers $(n_1 n_2 \ldots n_j)$ as a configuration of non-spurious single-particle shell model states. This state was then subject to a center translation τ_c by a Weyl operator W_{τ_c}. When transformed to the coordinates (zy) associated with the occupation numbers, the translated state was shown in proposition 6.9 to be precisely of the form required for the definition of the interaction and normalization operators. A straight-forward application of this viewpoint will lead to an interpretation of the interaction and normalization operators as matrix elements between j center-translated single-particle configurations. It proves convenient to replace the Weyl operator W_{τ_c} for a center translation by the operator

$$\Lambda_t \circ V_t = W_{\tau_c} \exp\left[\frac{1}{2} t \cdot \bar{t}\right]$$

which differs from W_{τ_c} by a normalization factor. By comparing the expressions of the coherent state e_z given in section 6.3 and the result of proposition 6.9 it is found that one should write

$$z_i = [n_i]^{1/2} t_i.$$

We prefer to maintain the variables t_i instead of z_i since most analytic expressions appear simpler in the variables t_i. Then we find

6.10 Proposition: The orbital state

$$l_z(x) = (S_{g_c(JQ)}(e_z v)) (x)$$

may be interpreted as a state $l(x)$ of n particles occupying j non-spurious single-particle shell configurations, subject to a center translation τ_c as given in definition 6.7

$$l_z(x) = (\Lambda_t \circ V_t l) (x)$$

where the j vectors z and t are related by

$$z_i = [n_i]^{1/2} t_i.$$

Using this interpretation for two different configurations labeled by ρ, σ respectively we find from the definition of the interaction and normalization operators in their orbital form

6.11 Proposition: Consider two configurations ρ, σ of composite nucleon systems with specified occupation numbers $(n_{\rho_1} n_{\rho_2} \ldots n_{\rho \tilde{j}})$ and $(n_{\sigma_1} n_{\sigma_2} \ldots n_{\sigma j})$ respectively. Choose for each configuration and each occupation number a single-particle shell configuration and denote the orbital state as l_ρ and l_σ respectively. Associate with the two configurations two center translation vectors τ_c and τ'_c respectively. Then the orbital interaction and normalization operators for the composite particles become

$$H_{\rho\sigma}(\tilde{z}_\rho, z_\sigma) = (|f_{\tilde{\rho}}| |f_\sigma|)^{-1/2} (\alpha^n l_\rho |(\Lambda_{\tilde{t}_\rho} \circ V_{\tilde{t}_\rho})^+ \circ c(q_\rho f_\rho r_\rho)$$
$$\circ H \circ c(r_\sigma f_\sigma q_\sigma) \circ (\Lambda_{t_\sigma} \circ V_{t_\sigma}) | \alpha^n l_\sigma)$$

and

$$N_{\rho\sigma}(\tilde{z}_\rho, z_\sigma) = \delta(f_\rho, f_\sigma) |f_\sigma|^{-1} \sum_r (\alpha^n l_\rho |(\Lambda_{\tilde{t}_\rho} \circ V_{\tilde{t}_\rho})^+ \circ c(q_\rho f_\sigma r)$$
$$\circ c(r f_\sigma q_\sigma) \circ (\Lambda_{t_\sigma} \circ V_{t_\sigma}) | \alpha^n l_\sigma)$$

where the complex vectors are related by

$$\tilde{z}_{\rho_i} = [\tilde{n}_{\rho_i}]^{1/2} \, \tilde{t}_{\rho_i} \qquad i = 1 \; 2 \ldots \tilde{j}$$

$$z_{\sigma_i} = [n_{\sigma_i}]^{1/2} \, t_{\sigma_i} \qquad i = 1 \; 2 \ldots j.$$

The present proposition is the key result for the analysis presented in the following sections. Note that in the definition of the interaction and normalization kernel the determination of the orbital state was left open up to the requirement of separability in the coordinates (zy). In the form of proposition 6.10, these kernels appear as matrix elements between standard shell configurations. This appearance is not changed under the application of the Weyl operator since this operator separates into parts acting on the individual particles. The degrees of freedom $z_1 z_2 \ldots z_j$ associated with composite particle motion appear as complex translation parameters in the Weyl operators. This has the additional advantage that operator products may be evaluated before computation of matrix elements. The interaction and normalization operator will be found to be rigorously translational-invariant. The single-particle viewpoint as developed in sections 2 and 3 will now be matched with the composite particle theory to provide the concepts and computational tools for the determination of composite particle dynamics.

6.6 Notes and References

The elimination of the internal degrees of freedom through a variational principle is treated by Wildermuth and Tang, [WI 77]. The states after this projection describe the relative motion of composite particles. In related methods, this projection is combined in one step with an integral transform. These methods are often referred to as generator coordinate methods, whereas the first method in the Schrödinger representation is called the resonating-group method. The method which combines the transformation to Bargmann space with the projection is called the complex generator coordinate method, it comes closest to the present approach and is described by Brink and Weiguny, [BR 68]. For earlier work on generator coordinates we refer to Hill, Wheeler and Griffin, [HI 53, GR 57]. The use of Bargmann space as a tool for nuclear theory is described in [KR 73a] and by Moshinsky, Kramer and Seligman, [KR 75].

7 Configurations of Simple Composite Nucleon Systems

7.1 Concepts and Motivation

Simple composite nucleon systems were characterized in section 6.2 by the assumption that the internal orbital state of each composite system be stable under internal permutations. The occupation numbers of these composite particles then form a weight $w = (w_1 w_2 \ldots w_j)$ and the stability group is the group of the weight $S(w)$. The orbital partition f is established through a Gelfand pattern q. To this assumption on the permutational structure of the orbital states we add the specification of any internal state as an unexcited oscillator state. With this choice we obtain in sections 7.2 and 7.3 closed analytic expressions for the normalization and interaction kernels. In section 7.4 we choose $j = 3$ and pass from the kernels of the operators to the oscillator representation. The oscillator representation will be used in section 10 to study states of the lightest nuclei.

7.2 Normalization Kernels

The weight $w = (w_1 w_2 \ldots w_j)$ is associated with an orbital state which is stable under the group of the weight $S(w)$ whose elements are all internal permutations. The orbital partition f is build up through a Gelfand pattern q. The normalization operator is the scalar product between this ket state and a similar bra state whose quantum numbers we denote by the sign $\sim$. Hence the bra state has weight $\tilde{w}$, stability group $S(\tilde{w})$ and a Gelfand pattern $\tilde{q}$. It must have the same orbital partition f since otherwise the scalar product vanishes. Due to proposition 6.11 the n-body states used in the construction of the normalization kernel are based on single-particle states with overlap integrals $\epsilon_{i\,l}$. The scalar product in question was then shown in section 3.9 to be a matrix element of the irreducible representation $D^f(\epsilon)$ of the general linear group $GL(j, \mathbb{C})$. This matrix element according to proposition 3.32 has the exchange or double coset decomposition

$$D^f_{\tilde{q}q}(\epsilon) = [\tilde{w}! \ w!]^{1/2} \sum_k d^f_{\tilde{q}q}(z_k) \, [k!]^{-1} \, \epsilon^k$$

where the basic exchange integral according to definition 3.30 is the expression

$$\epsilon^k = \prod_{i,\,l} (\epsilon_{i\,l})^{k_{i\,l}}$$

and the sum runs over all double cosets associated with the weights $\tilde{w}$ and w. According to proposition 6.11, this basic exchange integral becomes part of a kernel which we shall call the exchange contribution to the normalization operator. The single-particle overlap ϵ_{il} is simply given by the matrix elements of the operator

$$(\Lambda_{\widetilde{t}_i} \circ V_{\widetilde{t}_i})^+ \circ (\Lambda_{t_l} \circ V_{t_l})$$

which reflects the representation of translations to the center positions and momenta $\widetilde{z}_i = \sqrt{\widetilde{w}_i}\, \widetilde{t}_i$ and $z_l = \sqrt{w_l}\, t_l$ by Weyl operators. For simple composite particles we assume now that the states before translations are unexcited oscillator states. By noting that the Weyl operators yield coherent states

$$\Lambda_{t_l} \circ V_{t_l}|000) = |e_{t_l}), \quad \Lambda_{\widetilde{t}_i} \circ V_{\widetilde{t}_i}|000) = |e_{\widetilde{t}_i})$$

as explained in example 4.6 we obtain

$$\epsilon_{il} = (e_{\widetilde{t}_i}|e_{t_l}) = \exp[\widetilde{t}_i \cdot \overline{t}_l].$$

The exchange contribution to the normalization operator with these values becomes

$$N(k)(\widetilde{z}, z) = \epsilon^k = \exp[\widetilde{z} \cdot A(k)\, \overline{z}]$$

with the j $\times$ j matrix A(k) given by

$$A_{il}(k) = [\widetilde{w}_i w_l]^{-1/2}\, k_{il}$$

We now write the normalization operator in a more elaborate notation.

7.1 Proposition: The normalization operator in center coordinates for j simple composite particles has the exchange decomposition

$$(\alpha^n f\widetilde{q}|N(\widetilde{z}, z)|\alpha^n fq) = [\widetilde{w}!\, w!]^{1/2} \sum_k{}' \, d^f_{\widetilde{q}q}(z_k)\, [k!]^{-1}\, N(k)(\widetilde{z}, z)$$

with the exchange contributions given by

$$N(k)(\widetilde{z}, z) = \exp[\widetilde{z} \cdot A(k)\, \overline{z}].$$

To pass from center to cluster coordinates, we employ the transformation discussed in section 5.1. Since the transformation is an orthogonal point transformation, the new kernel is simply obtained by substitution.

7.2 Proposition: The normalization operator in cluster coordinates $\widetilde{s}$, s has the exchange decomposition given in proposition 7.1 with the exchange contribution replaced by

$$N(k)(\widetilde{s}, s) = \exp[\widetilde{s} \cdot B(k)\, \overline{s}]$$

where

$$B(k) = {}^t W_j\, A(k)\, W_j$$

and the matrices $\widetilde{W}_j$, W_j are specified in definition 5.4.

Next we show that the overall center-of-mass vectors s_j and $\widetilde{s}_j$ separate out from the kernel.

7.3 Proposition: The $j \times j$ matrix $B(k)$ has the block diagonal form

$$B(k) = \begin{bmatrix} E(k) & 0 \\ 0 & 1 \end{bmatrix}.$$

The normalization kernel in cluster coordinates factorizes into a reproducing kernel for the center-of-mass state and a kernel depending on all other coordinates,

$$N(\tilde{s}, s) = \exp[\tilde{s}_j \cdot \bar{s}_j] \, N'(\tilde{s}_1 \tilde{s}_2 \ldots \tilde{s}_{j-1}, s_1 s_2 \ldots s_{j-1})$$

Proof: First we prove the block diagonal form of the matrix $B(k)$. The last column of the matrix $B(k)$ is given by

$$B_{mj}(k) = \sideset{}{'}\sum_{i,l} (^t\tilde{W}_j)_{mi} [\tilde{w}_i w_l]^{-1/2} k_{il} (W_j)_{lj}.$$

From the explicit form of the orthogonal matrix W_j given in definition 5.4 one finds

$$\sideset{}{'}\sum_{l=1}^{j} [w_l]^{-1/2} k_{il}(W_j)_{lj} = [n]^{-1/2} \sideset{}{'}\sum_{l=1}^{j} k_{il} = [n]^{-1/2} \tilde{w}_i$$

where in the last step we used the relation of the numbers k_{il} to the weight components according to definition 2.13. Using this result we obtain

$$B_{mj}(k) = [n]^{-1/2} \sideset{}{'}\sum_{i=1}^{j} (^t\tilde{W}_j)_{mi} [\tilde{w}_i]^{1/2}.$$

From definition 5.4 one finds for $m \neq j$

$$B_{mj}(k) = [n]^{-1/2} \left\{ \left[\frac{\tilde{w}_{m+1}}{\tilde{q}_{m+1}\tilde{q}_m} \right]^{1/2} \sideset{}{'}\sum_{i=1}^{m} \tilde{w}_i - \left[\frac{\tilde{q}_m}{\tilde{q}_{m+1}} \right]^{1/2} [\tilde{w}_{m+1}]^{1/2} \right\} = 0$$

and for $m = j$

$$B_{jj}(k) = [n]^{-1} \sideset{}{'}\sum_{i=1}^{j} \tilde{w}_i = 1.$$

A similar result holds true for the last row of the matrix $B(k)$ and yields the block diagonal form of this matrix. Since the matrix element B_{jj} is independent of the double coset k, the exponential term associated with $\tilde{s}_i \cdot \bar{s}_j$ appears as a factor in the normalization kernel. $\square$

So far we have assumed that there are j composite particles both in the bra and ket configuration. The case of $\tilde{j}$ composite particles in the bra and j composite particles in the ket configuration is simply obtained by putting $|\tilde{j} - j|$ components of one of the weights equal to zero. Then the dependence on the corresponding center vectors drops out of the kernels, the matrix $A(k)$ may be replaced in non-square form by omitting the zero part and the matrices $W_{\tilde{j}}$, W_j serve to transform this non-square matrix to the representation in cluster coordinates.

Example 7.1: The normalization kernel for ^{4}He + ^{4}He.

To describe a system of two interacting ^{4}He nuclei, we choose internally unexcited oscillator states and the occupation numbers $\widetilde{w} = w = (4, 4)$. The only allowed orbital partition is f = [4 4] and the two Gelfand patterns are obtained from

$$\left(\begin{matrix} f \\ \widetilde{q} \end{matrix}\right) = \left(\begin{matrix} f \\ q \end{matrix}\right) = \begin{matrix} 4 & 4 \\ & 4 \end{matrix}$$

as $\widetilde{q} = q = 4$. The polynomial $D_{qq}^f(\epsilon)$ is of highest weight and we obtain from proposition 3.20

$$D_{4\ 4}^{[44]}(\epsilon) = (\Delta_{1\,2}^{1\,2})^4 = (\epsilon_{11}\epsilon_{22} - \epsilon_{12}\epsilon_{21})^4 .$$

The expansion yields

$$D_{4\ 4}^{[44]}(\epsilon) = \sum_{\alpha=0}^{4} (-1)^\alpha \binom{4}{\alpha} \epsilon_{11}^{4-\alpha}\epsilon_{12}^{\alpha} \epsilon_{21}^{\alpha} \epsilon_{22}^{4-\alpha}.$$

The double coset symbol k is recognized in this expansion as

$$k = \left\{ \begin{matrix} 4-\alpha & \alpha \\ \alpha & 4-\alpha \end{matrix} \right\}.$$

Insertion of the analytic form of the single-particle overlap integrals and transformation to two-center coordinates yields the normalization kernel as

$$(\alpha^8 [4\ 4]\ 4 \mid N(\widetilde{z}_1\widetilde{z}_2, z_1 z_2) \mid \alpha^8 [4\ 4]\ 4) = \sum_{\alpha=0}^{4} (-1)^\alpha \binom{4}{\alpha} \exp\left[\sum_{r,s=1}^{2} \widetilde{z}_r \cdot A_{rs}(k)\, \overline{z}_s \right]$$

where the matrix A(k) is given by

$$A(k) = \frac{1}{4}\left[\begin{matrix} 4-\alpha & \alpha \\ \alpha & 4-\alpha \end{matrix} \right].$$

Now we pass to the cluster coordinates which from example 5.2 are given by

$$s_1 = \sqrt{\frac{1}{2}}(z_1 - z_2)$$

$$s_2 = \sqrt{\frac{1}{2}}(z_1 + z_2).$$

The transformed kernel becomes

$$(\alpha^8 [4\ 4]\ 4 \mid N(\widetilde{s}_1\widetilde{s}_2, s_1 s_2) \mid \alpha^8 [4\ 4]\ 4) = \exp[\widetilde{s}_2 \cdot \overline{s}_2]\left[\exp\left[\frac{1}{4}\widetilde{s}_1 \cdot \overline{s}_1\right] \right.$$

$$\left. - \exp\left[-\frac{1}{4}\widetilde{s}_1 \cdot \overline{s}_1\right] \right]^4 = \exp[\widetilde{s}_2 \cdot \overline{s}_2] \sum_{\alpha=0}^{4} (-1)^\alpha \binom{4}{\alpha}\exp\left[\frac{4-2\alpha}{4}\widetilde{s}_1 \cdot \overline{s}_1\right].$$

Hence the center-of-mass vectors $\tilde{s}_2$, s_2 appear in the form of a unit operator. With respect to the relative coordinate between the two composite particles, the kernel is a sum of exponential terms in the scalar product $\tilde{s}_1 \cdot \bar{s}_1$. These terms are easily recognized as kernels of the complex dilatation operator considered in example 5.5. To obtain the operator properties of the kernel we write, dropping the dependence on $\tilde{s}_2 \cdot \bar{s}_2$,

$$(\alpha^8 [4\ 4]\ 4 | N'(\tilde{s}_1, s_1) | \alpha^8 [4\ 4]\ 4) = \sum_{N = 0}^{\infty} \eta_N [N!]^{-1} (\tilde{s}_1 \cdot \bar{s}_1)^N$$

and find

$$\eta_N = \sum_{\alpha = 0}^{4} (-1)^\alpha \binom{4}{\alpha} \left(1 - \frac{1}{2}\alpha\right)^N .$$

Noting that the integral operator

$$[N!]^{-1} (\tilde{s}_1 \cdot \bar{s}_1)^N = \sum_{LM}{}' P_{LM}^N (\tilde{s}_1) \overline{P_{LM}^N (s_1)}$$

is a sum of projection operators for harmonic oscillator states of the relative motion we find that the expansion of $N'(\tilde{s}_1, s_1)$ is an eigenfunction expansion of the operator with eigenvalues given by η_N. These eigenvalues are degenerate with respect to the labels L, M associated with a given N. The eigenvalues for N odd vanish and moreover, one finds $\eta_0 = \eta_2 = 0$. For large values of N the eigenvalues tend towards the value 2.

7.3 Interaction Kernels

The orbital interaction operator was introduced in section 6.3 as the matrix element of the n-body hamiltonian between appropriate many-body states. We shall assume that the hamiltonian contains at most two-body interactions. Then the analysis given in section 2.7 applies and proposition 2.60 yields the matrix elements of the full hamiltonian in terms of orbital matrix elements of the orbital part of the hamiltonian which acts on the last pair of particles. By proposition 6.11 the orbital bra and ket states have been interpreted as configurations built from single-particle states. Then the evaluation of the orbital matrix elements can be reduced from the n-body system to the two-body system with the help of fractional parentage coefficients. This reduction is given in proposition 3.33 when we choose $n'' = 2$. In order to keep the discussion general, we shall employ the density operators introduced in section 5.4. Thus, if $T(2)$ is the orbital two-body operator in question, we find its matrix elements through the evaluation of the reduced density operator $D(2)$. Let us assume that the operator $T(2)$ does not affect the dependence of the two-body state on the coordinate $x_1 + x_2$. This assumption holds true for most orbital two-body operators used in nuclear physics. Then the matrix elements of $T(2)$ between two-body states may be derived from its kernel as

$$T(2) = \int\int T(2) (\tilde{v}, v) d_{v\tilde{v}}(2) d\mu(v) d\mu(\tilde{v})$$

where $d_{v\tilde{v}}(2)$ is the reduced density operator introduced in definition 5.17. Hence, it suffices to consider the matrix elements of the operator $d_{v\tilde{v}}(2)$ between n-body states acting on the last pair of particles. To this operator we apply proposition 3.33 and get the expression

$$(\alpha^n \tilde{f}\, (f'f'')\, \tilde{q} \,\|d_{v\tilde{v}}(2)\,(\tilde{t}, t)\|\, \alpha^n f(f'f'')\, q)$$

$$= |f'|^{1/2} \sum_{\tilde{q}'q'\tilde{q}''q''} \{\langle \tilde{f}\tilde{q}\,|f\tilde{q}'f''\tilde{q}''\rangle\, D^{f'}_{\tilde{q}'q'}(\epsilon)$$

$$|f''|^{-1/2}\, (\alpha^2 f''\tilde{q}''\|\,d_{v\tilde{v}}(2)\,(\tilde{t}, t)\|\, \alpha^2 f''q'')\,\langle f'q'f''q''|\,fq\rangle\}.$$

The first and last coefficient in curly brackets are the fractional parentage coefficients discussed in section 3.7. The polynomial function $D^{f'}(\epsilon)$ is of the same type as the $D^f(\epsilon)$ appearing in the normalization kernel except for the fact that the double coset expansion is now based on the weights $\tilde{w}'$ and w'. Hence $D^{f'}(\epsilon)$ may be written as

$$D^{f'}_{\tilde{q}'q'}(\epsilon) = [\tilde{w}'!\,w'!]^{1/2} \sum_{k'} d^{f'}_{\tilde{q}'q'}(z_{k'})\,[k'!]^{-1}\,\epsilon^{k'}.$$

The single-particle overlap integrals are the same ones as before, and by the reasoning applied to the normalization kernel one finds

$$\epsilon^{k'} = \exp[\tilde{z}\cdot A(k')\,\bar{z}]$$

where $A(k')$ is the matrix $A(k)$ defined in section 7.2 but taken for the double coset k' and the weights $\tilde{w}'$ and w'.

The two-body matrix elements are characterized by Gelfand patterns $\tilde{q}''$ and q'' and by a partition $f'' = [2]$ or $[11]$. In section 3.4 it was shown that $\tilde{q}''$ and q'' are equivalent to the choice of index pairs il and rs for the corresponding single-particle states in bra and ket. In section 3.10 the partition f'' was established through appropriate linear combinations of the two-body matrix elements.

The analytic form of the matrix elements for the operator $d_{v\tilde{v}}(2)$ is obtained from its matrix elements between unexcited oscillator states shifted by Weyl operators. To find these matrix elements we use the kernel given in proposition 5.18 as a generating function and choose the centers il for the bra and the centers rs for the ket states. The two-body matrix element of the reduced density operator becomes

$$(\alpha^2\, il\,|d_{v\tilde{v}}(2)\,(\tilde{t}, t)|\,\alpha^2\, rs) = (000, 000\,|\,(\Lambda_{\tilde{t}} \circ V_{\tilde{t}})^+ \circ d_{v\tilde{v}}(2) \circ (\Lambda_t \circ V_t)|\,000, 000)$$

$$= \exp\left[\sqrt{\frac{1}{2}}\,(\tilde{t}_i - \tilde{t}_l)\cdot\tilde{v} + v\cdot\sqrt{\frac{1}{2}}\,(\bar{t}_r - \bar{t}_s) + \frac{1}{2}\,(\tilde{t}_i + \tilde{t}_l)\cdot(\bar{t}_r + \bar{t}_s)\right].$$

To introduce the orbital partition we have to take linear combinations symmetrized or antisymmetrized with respect to bra or ket states. From the explicit form of the matrix element one notices that the corresponding interchanges are equivalent to the transformations $v \to -v$ or $\tilde{v} \to -\tilde{v}$.

We distinguish now the various possibilities of the index pairs il, rs and find from proposition 3.33

7.4 Proposition: The reduced two-body matrix elements of the reduced two-body density operator are given by

$$(\alpha^2[2]\,ii\,|d_{v\tilde{v}}(2)\,(\tilde{t}, t)|\,\alpha^2[2]\,rr) = (\alpha^2\,ii\,|d_{oo}(2)\,(\tilde{t}, t)|\,\alpha^2\,rr),$$

$$(\alpha^2[2]\,il\,|d_{v\tilde{v}}(2)\,(\tilde{t}, t)|\,\alpha^2[2]\,rr)$$
$$= (\alpha^2\,il\,|\,\sqrt{\frac{1}{2}}\,(d_{o\tilde{v}}(2)\,(\tilde{t}, t) + d_{o\,-\tilde{v}}(2)\,(\tilde{t}, t))|\,\alpha^2\,rr),$$

$$(\alpha^2[2]\,ii\,|d_{v\tilde{v}}(2)\,(\tilde{t}, t)|\,\alpha^2[2]\,rs)$$
$$= \left(\alpha^2\,ii\,|\,\sqrt{\frac{1}{2}}\,(d_{vo}(2)\,(\tilde{t}, t) + d_{-vo}(2)\,(\tilde{t}, t))|\,\alpha^2\,rs\right),$$

$$(\alpha^2[2]\,il\,|d_{v\tilde{v}}(2)\,(\tilde{t}, t)|\,\alpha^2[2]\,rs)$$
$$= \left(\alpha^2\,il\,|\frac{1}{2}(d_{v\tilde{v}}(2)\,(\tilde{t}, t) + d_{v\tilde{v}}(2)\,(\tilde{t}, t) + d_{v\,-\tilde{v}}\,(2)\,(\tilde{t}, t) + d_{-v\,-\tilde{v}}(2)\,(\tilde{t}, t))|\,\alpha^2\,rs\right),$$

$$(\alpha^2[11]\,il\,|d_{v\tilde{v}}(2)\,(\tilde{t}, t)|\,\alpha^2[11]\,rs)$$
$$= \left(\alpha^2\,il\,|\frac{1}{2}(d_{v\tilde{v}}(2)\,(\tilde{t}, t) - d_{-v\tilde{v}}(2)\,(\tilde{t}, t) - d_{v\,-\tilde{v}}(2)\,(\tilde{t}, t) + d_{-v\,-\tilde{v}}(2)\,(\tilde{t}, t))|\,\alpha^2\,rs\right).$$

Thus, the analytic form of these matrix elements is immediately obtained once the matrix elements of $d_{v\tilde{v}}(2)$ are available for all pairs of indices. We shall indicate the appropriate linear combinations by considering only the matrix elements of $d_{v\tilde{v}}(2)$ and putting a bracket with index f'' at the relevant position.

We return to the matrix element of $d_{v\tilde{v}}(2)$ and rewrite it in the form

$$(\alpha^2\,il\,|d_{v\tilde{v}}(2)\,(\tilde{t}, t)|\,\alpha^2\,rs) = \exp[\tilde{t}_i \cdot \tilde{t}_r + \tilde{t}_l \cdot \tilde{t}_s] \times$$
$$\times \exp\left[-\frac{1}{2}(\tilde{t}_i - \tilde{t}_l) \cdot (\tilde{t}_r - \tilde{t}_s) + \sqrt{\frac{1}{2}}(\tilde{t}_i - \tilde{t}_l) \cdot \tilde{v} + v \cdot \sqrt{\frac{1}{2}}(\tilde{t}_r - \tilde{t}_s)\right].$$

Here we separated an exponential factor which may be combined with the expression coming from $D^f(\epsilon)$. If the weights $\tilde{w}''$ and w'' associated with $\tilde{q}''$ and q'' are used to define a $j \times j$ double coset k'', this exponential factor may by written as

$$\exp[\tilde{z} \cdot A(k'')\,\bar{z}].$$

We write $k' + k'' = k$ and note that from the definition of $A(k)$ in proposition 7.1 we have $A(k') + A(k'') = A(k)$. Clearly $k' + k''$ is a double coset symbol for the weights $\tilde{w}$ and w. The passage from center coordinates to cluster coordinates for these exponential terms proceeds as for the normalization and yields an exponential term

$$\exp[\tilde{s} \cdot B(k' + k'')\,\bar{s}]$$

with a block diagonal matrix $B(k' + k'')$,

$$B(k' + k'') = \begin{bmatrix} E(k' + k'') & 0 \\ 0 & 1 \end{bmatrix}.$$

This form of the matrix exhibits the same separation of the center-of-mass part of the kernel as it was found for the normalization kernel. For the remaining exponential terms we introduce the expansions

$$\sqrt{\frac{1}{2}}(\tilde{t}_i - \tilde{t}_l) = \sum_{m=1}^{j-1} c_m(\tilde{q}'') \tilde{s}_m$$

$$\sqrt{\frac{1}{2}}(t_r - t_s) = \sum_{m=1}^{j-1} b_m(q'') s_m$$

It is easily shown that these expansions do not involve the coordinates $\tilde{s}_j$ and s_j. With this notation it is now possible to write down the interaction kernel in cluster coordinates.

7.5 Proposition: The orbital interaction kernel for simple composite particles and for the Hamiltonian replaced by the reduced density operator is given by

$$(\alpha^n \tilde{f}(f'f'') \tilde{q} \| d_{v\tilde{v}}(2) (\tilde{s}, s) \| \alpha^n f(f'f'') q)$$

$$= |f'|^{1/2} \sum_{\tilde{q}'q'\tilde{q}''q''} \left\{ \langle \tilde{f}\tilde{q} | f'\tilde{q}'f''\tilde{q}'' \rangle \langle f'q'f''q'' | fq \rangle \right.$$

$$\left. [\tilde{w}'! \, w'!]^{1/2} \sum_{k'} d^{f'}_{\tilde{q}'q'}(z_{k'}) [k'!]^{-1} [d_{v\tilde{v}}(2) (k'k''\tilde{q}''q'') (\tilde{s}, s)]^{f''} \right\}$$

where the index f'' refers to the necessary (anti-)symmetrization discussed earlier in this section and where the exchange contributions are given by

$$d_{v\tilde{v}}(2) (k'k''\tilde{q}''q'') (\tilde{s}, s) = \exp\left[\sum_{i,l}^{j-1} \tilde{s}_i(B_{il}(k' + k'') - c_i(\tilde{q}'') b_l(q'')) \tilde{s}_l \right]$$

$$\times \exp\left[\sum_{i=1}^{j-1} c_i(\tilde{q}'') (\tilde{s}_i \cdot \bar{v}) + \sum_{l=1}^{j-1} b_l(q'') (v \cdot \tilde{s}_l) \right].$$

Finally we remark that the expressions may be adapted to the case $\tilde{j} \neq j$ by the procedure indicated at the end of section 7.2.

7.4 Configurations of three Simple Composite Nuclear Systems

We discuss in detail the configurations with three simple composite systems. The weights are of the form

$$\tilde{w} = (\tilde{w}_1 \tilde{w}_2 \tilde{w}_3), \quad w = (w_1 w_2 w_3)$$

and since any weight component must be smaller than or equal to four, these configurations cover states of up to $n = 12$ nucleons. The main point of the present analysis will be the passage to an oscillator representation for the normalization and interaction operator. In this section, we shall drop the dependence of the operators on the overall center-of-mass coordinate. We want to consider an expansion of the ket states in terms of the coupled states

$$[P_{L_1}^{N_1}(s_1) P_{L_2}^{N_2}(s_2)]_{LM} = \sum_{M_1 M_2} P_{L_1 M_1}^{N_1}(s_1) P_{L_2 M_2}^{N_2}(s_2) \langle L_1 M_1 L_2 M_2 \mid LM \rangle$$

and corresponding states for the bra of the form

$$[P_{\widetilde{L}_1}^{\widetilde{N}_1}(\widetilde{s}_1) P_{\widetilde{L}_2}^{\widetilde{N}_2}(\widetilde{s}_2)]_{\widetilde{L}\widetilde{M}} = \sum_{\widetilde{M}_1 \widetilde{M}_2} P_{\widetilde{L}_1 \widetilde{M}_1}^{\widetilde{N}_1}(\widetilde{s}_1) P_{\widetilde{L}_2 \widetilde{M}_2}^{\widetilde{N}_2}(\widetilde{s}_2) \langle \widetilde{L}_1 \widetilde{M}_1 \widetilde{L}_2 \widetilde{M}_2 \mid \widetilde{L}\widetilde{M} \rangle.$$

7.6 Proposition: The exchange part of the normalization kernel in the oscillator representation is given by

$$(\widetilde{N}_1 \widetilde{L}_1 \widetilde{N}_2 \widetilde{L}_2 \widetilde{L}\widetilde{M} \mid N(k) \mid N_1 L_1 N_2 L_2 LM)$$
$$= \delta(\widetilde{L}, L)\, \delta(\widetilde{M}, M)\, (\widetilde{N}_1 \widetilde{L}_1 \widetilde{N}_2 \widetilde{L}_2 L \mid S_{g_c(E'(k))} \mid N_1 L_1 N_2 L_2 L)$$

where the second line is a generalized transformation bracket given in proposition 5.7.

Proof: The exchange decomposition is not affected by a change of the representation. Hence it suffices to transform the exchange contribution $N(k)$ to the oscillator representation. The kernel $N(k)(\widetilde{s}, s)$ serves as a generating function for the oscillator representation and its expansion is the one considered in the derivation of the general transformation bracket according to proposition 5.7.   □

Now we proceed to the matrix elements of the reduced density operator in the oscillator representation. Again it suffices to expand the exchange contributions since the algebraic coefficients are not affected. The exchange part according to proposition 7.5 is the exponential of a quadratic and a linear part with respect to the coordinates $\widetilde{s}_1 \widetilde{s}_2 s_1 s_2$. The expansion of the exponential with quadratic terms yields again a general transformation bracket,

$$\exp\left[\sum_{i,\,l} \widetilde{s}_i \cdot E'_{il} s_j \right]$$

$$= \sum_{\widetilde{N}'_1 \widetilde{L}'_1 \widetilde{N}'_2 \widetilde{L}'_2 N'_1 L'_1 N'_2 L'_2 L' M'} \{ [P_{\widetilde{L}'_1}^{\widetilde{N}'_1}(\widetilde{s}_1) P_{\widetilde{L}'_2}^{\widetilde{N}'_2}(\widetilde{s}_2)]_{L'M'} \overline{[P_{L'_1}^{N'_1}(s_1) P_{L'_2}^{N'_2}(s_2)]_{L'M'}}$$
$$(\widetilde{N}'_1 \widetilde{L}'_1 \widetilde{N}'_2 \widetilde{L}'_2 L' \mid S_{g_c(E')} \mid N'_1 L'_1 N'_2 L'_2 L') \}$$

where the matrix E' is given by

$$E'_{il}(k', k''\widetilde{q}''q'') = E_{il}(k' + k'') - c_i(\widetilde{q}'') b_l(q'').$$

The exponential of the linear terms involving $\tilde{s}_1$ and $\tilde{s}_2$ has the expansion

$$\exp\left[(c_1\tilde{s}_1 + c_2\tilde{s}_2)\cdot\overline{\tilde{v}}\right]$$

$$= \sum_{\tilde{N}''\tilde{L}''\tilde{M}''\tilde{N}_1''\tilde{L}_1''\tilde{N}_2''\tilde{L}_2''} \{[P_{\tilde{L}_1''}^{\tilde{N}_1''}(\tilde{s}_1)\,P_{\tilde{L}_2''}^{\tilde{N}_2''}(\tilde{s}_2)]_{\tilde{L}''\tilde{M}''}(c_1)^{\tilde{N}_1''}(c_2)^{\tilde{N}_2''}$$

$$A(\tilde{N}_1''\tilde{L}_1''\tilde{N}_2''\tilde{L}_2'',\tilde{N}''\tilde{L}'')\,\overline{P_{\tilde{L}''\tilde{M}''}^{\tilde{N}''}(\tilde{v})}\}$$

where we used results given in proposition 4.34. Similarly we get

$$\exp\left[v\cdot(b_1\overline{\tilde{s}}_1 + b_2\overline{\tilde{s}}_2)\right]$$

$$= \sum_{N''L''M''N_1''L_1''N_2''L_2''} \{P_{L''M''}^{N''}(v)\,A(N_1''L_1''N_2''L_2'',N''L'')\,\overline{[P_{L_1''}^{N_1''}(s_1)\,P_{L_2''}^{N_2''}(s_2)]_{L''M''}}$$

$$(b_1)^{N_1''}(b_2)^{N_2''}\}.$$

Since the oscillator states in the four coordinates $\tilde{s}_1\tilde{s}_2 s_1 s_2$ appear each in two places, we must first recouple the angular momenta and then use the identity given in the proof of proposition 5.7 to derive the final expansion. These steps introduce two recouplings of four angular momenta and four coefficients A as defined in relation with proposition 4.33. Then we get

7.7 Proposition: The reduced two-body density operator for three simple composite nucleon systems in the oscillator representation has the exchange decomposition given in proposition 7.5 and the exchange contribution

$$(\tilde{N}_1\tilde{L}_1\tilde{N}_2\tilde{L}_2\tilde{L}\overline{M}|\,d_{v\tilde{v}}(2)\,(k'k''\overline{q}''q'')|N_1L_1N_2L_2LM)$$

$$= \sum_{\tilde{N}''\tilde{L}''\tilde{M}''N''L''M''L'M'} \{\overline{P_{\tilde{L}''\tilde{M}''}^{\tilde{N}''}(\tilde{v})}\,P_{L''M''}^{N''}(v)$$

$$\times \langle\tilde{L}\overline{M}|L'M'\tilde{L}''\tilde{M}''\rangle\,\langle L'M'L''M''|LM\rangle$$

$$\times (\tilde{N}_1\tilde{L}_1\tilde{N}_2\tilde{L}_2\tilde{L}\tilde{N}''\tilde{L}''L'|N_1L_1N_2L_2LN''L''L')\}$$

where the coefficient in the expansion is given by

$$(\tilde{N}_1\tilde{L}_1\tilde{N}_2\tilde{L}_2\tilde{L}\tilde{N}''\tilde{L}''L'|N_1L_1N_2L_2LN''L''L'_2)$$

$$= \sum_{\substack{\tilde{N}_1'\tilde{L}_1'\tilde{N}_1''\tilde{L}_1''\tilde{N}_2'\tilde{L}_2'\tilde{N}_2''\tilde{L}_2''\\N_1'L_1'N_1''L_2''N_2'L_2'N_2''L_2''}} \{A(\tilde{N}_1'\tilde{L}_1'\tilde{N}_1''\tilde{L}_1'',\tilde{N}_1\tilde{L}_1)\,A(\tilde{N}_2'\tilde{L}_2'\tilde{N}_2''\tilde{L}_2'',\tilde{N}_2\tilde{L}_2)$$

$$A(N_1'L_1'N_1''L_1'',N_1L_1)\,A(N_2'L_2'N_2''L_2'',N_2L_2)$$

$$A(\tilde{N}_1''\tilde{L}_1''\tilde{N}_2''\tilde{L}_2'',\tilde{N}''\tilde{L}'')\,A(N_1''L_1''N_2''L_2'',N''L'')$$

$$\langle\tilde{L}_1(\tilde{L}_1'\tilde{L}_1'')\,\tilde{L}_2(\tilde{L}_2'\tilde{L}_2'')\,\tilde{L}|L'(\tilde{L}_1'\tilde{L}_2')\,\tilde{L}''(\tilde{L}_1''\tilde{L}_2'')\,\tilde{L}\rangle$$

$$\langle L'(L_1'L_2')\,L''(L_1''L_2'')\,L|L_1(L_1'L_1'')\,L_2(L_2'L_2'')\,L\rangle$$

$$(c_1)^{\tilde{N}_1''}(c_2)^{\tilde{N}_2''}(b_1)^{N_1''}(b_2)^{N_2''}(\tilde{N}_1'\tilde{L}_1'\tilde{N}_2'\tilde{L}_2'\ L'|S_{g_c(E')}|N_1'L_1'N_2'L_2'L')\}.$$

Since we introduced the angular momenta, it is now appropriate to pass to reduced matrix elements with respect to angular momentum. Suppose that the operator $T(2)$ is a tensor operator of rank κ. Then proposition 7.7 may be rewritten in the form

$$(\widetilde{N}_1 \widetilde{L}_1 \widetilde{N}_2 \widetilde{L}_2 \widetilde{L} \| T^\kappa(2) \| N_1 L_1 N_2 L_2 L)$$

$$= \sum_{\widetilde{N}''\widetilde{L}''N''L''N'L'} \left\{ (\widetilde{N}''\widetilde{L}'' \| T^\kappa(2) \| N''L'') \right.$$

$$(\widetilde{N}_1 \widetilde{L}_1 \widetilde{N}_2 \widetilde{L}_2 \widetilde{L} \widetilde{N}''\widetilde{L}''L' | N_1 L_1 N_2 L_2 L N''L''L')$$

$$\left. (-1)^{L'+L''+\widetilde{L}+\kappa} [(2\widetilde{L}+1)(2L+1)]^{1/2} \begin{Bmatrix} L'' & L & L' \\ \widetilde{L} & \widetilde{L}'' & \kappa \end{Bmatrix} \right\}$$

where

$$(\widetilde{N}''\widetilde{L}'' \| T^\kappa(2) \| N''L'') = \sum_{Q\widetilde{M}''M''} \left\{ [2\kappa+1]^{1/2} \langle \kappa Q | \widetilde{L}''\widetilde{M}''L'' - M'' \rangle (-1)^{L''-M''} \right.$$

$$\left. \int \overline{P^{\widetilde{N}''}_{\widetilde{L}''\widetilde{M}''}(\widetilde{v})} \, T^\kappa(2)\,(\widetilde{v}, v)\, P^{N''}_{L''M''}(v)\, d\mu(\widetilde{v})\, d\mu(v) \right\}$$

and the notation is taken from Edmonds [ED 57].

7.5 Notes and References

Some aspects of composite particle theory in relation to harmonic oscillator states are treated by Kramer and Moshinsky, [KR 68b], and in [KR 73a]. A detailed algebraic theory of three-cluster configurations is developed in [KR 73]. Its results are rederived from the Bargmann representation in section 7.4. The Bargmann representation for simple composite particles is considered in [KR 73a] and [KR 75].

8 Interaction of Composite Nucleon Systems with Internal Shell Structure

8.1 Concepts and Motivation

In the present section, we extend the study of composite nucleon systems to more complex internal states. In section 8.2, we discuss algebraic and analytic properties of the overlap matrix between single-particle states. By a modification of the single-particle basis, we arrive at a new biorthogonal basis which leads to a simpler form of the matrix ϵ. This modification is implemented through the generalized Weyl operators introduced in section 4.4. For three important configurations we determine the matrix ϵ explicitly. In sections 8.3 and 8.4, we examine the interaction of a simple composite particle with a composite particle having an internal closed oscillator shell. The corresponding configuration covers the interaction of a single nucleon, a deuteron, a ^{3}H, ^{3}He or a ^{4}He nucleus with the closed-shell nuclei ^{4}He, ^{16}O and ^{40}Ca. We obtain the normalization kernel, examine its exchange decomposition and compute its eigenfunctions and eigenvalues. The eigenvalues reflect the action of the Pauli principle on the composite particle interaction as a function of the relative excitation and the mass numbers of the fragments. In section 8.5, we study the configuration $s^4 p^{12} + s^4 p^{12}$ which covers the interaction of ^{16}O + ^{16}O. Particular emphasis is given to the exchange properties of the normalization operator and to the accessibility of compound states in ^{32}S. The interaction of a simple composite particle with a composite particle having an open oscillator shell is examined in section 8.6. It is shown that the necessary modifications of the scheme involve shell model concepts related to the introduction of angular momentum for shell configurations. The configurations are arranged in the order of increasing complexity. The analysis exhibits the interplay between the various algebraic and analytic concepts introduced earlier and shows that insight into the physics of these configurations can already be gained from the properties of the normalization operator.

8.2 Single-Particle Bases and their Overlap Matrix

The orbital n-body states which we are going to consider are built by the occupation of j single-particle states. The overlap matrix ϵ consists of all scalar products between j bra and j ket states. We collect in this section some algebraic and analytic properties of this matrix.

8.1 Proposition: Let ϵ be a $j \times j$ matrix partitioned into blocks according to

$$\epsilon = \begin{bmatrix} \gamma & \beta \\ \alpha & \delta \end{bmatrix}$$

where the dimension of the blocks $\gamma\beta\alpha\delta$ is $r \times r, r \times (j-r), (j-r) \times r$, and $(j-r) \times (j-r)$ respectively and where γ is nonsingular. Then the matrix ϵ may be written as a product of three partitioned matrices,

$$\epsilon = \begin{bmatrix} 1 & 0 \\ A & 1 \end{bmatrix} \begin{bmatrix} C & 0 \\ 0 & D \end{bmatrix} \begin{bmatrix} 1 & B \\ 0 & 1 \end{bmatrix}$$

where

$$A = \alpha\gamma^{-1} \quad B = \gamma^{-1}\beta \quad C = \gamma \quad D = \delta - \alpha\gamma^{-1}\beta.$$

Proof: Since γ is invertible, the blocks ABCD are well defined. The results is verified by block matrix multiplication.   □

8.2 Definition: Consider a fixed pair of bra and ket centers associated with shifts $\tilde{t}$ and t in phase space. The modified ket and bra basis are given by the replacements

$$\Lambda_t \circ V_t \,|\, NLM) \to \Lambda_t \circ V_{\tilde{t}} \,|\, NLM)$$

$$\Lambda_{\tilde{t}} \circ V_{\tilde{t}} \,|\, \widetilde{N}\widetilde{L}\widetilde{M}) \to \Lambda_{\tilde{t}} \circ V_t \,|\, \widetilde{N}\widetilde{L}\widetilde{M}).$$

8.3 Proposition: For two centers as considered in definition 8.2 and a fixed set of j (orthogonal) oscillator states, the overlap matrix is given by

$$\epsilon = I_j \exp[\tilde{t} \cdot \bar{t}].$$

The two bases are said to be biorthogonal.

Proof: The overlap matrix is the matrix of a product of generalized Weyl operators. This product may be rewritten by application of the rules given in proposition 4.21 as

$$(\Lambda_{\tilde{t}} \circ V_t)^+ (\Lambda_t \circ V_{\tilde{t}}) = \Lambda_{-t} \circ V_{-\tilde{t}} \circ \Lambda_t \circ V_{\tilde{t}} = \Lambda_0 \circ V_0 \exp[\tilde{t} \cdot \bar{t}]$$

Since this is the unit operator multiplied by a factor, the matrix ϵ has the form claimed in the proposition.   □

If in a configuration of several centers in the bra and ket we introduce biorthogonal bases for all pairs of centers labelled by $\tilde{t}_1 t_1, \tilde{t}_2 t_2, \ldots, \tilde{t}_j t_j$, the diagonal blocks of the matrix ϵ become multiples of the unit matrix. The situation is different if we choose pairs of centers with different index.

8.4 Proposition: The overlap between biorthogonal bases belonging to the bra center i and the ket center l, $i \neq l$, is determined by the matrix elements of the operator

$$\Lambda_{t_l - t_i} \circ V_{\tilde{t}_l - \tilde{t}_i} \exp[\tilde{t}_i \cdot \bar{t}_l].$$

Proof: The product of operators entering the overlap matrix is given by

$$((\Lambda_{\tilde{t}_i} \circ V_{t_i})^+ \circ (\Lambda_{t_l} \circ V_{\tilde{t}_l}) = \Lambda_{-t_i} \circ V_{-\tilde{t}_i} \circ \Lambda_{t_l} \circ V_{\tilde{t}_l} = \Lambda_{t_l - t_i} \circ V_{\tilde{t}_l - \tilde{t}_i} \exp[\tilde{t}_i \cdot \bar{t}_l]$$

where use was made of proposition 4.21.

The matrix of the remaining general Weyl operators between oscillator states was given in propositions 4.35 and 4.36.   □

We now discuss three specific single-particle bases. For short we shall denote the single-particle oscillator states for $N = 0$ by s, for $N = 1$ by p and for $N = 2$ by sd. By a plus sign we shall separate the states at different centers.

Case I: The Two-Center Basis sp + s

We choose two centers in the bra and ket configuration. At center 1 we use the four oscillator states

NLM = 000,   11-1,   110,   111   and at center 2 a single oscillator state

NLM = 000.

The total number of single-particle states is 5 and hence, the matrix ϵ belongs to the group $GL(5, \mathbb{C})$. The matrix ϵ is conveniently partioned in the way specified in proposition 8.1 as

$$\epsilon = \begin{bmatrix} \gamma & \beta \\ \alpha & \delta \end{bmatrix}$$

where γ is of dimension 4×4 and refers to the first four single-particle states associated with bra and ket centers 1. According to proposition 8.3, the blocks γ and δ are given by multiples of the identity matrix,

$$\gamma = I_4 \exp \tilde{t}_1 \cdot \bar{t}_1 \qquad \delta = I \exp \tilde{t}_2 \cdot \bar{t}_2 .$$

The block α contains the matrix elements

$$(000| \Lambda_{t_1 - t_2} \circ V_{\tilde{t}_1 - \tilde{t}_2} |NLM) \exp [\tilde{t}_2 \cdot \bar{t}_1] = P_{LM}^N (\tilde{t}_2 - \tilde{t}_1) \exp [\tilde{t}_2 \cdot \bar{t}_1]$$

Here we use proposition 4.35 and the expression is valid for any state $|NLM)$. The 1×4 block α is given by choosing NLM = 000, 11-1, 110, 111. The block β contains the matrix elements

$$(NLM| \Lambda_{t_2 - t_1} \circ V_{\tilde{t}_2 - \tilde{t}_1} |000) \exp [\tilde{t}_1 \cdot \bar{t}_2] = \overline{P_{LM}^N (t_2 - t_1)} \exp [\tilde{t}_1 \cdot \bar{t}_2]$$

Again we use proposition 4.35 and get the 4×1 block β by choosing the four values of NLM. This completes the determination of the overlap matrix.

We now derive the factorization of ϵ according to proposition 8.1. The block γ is invertible and we get

$$A = \alpha \gamma^{-1} = \alpha \exp [-\tilde{t}_1 \cdot \bar{t}_1]$$

$$B = \gamma^{-1} \beta = \beta \exp [-\tilde{t}_1 \cdot \bar{t}_1]$$

$$C = \gamma = I_4 \exp [\tilde{t}_1 \cdot \bar{t}_1]$$

$$D = \exp \tilde{t}_2 \cdot \bar{t}_2 - \exp [-\tilde{t}_1 \cdot \bar{t}_1] \exp [\tilde{t}_1 \cdot \bar{t}_2 + \tilde{t}_2 \cdot \bar{t}_1] \left[1 + \sum_{M=-1}^{+1} P_{1M}^1 (\tilde{t}_2 - \tilde{t}_1) \overline{P_{1M}^1 (t_2 - t_1)} \right]$$

$$= \exp [\tilde{t}_2 \cdot \bar{t}_2] - \exp [-\tilde{t}_1 \cdot \bar{t}_1 + \tilde{t}_1 \cdot \bar{t}_2 + \tilde{t}_2 \cdot \bar{t}_1] [1 + (\tilde{t}_2 - \tilde{t}_1) \cdot (\bar{t}_2 - \bar{t}_1)].$$

In the last line, we used the identity given in proposition 4.34.

Case II: The Two-Center Basis sp.. + s

We generalize case I by considering at center 1 all oscillator states up to excitation $\overline{N}_1$. At center 2 we again take the excitation zero. From the added degeneracy of oscillator levels we find for the total number of states

$$j = \frac{1}{6}(\overline{N}_1 + 1)(\overline{N}_1 + 2)(\overline{N}_1 + 3) + 1$$

The matrix ϵ is conveniently partitioned according to $j = (j - 1) + 1$. Then the blocks γ and δ become

$$\gamma = I_{j-1} \exp[\tilde{t}_1 \cdot \overline{t}_1] \quad \delta = \exp[\tilde{t}_2 \cdot \overline{t}_2]$$

The $1 \times (j - 1)$ block α has precisely the same elements as given under case I, but now the values NLM extend up to the excitation $\overline{N}_1$. The $(j - 1) \times 1$ block β is obtained by the corresponding extension. Now, we compute the blocks for the factorized form of ϵ. We find

$$A = \alpha \exp[-\tilde{t}_1 \cdot \overline{t}_1]$$
$$B = \beta \exp[-\tilde{t}_1 \cdot \overline{t}_1]$$
$$C = \gamma = I_{j-1} \exp[\tilde{t}_1 \cdot \overline{t}_1]$$
$$D = \exp[\tilde{t}_2 \cdot \overline{t}_2] - \exp[-\tilde{t}_1 \cdot \overline{t}_1 + \tilde{t}_1 \cdot \overline{t}_2 + \tilde{t}_2 \cdot \overline{t}_1]\left[\sum_{N=0}^{\overline{N}_1} (N!)^{-1}((\tilde{t}_1 - \tilde{t}_2)\cdot(\overline{t_1 - t_2}))^N\right] .$$

The polynomial factor in the second term is obtained from the identity given in proposition 4.34.

Finally, we compute the determinant of the overlap matrix ϵ. When ϵ is written in factorized form, the left- and right-hand matrix factors are triangular with entries one on the diagonal. Their determinant equals one and the determinant of ϵ is the product of the determinants of the blocks C and D. Thus the determinant of ϵ becomes

$$\Delta_{12\ldots j}^{12\ldots j} = \exp[(j - 1)\tilde{t}_1 \cdot \overline{t}_1]$$

$$\times \left\{\exp \tilde{t}_2 \cdot \overline{t}_2 - \exp[-\tilde{t}_1 \cdot \overline{t}_1 + \tilde{t}_1 \cdot \overline{t}_2 + \tilde{t}_2 \cdot \overline{t}_1] \sum_{N=0}^{\overline{N}_1} (N!)^{-1}((\tilde{t}_1 - \tilde{t}_2)(\overline{t_1 - t_2}))^N\right\}$$

For later use, we introduce the new variables

$$\tilde{t} = (\tilde{t}_1 - \tilde{t}_2), \quad t = t_1 - t_2$$

and a function $q_m(\xi)$.

8.5 Definition: The analytic function $q_m(\xi)$ is defined by the power series

$$q_m(\xi) = \sum_{\omega=m}^{\infty} (\omega!)^{-1} \xi^{\omega}$$

Then we find

8.6 Proposition: The determinant of the overlap matrix ϵ for the single-particle basis of case II is given by

$$\Delta^{12\cdots j}_{12\cdots j} = \exp\left[(j-1)\,\tilde{t}_1\cdot\bar{t}_1 + \tilde{t}_2\cdot\bar{t}_2 - \tilde{t}\cdot\bar{t}\right] q_{\bar{N}_1+1}(\tilde{t}\cdot\bar{t})$$

Case III: The Two-Center Configuration sp + sp

Here we use both at centers 1 and 2 the 4 single-particle states $NLM = 000$, $11\text{-}1$, 110, 111. The 8×8 matrix ϵ belongs to the group $GL(8, \mathbb{C})$ and is conveniently partitioned according to $8 = 4 + 4$. For the blocks γ and δ we obtain

$$\gamma = I_4 \exp\tilde{t}_1\cdot\bar{t}_1 \qquad \delta = I_4 \exp\tilde{t}_2\cdot\bar{t}_2.$$

The computation of the blocks α and β is more involved. Here we need according to proposition 8.4 the matrix elements of the generalized Weyl operator between the four oscillator states. From proposition 4.36 this matrix is the product of the matrices for the operators Λ and V. We introduce for the computation of the matrix of $\Lambda_t \circ V_{\tilde{\tau}}$ the short-hand notation

$$P^1_{1M}(x) = x_M.$$

Then the 4×4 matrix of $\Lambda_t \circ V_{\tilde{\tau}}$ becomes

$$(|\,\Lambda_t \circ V_{\tilde{\tau}}\,|) = \begin{bmatrix} 1 & 0 & 0 & 0 \\ \bar{t}_{-1} & 1 & 0 & 0 \\ \bar{t}_0 & 0 & 1 & 0 \\ \bar{t}_1 & 0 & 0 & 1 \end{bmatrix} \begin{bmatrix} 1 & -\tilde{t}_{-1} & -\tilde{t}_0 & -\tilde{t}_1 \\ 0 & 1 & 0 & 0 \\ 0 & 0 & 1 & 0 \\ 0 & 0 & 0 & 1 \end{bmatrix}$$

which is the product of a lower and an upper triangular matrix. The block α of the matrix ϵ is now obtained as

$$\alpha = (|\,\Lambda_{t_1-t_2} \circ V_{\tilde{\tau}_1-\tilde{\tau}_2}\,|) \exp[\tilde{t}_2\cdot\bar{t}_1]$$

and similarly, the block β is given by

$$\beta = (|\,\Lambda_{t_2-t_1} \circ V_{\tilde{\tau}_2-\tilde{\tau}_1}\,|) \exp[\tilde{t}_1\cdot\bar{t}_2].$$

Now we compute the determinant of the overlap matrix ϵ. By similar arguments as given for case II, this determinant is the product of the determinants of the 4×4 matrices

$$C = \gamma = I_4 \exp\tilde{t}_1\cdot\bar{t}_1$$

and

$$D = \delta - \alpha\gamma^{-1}\beta = I_4 \exp\tilde{t}_2\cdot\bar{t}_2 - \exp[-\tilde{t}_1\cdot\bar{t}_1]\,\alpha\beta.$$

So the only non-trivial computation to be carried out is to determine the determinant of D from the known matrices α and β as given above. The result is expressible in terms of exponentials and the functions q_m given in definition 8.5.

8.7 Proposition: The determinant of the overlap matrix ϵ for the case III has the value

$$\Delta^{1\,2\ldots 8}_{1\,2\ldots 8} = \exp\left[4\,\tilde{t}_1 \cdot \bar{t}_1 + 4\,\tilde{t}_2 \cdot \bar{t}_2 - 2\,\tilde{t} \cdot \bar{t}\right]$$
$$\{q_6(2\tilde{t} \cdot \bar{t}) + q_6(-2\tilde{t} \cdot \bar{t}) - 4\,q_6(\tilde{t} \cdot \bar{t}) - 4\,q_6(-\tilde{t} \cdot \bar{t})$$
$$- (\tilde{t} \cdot \bar{t})^2\,(q_4(\tilde{t} \cdot \bar{t}) + q_4(-\tilde{t} \cdot \bar{t}))\}$$

8.3 The Normalization Operator for Two-Center Configurations with a Closed Shell and a Simple Composite Particle Configuration

We consider now a specific two-center configuration and the corresponding normalization operator.

At center 2 we take a simple composite system occupied by $\tilde{n}_2 = n_2$ nucleons. At center 1 we assume that all shells of an harmonic oscillator have been filled up to the excitation $\bar{N}_1$. The number of single-particle states at center 1 is $j - 1$ and is related to $\bar{N}_1$ through the added degeneracy of the oscillator levels,

$$j - 1 = \frac{1}{6}(\bar{N}_1 + 1)(\bar{N}_1 + 2)(\bar{N}_1 + 3).$$

Any single-particle state at center 1 is occupied by four nucleons and hence, the total number of nucleons at center 1 is

$$\tilde{n}_1 = n_1 = 4(j - 1).$$

The weight of n associated with the configuration is

$$\tilde{w} = w = (4\ 4 \ldots 4\ n_2) = (4^{j-1}\,n_2).$$

and the only orbital partition which is allowed on physical grounds is

$$f = [4^{j-1}\,n_2].$$

Hence the configuration is of maximal weight both in bra and ket and the Gelfand patterns $\tilde{q}$ and q are of the form given in proposition 3.19,

$$\tilde{q} = q = 4\ 4\ 4\ \ .\ .\ 4$$
$$4\ 4\ 4\ .\ 4$$
$$\cdot\quad\cdot$$
$$4$$

In a short-hand notation, we write the total configuration for $\bar{N}_1 = 0$ as $s^4 + s^{n_2}$, for $\bar{N}_1 = 1$ as $s^4 p^{12} + s^{n_2}$ and for $\bar{N}_1 = 2$ as $s^4 p^{12}(sd)^{24} + s^{n_2}$.

Now we consider the normalization operator for these configurations. This kernel according to section 3.9 is given by the irreducible representation $D^f(\epsilon)$ of the group $GL(j, \mathbb{C})$. For $f = [4^{j-1}\,n_2]$ and highest weights we find from proposition 3.20

$$D^{[4^{j-1}\,n_2]}_{q_{max},\,q_{max}}(\epsilon) = (\Delta^{1\,2\ldots j-1}_{1\,2\ldots j-1})^{4-n_2}\,(\Delta^{1\,2\ldots j}_{1\,2\ldots j})^{n_2}.$$

The matrix ϵ was discussed as case II in section 8.2. Its determinant was obtained as

$$\Delta_{12\cdots j}^{12\cdots j} = \exp\left[(j-1)\tilde{t}_1\cdot\bar{t}_1 + \tilde{t}_2\cdot\bar{t}_2\right]\exp\left[-\tilde{t}\cdot\bar{t}\right] q_{\bar{N}_1+1}(\tilde{t}\cdot\bar{t}).$$

The determinant of the matrix which contains only the first $j-1$ rows and columns of ϵ is just the determinant of the block $\gamma = C$ introduced in section 8.2. This block is a multiple of the unit matrix with determinant

$$\Delta_{12\cdots j-1}^{12\cdots j-1} = \exp\left[(j-1)\tilde{t}_1\cdot\bar{t}_1\right]$$

With these expressions the representation D^f becomes

$$D_{\tilde{q}_{max}\,q_{max}}^{[4^{j-1}\,n_2]}(\epsilon) = \exp\left[4(j-1)\tilde{t}_1\cdot\bar{t}_1 + n_2\tilde{t}_2\cdot\bar{t}_2 - n_2\tilde{t}\cdot\bar{t}\right]\left[q_{\bar{N}_1+1}(\tilde{t}\cdot\bar{t})\right]^{n_2}.$$

The transformation to center coordinates is given by

$$z_1 = \sqrt{n_1}\,t_1 \qquad z_2 = \sqrt{n_2}\,t_2.$$

Now we pass to cluster coordinates $s_1 s_2$ which are given from example 5.2 by

$$s_1 = \left[\frac{n_2}{n}\right]^{1/2} z_1 - \left[\frac{n_1}{n}\right]^{1/2} z_2$$

$$s_2 = \left[\frac{n_1}{n}\right]^{1/2} z_1 + \left[\frac{n_2}{n}\right]^{1/2} z_2.$$

The combination of both transformations yields the identities

$$t_1 - t_2 = [n_1]^{-1/2} z_1 - [n_2]^{-1/2} z_2 = \left[\frac{n_1 n_2}{n}\right]^{-1/2} s_1$$

$$\tilde{t}\cdot\bar{t} = \left(\frac{n_1 n_2}{n}\right)^{-1} \tilde{s}_1\cdot\bar{s}_1$$

and the orthogonality of the transformation gives

$$n_1\tilde{t}_1\cdot\bar{t}_1 + n_2\tilde{t}_2\cdot\bar{t}_2 = \tilde{s}_1\cdot\bar{s}_1 + \tilde{s}_2\cdot\bar{s}_2.$$

These expressions appear in the normalization kernel and allow us to pass to cluster coordinates.

8.8 Proposition: For a configuration of two composite particles with closed shell and simple internal configuration, respectively, the normalization operator in cluster coordinates is given by

$$(\alpha^{4(j-1)+n_2} f\tilde{q} | N(\tilde{s}_1\tilde{s}_2, s_1 s_2) | \alpha^{4(j-1)+n_2} f q) = \exp\left[\tilde{s}_2\cdot\bar{s}_2\right] N(\tilde{s}_1, s_1)$$

where the kernel for the relative motion is

$$N(\tilde{s}_1, s_1) = \exp\left[\left(1 - n_2\frac{n}{n_1 n_2}\right)\tilde{s}_1\cdot\bar{s}_1\right]\left[q_{\bar{N}_1+1}\left(\frac{n}{n_1 n_2}\tilde{s}_1\cdot\bar{s}_1\right)\right]^{n_2}.$$

We proceed now to a more detailed examination of the properties of the operator $N(\widetilde{s}_1, s_1)$. First we derive an auxiliary result:

8.9 Proposition: The powers of the function $q_{m+1}(\xi)$ admit the expansion

$$[q_{m+1}(\xi)]^\lambda = \sum_{\alpha=0}^{\lambda} \sum_{\rho=0}^{m\alpha} \binom{\lambda}{\alpha} (-1)^\alpha \, a(m, \alpha, \rho) \, \xi^\rho \exp(\lambda - \alpha) \, \xi$$

where

$$a(m, \alpha, \rho) = \sum_{\alpha_0 \alpha_1 \cdots \alpha_m} \left\{ \alpha! \, [\alpha_0! \, (1!)^{\alpha_1} \alpha_1! \, (2!)^{\alpha_2} \alpha_2! \ldots (m!)^{\alpha_m} \alpha_m!]^{-1} \right.$$

$$\left. \delta \left(\sum_{i=0}^{m} i\alpha_i, \rho \right) \delta \left(\sum_{i=0}^{m} \alpha_i, \alpha \right) \right\}.$$

Proof: From definition 8.5 one may write

$$q_{m+1}(\xi) = \exp \xi - \sum_{\nu=0}^{m} (\nu!)^{-1} \, \xi^\nu.$$

This expression yields

$$[q_{m+1}(\xi)]^\lambda = \sum_{\alpha=0}^{\lambda} \binom{\lambda}{\alpha} (-1)^\alpha \left(\sum_{\nu=0}^{m} (\nu!)^{-1} \, \xi^\nu \right)^\alpha \exp(\lambda - \alpha) \, \xi.$$

The coefficients $a(m, \alpha, \rho)$ arise from the power

$$\left(\sum_{\nu=0}^{m} (\nu!)^{-1} \, \xi^\nu \right)^\alpha = \sum_{\rho=0}^{m\alpha} a(m, \alpha, \rho) \, \xi^\rho$$

and are seen from a multinomial expansion to have the values given above.   □

Now we are prepared to prove

8.10 Proposition: The normalization operator $N(\widetilde{s}_1, s_1)$ derived in proposition 8.8 has the oscillator states of the relative motion as its eigenstates. The eigenvalues η_N are degenerate and depend only on the total excitation N, they are explicitly given by

$$\eta_N = \sum_{\alpha=0}^{n_2} \sum_{\rho=0}^{\overline{N}_1\alpha} \binom{n_2}{\alpha} a(\overline{N}_1, \alpha, \rho) \frac{N!}{(N-\rho)!} \left(\frac{n}{n_1 n_2} \right)^\rho \left(1 - \alpha \frac{n}{n_1 n_2} \right)^{N-\rho} (-1)^\alpha$$

For $N < n_2(\overline{N}_1 + 1)$ these eigenvalues are equal to zero.

Proof: With the new variables $\xi = \widetilde{s}_1 \cdot \overline{s}_1$ and $\gamma = \dfrac{n}{n_1 n_2}$ the kernel becomes

$$\exp[(1 - n_2\gamma) \xi] \, [q_{\overline{N}_1+1}(\gamma\xi)]^{n_2}$$

$$= \sum_{\alpha=0}^{n_2} \sum_{\rho=0}^{\overline{N}_1\alpha} \binom{n_2}{\alpha} (-1)^\alpha \, a(\overline{N}_1, \alpha, \rho) \, \gamma^\rho \xi^\rho \exp[(1 - \alpha\gamma) \xi]$$

where we used proposition 8.9. With the additional expansion

$$\xi^\rho \exp\left[(1 - \alpha\gamma)\,\xi\right] = \sum_{N=\rho}^{\infty} \left\{\frac{N!}{(N-\rho)!}\,(1 - \alpha\gamma)^{N-\rho}\right\} (N!)^{-1}\,\xi^N$$

one finds

$$\exp\left[(1 - n_2\gamma)\,\xi\right] \left[q_{\overline{N}_1+1}(\gamma\xi)\right]^{n_2} = \sum_{N}^{\infty} \eta_N\,(N!)^{-1}\,\xi^N$$

where η_N has the value given in the proposition 8.10.

Returning now to the original variables we get

$$N(\widetilde{s}_1, s_1) = \sum_{N}^{\infty} \eta_N\,(N!)^{-1}\,(\widetilde{s}_1 \cdot \overline{s}_1)^N = \sum_{N=0}^{\infty} \eta_N \sum_{LM} P_{LM}^N(\widetilde{s}_1)\,\overline{P_{LM}^N(s_1)}$$

where we used proposition 4.34. Clearly this is the eigenfunction expansion of the kernel. To determine those powers for which η_N must be equal to zero we note that the power series of $\left[q_{\overline{N}_1+1}(\xi)\right]^{n_2}$ starts at the power $(\overline{N}_1 + 1)\,n_2$. This power determines the lowest power in the expansion of the full kernel and hence the lowest value of N as $(\overline{N}_1 + 1)\,n_2$. $\square$

The lowest non-vanishing eigenvalue $\eta_{(\overline{N}_1+1)\,n_2}$ is immediately computed by noting that it comes from the lowest power of $\left[q_{\overline{N}_1+1}(\xi)\right]^{n_2}$. This gives

$$\eta_{(\overline{N}_1+1)\,n_2} = \left[\frac{n_1 + n_2}{n_1 n_2}\right]^{n_2(\overline{N}_1+1)} \frac{[n_2(\overline{N}_1 + 1)]!}{[(\overline{N}_1 + 1)!]^{n_2}}$$

where n_1 and $\overline{N}_1$ are related through the added degeneracy of the oscillator levels.

The vanishing of the eigenvalues η_N for the lowest excitation is a direct consequence of the exchange properties of the kernel. The exchange property is recognized in the summation index α appearing in the expansion of $\left[q_{\overline{N}_1+1}(\gamma\xi)\right]^{n_2}$ as given in propositions 8.9 and 8.10. This index ranges from $\alpha = 0$ to $\alpha = n_2$ and may be related to a double coset symbol of the type

$$\left\{ \begin{matrix} n_1 - \alpha & \alpha \\ \alpha & n_2 - \alpha \end{matrix} \right\}$$

which describes the exchange between the two composite particles. The value $\alpha = 0$ corresponds to the "direct" or "no-exchange" term and contributes the value 1 to η_N for N = 0 1 2 ....

The vanishing of the eigenvalues for $N < (\overline{N}_1 + 1)\,n_2$ is in agreement with the reasoning from the shell model which predicts that the additional n_2 particles must at least move into the next higher oscillator shell. The quantitative new feature is the deviation of the normalization operator from a projection operator of the type

$$P(\widetilde{s}_1, \overline{s}_1) = q_{(\overline{N}_1+1)\,n_2}(\widetilde{s}_1 \cdot \overline{s}_1) = \sum_{N=(\overline{N}_1+1)\,n_2}^{\infty} (N!)^{-1}\,(\widetilde{s}_1 \cdot \overline{s}_1)^N$$

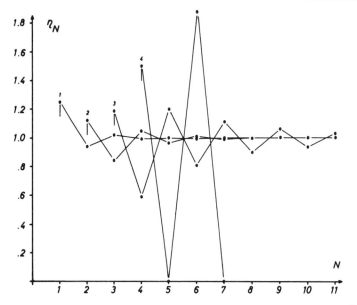

Fig. 8.1 Eigenvalues η_N of the normalization operator for the configuration $s^4 + s^{n_2}$ and $n_2 = 1, 2, 3, 4$ as a function of the relative oscillator excitation N.

which would have all eigenvalues equal to one for $N \geqslant (\bar{N}_1 + 1)\, n_2$. The dependence of the eigenvalues η_N of the normalization operator on the numbers $\bar{N}_1$, n_1 and n_2 is shown in fig. 8.1.

8.4 The Interaction Kernel for Two-Center Configurations with a Closed Shell and a Simple Composite Particle Configuration

The derivation of a condensed analytic expression for the normalization kernel in section 8.3 was based in part on the property that the corresponding representations of the group $GL(j, \mathbb{C})$ were of highest weight. This highest weight property will now again be used to derive simple analytic expressions for the interaction kernels. In section 8.2, we obtained for the overlap matrix ϵ a product form of the type

$$\epsilon = \begin{bmatrix} 1 & 0 \\ A & 1 \end{bmatrix} \begin{bmatrix} C & 0 \\ 0 & D \end{bmatrix} \begin{bmatrix} 1 & B \\ 0 & 1 \end{bmatrix}.$$

In case II the second factor is a diagonal matrix. Now we employ proposition 3.34 for the orbital reduced matrix elements and take

$$\epsilon_1 = \begin{bmatrix} 1 & 0 \\ A & 1 \end{bmatrix} \quad \epsilon_2 = \begin{bmatrix} C & 0 \\ 0 & D \end{bmatrix} \begin{bmatrix} 1 & B \\ 0 & 1 \end{bmatrix}.$$

8.11 Proposition: For upper (lower) triangular matrices, the irreducible representations of $GL(j, \mathbb{C})$ obey

$$D^f_{\tilde{q}, q_{max}}\left(\begin{bmatrix} 1 & B \\ 0 & 1 \end{bmatrix}\right) = \delta_{\tilde{q}, q_{max}}$$

$$D^f_{q_{max}, q'}\left(\begin{bmatrix} 1 & 0 \\ A & 1 \end{bmatrix}\right) = \delta_{q_{max}, q'}.$$

Proof: Consider the Gelfand polynomial of highest weight given in proposition 3.20. If the matrix z is replaced by

$$z' = \begin{vmatrix} 1 & B \\ 0 & 1 \end{vmatrix} z$$

all determinants $\Delta^{12\cdots i}_{12\cdots i}$ retain their original value due to the triangular form of the matrix. Hence the Gelfand polynomial of highest weight is invariant under this transformation. A similar proof applies upon multiplication with a lower triangular matrix from the right.   □

We are now prepared to prove

8.12 Proposition: The orbital interaction kernel in a two-center configuration is given by

$$(\alpha^n f(f'f'') \tilde{q} \| T(2) \| \alpha^n f(f'f'') q)$$

$$= |f'|^{1/2} \sum_{q'q''} \{\langle fq|f'q'f''q''\rangle \{\alpha^2 f''q'' \| T(2) \| \alpha^2 f''q''\}\langle f'q'f''q''|fq\rangle\}$$

$$D^f_{q_{max} q_{max}}(\epsilon)$$

where

$$\{\alpha^2 f''q'' \| T(2) \| \alpha^2 f''q''\} = \sum_{\tilde{q}''\tilde{q}''} D^{f''}_{q''\tilde{q}}(\epsilon_1^{-1})(\alpha^2 f''\tilde{\tilde{q}}'' \| T(2) \| \alpha^2 f''\tilde{q}'') D^{f''}_{\tilde{q}''q''}(\epsilon_2^{-1})$$

and

$$\epsilon_1 = \begin{bmatrix} 1 & 0 \\ A & 1 \end{bmatrix} \quad \epsilon_2 = \begin{bmatrix} C & 0 \\ 0 & D \end{bmatrix}\begin{bmatrix} 1 & B \\ 0 & 1 \end{bmatrix}.$$

Proof: We start from the expression for the reduced matrix elements given in proposition 3.34. From proposition 8.11 we know that the triangular transformations do not affect the highest weight states. When the first diagonal matrix factor of the matrix ϵ_2 is applied to a highest weight state, it yields a scalar factor times the highest weight state. This factor must coincide with $D^f_{q_{max}, q_{max}}(\epsilon)$ since the matrix ϵ is the product of ϵ_1 and ϵ_2. Hence, it follows that

$$D^f_{q_{max}q'}(\epsilon_1) = \delta(q_{max}, q')$$

$$D^f_{\tilde{q}q_{max}}(\epsilon_2) = \delta(\tilde{q}, q_{max}) D^f_{q_{max}q_{max}}\left(\begin{bmatrix} C & 0 \\ 0 & D \end{bmatrix}\right)$$

and the last factor is just the matrix element of $D^f(\epsilon)$ which underlies the normalization kernel. The use of these values in proposition 3.34 yields the simplified expressions given above.   □

The expression derived in proposition 8.12 has a number of remarkable features. We avoid completely the computation of the representation $D^{f'}(\epsilon)$ and instead need only the much simpler representation $D^{f''}$ for $f'' = [2]$ or $[11]$. These representations were determined in section 3.4. The inversion of the matrices ϵ_1 and ϵ_2 offers no problem because of their triangular properties. For the interaction operator, we may introduce the reduced two-body density operator discussed in section 5.4. Its matrix elements up to the p-shell were derived in section 5.4. So the only algebraic coefficients needed in the computation are the fractional parentage coefficients. These coefficients are collected in Table 8.1. For the special case $n_2 = 4$ the computation is greatly simplified on the basis of proposition 8.14 derived in section 8.5. The following example illustrates the procedure for the simplest possible configuration.

Example 8.1: The configuration $s^4 + s^{n_2}$

The number of states is $j = 2$ and the overlap matrix has the form

$$\epsilon = \begin{bmatrix} \epsilon_{11} & \epsilon_{12} \\ \epsilon_{21} & \epsilon_{22} \end{bmatrix} = \begin{bmatrix} 1 & 0 \\ \epsilon_{11}^{-1}\epsilon_{21} & 1 \end{bmatrix} \begin{bmatrix} \epsilon_{11} & 0 \\ 0 & \epsilon_{11}^{-1}\Delta_{12}^{12} \end{bmatrix} \begin{bmatrix} 1 & \epsilon_{11}^{-1}\epsilon_{12} \\ 0 & 1 \end{bmatrix} .$$

The matrices ϵ_1, ϵ_2 and their inverses are given by

$$\epsilon_1 = \begin{bmatrix} 1 & 0 \\ \epsilon_{11}^{-1}\epsilon_{21} & 1 \end{bmatrix} \qquad \epsilon_1^{-1} = \begin{bmatrix} 1 & 0 \\ -\epsilon_{11}^{-1}\epsilon_{21} & 1 \end{bmatrix}$$

$$\epsilon_2 = \begin{bmatrix} \epsilon_{11} & \epsilon_{12} \\ 0 & \epsilon_{11}^{-1}\Delta_{12}^{12} \end{bmatrix} \qquad \epsilon_2^{-1} = \begin{bmatrix} \epsilon_{11}^{-1} & -\epsilon_{12}(\Delta_{12}^{12})^{-1} \\ 0 & \epsilon_{11}(\Delta_{12}^{12})^{-1} \end{bmatrix}$$

Now we evaluate the matrices $D^{f''}$ for ϵ_1^{-1} and ϵ_2^{-1}. The representation $D^{[2]}$ of $GL(2, \mathbb{C})$ is three-dimensional and we label its rows and columns by the index pairs 11, 12 and 22. From the general expression given in section 3.4 we have

		11	12	22
$D^{[2]}(\epsilon):$	11	$\epsilon_{11}\epsilon_{11}$	$\sqrt{2}\,\epsilon_{11}\epsilon_{12}$	$\epsilon_{12}\epsilon_{12}$
	12	$\sqrt{2}\,\epsilon_{11}\epsilon_{21}$	$\epsilon_{11}\epsilon_{22} + \epsilon_{12}\epsilon_{21}$	$\sqrt{2}\,\epsilon_{12}\epsilon_{22}$
	22	$\epsilon_{21}\epsilon_{21}$	$\sqrt{2}\,\epsilon_{21}\epsilon_{22}$	$\epsilon_{22}\epsilon_{22}$

This yields in the two special cases

$$D^{[2]}(\epsilon_1^{-1}) = \begin{bmatrix} 1 & 0 & 0 \\ -\sqrt{2}\,\epsilon_{11}^{-1}\epsilon_{21} & 1 & 0 \\ \epsilon_{11}^{-2}\epsilon_{21}^2 & -\sqrt{2}\,\epsilon_{11}^{-1}\epsilon_{21} & 1 \end{bmatrix}$$

$$D^{[2]}(\epsilon_2^{-1}) = \begin{bmatrix} \epsilon_{11}^{-2} & -\sqrt{2}\,\epsilon_{12}\epsilon_{11}^{-1}(\Delta_{12}^{12})^{-1} & \epsilon_{12}^2(\Delta_{12}^{12})^{-2} \\ 0 & (\Delta_{12}^{12})^{-1} & -\sqrt{2}\,\epsilon_{12}\epsilon_{11}(\Delta_{12}^{12})^{-2} \\ 0 & 0 & \epsilon_{11}^2(\Delta_{12}^{12})^{-2} \end{bmatrix} .$$

Table 8.1 The squared 9f symbols needed for the fractional parentage coefficients of the configuration $[4^{j-2}\,4\,n_2]$. The integers j and n_2 take the values $j \geqslant 2$, $n_2 = 1\ 2\ 3\ 4$.

Squared $9f$ *symbol*	*Ranges of* j *and* n_2
$\begin{bmatrix} 4^{j-2}\,4\,n_2 & 4^{j-2}\,4 & n_2 \\ 4^{j-2}\,4\,n_2-2 & 4^{j-2}\,2 & n_2 \\ 2 & 2 & 0 \end{bmatrix}^2 = \dfrac{1}{6}\dfrac{n_2(n_2-1)}{(6-n_2)(5-n_2)}$	$j \geqslant 2$ $n_2 = 2\ 3\ 4$
$\begin{bmatrix} 4^{j-2}\,4\,n_2 & 4^{j-2}\,4 & n_2 \\ 4^{j-2}\,4\,n_2-2 & 4^{j-2}\,3 & n_2-1 \\ 2 & 1 & 1 \end{bmatrix}^2 = \dfrac{1}{4}\dfrac{(n_2-1)}{(6-n_2)}$	$j \geqslant 2$ $n_2 = 2\ 3\ 4$
$\begin{bmatrix} 4^{j-2}\,4\,n_2 & 4^{j-2}\,4 & n_2 \\ 4^{j-2}\,4\,n_2-2 & 4^{j-2}\,4 & n_2-2 \\ 2 & 0 & 2 \end{bmatrix}^2 = 1$	$j \geqslant 2$ $n_2 = 2\ 3\ 4$
$\begin{bmatrix} 4^{j-2}\,4\,n_2 & 4^{j-2}\,4 & n_2 \\ 4^{j-2}\,3\,n_2\mp1 & 4^{j-2}\,2 & n_2 \\ 2 & 2 & 0 \end{bmatrix}^2 = \dfrac{5}{6}\dfrac{n_2}{(6-n_2)}$	$j \geqslant 2$ $n_2 = 1\ 2\ 3$
$\begin{bmatrix} 4^{j-2}\,4\,n_2 & 4^{j-2}\,4 & n_2 \\ 4^{j-2}\,3\,n_2-1 & 4^{j-2}\,3 & n_2-1 \\ 2 & 1 & 1 \end{bmatrix}^2 = \dfrac{5}{8}\dfrac{(4-n_2)}{(6-n_2)}$	$j \geqslant 2$ $n_2 = 1\ 2\ 3$
$\begin{bmatrix} 4^{j-2}\,4\,n_2 & 4^{j-2}\,4 & n_2 \\ 4^{j-2}\,2\,n_2 & 4^{j-2}\,2 & n_2 \\ 2 & 2 & 0 \end{bmatrix}^2 = \dfrac{5}{3}\dfrac{(3-n_2)}{(5-n_2)}$	$j \geqslant 2$ $n_2 = 1\ 2$
$\begin{bmatrix} 4^{j-2}\,4\,n_2 & 4^{j-2}\,4 & n_2 \\ 4^{j-2}\,3\,n_2-1 & 4^{j-3}\,3\,3 & n_2 \\ 1\,1 & 1\,1 & 0 \end{bmatrix}^2 = \dfrac{1}{2}\dfrac{n_2}{(6-n_2)}$	$j \geqslant 3$ $n_2 = 1\ 2\ 3\ 4$
$\begin{bmatrix} 4^{j-2}\,4\,n_2 & 4^{j-2}\,4 & n_2 \\ 4^{j-2}\,3\,n_2-1 & 4^{j-2}\,3 & n_2-1 \\ 1\,1 & 1 & 1 \end{bmatrix}^2 = \dfrac{5}{8}$	$j \geqslant 2$ $n_2 = 1\ 2\ 3\ 4$
$\begin{bmatrix} 4^{j-2}\,4\,n_2 & 4^{j-2}\,4 & n_2 \\ 4^{j-3}\,3\,3\,n_2 & 4^{j-3}\,3\,3 & n_2 \\ 1\,1 & 1\,1 & 0 \end{bmatrix}^2 = \dfrac{3}{2}\dfrac{(4-n_2)}{(6-n_2)}$	$j \geqslant 3$ $n_2 = 1\ 2\ 3$

In a similar fashion one finds for the one-dimensional representation $D^{[11]}$

$$D^{[11]}(\epsilon_1^{-1}) = 1$$

$$D^{[11]}(\epsilon_2^{-1}) = (\Delta_{12}^{12})^{-1}$$

The inverse powers of the determinant Δ_{12}^{12} appearing in these expressions are no problem since these expressions are multiplied by

$$D_{q_{max} q_{max}}^{[4 n_2]}(\epsilon) = (\epsilon_{11})^{4-n_2} (\Delta_{12}^{12})^{n_2}.$$

We need now the fractional parentage coefficients of $GL(2, \mathbb{C})$ for this configuration. These coefficients are just the ordinary Wigner coefficients of the group $U(2)$ or $SU(2)$. The correspondence between the notation in terms of a Gelfand pattern and of an angular momentum j with component m is given by

$$
\begin{matrix}
f_1 \; f_2 & j = \dfrac{1}{2}(f_1 - f_2) \\
 \\
w_1 & m = w_1 - \dfrac{1}{2}(f_1 + f_2).
\end{matrix}
$$

We obtain the correspondence

$$\left\langle \begin{matrix} f_1' f_2' & f_1'' f_2'' \\ w_1' & w_1'' \end{matrix} \;\middle|\; \begin{matrix} f_1 f_2 \\ w_1 \end{matrix} \right\rangle = \langle j'm' \, j''m'' | jm \rangle.$$

For the special configurations we have $f = [4 n_2]$ and $w_1 = 4$. For even interactions we have $f'' = [20]$ and hence $j'' = 1$, $m'' = w_1'' - 1$. The corresponding Wigner coefficients are given in terms of 3j symbols by Edmonds [ED 57, p. 45], and read

$$
\left\langle \begin{matrix} f_1' f_2' & 2 \; 0 \\ w_1' & w_1'' \end{matrix} \;\middle|\; \begin{matrix} 4 \; n_2 \\ 4 \end{matrix} \right\rangle
$$
$$
= (-1)^{q-w_1''+1} \left| \frac{(4 - n_2 + 1)! \, (q + 1)! \, (4 - n_2 + q - w_1'' + 1)! \, w_1''!}{(4 - n_2 + q + 2)! \, (1 - q)! \, (4 - n_2 + q - 1)! \, (q + w_1'' - 1)! \, (2 - w_1'')!} \right|^{1/2}
$$

where we defined $q = \dfrac{1}{2}(f_1' - f_2' - f_1 + f_2)$ and q takes the values $q = 1, 0, -1$. The three possibilities $w_1'' = 2, 1, 0$ correspond to the index pairs $11, 12, 22$ in the matrices given above, and the Wigner coefficients for these three cases become

$$
\left\langle \begin{matrix} f_1' f_2' & 2 \; 0 \\ 2 & 2 \end{matrix} \;\middle|\; \begin{matrix} 4 \; n_2 \\ 4 \end{matrix} \right\rangle = (-1)^{q+1} \left[\frac{(4 - n_2 + 1)! \, 2}{(4 - n_2 + q + 2)! \, (1 - q)!} \right]^{1/2}
$$

$$
\left\langle \begin{matrix} f_1' f_2' & 2 \; 0 \\ 3 & 1 \end{matrix} \;\middle|\; \begin{matrix} 4 \; n_2 \\ 4 \end{matrix} \right\rangle = (-1)^{q} \left[\frac{(4 - n_2 + 1)! \, (4 - n_2 + q) \, (q + 1)}{(4 - n_2 + q + 2)! \, (1 - q)!} \right]^{1/2}
$$

$$
\left\langle \begin{matrix} f_1' f_2' & 2 \; 0 \\ 4 & 0 \end{matrix} \;\middle|\; \begin{matrix} 4 \; n_2 \\ 4 \end{matrix} \right\rangle = (-1)^{q+1} \left[\frac{(4 - n_2 + 1)! \, (4 - n_2 + q) \, (4 - n_2 + q + 1) \, q(q + 1)}{(4 - n_2 + q + 2)! \, (1 - q)! \, 2} \right]^{1/2}
$$

For odd interactions we have $f'' = [11]$ and hence $j'' = 0$ which implies $j' = j$. There is a single Wigner coefficient given by

$$\left\langle \begin{array}{ccc} 3 & n_2 - 1 & 1\ 1 \\ & 3 & 1 \end{array} \Bigg| \begin{array}{c} 4\ n_2 \\ 4 \end{array} \right\rangle = \langle jm\ 00 | jm \rangle = 1.$$

With these expressions one gets the general form of the interaction operator in terms of the single-particle overlaps ϵ_{il} and the two-body matrix elements. The analytic form of these overlaps and of the two-body matrix elements were given in section 7.3 and allow us to complete the computation of the interaction operator in analytic form.

We give now an explanation for the use of Table 8.1. The fractional parentage coefficients for the orbital partition $f = [4^{j-1} n_2]$ and the Gelfand pattern of maximum weight may be expressed with the help of reduced Wigner coefficients as

$$\langle f'q'\ f''q'' | [4^{j-1} n_2]\ q_{max} \rangle$$

$$= \left\langle \begin{array}{cc} f' & f'' \\ f'_{j-1} & f''_{j-1} \end{array} \Bigg| \begin{array}{c} 4^{j-1} n_2 \\ 4^{j-1} \end{array} \right\rangle$$

$$\langle f'_{j-1} q'_{j-1} f'' q''_{j-1} | 4^{j-1} q_{j-1\ max} \rangle.$$

The square of the second Wigner coefficient of the group $GL(j - 1, \mathbb{C})$ is given from section 3.6 and proposition 3.10 by

$$\langle f'_{j-1} q'_{j-1} f'' q''_{j-1} | 4^{j-1} q_{j-1\ max} \rangle^2 = \dim^{-1}(f'', j-1)$$

$$= \begin{cases} \left(\frac{1}{2}(j-1)j \right)^{-1} & \text{for} \quad f'' = [2] \\ \left(\frac{1}{2}(j-1)(j-2) \right)^{-1} & \text{for} \quad f'' = [11]. \end{cases}$$

The first factor is the reduced Wigner coefficient and is related from proposition 3.29' to a 9f symbol as

$$\left\langle \begin{array}{cc} f' & f'' \\ f'_{j-1} & f''_{j-1} \end{array} \Bigg| \begin{array}{c} 4^{j-1} n_2 \\ 4^{j-1} \end{array} \right\rangle$$

$$= \lambda^{-1}_{[4^{j-1} n_2]} \lambda_{f'} \lambda_{f''} \lambda_{[4^{j-1}]} \lambda^{-1}_{f'_{j-1}} \lambda^{-1}_{f''_{j-1}} \left[\frac{w_j!}{w'_j!\ w''_j!} \right]^{1/2}$$

$$\begin{bmatrix} 4^{j-1} n_2 & 4^{j-1} & w_j \\ f' & f'_{j-1} & w'_j \\ f'' & f''_{j-1} & w''_j \end{bmatrix}$$

where now $w_j = n_2$. The factors λ are easily calculated from proposition 2.56. In Table 8.1, we give the values of the squares for the 9 possible 9f symbols for all possible pairs $f'f''$ and for $n_2 = 1\ 2\ 3\ 4$. These values do not depend on the number j and therefore apply to the three configurations $s^4 + s^{n_2}$, $s^4 p^{12} + s^{n_2}$ and $s^4 p^{12} (sd)^{24} + s^{n_2}$ which cover the interaction of ^{4}He, ^{16}O and ^{40}Ca with a single nucleon, ^{2}H, ^{3}H or ^{3}He and ^{4}He.

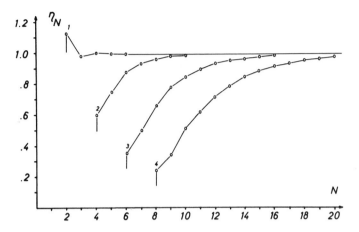

Fig. 8.2 Eigenvalues η_N of the normalization operator for the configuration $s^4 p^{12} + s^{n_2}$ and $n_2 = 1, 2,$ 3, 4 as a function of the relative oscillator excitation N.

8.5 Two Composite Particles with Closed-Shell Configurations

As an example of a system with two complex composite particles we take the configuration $s^4 p^{12} + s^4 p^{12}$ which describes the dynamics of two ^{16}O nuclei in the internal oscillator shell approximation. The overlap matrix ϵ and its determinant were computed as case III of section 8.2. The determinant was found to be

$$\Delta_{1\,2\ldots 8}^{1\,2\ldots 8} = \exp[4\,\tilde{t}_1 \cdot \bar{t}_1 + 4\,\tilde{t}_2 \cdot \bar{t}_2 - 2\,\tilde{t} \cdot \bar{t}]$$
$$[q_6(2\tilde{t} \cdot \bar{t}) + q_6(-2\tilde{t} \cdot \bar{t}) - 4\,q_6(\tilde{t} \cdot \bar{t}) - 4\,q_6(-\tilde{t} \cdot \bar{t})$$
$$- (\tilde{t} \cdot \bar{t})^2\, q_4(\tilde{t} \cdot \bar{t}) - (\tilde{t} \cdot \bar{t})^2\, q_4(-\tilde{t} \cdot \bar{t})].$$

We pass to cluster coordinates by noting that for $n_1 = n_2 = 16$

$$\tilde{t}_1 \cdot \bar{t}_1 + \tilde{t}_2 \cdot \bar{t}_1 = \frac{1}{16}(\tilde{s}_1 \cdot \bar{s}_1) + \frac{1}{16}\tilde{s}_2 \cdot \bar{s}_2$$

and

$$\tilde{t} \cdot \bar{t} = (\tilde{t}_2 - \tilde{t}_1) \cdot (\bar{t}_2 - \bar{t}_1) = \frac{1}{8}\tilde{s}_1 \cdot \bar{s}_1$$

The corresponding substitutions yield

$$\Delta_{1\,2\ldots 8}^{1\,2\ldots 8} = \exp\left[\frac{1}{4}\tilde{s}_2 \cdot \bar{s}_2\right]$$
$$\left[q_6\left(\frac{1}{4}\tilde{s}_1 \cdot \bar{s}_1\right) + q_6\left(-\frac{1}{4}\tilde{s}_1 \cdot \bar{s}_1\right) - 4\,q_6\left(\frac{1}{8}\tilde{s}_1 \cdot \bar{s}_1\right) - 4\,q_6\left(-\frac{1}{8}\tilde{s}_1 \cdot \bar{s}_1\right)\right.$$
$$\left. - \frac{1}{64}(\tilde{s}_1 \cdot \bar{s}_1)^2\, q_4\left(\frac{1}{8}\tilde{s}_1 \cdot \bar{s}_1\right) - \frac{1}{64}(\tilde{s}_1 \cdot \bar{s}_1)^2\, q_4\left(-\frac{1}{8}\tilde{s}_1 \cdot \bar{s}_1\right)\right]$$

The orbital partition is $f = [4^8]$ and the normalization kernel is given by

$$D^{[4^8]}_{q_{max} \, q_{max}} (\epsilon) = (\Delta^{1\,2\,\cdots\,8}_{1\,2\,\cdots\,8})^4$$

Substitution of the determinant yields, after dropping the center-of-mass term $\exp[\tilde{s}_2 \cdot \bar{s}_2]$,

8.13 Proposition: The normalization kernel for the configuration $s^4 p^{12} + s^4 p^{12}$ is given by

$$(\alpha^{32} [4^8] \, q_{max} \, | \, N(s_1, \bar{s}_1) | \, \alpha^{32} [4^8] \, q_{max})$$

$$= \left[q_6 \left(\frac{1}{4} \tilde{s}_1 \cdot \bar{s}_1 \right) + q_6 \left(-\frac{1}{4} \tilde{s}_1 \cdot \bar{s}_1 \right) - 4 q_6 \left(\frac{1}{8} \tilde{s}_1 \cdot \bar{s}_1 \right) - 4 q_6 \left(-\frac{1}{8} \tilde{s}_1 \cdot \bar{s}_1 \right) \right.$$

$$\left. - \frac{1}{64} (\tilde{s}_1 \cdot \bar{s}_1)^2 \, q_4 \left(\frac{1}{8} \tilde{s}_1 \cdot \bar{s}_1 \right) - \frac{1}{64} (\tilde{s}_1 \cdot \bar{s}_1)^2 \, q_4 \left(-\frac{1}{8} \tilde{s}_1 \cdot \bar{s}_1 \right) \right]^4 .$$

We first discuss the exchange contributions appearing in this kernel. If we consider for the moment the determinant itself, it describes a system which could be denoted as $sp^3 + sp^3$ and would not correspond to a configuration of interest in nuclear physics. Nevertheless, the exchange decomposition of this system can be recognized in the expression for the determinant. The individual terms are associated with the double coset symbols

$$\begin{Bmatrix} 4 & 0 \\ 0 & 4 \end{Bmatrix} \begin{Bmatrix} 0 & 4 \\ 4 & 0 \end{Bmatrix} \begin{Bmatrix} 3 & 1 \\ 1 & 3 \end{Bmatrix} \begin{Bmatrix} 1 & 3 \\ 3 & 1 \end{Bmatrix} \begin{Bmatrix} 2 & 2 \\ 2 & 2 \end{Bmatrix}$$

in that order with two terms for the last symbol. The determinant itself has in its expansion only even powers of $\tilde{t} \cdot \bar{t}$ which implies that only even oscillator states would yield non-vanishing eigenvalues of the kernel. Returning now to the physical configuration $s^4 p^{12} + s^4 p^{12}$, the exchange decomposition would be obtained upon writing out the fourth power of the determinant in full detail. We shall not do this here but note that, from the definition of the function q, the first two terms when raised to the fourth power contribute exponential terms of the form

$$\exp [\pm \tilde{s}_1 \cdot \bar{s}_1]$$

which correspond to the double coset symbols

$$\begin{Bmatrix} 16 & 0 \\ 0 & 16 \end{Bmatrix} \begin{Bmatrix} 0 & 16 \\ 16 & 0 \end{Bmatrix}$$

respectively.

By carrying out a full expansion of the kernel in the form

$$N'(\tilde{s}_1, \bar{s}_1) = \sum_{N = \underline{N}}^{\infty} \eta_N \frac{(\tilde{s}_1 \cdot \bar{s}_1)^N}{N!}$$

we obtain the eigenstates and eigenvalues of the normalization kernel. First of all, we note that $\underline{N} = 24$ since we are taking the fourth power of a series starting at the sixth power.

Note that this minimal excitation is four units of $\hbar\omega$ higher than a simple shell-model estimate. In this estimate, one would argue that the lowest overall configuration of 32 nucleons at a single center must have $1 \cdot 3 \cdot 4 + 2 \cdot 16 = 44$ units of $\hbar\omega$ corresponding to the configuration $s^4 p^{12} (sd)^{16}$. Subtracting from this number twice the internal oscillator excitation of two $s^4 p^{12}$ configurations one arrives at the estimate

$$N_{min} = 44 - 2 \cdot 12 = 20$$

for the lowest excitation of the relative motion. If the orbital symmetry and $U(3)$ symmetry in the sd-shell are taken into account, it is found that the configuration $s^4 p^{12} (sd)^{16}$ can not accommodate the orbital partition $f = [4^8]$. The conclusion for the physics of the $^{16}O + {}^{16}O$ system is that the lowest shell model states of ^{32}S are not accessible through the collision in this channel. The argument depends on the assumption of fixed internal states and would no longer be valid if these internal states would be deformed in the near collision region.

The full normalization kernel has non-vanishing eigenvalues only for even oscillator states of the relative motion. The lowest eigenvalues are easily computed, they are given by

$$\eta_{24} = 0,006336$$
$$\eta_{26} = 0,030030$$
$$\eta_{28} = 0,080780.$$

For large N, the no-exchange and the 16-nucleon exchange term dominate and the eigenvalues approach the value 2 for even N.

We now turn to the interaction operator for the system $s^4 p^{12} + s^4 p^{12}$. We have highest weight configurations and hence can apply proposition 8.12 to this configuration. The matrices ϵ_1 and ϵ_2 may be chosen as

$$\epsilon_1 = \begin{bmatrix} 1 & 0 \\ A & 1 \end{bmatrix} \quad \epsilon_2 = \begin{bmatrix} C & 0 \\ 0 & D \end{bmatrix} \begin{bmatrix} 1 & B \\ 0 & 1 \end{bmatrix}$$

with blocks which were explicitly given under case III in section 8.2. The present configuration with respect to the group $GL(8, \mathbb{C})$ is extremely simple since it corresponds to a single block partition $f = [4^8]$. The Wigner coefficients are simply given from the remarks following proposition 3.25' by

$$\langle f'q'f''q'' \,|\, [4^8] \, q_{max} \rangle = (\pm 1) \, \dim^{-1/2} ([f''], 8).$$

Since the square of the coefficient appears, the sign is of no importance. Insertion of these Wigner coefficients leads to

8.14 Proposition: The interaction operator for the configuration $f = [4^j]$ is given by

$$(\alpha^n [4^j] \, (f'f'') \, q_{max} \,\|\, T(2) \,\|\, \alpha^n [4^j] \, (f'f'') \, q_{max}) = |f'|^{-1/2} \dim^{-1} (f'', j) \, (\Delta^{1\,2\,\cdots\,j}_{1\,2\,\cdots\,j})^4$$

$$\sum_{\tilde{q}''\tilde{\tilde{q}}''} D^{f''}_{\tilde{q}''\tilde{\tilde{q}}''}(\epsilon^{-1}) \, (\alpha^2 f'' \tilde{\tilde{q}}'' \,\|\, T(2) \,\|\, \alpha^2 f'' \tilde{\tilde{q}}'').$$

Proof: We start with the expression given in proposition 8.12. Since the product of Wigner coefficients as given above does not depend on the labels q'', their product may be taken in front of the sum. The sum over q'' yields

$$\sum_{q''} \{\alpha^2 f'' q'' \| T(2) \| \alpha^2 f'' q''\}$$

$$= \sum_{\tilde{q}'' \tilde{\tilde{q}}'' q''} D^{f''}_{q'' \tilde{q}''}(\epsilon_1^{-1})\,(\alpha^2 f'' \tilde{\tilde{q}}'' \| T(2) \| \alpha^2 f'' \tilde{q}'')\, D^{f''}_{\tilde{q}'' q''}(\epsilon_2^{-1})q$$

$$= \sum_{\tilde{q}'' \tilde{\tilde{q}}''} D^{f''}_{\tilde{\tilde{q}}'' \tilde{q}}((\epsilon_1 \epsilon_2)^{-1})\,(\alpha^2 f'' \tilde{\tilde{q}} \| T(2) \| \alpha^2 f'' \tilde{q}'').$$

and since $\epsilon = \epsilon_1 \epsilon_2$ we get the result.   □

Proposition 8.14 was derived in a slightly different way in section 3.11. The result of proposition 3.35 is recovered upon writing

$$D^{f''}_{\tilde{q}'' \tilde{q}}(\epsilon^{-1}) = D^{f''}_{\tilde{q}'' \tilde{q}''}(^{t}\epsilon^{-1}) = (\Delta^{1\,2\,\cdots\,j}_{1\,2\,\cdots\,j})^{-2}\, D^{f''}_{\tilde{q}'' \tilde{q}''}(\beta).$$

Proposition 8.14 applies in particular to the configuration $s^4 p^{12} + s^4 p^{12}$ with $j = 8$. The explicit expressions were given in general in section 3.11 and we shall not repeat them here. The matrix β is obtained from the algebraic complements of the matrix ϵ. Alternatively, the matrix ϵ^{-1} may be directly computed from the factorized form of ϵ.

8.6 Two-Center Configurations with an Open Shell and a Simple Composite-Particle Configuration

As an example of a configuration where one composite particle has an internal open-shell structure we consider the configuration $s^4 p^b + s^4$. There are five single-particles states and we are dealing with the group $GL(5, \mathbb{C})$. The orbital partition at the first center may be taken as $f_1 = [4 h_1 h_2 h_3]$ where $h = [h_1 h_2 h_3]$ is the orbital partition in the p-shell for the configuration p^b. The new point in the analysis is that we do not want to use the Gelfand pattern to characterize the states in the p-shell. Rather we would like to introduce the orbital angular momentum L with component M at center 1. Expressed in terms of representations of groups, we would like to introduce the group $SO(3, \mathbb{R})$ as the sub-group of the unitary group $U(3)$ associated with the oscillator states in the p-shell. The states characterized in this fashion have the form

$$|\alpha^b [h_1 h_2 h_3]\, \Omega\, LM\rangle$$

where the label Ω serves to distinguish between repeated values of the orbital angular momentum. Note that these states can in principle be expanded in terms of Gelfand states for the p-shell. For the full group $GL(5, \mathbb{C})$ the representations inherit their labels from the unitary subgroup $U(5)$. Therefore, what we have to do is to replace the Gelfand label q by an index scheme containing the representation $[h_1 h_2 h_3]$ of the group $U(3)$ and the angular momentum. We are at liberty to start at center 1 with the states in the p-shell.

Then, the new label for the representations of the group $GL(5, \mathbb{C})$ takes the form

$$
\begin{array}{ccc}
4 & h_1 & h_2 & h_3 \\
h_1 & h_2 & h_3 & = q \\
\Omega & L & M &
\end{array}
$$

where we generalized the meaning of the letter q. This leads to

8.15 Proposition: The normalization kernel for the configuration $s^4 p^b + s^4$ is given by

$$
(\alpha^{8+b} [4\,4\,h_1 h_2 h_3] \, \tilde{q} \,|\, N(\tilde{t}_1 \tilde{t}_2, t_1 t_2)|\, \alpha^{8+b} [4\,4\,h_1 h_2 h_3] \, q) = D_{\tilde{q}q}^{[4\,4\,h_1 h_2 h_3]}(\epsilon)
$$

where the labels $\tilde{q}, q$ are of the form

$$
\tilde{q} = \begin{array}{ccc}
4 & h_1 & h_2 & h_3 \\
h_1 & h_2 & h_3 \\
\tilde{\Omega} & \tilde{L} & \tilde{M}
\end{array}
\qquad
q = \begin{array}{ccc}
4 & h_1 & h_2 & h_3 \\
h_1 & h_2 & h_3 \\
\Omega & L & M
\end{array}
$$

and $\epsilon \in GL(5, \mathbb{C})$ is the overlap matrix given in case I of section 8.2.

The procedure for the computation of this expression depends on the specific configuration. In principle, the computation is possible through the use of the Gelfand scheme and an appropriate transformation to the present scheme. In practice, one would like to have more direct methods. One important observation in this respect is the fact that the matrix ϵ has an extremely simple and almost diagonal form. The computation of the interaction kernel follows in principle the same steps as before. The fractional parentage coefficients must now be taken in the new labelling scheme based on angular momentum. Although the computations are more involved, they do not require new tools beyond the ones known from the oscillator shell model. The results of the analysis go of course beyond the shell model which is usually considered at a single center.

Now we construct the explicit form of the normalization operator for the special case where $h = [h_1 h_2 h_3] = [b\,0\,0]$. In this case, we need no label Ω and the orbital angular momentum is given by

$$
L = b, \quad b-2, \ldots \begin{cases} 0 \\ 1 \end{cases}.
$$

In example 3.1 of section 3.8 we gave the algebraic form of $D^f(\epsilon)$ for the representation $f = [4\,4\,b\,0\,0]$ of $GL(5, \mathbb{C})$, based on the bordered decomposition according to proposition 3.30. If now we introduce, with respect to the subgroup $GL(3, \mathbb{C})$, instead of the Gelfand labels $\tilde{q}_3, q_3$ the orbital angular momenta

$$
\tilde{q}_3 \rightarrow \tilde{L}\tilde{M}, \quad q_3 \rightarrow LM,
$$

the form of $D^f(\epsilon)$ in this scheme is obtained by introducing instead of the term

$$
(s_3!)^{-1} (\epsilon_{35})^{s_3} (\epsilon_{53})^{s_3}
$$

with $s_3 = k_{35} = k_{53}$ the sum

$$\sum_{L'M'\widetilde{L}''\widetilde{M}''L''M''} \{\langle b\widetilde{L}\widetilde{M}|a_3 L'M's_3\widetilde{L}''\widetilde{M}''\rangle P^{s_3}_{\widetilde{L}''\widetilde{M}''\cdot}(\epsilon_{15}\epsilon_{25}\epsilon_{35})$$

$$P^{s_3}_{\cdot L''M''}(\epsilon_{51}\epsilon_{52}\epsilon_{53}) \langle a_3 L'M's_3 L''M''|bLM\rangle\}$$

Here the coefficients are the Wigner coefficients of the group $U(3)$ in the chain $U(3) > SO(3, \mathbb{R})$ corresponding to the angular momentum reduction discussed in section 4.6, and the polynomials are the single-particle oscillator states with angular momentum given in proposition 4.31 of section 4.6. Since the analytic form of the overlaps ϵ was derived under case I of section 8.1, we may write

$$P^{s_3}_{\widetilde{L}''\widetilde{M}''\cdot}(\epsilon_{15}\epsilon_{25}\epsilon_{35}) = \overline{P^{s_3}_{\widetilde{L}''\widetilde{M}''}(t_2 - t_1)} \exp[s_3\widetilde{t}_1 \cdot \widetilde{t}_2],$$

$$P^{s_3}_{\cdot L''M''}(\epsilon_{51}\epsilon_{52}\epsilon_{53}) = P^{s_3}_{L''M''}(\widetilde{t}_2 - \widetilde{t}_1) \exp[s_3\widetilde{t}_2 \cdot \widetilde{t}_1].$$

Similarly we have

$$\epsilon_{11} = \exp\widetilde{t}_1 \cdot \widetilde{t}_1 \qquad \epsilon_{55} = \exp\widetilde{t}_2 \cdot \widetilde{t}_2$$

$$\epsilon_{45} = \exp\widetilde{t}_1 \cdot \widetilde{t}_2 \qquad \epsilon_{54} = \exp\widetilde{t}_2 \cdot \widetilde{t}_1.$$

Then the normalization operator of the configuration is given by

8.15 Proposition: The normalization kernel for the two-center configuration $s^4 p^b + s^4$ is given by

$$(\alpha^{8+b}[4\,4\,b]\,\widetilde{q}|N(\widetilde{t}_1\widetilde{t}_2, t_1 t_2)|\alpha^{8+b}[4\,4\,b]\,q)$$

$$= \sum_{k_{55}a_3 L'M's_3\,\widetilde{L}''\widetilde{M}''L''M''} \left\{(-1)^{k_{55}} \frac{(4-s_3)!\,b!}{(4-k_{55}-s_3)!\,k_{55}!\,(b-s_3)!}\right.$$

$$\exp[(4+b)\widetilde{t}_1 \cdot \widetilde{t}_1 + 4\widetilde{t}_2 \cdot \widetilde{t}_2 - (4-k_{55}-s_3)(\widetilde{t}_1-\widetilde{t}_2)\cdot(\widetilde{t}_1-\widetilde{t}_2)]$$

$$\langle b\widetilde{L}\widetilde{M}|a_3 L'M's_3\widetilde{L}''\widetilde{M}''\rangle \overline{P^{s_3}_{\widetilde{L}''\widetilde{M}''}(t_2 - t_1)}$$

$$\left. P^{s_3}_{L''M''}(\widetilde{t}_2 - \widetilde{t}_1) \langle a_3 L'M's_3 L''M''|bLM\rangle\right\}$$

One recognizes in the first part of the exponential the part which, after introduction of the coordinates s_1 and s_2, allows for the removal of the center-of-mass motion.

8.7 Notes and References

There are by now many theoretical studies of the interaction between complex nuclei on the basis of microscopic theories. In many cases these studies are restricted to the orbital partition $f = [4^j]$ which was shown in this and preceding sections to yield particularly simple results.

Alternative methods for obtaining the interaction and normalization kernels are treated by Sünkel and Wildermuth [SU 72], by Horiuchi [HO 77], and by Hecht and Zahn [HE 78].

9 Internal Radius and Dilatation

9.1 Oscillator States of Different Frequencies

At some places in the preceding sections full use has been made of harmonic oscillator state wave functions. But no attention was directed to the internal width of the different composite particle systems. The frequencies of the oscillator states in different degrees of freedom were all chosen to be equal. It was possible therefore to transform from one set of coordinates to another, for example from cluster coordinates to single-particle coordinates, by orthogonal transformations. Even in Bargmann space these could be performed by substitution without explicitly using integral transforms (see section 5.1).

But especially for systems consisting of composite particles of very different size and occupation number like the system consisting of a ^{40}Ca and ^{4}He nucleus this approximation may be insufficient, and even in cluster model calculations of the lightest nuclei states consisting of simple composite systems with different oscillator width have been used.

In section 5.2 it has been shown that it is possible to pass from one frequency to another by applying a real dilatation to space coordinates which then are completed to a real symplectic transformation. These transformations are represented by linear operators on the Hilbert space of the Schrödinger representation or in Bargmann space. In Bargmann space the unitary operator representing a dilatation D is described by the kernel (see 5.2)

$$S_{g_c(D)}(\tilde{x}, x) = \left[\det \left(\frac{D + D^{-1}}{2} \right) \right]^{-1/2} \exp \left[\frac{1}{2} \tilde{x} \cdot (D - D^{-1})(D + D^{-1})^{-1} \tilde{x} \right.$$
$$\left. + 2 \tilde{x} \cdot (D + D^{-1})^{-1} \bar{x} - \frac{1}{2} \bar{x} \cdot (D - D^{-1})(D + D^{-1})^{-1} \bar{x} \right].$$

Certainly this integral transform can be applied to any wave function and yields a dilatation of the r.m.s. radius of the system described by this wave function.

In this section, we apply as an example dilatations to simple composite systems which have been considered in section 7. We deal with such transformations only where all three space coordinates are dilated by the same parameter. Everything connected with angular momentum is handled in the same way as in previous sections and the vector of all three space coordinates will be denoted by one and the same letter.

9.2 Dilatations in Different Coordinate Systems

With the notation of section 6 we consider a system of n particles divided into j subsystems each with occupation number n_i. The whole system is classified by a weight $(w_1 \ldots w_j)$ of n.

It has been shown in section 5.1 that even in Bargmann space one can pass from cluster coordinates via center coordinates to single particle coordinates by the orthogonal transformations JQW. The matrix $W = W_j \oplus I_{n-j}$ (see definition 5.4) transforms the relative co-ordinates s into coordinates z leading to the centers of the subsystems and I_{n-j} is a unit matrix in $(n-j)$ dimensions which transforms internal coordinates into themselves. Q is a permutation matrix which rearranges the center coordinates (see Definition 5.2).

$J = \overset{j}{\underset{\nu=1}{\oplus}} I_{w_\nu}$ is a direct sum of Jacobi matrices and transforms center coordinates into single particle coordinates (see definition 5.1).

We assume that all internal coordinates which belong to the same composite particle are dilated by the same real parameter d^ν. The relative coordinates may be dilated by different real parameters d_{s_ν} where the index s_ν refers to the relative coordinate s_ν. In some cases, so for example in scattering problems, these parameters are arbitrary and may be adapted to a standard frequency, in other cases they are suggested by the physical situation. This is usually the case in bound state problems.

9.1 Definition: Using cluster coordinates in space the dilatation of a composite particle systems is described by a diagonal matrix which splits formally into a direct sum

$$D = D_j \oplus \overset{j}{\underset{\nu=1}{\oplus}} D^\nu$$

The diagonal matrix $((D_j)_{ik}) = (d_{s_i}\delta_{ik})$, $i, k = 1\,2\ldots j$ dilates relative coordinates and the $(n_\nu - 1) \times (n_\nu - 1)$ diagonal matrices $(D_{ik}^\nu) = (d^\nu \delta_{ik})$, $\nu = 1\,2\ldots j$; $i, k = 1\,2\ldots n_\nu - 1$ dilate every subsystem by a common parameter d^ν.

Very helpful will be the following almost trivial propositions. The first one relates representations of canonical transformations as applied to wave functions and as applied to integral kernels.

9.2 Proposition: Given a linear operator K with kernel $K(x, x')$ in Bargmann space B and an arbitrary real symplectic transformation g. For $f \in B$ we define

$$f_g(x) = \int S_{g_c}(x, x')\, f(x')\, d\mu(x')$$

with S_{g_c} as in 4.27. Then

$$(K f_g)\,(x) = (K_g f)\,(x)$$

where K_g is the linear operator with kernel

$$K_g(x, x') = \int K(x, x'')\, S_{g_c}(x'', x')\, d\mu(x'').$$

The second proposition describes kernels of splitting point transformations:

9.3 Proposition: Consider a point transformation B which splits into the direct sum $B_1 \oplus B_2$. Then the corresponding kernel of B in Bargmann space splits into the product of the kernels corresponding to B_1 and B_2 respectively,

$$S_{g_c(B)}(\tilde{x}, x) = S_{g_c(B_1)}(\tilde{x}_1, x_1)\, S_{g_c(B_2)}(\tilde{x}_2, x_2).$$

x_i are coordinates in those linear subspaces where B_i does not act trivially.

The proof of the first proposition follows immediately if one changes the order of integration, and the second proposition is verified by writing the kernels explicitly according to proposition 4.28.

Proposition 9.3 shows that we can transfer dilatations of states to (inverse) dilatations of kernels. This allows us to calculate matrix elements of operators between dilated oscillators by Taylor expansion of dilated integral kernels.

Remark: A dilatation of all coordinates by the same parameter would cause an integral transformation in Bargmann space. On the other hand, this would only mean the introduction of a new state which could be done in the Schrödinger representation beforehand and, therefore, dilatations of this kind will not be considered.

We have already refered to the transformations W, J and Q defined in section 5 which describe transformations between different coordinate sets. All these transformations are orthogonal. If dilatations are taken into account we must multiply these transformations by the matrix D of definition 9.1 from the right. So instead of W (or QW) or JQW we have WD (or QWD) or JQWD respectively. Obviously the next step should be matrix multiplication and calculation of the kernels of S_g according to 4.28. But this turns out to be rather tedious especially since the matrix JQWD must be inverted. This means the inversion of an n X n matrix.

We know from sections 7 and 8 that many calculations for composite particle systems turn out to be much easier if they are performed on center coordinates or single particle coordinates. In both cases all coordinates refering to the same subsystem ought to be dilated by the same parameter. Unfortunately, this is not the case if we dilate by the matrix D. Therefore we shall introduce a new dilatation matrix associated to D.

9.4 Definition: The matrix which dilates all single particle coordinates refering to the same subsystem by the same parameter d^i will be denoted by Δ.

This dilatation matrix has the form

$$\Delta = \overset{j}{\underset{\nu=1}{\oplus}} \Delta^\nu$$

where $(\Delta^\nu_{ik}) = (d^\nu \delta_{ik})$ with $\nu = 1 \, 2 \ldots j$ and $i, k = 1 \, 2 \ldots n_\nu$.

We want to calculate matrix elements of an integral operator K which is represented by its kernel $K(\tilde{x}, x)$ in single particle coordinates $\tilde{x}$ and x between composite particle wave functions which are given in cluster coordinates $\tilde{s}, \tilde{y}$ and s, y. Transferring the dilatation to the kernel we obtain a new kernel in cluster coordinates

$$K_{\tilde{D}D}(\tilde{s}\tilde{y}, sy) = \int S_{g_c((\tilde{J}\tilde{Q}\tilde{W}\tilde{D})^{-1})}(\tilde{s}\tilde{y}, \tilde{x}) \, K(\tilde{x}, x) \, S_{g_c(JQWD)}(x, sy) \, d\mu(\tilde{x}) \, d\mu(x).$$

On the right-hand side we will now introduce between the operators K and S_{g_c} the unit operator in form of

$$S_{g_c(\Delta \Delta^{-1})} = S_{g_c(\Delta)} \circ S_{g_c(\Delta^{-1})}$$

and combine $S_{g_c(\Delta^{-1})}$ and $S_{g_c(JQWD)}$ to $S_{g_c(L)}$ where $L = \Delta^{-1} JQWD$. We have

$$\Delta J = \begin{bmatrix} d^1 I_{n_1} & & 0 \\ & \ddots & \\ 0 & & d^j I_{n_j} \end{bmatrix} \begin{bmatrix} J_{n_1} & & 0 \\ & \ddots & \\ 0 & & J_{n_j} \end{bmatrix}$$

$$= \begin{bmatrix} J_{n_1} & & 0 \\ & \ddots & \\ 0 & & J_{n_j} \end{bmatrix} \begin{bmatrix} d^1 I_{n_1} & & 0 \\ & \ddots & \\ 0 & & d^j I_{n_j} \end{bmatrix} = J\Delta.$$

Both matrices Δ and J have the same block structure and the Δ^i are scalar multiples of unit matrices. We define a matrix $\Delta_Q = Q^{-1} \Delta Q$. This matrix is again a diagonal matrix but its diagonal elements have been rearranged,

$$\Delta_Q = \begin{bmatrix} d^1 & & & & & 0 \\ & \ddots & & & & \\ & & d^j & & & \\ & & & D^1 & & \\ & & & & \ddots & \\ 0 & & & & & D^j \end{bmatrix}.$$

The submatrices D^i are the same as those in the matrix D.

9.5 Proposition: The dilatation of composite nucleon systems can be decomposed into a dilatation Δ of the clusters in single particle coordinates as defined in 9.4 and a point transformation $L = JQW_D$. The matrix $W_D = \Delta_Q^{-1} WD$ splits into a direct sum

$$W_D = (W_D)_j \oplus I_{n-j} = ((\Delta_Q^{-1})_j W_j D_j) \oplus I_{n-j}$$

where $(W_D)_j$ is a $j \times j$ matrix and I_{n-j} the $(n-j) \times (n-j)$ unit matrix.

Proof: That the transformation decomposes has already been shown. Further we have the identities

$$L = \Delta^{-1} JQWD = J \Delta^{-1} QWD = J(QQ^{-1}) \Delta^{-1} QWD$$
$$= JQ(Q^{-1} \Delta^{-1} Q) WD$$
$$= JQ(\Delta_Q)^{-1} WD$$

Since W reduces to $W_j \oplus I_{n-j}$ and since Δ_Q splits into

$$\Delta_Q = \begin{bmatrix} d^1 & & \\ & \ddots & \\ & & d^j \end{bmatrix} \oplus \bigoplus_{i=1}^{j} D^i,$$

W_D has the desired form. $\square$

If we compare this result with 5.4 we see that only W_j has to be substituted by $(W_D)_j$. J and Q are still the same, only the transformation $(W_D)_j$ is no longer orthogonal and therefore in Bargmann space yields an integral transform. Because of proposition 9.3 we can summarize this in

9.6 Proposition: The kernel of the transformation W_D is given by

$$S_{g_c(W_D)}(zy', sy) = S_{g_c((W_D)_j)}(z, s) \exp[y' \cdot \overline{y}].$$

The only non-trivial transformation is the one corresponding to $(W_D)_j$. To obtain λ^{-1} this matrix must be inverted. But it is now only an $j \times j$ matrix instead of the $n \times n$ matrix $JQWD$.

Everything which has been derived here for the right hand side can be immediately applied to the left hand side. Only every matrix must be substituted by its inverse.

The transformation of the operator K into the operator $K_{\widetilde{D}D}$ may be rather complicated. It is easy if K is an element of the semigroups defined in 5.13. Then the corresponding matrix g_c can be calculated and the integration can be performed using the representation property

$$S_{g_c} \circ S_{g_c'} = S_{g_c g_c'}.$$

Unfortunately, this is not always the case in applications. Nevertheless, the integral transform can be calculated explicitly if the kernel K is given for example in the general form

$$K(\widetilde{x}, x) = c \exp\left[\frac{1}{2} \widetilde{x} \cdot F \widetilde{x} + \widetilde{x} \cdot G \overline{x} - \frac{1}{2} \overline{x} \cdot H \overline{x}\right].$$

where G is not necessarily invertible. Clearly F and H are symmetric. If they are not they can be symmetrized at once without changing the operator. But the spaces of $\widetilde{x}$ and x need not have the same dimension. The result of the integration is given by the following proposition.

9.7 Proposition: Consider two integral transforms

$$K_1: \ B \to B'$$
$$K_2: \ B' \to B''$$

of Bargmann spaces B, B', B'' over $\mathbb{C}^n, \mathbb{C}^{n'}, \mathbb{C}^{n''}$ respectively where n, n' and n'' need not coincide. Let

$$K_i(\widetilde{x}, x) = \exp\left[\frac{1}{2} \widetilde{x} \cdot F_i \widetilde{x} + \widetilde{x} \cdot G_i \overline{x} - \frac{1}{2} \overline{x} \cdot H_i \overline{x}\right]$$

be the kernels of these transformations. Then the kernel of $K_1 \circ K_2$ is given by

$$(K_1 \circ K_2)(\widetilde{x}, x) = K(\widetilde{x}, x) = C \exp\left[\frac{1}{2} \widetilde{x} \cdot F \widetilde{x} + \widetilde{x} \cdot G \overline{x} - \frac{1}{2} \overline{x} \cdot H \overline{x}\right]$$

with

$$C = (\det(1 + F_2 H_1))^{-1/2}$$
$$F = F_1 + G_1(1 + F_2 H_1)^{-1} F_2{}^t G_1$$
$$G = G_1(1 + F_2 H_1)^{-1} G_2$$
$$H = H_2 + {}^t G_2 H_1(1 + F_2 H_1)^{-1} G_2$$

if $(1 + F_2 H_1)$ is invertible and the condition $1 - \frac{1}{4}(F_2 - \overline{H}_1)(\overline{F}_2 - H_1) > 0$ is fulfilled.

The proof requires the integration of an exponential of an inhomogenous form of second order in complex phase space. This integral has been solved by Itzykson [IT 67].

9.8 Proposition: We have

$$\int \exp\left[\frac{1}{2} x \cdot \gamma x + \frac{1}{2}\overline{x} \cdot \overline{\delta}\,\overline{x} + ax + \overline{b}\overline{x}\right] d\mu(x) = (\det(1 - \gamma\overline{\delta}))^{-1/2}$$

$$\exp\left[\frac{1}{2} a \cdot \overline{\delta}(1 - \gamma\overline{\delta})^{-1} a + \overline{b} \cdot (1 - \gamma\overline{\delta})^{-1} a + \frac{1}{2}\overline{b} \cdot (1 - \gamma\overline{\delta})^{-1} \gamma\overline{b}\right]$$

if $(1 - \frac{1}{4}(\gamma + \delta)(\overline{\gamma} + \overline{\delta})) > 0$.

The sign of the square root of the determinant $(1 - \gamma\overline{\delta})$ is a priori not uniquely determined and therefore, also the sign of the constant C in proposition 9.7. This problem is closely related to the introduction of metaplectic representations mentioned at the beginning of section 4. But at least as long as one of the integrals represents a real point transformation, the sign can be chosen to be positive.

9.3 Dilatations of Simple Composite Nucleon Systems

We have shown in the preceding section that even in situations where dilatations are present we can transform states given in cluster coordinates into states given in center and internal coordinates by the integral transformation $S_{g_c(W_D)}$ of proposition 9.6. Therefore, as in section 6.3 we can start at once with wave functions described in center coordinates and since we are interested in kernels we start with a wave function

$$h(zy) = e_{z'}(z)\, v(y)$$

This wave function is transformed by $S_{g_c(JQ)}$ to a description in single particle coordinates x':

$$l_{z'}(x') = (S_{g_c(JQ)}(e_{z'}v))(x').$$

But now between the operator K and the wave function we are left with the dilatation Δ with integral kernel $S_{g_c(\Delta)}(x, x')$. This kernel will be applied to single particle wave functions.

The matrix Δ is a diagonal matrix and therefore by proposition 9.6 its kernel is a product of kernels

$$S_{g_c(\Delta)} = \prod_{i=1}^{n} S_{g_c(\Delta_{ii})}(x_i, x_i').$$

Each dilatation operator $S_{g_c(\Delta_{ii})}$ is applied to one single particle wave function. We can at once use this to calculate the single particle overlap integrals ϵ_{il} of section 7.2. We have

$$(S_{g_c(\Delta_{ii})} e_{t_l}) (x_i') = (S_{g_c(d^l)} e_{t_l}) (x_i') = f_{t_l, d^l}(x_i').$$

The first identity follows from the fact that all single particle coordinates refering to the same subsystem are dilated by the same parameter (see definition 9.5).

The same applies to the left hand side and we obtain

$$\epsilon_{il} = (f_{\tilde{t}_i, \tilde{d}^i} \mid f_{t_l, d^l})$$
$$= (S_{g_c(\tilde{d}^i)} e_{t_i} \mid S_{g_c(d^l)} e_{t_l})$$
$$= (e_{\tilde{t}_i} \mid S_{g_c((\tilde{d}^i)^{-1})} \circ S_{g_c(d^l)} e_{t_l})$$
$$= (e_{\tilde{t}_i} \mid S_{g_c(d^l/\tilde{d}^i)} e_{t_l})$$

Here the third identity follows from the fact that the adjoint of an integral transform of a canonical transformation coincides with the integral transform of the inverse of the canonical transformation.

Finally with

$$S_{g_c(d)} (\tilde{x}, x) = \left[\frac{1}{2}(d + d^{-1}) \right]^{-3/2} \exp \left[\frac{1}{2} \frac{d^2 - 1}{d^2 + 1} \tilde{x} \cdot \tilde{x} + \frac{2d}{d^2 + 1} \tilde{x} \cdot \overline{x} - \frac{1}{2} \frac{d^2 - 1}{d^2 + 1} \overline{x} \cdot \overline{x} \right]$$

we obtain

9.9 Proposition: The single-particle overlap matrix elements of dilated simple composite particle systems are

$$\epsilon_{il} = | d_{il}^+ |^{-3/2} \exp \left[\frac{1}{2} \frac{f_{il}}{\tilde{n}_i} \tilde{z}_i \cdot \tilde{z}_i + \frac{h_{il}}{[\tilde{n}_i n_l]^{1/2}} \tilde{z}_i \cdot \overline{z}_l - \frac{1}{2} \frac{f_{il}}{n_l} \overline{z}_l \cdot \overline{z}_l \right]$$

with

$$d_{il}^+ = \frac{1}{2} \left(\frac{d^l}{\tilde{d}^i} + \frac{\tilde{d}^i}{d^l} \right)$$
$$f_{il} = ((\tilde{d}^i)^2 - (d^l)^2) ((\tilde{d}^i)^2 + (d^l)^2)^{-1}$$
$$h_{il} = (d_{il}^+)^{-1} .$$

For $\tilde{d}^i = d^l$ the matrix elements coincide with the undilated ones of section 7.2 which must be the case since the integral transforms represent unitary operators.

In order to calculate the whole normalization kernel for simple composite particles it is possible to proceed in the same way as in section 7.2. It is only necessary to substitute the single particle matrix elements.

To determine matrix elements we should like to limit our considerations to density operators as we have done in section 7. But unfortunately, dilatations of density operators do not seem to give simple expressions. Therefore, we shall restrict ourselves to the calculation of a little less complicated matrix elements of Gaussian interactions, which can be represented by elements of the semigroup $Sp(2m, \mathbb{C}) \cap U^{\geqslant}(m, m)$ (see section 5.3). In fact, to a certain degree Gaussian interactions play a similar role as density operators since many interactions can be calculated by them. So for example we get the kinetic energy by differentiation.

Let $V(x) = V_0 \exp -\frac{1}{2} \gamma \xi^2$ be a local (one-dimensional) Gaussian interaction in Schrödinger representation which up to a constant factor represents the matrix

$$g = \begin{bmatrix} 1 & 0 \\ -i\gamma & 1 \end{bmatrix}.$$

We set $V_0 = 1$ in order to simplify the notation of the following. There corresponds a kernel in Bargmann space to $V(x)$ which, according to section 5.3, example 5.4, is given by

$$K(\tilde{x}, x) = \left[\frac{2+\gamma}{2}\right]^{-3/2} \exp\left[-\frac{1}{2}\frac{\gamma}{2+\gamma}\tilde{x}\cdot\tilde{x} + \frac{2}{2+\gamma}\tilde{x}\cdot x - \frac{1}{2}\frac{\gamma}{2+\gamma}x\cdot x\right].$$

In complex phase space, this kernel represents the complex symplectic transformation:

$$g_c = \frac{1}{2}\begin{bmatrix} 2+\gamma & \gamma \\ -\gamma & 2-\gamma \end{bmatrix}.$$

The expressions of section 7.3 consist of sums of products of fractional parentage coefficients $\langle f'q'f''q'' | fq \rangle$, reduced matrix elements of reduced two-particle density operators and polynomial functions $D^{f'}(\epsilon)$. The latter are of the same type as the $D^f(\epsilon)$ in the normalisation kernel. Here we need only to insert dilated single-particle overlap integrals which have just been calculated. We replace the reduced two-particle density operators by Gaussian interaction kernels, or in other words, we insert from the beginning a Gaussian interaction kernel in the relation $(f|K|h) = \text{trace } K \circ D$ of section 5.4. In the sequel, we set 1 resp. 2 for all indices involved in the interaction.

Let us assume that the Gaussian interaction depends only on the relative coordinates. With respect to the center-of-mass coordinates we have unit operators. We transform this kernel to single-particle coordinates and then apply the dilatations according to proposition 9.3. At this place, it is advisable first to calculate the matrix corresponding to the dilated interaction kernel in real phase space. Then, in relative coordinates the kernel represents the matrix

$$g_\gamma = \begin{bmatrix} 1 & 0 & 0 & 0 \\ 0 & 1 & 0 & 0 \\ -i\gamma & 0 & 1 & 0 \\ 0 & 0 & 0 & 1 \end{bmatrix},$$

This we transform to single-particle coordinates by

$$\xi = J_2^{-1} \sigma \quad \text{with} \quad J_2 = \left[\frac{1}{2}\right]^{1/2}\begin{bmatrix} 1 & -1 \\ 1 & 1 \end{bmatrix}$$

and dilate by the matrices

$$\tilde{\Delta} = \begin{bmatrix} \tilde{d}^1 & 0 \\ 0 & \tilde{d}^2 \end{bmatrix} \quad \Delta = \begin{bmatrix} d^1 & 0 \\ 0 & d^2 \end{bmatrix}.$$

Thus we obtain a matrix

$$t = g(\widetilde{\Delta}^{-1} J_2^{-1}) \, g_\gamma \, g(J_2 \Delta)$$

Remember that dilations on the left are caused by reciprocal matrices.

Let

$$t_c = \begin{bmatrix} \lambda & \mu \\ \nu & \rho \end{bmatrix}$$

be the matrix in complex phase space corresponding to t, then

$$\lambda = \frac{1}{2}(\Delta_+ + \gamma C_0)$$

$$\mu = \frac{1}{2}(\Delta_- + \gamma C_0)$$

$$\nu = \frac{1}{2}(\Delta_- - \gamma C_0)$$

with the 2×2 matrix

$$C_0 = \widetilde{\Delta} J_2^{-1} \begin{bmatrix} 1 & 0 \\ 0 & 0 \end{bmatrix} J_2 \Delta = \frac{1}{2} \begin{bmatrix} \widetilde{d}^1 d^1 & -\widetilde{d}^1 d^2 \\ -\widetilde{d}^2 d^1 & \widetilde{d}^2 d^2 \end{bmatrix}$$

and the 2×2 diagonal matrices

$$\Delta_\pm = (\widetilde{\Delta}^{-1} \Delta \pm \widetilde{\Delta} \Delta^{-1})$$

For the calculation of the integral transform we need the matrix

$$\lambda^{-1} = 2\Delta_+^{-1} - 2\gamma \Delta_+^{-1} C_0 \Delta_+^{-1} (1 + \gamma\,{}^t d \Delta_+^{-1} \widetilde{d})^{-1}$$

and the determinant

$$\det(\lambda) = \frac{1}{4} \det(\Delta_+) (1 + \gamma\,{}^t d \Delta_+^{-1} \widetilde{d})$$

where we introduced the two-dimensional vectors

$$\widetilde{d} = \sqrt{\frac{1}{2}} \begin{bmatrix} \widetilde{d}^1 \\ -\widetilde{d}^2 \end{bmatrix} \quad \text{and} \quad d = \sqrt{\frac{1}{2}} \begin{bmatrix} d^1 \\ -d^2 \end{bmatrix}.$$

Multiplication of λ^{-1} and ν or μ gives the kernel of theorem 5.14.

9.4 Notes and References

The use of dilatations for changing the frequency of oscillator states is pointed out in [KR 75]. Seligman and Zahn [SE 76] employ dilatations for the description of composite particles with different radii. Sünkel [SU 76] used a different integral transform to single-particle states and studied the reaction $^{40}Ca + {}^4He$ with different radii for the fragments.

10 Configurations of Three Simple Composite Particles and the Structure of Nuclei with Mass Numbers A = 4-10

10.1 Concepts and Motivation

Most of the phenomena called states in light nuclei really are more or less broad and overlapping resonances. They should be treated in a microscopic reaction theory, but the problems involved become enormous when several channels are open. Therefore things are simplified drastically if in a quasibound approach square integrable functions are used only. Then the A-body hamiltonian can be diagonalized in order to derive observable quantities from the resulting set of eigenstates. But still there is the fundamental dilemma of using a finite model space without being able to estimate the effect of the remaining part of the total Hilbert space. Now, if we finally remember that the nuclear interaction is not yet known completely, it is not very surprising to see no full agreement between calculated quantities and those derived from experiment (assuming for the moment the analysis of experimental data itself would be free of ambiguities).

The question of main interest therefore is, in what way discrepancies are related to one or the other of the uncertainties just noted. Looking at the structure problem in light nuclei from this point of view, it seems necessary to subject any model space to an extensive test, which hopefully may reveal the origins of some of the inconsistencies.

Bearing these remarks in mind we present here results obtained with configurations of three simple composite particles. The states in the model space are characterized by orbital partitions equivalent to the supermultiplet quantum numbers and by oscillator quantum numbers. A finite-dimensional state space is obtained by restricting the overall oscillator excitation to values smaller than some N_{max}.

The viewpoints and intentions of the work reported here can be specified as follows:

(i) We start with the space of A-particle oscillator functions up to excitation $N_{max} \hbar \omega$. But in contrast to the shell model this space is thought to be generated from the beginning by states with definite orbital symmetries $f = [f_1 f_2 \dots]$. Then from such a properly classified basis it is possible to select special realizations of a few orbital partitions only. Just this is done by the composite particle ansatz if understood from a group theoretical point of view. The resulting model space will be briefly described in section 10.2.

(ii) Before applying the model space its convergence properties and efficiency will be investigated. The results of section 10.4 can then serve as a basis for further inferences.

(iii) The model space in its simplest form covers essential parts of the $s^4 p^{A-4}$-shell model space. Thus, as we shall see repeatedly, we are in a position to get an idea of the efficiency of shell model fits.

(iv) Much effort has been undertaken to avoid additional ambiguities. The center-of-mass motion is eliminated from the beginning. Assuming then the A-body hamiltonian to be composed of two-body interactions, its matrix elements between basis functions are expressed completely in terms of two-body matrix elements. Once the basis functions are given, there are no further approximations. Some remarks concerning the computation of matrix elements will be made in section 10.3.

(v) The stability of the model space with respect to some widely used two-body interactions will be checked. In addition, because the dependence of our final results on the interaction will not be obscured by the presence of adjustable parameters, it may be possible to draw some conclusions about the interactions themselves. The interaction matrix elements used are specified in section 10.3.

(vi) The calculated eigenstates will show significant f LS-structures. Whereas the meaning of L and S in reaction processes is well known, it was pointed out once more by John and Seligman [JO 74], that the supermultiplet quantum number plays an important role too. Because the comparison of calculated quasibound energies with derived resonance energies is only of restricted value, we will try instead to discuss the structure of eigenstates with respect to the presence of related open channels.

(vii) So far, numerical results are available for the mass region $A = 4 - 10$, including however spectra of states with normal and non-normal parity. Thus, in shell model language, nuclei are covered from the closed-shell ^{4}He up to ^{10}B, lying in the middle of the p-shell. At least in case of non-normal parity such a program has never been performed. The data will be presented in 10.8. We compare different interactions and discuss to some extent agreements and discrepancies with other model calculations and with results derived from experiment.

10.2 The Model Space

States of A nucleons with orbital symmetry $f = [f_1 f_2 \dots]$ may be constructed directly by starting with configurations of j composite particles. Given any specific splitting $A = w_1 + w_2 + \dots w_j$, the composite particles are assumed to be unchanged under internal permutations and hence correspond to weights $w = (w_1, w_2, \dots, w_j)$. Because of the Pauli principle we must have $w_i \leqslant 4$. Thus, in the ansatz we start with representations of very special subgroups of $S(n)$. Littlewoods rules then tell us that only a very restricted set of representations of the whole group $S(n)$ can be induced, the one with the highest complexity being $f = [w_1 w_2 \dots w_j]$. This is just what we want for physical reasons, according to the supermultiplet models. On the other hand, we could have induced the same partitions with any finer splitting of more than j clusters. But this is what we do not want in order to avoid the well-known state explosion. Applied to the mass region considered in this work we decide to choose $j = 3$. This number will be kept fixed throughout, allowing however for all possible splittings of A into three weight components.

The orbital functions are further specified according to the oscillator model. After separating the center-of-mass vector, a 3-cluster state is taken to be a function of $A - 3$ internal relative vectors within the composite particles and two relative vectors s_1, s_2 between the centers-of-mass of the composite particles. The state dependence is described by oscillator functions of a single frequency ω. Whereas internal vectors are unexcited, s_1 and s_2 carry oscillator excitations of N_1, N_2 quanta and angular momenta L_1, L_2. Orbital angular momentum is established by coupling $L = L_1 + L_2$. Each orbital symmetry requires a minimum amount of total excitation $N_0 = N_1 + N_2$. For given N and L we consider all possible combinations $N_1 L_1 N_2 L_2$. States of different parity are obtained by choosing N even or odd.

Finally, in order to get antisymmetric states we must couple with spin-isospin functions of symmetry $\hat{f}$ associate to f, thereby determining all possible ST-combinations of total spin and isospin.

Given then specific values of parity ($\pi = \pm 1$), total angular momentum $J = L + S$ and isospin T (if, as here, no isospin mixing is taken into account), we obtain a basic set of antisymmetric states of the form

$$|(\alpha\gamma)^A f[1^n] qN_1 L_1 N_2 L_2 LSJM_J TM_T)$$

$$= |f|^{-1/2} \sum_r [|\alpha^A f r q N_1 L_1 N_2 L_2 L)| \gamma^A \hat{f} \hat{r} STM_T)]_{JM_J}$$

which are coupled with respect to orbital and spin-isospin permutational symmetry as explained in section 2.6. The orbital states are constructed by application of Young operators $c(rfq)$ to orbital A-nucleon states which in cluster coordinates are given by

$$[P_{L_1}^{N_1}(s_1) P_{L_2}^{N_2}(s_2)]_{LM_L}.$$

We emphasize that these states are still A-nucleon states in Bargmann space where independence of internal coordinates y indicates that the corresponding states are unexcited. The Gelfand label q incorporates the chosen weight $w = (w_1 w_2 w_3)$ and one intermediate partition which serves to distinguish possibly linear independent states of the same weight w and partition f.

Example 10.1: The system of A = 7 *nucleons*

The possible weights with three or less components are

$$w = (43), (421), (331), (322)$$

and all weights obtained by permutation of components. The allowed orbital partitions are

$$f = [43], [421], [331], [322]$$

For the partition f = [43], the number of Gelfand patterns equals the dimension of the irreducible representation $D^{[43]}$ of GL(3, $\mathbb{C}$) which according to proposition 3.10 is given by

$$\dim([43], 3) = \frac{\begin{array}{|c|c|c|c|} \hline 3 & 4 & 5 & 6 \\ \hline 2 & 3 & 4 \\ \hline \end{array}}{\begin{array}{|c|c|c|c|} \hline 5 & 4 & 3 & 1 \\ \hline 3 & 2 & 1 \\ \hline \end{array}} = 24$$

We need these Gelfand patterns only for the four weights given above since a permutation of weight components would not yield new states. The possible Gelfand states for these four weights and the partition $f = [43]$ are given by

w: (43)   (421)   (331)   (322)

q: $\begin{matrix} 4 & 3 \\ & 4 \end{matrix}$ $\begin{matrix} 4 & 2 \\ & 4 \end{matrix}$ $\begin{matrix} 4 & 2 \\ & 3 \end{matrix}$ $\begin{matrix} 3 & 3 \\ & 3 \end{matrix}$ $\begin{matrix} 4 & 1 \\ & 3 \end{matrix}$ $\begin{matrix} 3 & 2 \\ & 3 \end{matrix}$

Next we choose the oscillator excitations for the two vectors s_1, s_2. From the shell model we know that $N_0 = 3$ in this case is the minimum excitation.

The antisymmetric states are strictly orthogonal with respect to the orbital partition f, the total orbital angular momentum L, total spin S, total angular momentum J and the total isospin T. The orbital states are strictly orthogonal with respect to the label r which distinguishes different partners of the representation d^f of the orbital symmetric group S(n). They are also orthogonal with respect to the total number of oscillator quanta $N = N_1 + N_2$. The orbital states are not orthogonal with respect to the underlying weights w and Gelfand patterns q. They are not orthogonal with respect to the oscillator excitations $N_1 N_2$ and the orbital angular momenta $L_1 L_2$ associated with the vectors $s_1 s_2$. All these latter quantum numbers belong to operators which do not commute with permutations and hence with the orbital Young operators $c(rfq)$.

The normalization operator for the whole set of configurations of three simple composite particles inherits these quantum numbers from the A-nucleon states. Hence it is block diagonal with respect to the orbital partition f and the total orbital angular momentum L, independent of spin and isospin, and diagonal with respect to the total number of oscillator quanta N. The columns and rows of the finite-dimensional blocks of the normalization operator are then characterized by the labels $qN_1 L_1 N_2 L_2$. The matrix elements in these blocks are computed on the basis of the exchange decomposition given in proposition 7.1 and the exchange part of the normalization operator given in proposition 7.6. The computation of the numbers $d^f_{qq}(z_k)$ needed in proposition 7.1 is based on the methods of section 2 and in particular of section 2.5. The transformation brackets needed in proposition 7.6 are computed from proposition 5.7. The 2×2 matrix $E(k)$ is constructed according to proposition 7.3 from the matrices given in definition 5.4 and from the double coset symbol k.

The diagonalization of these finite dimensional blocks determines the eigenvalues and eigenstates of the normalization operator. The eigenstates with eigenvalues equal to zero are redundant and do not enter the composite particle dynamics. The eigenstates with non-vanishing eigenvalues provide a basis of the model space. By exhausting all combinations $N_1 L_1 N_2 L_2$ up to $N = N_1 + N_2 = N_{max}$ we get a model space of finite dimension.

10.3 The Interaction

The hamiltonian of the A-nucleon system is considered as being given with strict translational invariance and two-body interactions between all pairs of nucleons. The two-body interaction with respect to permutational symmetry is composed of products of orbital operators $T(2)$ and spin-isospin operators $U(2)$. Due to invariance under permutations and parity, the orbital two-body operators may be taken as even or odd. With respect to the rotation group, the interaction must be an invariant sum of products of orbital and spin-isospin tensor operators of rank κ. The rank κ is zero for central, one for spin-orbit and two for tensor interactions. The separation of the orbital and the spin-isospin matrix elements is performed through the method of the last pair explained in section 2.7 and by the application of angular momentum techniques with respect to the angular momenta LSJ and the tensors $T^\kappa(2)$ and $U^\kappa(2)$ as explained by Edmonds [ED 57].

The interaction operator of the composite particle configuration on this basis becomes a sum of products of orbital and spin-isospin contributions. The orbital part of this operator is obtained by taking the trace of the reduced two-body density operator with the given orbital operator $T(2)$. In the oscillator representation it was shown in section 7.4 that the orbital interaction operator becomes an algebraic expression which involves the reduced orbital two-body matrix elements

$$(\widetilde{N}''\widetilde{L}'' \| T^\kappa(2) \| N''L'').$$

This reduction to the two-body oscillator matrix elements involves three steps. After identification of the two weights $\widetilde{w}$ and w and the orbital partitions $\widetilde{f}$ and f, an exchange decomposition is performed according to proposition 7.5. This decomposition requires, in addition to the expressions encountered already for the normalization operator, the computation of the fractional parentage coefficients.

The second, much simpler step is the determination of the matrices B and the coefficients c_m and b_m entering in proposition 7.5. The third stage is the evaluation of the coefficients appearing in proposition 7.7 for the chosen oscillator configuration.

The kinetic energy may be treated by the same method after elimination of the total momentum and the associate kinetic energy. Instead of computing the two-body matrix elements for a parametrized interaction, we use in the present calculation directly the oscillator matrix elements determined by various authors. Tabulated two-body oscillator matrix elements are available from:

SWTH: Shakin, Waghmare, Tomaselli, Hull [SH 67]

EJMSS: Elliott, Jackson, Mavromatis, Sanderson, Singh [EL 68]

SOM: Sommer [SO 73]

GFA/OR
GFA/EH :   Galonska, Faessler, Appel [GA 70]

RM: Ripa and Maqueda [RI 71].

The oscillator parameter b varies in steps between 1.4 fm and 2.2 fm, usually values are given for $\widetilde{n}$, $n \leqslant 4$ where $n = \frac{1}{2}(N - L)$ and L', $L \leqslant 2$. This gives a total number of 175 different matrix elements, which enter the calculations. GFA did not determine S–D matrix elements, therefore, in this case, we have taken those of EJMSS.

The SWTH matrix elements are derived from the Yale potential in the unitary-model approach, whereas all the others are connected with the nucleon-nucleon phase shifts either using Born approximation or some kind of smooth auxiliary potential. Later on it will be necessary to discuss the ^{3}S and ^{3}S–^{3}D matrix elements, which are therefore tabulated in Table 10.1.

By combining all these steps, the interaction kernel is obtained in the original, partially nonorthogonal basis. The generalized linear eigenvalue problem involving both the interaction and the normalization (finite matrix) operator can now be solved by use of the non-redundant eigenstates of the normalization operator. In the following sections we shall study the properties of the eigenvalues and eigenstates for the mass numbers $A = 4 \ldots 10$.

Table 10.1 Upper part $^3S_1 - {}^3S_1$, lower part $^3S_1 - {}^3D_1$ two-body matrix elements for different interactions

$\tilde{n}$	n	SOM b = 1.5 fm	SWTH b = 1.5 fm	EJMSS b = 1.5 fm	RM b = 1.6 fm
0	0	− 10.965	− 10.60	− 9.97	− 10.65
0	1	− 6.355	− 7.92	− 6.82	− 3.64
0	2	− 3.420	− 4.69	−	− 1.40
0	3	− 1.395	− 1.81	−	− 0.04
1	1	− 6.843	− 6.84	− 5.86	− 7.26
1	2	− 4.102	− 4.00	− 3.18	− 1.96
1	3	− 1.750	− 1.38	−	− 0.07
2	2	− 3.834	− 2.34	− 2.69	− 4.84
2	3	− 1.874	− 0.40	− 1.00	− 0.20
3	3	− 1.547	0.74	− 0.27	− 2.63
0	0	− 0.605	− 9.21	− 7.72	− 1.13
0	1	− 0.893	− 12.50	−	− 1.50
0	2	− 1.13	− 14.49	−	− 1.71
0	3	− 1.361	− 15.60	−	− 1.87
1	0	− 0.377	− 4.16	− 0.66	− 0.44
1	1	− 0.774	− 8.49	− 3.94	− 1.03
1	2	− 1.165	− 11.60	−	− 1.48
1	3	− 1.547	− 13.70	−	− 1.80
2	0	− 0.316	− 2.02	0.93	− 0.24
2	1	− 0.696	− 4.56	0.81	− 0.61
2	2	− 1.147	− 7.62	− 2.43	− 1.06
2	3	− 1.639	− 10.20	−	− 1.45
3	0	− 0.377	− 0.98	−	− 0.19
3	1	− 0.710	− 2.33	1.01	− 0.41
3	2	− 1.188	− 4.28	− 0.76	− 0.70
3	3	− 1.762	− 6.61	− 3.94	− 1.03

10.4 Convergence Properties of the Model Space

We have pointed out at the beginning that no variational procedure is an approximative method in the usual sense, because there is no estimation of goodness. Stricly speaking we are not even protected against fallacies. So much the more the convergence properties of a model space should be investigated as far as possible.

We extend the model space successively by adding relatively small groups of correlated functions. An example is shown in fig. 10.1 for ^{6}Li with the SOM interaction. In an absolute energy scale there are columns of levels from left to right, which are obtained in the following way: Starting with a space of states with partition [42] and N = 2 oscillator quanta we get the levels in the first column. In the next step we add states with the same excitation, but orbital partition [411], leading to the spectrum shown in the second column from the left. Continuing this way, as it is indicated in the notation of fig. 10.1, we finally end up with the model space of all possible configurations of three composited particles with partitions [42], [411], [33] and at most 8 quanta oscillator excitation. The dimension of the space is 145 in the case of JT = 10.

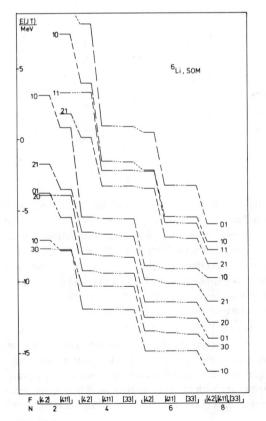

Figs. 10.1–10.3

States of positive parity in ^{6}Li under extension of the model space

Fig. 10.1

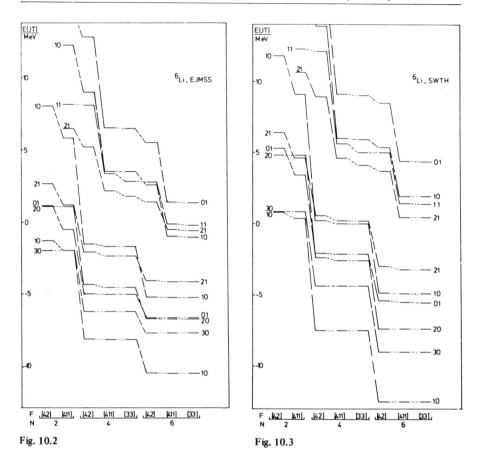

Fig. 10.2   **Fig. 10.3**

A first look at fig. 10.1 shows that the convergence behaviour may have two aspects. The first one is connected with the absolute position in energy of the total spectrum, that is with the binding energy. Here we obviously are far away from a static situation. The gain in energy of about 1.5 MeV when adding excitations of 8 quanta is to be compared with a probability of only 2 p.c. for finding such an excitation in the ground state eigenfunction. Absolute energies hence are generated by contributions of a large number of small components in the wave-functions. But it may be realistic to assume that this effect of short-range correlations can be taken into account within an effective interaction.

Now let us look at the excited states of ^{6}Li in figs. 10.1–10.3. For $N = N_0 = 2$ all three interactions produce almost identical spectra which in this case are exactly the $s^4 p^2$-shell model results. Two supermultiplets are fairly well separated, the splittings however being comparatively large and of the same order of magnitude in both cases. In addition, we observe appreciable mixing between states with different partitions. When adding now functions with higher oscillator excitations this first result is modified considerably. But now the most interesting fact is that, irrespective of the special interaction, the changes tend to consolidate the supermultiplet structure. Since the interaction between the two supermultiplets rapidly disappears, the higher excitations so to say determine the level arrangement inside two independent groups of states, the relative position of the groups remaining almost stable. The large splitting inside a supermultiplet f at the beginning, caused by spin-isospin dependent interactions, seems to be revised subsequently through the common effect of a large number of functions with higher oscillator excitations, but the same orbital partition f.

Of course, we can not prove anything about the "real" final states. But what could many-composite-particle states with high oscillator excitations bring about other than the same global effect just observed? There may be special situations, e.g., if high orbital angular momenta are involved, which require a splitting into more than three composite particles. In general, however, we believe that we reproduce the correct trend of the convergence.

In all nuclei considered here, we observe a similar convergence behaviour, on the basis of which we can make some extrapolations. The stability of the relative position of supermultiplet centers indicates that the position in energy is essentially determined by the supermultiplet quantum number f itself. Indeed, given two supermultiplets $f' = [f'_1 f'_2 \ldots]$ and $f = [f_1 f_2 \ldots]$, we get the following simple estimate by counting the number of surplus nucleon pairs in a relative even state:

$$E(f') - E(f) = 7[q^{f'} - q^f] \text{ MeV} \qquad (*)$$

with

$$q^f = \frac{1}{4} n(n-1) + \frac{1}{4}[f_1(f_1 - 1) + f_2(f_2 - 3) + \ldots f_j(f_j - 2j + 1)].$$

In Table 10.2 the distances of some calculated supermultiplet centers are compared with values following from (*). We may recall here once more the work of Franzini and Radicati [FR 63], who succeeded in fitting the ground state energies of many nuclei using the supermultiplet quantum number f.

Table 10.2 Energy differences (in MeV) of some calculated supermultiplet centers as compared with values following from (*)

f'	f	$E(f') - E(f)$ (*)	$E(f') - E(f)$ calc.
[31]	[4]	14	13.5
[22]	[31]	7	6.9
[32]	[41]	10.5	10.45
[411]	[42]	7	6.6
[421]	[43]	10.5	9.74
[431]	[44]	14	13.8
[422]	[431]	7	5.8
[432]	[441]	10.5	11.2
[442]	[433]	7	7.8

Table 10.3 Contributions (in percent) of different supermultiplets to the supermultiplet expansion of calculated wave functions in the lowest states of ^{6}Li. SOM, EJMSS and SWTH denote the two-body interactions used

SOM			EJMSS			SWTH			
[42]	[411]	[33]	[42]	[411]	[33]	[42]	[411]	[33]	JT
98	2	0	99	1	0	99	1	0	10
100	0	0	100	0	0	100	0	0	30
94	6	0	97	3	0	95	5	0	01
100	0	0	99	1	0	100	0	0	20
85	15	0	93	7	0	86	14	0	21
85	15	0	98	2	0	95	5	0	10*
15	85	0	7	93	0	13	87	0	21*
0	100	0	0	100	0	0	99	1	11
15	85	0	5	95	0	6	94	0	10**
5	95	0	5	95	0	6	94	0	01*
97	3	0	95	5	0	100	0	0	10***
100	0	0	100	0	0	100	0	0	30*
93	7	0	91	9	0				01**

Table 10.3 shows the supermultiplet structure of the states in figs. 10.1−10.3, Table 10.4 the somewhat more complicated situation for the lowest states with dominantly four quanta excitation in ^{8}Be, calculated with SOM. On the basis of the arguments given above we can for example predict the next higher supermultiplet in ^{8}Be to be [4211] with an excitation energy of about 25−30 MeV. It can not be realized as a three-cluster configuration, although it is contained in the $s^4 p^4$-shell model space. Indeed, as shown in section 2.8, the Cohen-Kurath interaction produces states in ^{8}Be with f = [4211] above 30 MeV.

Before summarizing our results we should perhaps look once more at the interaction problem. We must use matrix elements between highly excited two-particle states and these are subject to large errors, especially in the case of the important ^{3}S and ^{3}S−^{3}D interactions. Comparing figs. 10.1−10.3 we therefore observe some more or less systematic differences, but until we refer to experiment there is no possibility of further discussion.

Our conclusion at present is as follows: The constituents of the spectra in the light nuclei considered here are supermultiplets, characterized by partitions f of at most three rows. The relative position of two supermultiplets seems to be some kind of "fundamental" quantity, which can be determined by simple rules. Initially, in the lowest order (= $s^4 p^{A-4}$-shell) model space, the supermultiplet splitting which results from spin-isospin dependent forces, is overestimated. This will be revised by taking into account functions with higher oscillator excitations, but the same orbital partition. No definite extrapolations are possible, but the convergence behaviour is recognizable in a model space of configurations of three composite particles with oscillator excitations up to $(N_0 + 4)\hbar\omega$.

Table 10.4 Supermultiplet expansion in the lowest states of ^{8}Be for the SOM interaction

JT	[44]	[431]	[422]	JT	[44]	[431]	[422]
00	98	2	0	30*	0	55	45
20	98	2	0	20***	1	22	77
40	89	11	0	21**	0	99	1
20*	0	89	11	11**	0	98	2
21	0	99	1	41	0	100	0
10	0	94	6	40*	6	58	46
11	0	96	4	31*	0	88	12
30	0	100	0	20****	2	83	15
31	0	99	1	00**	1	3	96
10*	0	100	0	30**	0	43	57
40*	4	29	67	11***	0	6	94
20**	1	84	15	31**	0	77	23
00*	5	75	20	21***	0	90	10
21*	0	100	0	31***	0	36	64
11*	0	95	5	00***	91	5	4
01	0	100	0	31**	0	8	92
				20*****	9	3	87

10.5 Comparison with Shell Model Results

In the literature there are only two other computations which can be cited in connection with the discussion of the last section, namely the work of the Manchester group [IR 73] and the perturbation theoretic approach of Hauge and Maripuu [HA 73]. We will compare our results with theirs in the case of ^{6}Li.

The Manchester group uses the space $(os)^{\geq 2} (op, 1s, od)^{\geq 4}$ and the Reid soft core interaction. But, in contrast to us, they try to calculate absolute energies. To this end some kind of tensor correlation α is introduced, which effectively leads to a considerable enhancement of the $^3S_1$ interaction. In fig. 10.4 the level energies are given as a function of α. The calculated binding energy is comparable with the experimental value (E = 31.99 MeV) for $\alpha = 0.085$, for $\alpha = 0.1$ it is E = 47.1 MeV. The energies of the 01 and 20 states are not well defined because center-of-mass fluctuations are present in the model space used.

Hauge and Maripuu use $s^4 p^2$-configurations and the EJMSS matrix elements. Second order terms of all possible $2\hbar\omega$ corrections are then calculated via degenerate perturbation theory. Fig. 10.4 shows the calculated level energies as a function of the single-particle energy splitting.

We cite still another work of Cooper, Seaborn and Williams [CO 71]. They also use $s^4 p^2$-configurations and EJMSS, but calculate the interaction of the individual p-shell nucleons with the s^4-core. Two solutions are given, one of which (b) is obtained by strengthening the $^3S_1$ matrix elements by 35 p.c. This procedure has been introduced by Gunye et al. [GU 69] to improve the results of Hartree-Fock calculations.

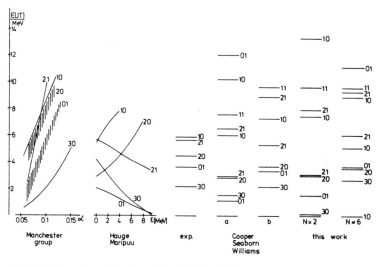

Fig. 10.4 Comparison of shell model calculations in ^{6}Li with the present work

Table 10.5 Experimental binding energies and calculated ground state energies (in MeV) with different interactions for nuclei A = 4 – 11

A	exp.	SOM	SWTH	EJMSS	GFA/OR	RM
4	28	14.7	16.1	16.5	14.4	28.7
5	27.34	9.	7.4	8.4	8.6	24.5
6	31.99	11.8	7.6	8.3	9.1	34.3
7	39.25	16.	8.1	11.2	6.9	39.5
8	56.5	28.2	18.5	22.5	17.4	56.2
9	58.2	28.1	9.5	16.4	10.5	57.
10	64.8	33.7	9.5	18.3		65.6
11	76	42.7	14.8	23.9	17.2	77.

10.6 Absolute Energies

In Table 10.5, ground-state energies (in MeV) are quoted which have been calculated in the space with excitations up to $N_0 + 2$ quanta.

The values obtained in this restricted space already are comparable with Hartree-Fock results. Gunye, Law and Bhaduri, [GU 69], report:

	A = 7	A = 8	A = 9
SWTH	12.5	22.5	21.45
EJMSS	7.07	15.85	14.87

It is interesting to observe that we get more binding with EJMSS than with SWTH. The different A-dependence may also be noted.

Perhaps we can divide the variety of results in Table 10.5 into three groups. The RM interaction seems to give an excellent fit to the binding energies of all the nuclei considered here, but the same interaction will give in no single nucleus a reasonable spectrum. The large central contribution obviously leads to drastic overbinding. Underbinding on the other hand occurs with SWTH, EJMSS and GFA, but the situation nevertheless is much better in this case, because excited states are reproduced fairly well. Thus we remain with the SOM interaction. Before making further comments we must anticipate the fact that just with this interaction we get the most consistent set of data in any regard. Here we get in most nuclei about 50 p.c. of the ground state energy, the difference from nucleus to nucleus being systematic. But looking now again into Table 10.5 we are led to the famous tensor interaction problem. The expectation value for this force in the ^{4}He ground state is -0.13 with SOM, -20.5 MeV with SWTH. The presence of the long-range S–D interaction is also evident in fig. 10.5. Indeed, the two-body S–D matrix elements of SOM and SWTH differ by an order of magnitude as is seen in Table 10.1. In section 10.8 we will have occasion to discuss this problem further.

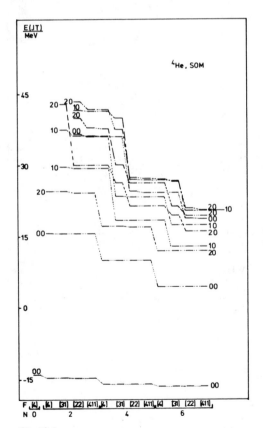

Figs. 10.5–10.7

States of positive parity in ^{4}He under extension of the model space

Fig. 10.5

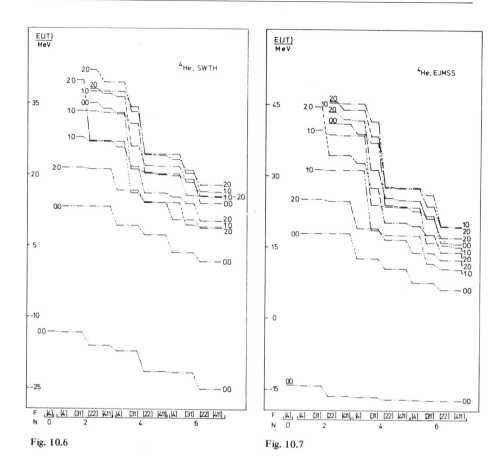

Fig. 10.6   **Fig. 10.7**

Table 10.6 Experimental and calculated excitation energies of the first non-normal parity state for nuclei A = 4–10. All energies are relative to the ground states quoted in Table 10.5

A	exp.	J T	SOM	SWTH	EJMSS
4	21.2	0 0	19.8	20.	
5	?	$\frac{1}{2}\frac{1}{2}$	8.8	8.6	6.2
6	?	2 0	12.8	12.7	12.9
7	?	$\frac{1}{2}\frac{1}{2}$	15.	14.1	15.
8	18.9	2 0	21.7	25.5	25.7
9	1.68	$\frac{1}{2}\frac{1}{2}$	8.1	7.8	8.7
10	5.11	2 0	10.4	9.8	10.6
11	6.8	$\frac{1}{2}\frac{1}{2}$		15.	

The general results about the relative position of non-normal parity states can also be mentioned in this section. Calculating these states in a space with excitations $N_0 + 1$ and $N_0 + 3$ quanta, we obtain the excitation energies relative to the ground states given in Table 10.6.

The values given here can only be regarded as first estimates. It is tempting, however, to use the structure which obviously is present in the Table to make some statements about the first non-normal parity levels in A = 5, 6, 7. The values for A = 8 ... 11 suggest a dependence on the mass number modulo 4.

10.7 The Oscillator Parameter b

Because so far we did not calculate radii or other quantities, which test wavefunctions, a systematic study of the b-dependence is not possible.

First of all we observe reasonable spectra for all nuclei with b between 1.4 fm and 1.6 fm, indicating no remarkable changes in the nuclear sizes. This has also been reported by Wilkinson and Mafethe [WI 66] for the entire p-shell. Various electron scattering determinations of b give values around b = 1.5 fm.

Now, as an example, we look at the b-dependence of the lowest ^{6}Li states in fig. 10.8. Again we can separate two distinct effects as in section 10.4. The model space is far from being complete because there is still an appreciable change in the ground state energy. On the other hand, the relative positions of the levels are fairly stable, that is, our wavefunctions certainly contain most of the important components. If we can recognize some common b-dependence in a spectrum it is perhaps possible to discriminate some states which are not approximated well.

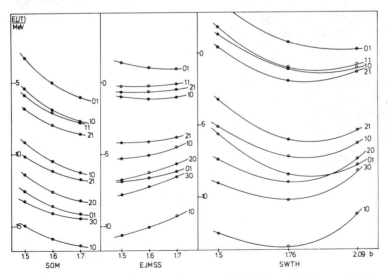

Fig. 10.8 States of positive parity in ^{6}Li as a function of the oscillator parameter b

10.8 Results on Nuclei with A = 4–10

So far we did not refer to experiment. If this is now done we are nevertheless mainly interested in the general model space problem. We can not fit anything but only test if the convergence behaviour observed in section 10.4 leads to realistic results concerning the structure and position of excited states. Unfortunately, this test is obstructed by at least two facts. First of all the convergence behaviour is inseparably connected with the interaction. Therefore, it is not possible to ascribe observed discrepancies either to the model space or to the interaction. On the other hand, if with a special interaction there are coincidences with experimental facts, this proves only some kind of effectiveness of this interaction with respect to the model space. The second difficulty of course is the lack of particle-bound states in these nuclei.

Therefore, we do not present final fits, but try to discuss all calculated data.

The experimental levels shown in the figures are taken from Ajzenberg-Selove and Lauritsen [AJ 74]. For A = 4 we use the compilation of Fiarman and Meyerhof [FI 73]. In any case only levels with definite parity are listed. Resonances observed by other authors are discussed in the text.

For each nucleus the spectra of the two parities are presented separately and we usually take the first known level as reference. The reference energy is described in the text as E(JTfLS). For states calculated with the SOM interaction we quote one or two fLS components such that the probability for finding any other fLS value is less than 10 p.c.

All calculations have been done with value b = 1.5 fm for the oscillator length parameter. Interactions used are indicated by abbreviations introduced in section 10.4.

If available we include tables which contain expectation values of the central, spin-orbit and tensor components of the interaction (κ = 0, 1, 2). Other tables give predictions and observations of particular resonances.

Results from the following other calculations are included in figures:

B. S. Cooper et al. [CO 71] (see also section 10.5)
P. P. Szydlik et al. [SZ 72]
R. F. Wagner and C. Werntz [WA 71]
B. S. Cooper and J. M. Eisenberg [CO 68a]
A. Aswad et al. [AS 73]
L. Grünbaum and M. Tomaselli [GR 71]
P. S. Hauge and S. Maripuu [HA 73] (see also section 10.5)
R. Saayman et al. [SA 73]

States of Positive Parity in ⁴He

$N_{max} = 6$, f = [4], [31], [22], [211]

JT = 00, 10, 20   Table 10.7, figs. 10.5–10.7, 10.9

In fig. 10.9 we choose E(0* 0 [4] 00) = 20.1 MeV as suggested by comparing figs. 10.5–10.7. The calculated 0⁺ state at E = 20.1 MeV corresponds to the only known sharp resonance. It differs from the ground state mainly by a dominant excitation of two oscillator quanta. A broad resonance at E = 25.5 MeV has been reported by [LI 72] with tentative assignment JT = 00 or 10. The present computation gives no evidence for a J = 0⁺ state in this region. However, figs. 10.5–10.7 show that in deviation from the shell model a state of JT = 10 moves into the energy region in question. This state has almost pure [31] symmetry. The two calculated states with JT = 20 differ in particular in their symmetry [4] and [22]. For the symmetry [4] we do not expect a resonance at this excitation. It can be seen from figs. 10.5–10.7 that the state with JT = 20, f = [22] moves down from a very high initial energy. Nevertheless the final energy in our opinion is still too high to justify an identification with the anomaly above the d–d threshold discussed in [GU 74]. We would prefer to relate this computed state with a resonance at E = 29 MeV proposed in earlier work by Werntz and Meyerhof [WE 68] and later on located by Fiarman and Meyerhof [FI 73] at E = 33 MeV. Szydlik et al. [SZ 72] calculated states in ⁴He using an oscillator basis and the EJMSS interaction. Their computation is comparable to our lowest order calculation (N = 2).

Table 10.7 Calculated contributions of central, spin-orbit and tensor interactions (κ = 0, 1, 2) for the lowest states of positive parity in ⁴He

JTf	SOM			SWTH			EJMSS		
	$\kappa = 0$	$\kappa = 1$	$\kappa = 2$	$\kappa = 0$	$\kappa = 2$	$\kappa = 2$	$\kappa = 0$	$\kappa = 1$	$\kappa = 2$
00	− 16.41	− 0.	− 0.13	− 5.68	− 0.5	− 20.5	− 12.15	0.18	− 5.4
00*	4.61	0.	− 0.1	8.43	0.3	− 7.1	· 8.89	− 0.05	− 5.7
10	13.6	0.	− 0.6	15.04	0.1	− 6.2	15.66	− 0.13	− 4.95
20 [4]	12.19	0.	− 0.25	16.78	0.	− 8.1	18.9	− 0.18	− 6.34
20 [22]	17.89	0.	− 1.64	21.66	− 0.03	− 11.4	22.26	− 0.11	− 8.3

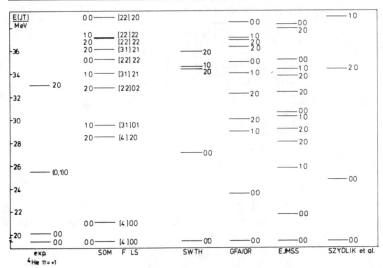

Fig. 10.9

States of positive parity in ⁴He

States of Negative Parity in ^{4}He

N_{max} = 5, f = [4], [31], [22], [211]

JT = 00, 10, 20, 01, 11, 21

Table 10.8, figs. 10.10–10.12

We choose $E(00\,[31]\,11)$ = 21.2 MeV. For N = 1 the model space contains only f = [31] which gives rise to two triplets LS = 11 and T = 0,1 and to an additional state LS = 10, T = 1. Resonances corresponding to these assignments have been analyzed, but only those with JT = 00, 20 have been unambiguously identified. Comparing the spacing of these two resonances with the computations we find good agreement only for the SOM and GFA/EH interactions. Table 10.8 shows that the SWTH interaction overestimates the tensor contribution and hence leads to a larger spacing of these states. For the higher resonances there exist two sets of resonance energies obtained from phase-shift analysis due to Werntz and Meyerhof [WE 68] and to Fiarman and Meyerhof [FI 73]. They are indicated in fig. 10.10 by broken and solid lines respectively. The computation with SOM and GFA/EH interactions for T = 1 levels show a splitting comparable to these data and an average position which favours the older analysis. Both computations give the JT = 10 level at about the same position but considerably lower than SWTH or the shell model calculation of Szydlik et al. [SZ 72]. We remark that under increase of the model space this level moves down with respect to the lowest level. It would be interesting to know if this result is related to the J = 1⁻ level proposed by Seiler [SE 75] and Ying [YI 73] as an alternative explanation for the anomaly above the d-d-level.

Shell model computations as [SZ 72] are comparable to our computations of order N = 1 as given in fig. 10.10.

Table 10.8 Calculated contributions of central, spin-orbit and tensor interactions (κ = 0, 1, 2) for the lowest states of negative parity in ^{4}He

JT	SOM			SWTH		
	$\kappa = 0$	$\kappa = 1$	$\kappa = 2$	$\kappa = 0$	$\kappa = 1$	$\kappa = 2$
00	5.43	1.5	− 3.6	11.98	1.9	− 15.3
20	5.54	− 0.9	− 0.45	12.1	− 1.	− 10.1
21	6.43	− 1.	− 0.2	10.88	− 1.	− 6.2
01	6.4	1.16	− 1.22	10.43	1.3	− 6.4
11	6.81	− 0.23	0.21	10.77	0.1	− 6.3
10	5.65	0.4	1.25	11.07	0.3	− 6.2
11	7.48	0.5	− 0.1	9.71	0.24	− 2.4

Figs. 10.11, 10.12 States of negative parity in ^{4}He under extension of the model space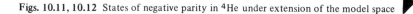

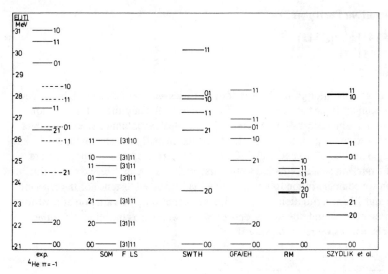

Fig. 10.10
States of negative
parity in ⁴He

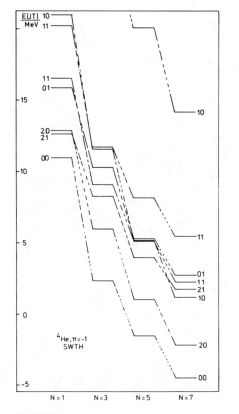

Fig. 10.11

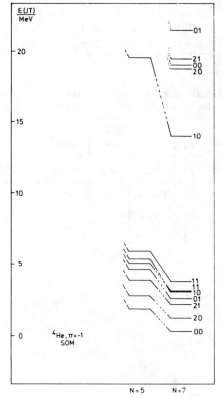

Fig. 10.12

States of Negative Parity in ^{5}He

$N_{max} = 5$, $f = [41], [32], [311]$

$2J\,2T = 11, 31, 51, 71$

Table 10.9, fig. 10.13

The relative separation of the lowest doublet varies with the interaction but is due mainly to the spin-orbit part as can be seen from Table 10.9. Only the RM interaction shows almost no doublet separation. At about $E = 20$ MeV, we obtain a second doublet with a dominant excitation of $N = 3$ quanta. A resonance at $E = 20$ MeV with $J = \frac{3}{2}^-$ has been found by Schröder, Kern and Fick [SC 74], and interpreted as a compound state consisting of a nucleon weakly coupled to the first excited state of ^{4}He. To check this interpretation we compare in the following Table the calculated distance of the relevant levels in ^{4}He and ^{5}He as a function of the oscillator excitation. The variation at least for the SWTH interaction found does not support a weak coupling assumption. For other evidence on resonances we refer to [SE 75].

| | ^{4}He: $E(0^*) - E(0)$ | | ^{5}He: $E(0^*) - E(0)$ | |
	N = 2	N = 4	N = 3	N = 5
SOM	30.5	25.7	28.3	22.3
SWTH	29.4	28.9	28.1	22.5

Table 10.9 Calculated contributions of central, spin-orbit and tensor interactions ($\kappa = 0, 1, 2$) for the lowest states of negative parity in ^{5}He

| | SOM | | | SWTH | | | EJMSS | | |
J T	$\kappa = 0$	$\kappa = 1$	$\kappa = 2$	$\kappa = 0$	$\kappa = 1$	$\kappa = 2$	$\kappa = 0$	$\kappa = 1$	$\kappa = 2$
$\frac{3}{2}\frac{1}{2}$	-10.74	-1.2	-0.06	-4.86	-1.11	-5.78	-6.63	-0.61	-2.78
$\frac{1}{2}\frac{1}{2}$	-10.64	1.2	-0.08	-5.29	1.19	-5.18	-6.6	-0.1	-2.57
$\frac{3}{2}\frac{1}{2}$	15.91	-1.88	-0.11	14.99	-1.21	-3.12	16.93	-2.03	-1.38

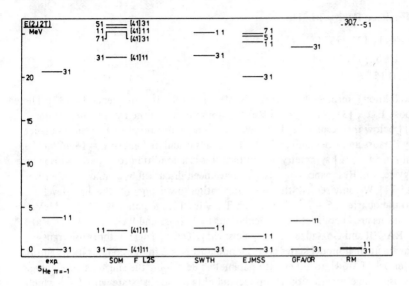

Fig. 10.13 States of negative parity in ^{5}He

States of Positive Parity in ^{5}He

$N_{max} = 6$, $f = [41], [32], [311]$

$2J\,2T = 11, 31, 51, 71, 13, 33, 53, 73$

Figs. 10.14, 10.15

The well-known resonance at $E = 16.76$ MeV has $LS = 0\,\frac{3}{2}$ and hence $f = [32]$. Therefore we choose $E\,(\frac{3}{2}\,\frac{1}{2}\,[31]\,11) = 16.76$ MeV. Our computation then yields three states with $f = [41]$ below this resonance. The lowest one may correspond to a broad resonance proposed by Strauss and Friedland [ST 72]. The levels calculated above $E = 16.76$ MeV all show almost pure $f = [32]$ symmetry and in turn this is a condition for a narrow resonance in this energy region. Resonances of this type have been discussed by a number of authors, compare [AJ 74]. We only remark that we find a rather low energy for the $J = \frac{7}{2}$ level belonging to the quartet $LS = 2\,\frac{3}{2}$. The lowest $T = \frac{3}{2}$ level is predicted at $E = 20.7$ MeV. Our computations are in conflict with calculations by Wagner and Werntz [WA 71], Ramarataram [RA 70] and Gogsadze and Kopaleishvili [GO 69]. These authors use translationally invariant shell model states corresponding to $N = 2$ in our computations and the Tabakin potential [TA 64], together with parameters describing the single-particle energies. They find considerable supermultiplet mixing and obtain a lowest state with $J = \frac{3}{2}$ which is then identified with the level at $E = 16.76$ MeV. This state according to [GO 69] has 25 % admixture of $F = [41]$. We believe that a narrow resonance at this energy must correspond to the onset of a new supermultiplet with almost no admixture. Moreover with the present interactions we never found an inversion of the natural order of the supermultiplets as would be implied by these shell model calculations. Therefore we propose that most narrow resonances above $E = 16.8$ MeV should have $f = [32]$ whereas resonances with $f = [41]$ should be broader.

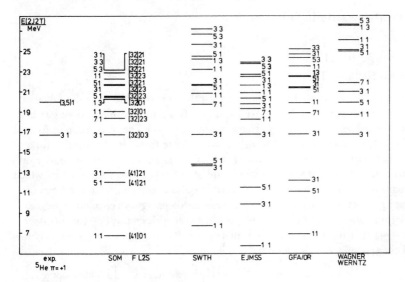

Fig. 10.14 States of positive parity in ^{5}He

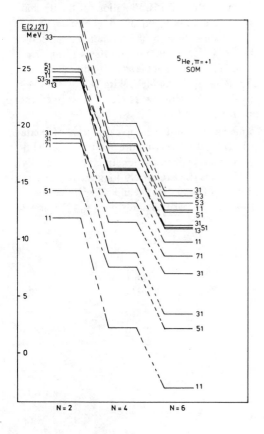

Fig. 10.15

States of positive parity in ^{5}He under extension of the model space

States of Positive Parity in ^{6}Li

$N_{max} = 6$, $f = [42], [411], [33]$

$JT = 00, 10, 20, 30, 01, 11, 21, 31$

Tables 10.3, 10.10, figs. 10.1–10.3, 10.16

The numbers in Table 10.3 once more suggest that a reasonable force should be somewhat in between SOM and SWTH. With this qualification the computations give a good account of the six lowest states characterized by $f = [42]$. The next group of four levels has $f = [411]$. Gruebler et al. [GR 70] found evidence from ^{4}He-d scattering for a broad resonance at about $E = 9$ MeV with $JT = 10$. Our assignment of this resonance gives unambiguously $fLS = [411]$ 10 with 8 % admixture of $fLS = [42]$ 10. This structure which cannot be built in the ^{4}He-d channel would account quite well for the characteristics of the resonance given in [GR 70]. Comparing the excitation energy we conclude that the SOM interaction should describe reasonably well the average level position for the super-multiplet $f = [411]$. This implies that the triplet of $T = 1$ levels appears comparatively low and should correspond to levels found in ^{6}B at energies $E = 2 \ldots 6$ MeV.

Indications of resonances above the ^{3}He–^{3}H threshold at $E = 15.8$ MeV come from two sources. From astrophysical considerations it was proposed that a narrow resonance with $JT = 01$ should occur right above this threshold [FE 75]. Violations of the Barshay-Temmer theorem in the ^{3}H(^{3}He, d) ^{4}He reaction have been explained by Nocken [NO 73] as due to a $JT = 21$ resonance at $E = 16 \ldots 17$ MeV. None of the computed levels shown in fig. 10.16 can account for this structure and we looked into higher states arising from at least $N = 4$. With the SOM interaction and $N_{max} = 6$ we get levels with dominantly $f = [42]$, $JT = 01$ at $E = 27.3$ MeV and $JT = 21$ at $E = 29.4$ MeV. With $N_{max} = 8$ these levels are expected to more down to about $E = 27$ MeV or $E = 24$ MeV. These levels cannot be excluded as candidates for the violation in question.

Thompson and Tang [TH 68] performed a resonanting group calculation of excited states in ^{6}Li. They predict six excited levels with ^{3}H + ^{3}He structure and the same JTLS-content as the lowest states considered above. States of this cluster structure necessarily belong to $f = [42]$ since the partition $f = [33]$ gives rise exclusively to negative parity states. In the present computation we allow for mixing of both ^{4}He + d and ^{3}H + ^{3}He cluster structures and find only a single group of six positive parity states with $f = [42]$ below the ^{3}H + ^{3}He threshold.

Table 10.10 Calculated contributions of central, spin-orbit and tensor interactions ($\kappa = 0, 1, 2$) for the lowest states of positive parity in ^{6}Li

JT	SOM			SWTH			EJMSS		
	$\kappa = 0$	$\kappa = 1$	$\kappa = 2$	$\kappa = 0$	$\kappa = 1$	$\kappa = 2$	$\kappa = 0$	$\kappa = 1$	$\kappa = 2$
10	− 14.08	− 0.77	− 0.04	− 3.95	− 0.62	− 7.92	− 7.12	− 0.60	− 2.90
30	− 11.18	− 2.31	− 0.21	− 1.32	− 2.09	− 5.62	− 4.04	− 1.82	− 1.93
01	− 11.31	− 1.31	0.06	− 4.32	− 1.3	0.04	− 5.92	− 0.92	0.03
20	11.12	0.48	− 0.77	− 1.17	0.16	− 6.39	− 3.45	− 0.21	− 3.21
21	− 8.66	− 1.47	− 0.	− 1.55	− 1.54	− 0.15	− 2.97	− 1.16	− 0.08
10*	− 10.18	0.66	0.37	− 0.99	0.97	− 5.07	− 3.3	0.72	− 2.73
21*	− 6.32	− 0.56	0.06	1.84	− 0.73	− 0.72	1.01	− 0.78	0.89
11*	− 5.78	0.54	− 0.61	2.54	0.44	− 1.68	1.25	− 0.02	− 1.52
10**	− 6.41	0.94	0.04	2.02	0.10	− 0.29	− 0.45	− 0.51	− 0.15
01*	− 5.78	1.87	0.63	2.14	1.73	0.41	1.16	− 0.06	0.26

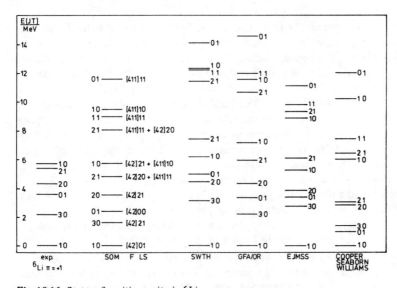

Fig. 10.16 States of positive parity in ^{6}Li

States of Negative Parity in ^{6}Li

N_{max} = 5, f = [42], [33], [411]

JT = 00, 10, 20, 30, 01, 11, 21, 31, 41

Table 10.11, fig. 10.17

From the following discussion we conclude that the energy scale in fig. 10.17 should be fixed as E(20 [42] 11) = 11 MeV. The calculated spectrum shows a group of low states with f = [42], a variety of states with f = [411] and a few states with f = [33]. There are also higher states with f = [42] which are not given in fig. 10.17. The lowest states form a triplet with LS = 11, JT = 20, 10, 00. A single-level analysis due to Senhouse and Tombrello [SE 64] indicates the possible presence of these levels at E = 6.6, 7.8 and 9 MeV. Note that these states by E1 transitions cannot decay to the lowest positive parity states in ^{6}Li without a change of the total spin.

Evidence for states with f = [411] could be obtained from their excitation by E1 radiation in the ^{6}Li(γ, n) reaction. The experimental spectra [HA 65a] show various maxima between E = 12 MeV and E = 22 MeV which could be related to groups of states with f = [411]. Above E = 22 MeV we expect contributions from higher supermultiplets as f = [321].

Of particular interest are the states with f = [33] which are found to have little mixing with f = [411]. The partition f = [33] couples strongly to the odd orbital angular momentum states in the ^{3}He + ^{3}H channel. Evidence for this partition comes from the elastic reaction and from γ-transitions. A phase-shift analysis of the reaction ^{3}H(^{3}He, ^{3}He) due to [VL 77] shows resonances JT = 21.01 at E = 21.0 MeV and E = 21.5 MeV respectively for L = 1 and resonances JT = 41,31 at E = 25.7 MeV and E = 26.7 MeV respectively for L = 3. Comparing the present computation we identify the state JT = 21 as 21 [33] 11 and place it at E = 21.0 MeV. Table 10.11 shows the calculated levels for f = [33] along with the experimental results. This table is based on a recalculation with higher angular momenta and differs in some details from the scheme displayed in Fig. 10.17. The four resonances of [VL 77] are reasonably well represented. For the computed levels with JT = 11, 10, 21 one should compare the phase shifts given by [VL 77]. The reported anomaly in the complex phase shift $^1F_3$ could be correlated with the presence of the state JT = 30 computed at E = 28.4 MeV. Since our computations yield a systematic energy difference between T = 0 and T = 1 states, this state may be located at an energy about 1 MeV lower.

For the γ-transitions we apply the following rules: states with a dominant partition should differ at most in the position of a single box. For E1 transitions, we have the selection rules $\Delta J = 0, \pm 1$, $\Delta L = 0, \pm 1$ and parity change. Moreover, we assume $\Delta S = 0$ which holds true for the bigger part of the E1 transition operator. For the self-conjugate nucleus ^{6}Li we have in addition $\Delta T \neq 0$. The coupling of reaction channels to resonances is favoured if the orbital partition of the resonance is induced by the fragment partitions in the reaction channel. Thus, the channel ^{3}He + ^{3}H for odd parity couples to resonances of partition f = [33]. Coupling to the partition f = [411] would appear only through corresponding admixtures in the resonance.

The reaction ^{3}H(^{3}He, γ) was studied in [VE 71] and [VE 73]. These authors analyzed the γ-transitions to the first five levels in ^{6}Li, π = + 1 which they denote as $\gamma_0\gamma_1\gamma_2\gamma_3\gamma_4$.

In [VE 71] the experimental results were interpreted in terms of resonances JT = 41 at E = 26.1 MeV and JT = 31 at E = 26.6 MeV. In [VE 73] the interpretation of the lower resonance was modified on the basis of a direct capture calculation. It was argued that the resonance should differ in structure from the entrance channel, and a structure α + p + n was proposed with JT = (2 3 4) 1 at an energy E = 25.1 MeV. From the induction rules, the structure α + p + n yields the orbital partitions f = [42] and f = [411]. The first partition has ST = 01, 10 and therefore does not yield the transition. The partition f = [411] is fully included in the present calculation. The mixture between f = [33] and f = [411] if found to be a few percent in this energy region. From this and from the results found by [VL 77] we conclude in contrast to [VE 73] that all resonances found from the channel ^{3}He + ^{3}H have the partition f = [33]. The assignment of the resonances at E = 21; 21.5 MeV is supported by the resonance in the reaction ^{6}Li(γ, ^{3}H) reported by [MU 70].

Table 10.11 Calculated negative parity states in ^{6}Li of partition f = [33] and predicted γ-transitions to low positive parity states in ^{6}Li compared with experimental results on the reactions ^{3}H(^{3}He, ^{3}He) ^{3}H by [VL 77] and ^{3}H(^{3}He, γ) ^{6}Li by [VE 73]

Calculation			^{3}H(^{3}He, ^{3}He) ^{3}H		^{3}H(^{3}He, γ) ^{6}Li		
E	JTfLS	decay	E	JT, LS	E	JT, LS	decay
28.4	30 [33] 30	γ_4			26.6	30, (13) 0	γ_4
27.8	21 [33] 31	$\gamma_1\gamma_3$					
27.8	31 [33] 31	$\gamma_1\gamma_3$	26.7	31,31	26.6	31, (13) 1	γ_3
25	41 [33] 31	γ_1	25.7	41,31	25.1	(234) 1, 13	γ_1
23.6	10 [33] 10	γ_0					
23.0	11 [33] 11	γ_0					
21.2	01 [33] 11	γ_0	21.5	01.11			
21.0	21 [33] 11	$\gamma_0\gamma_1$	21.0	21.11			

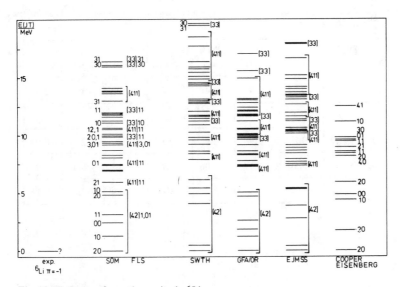

Fig. 10.17 States of negative parity in ^{6}Li

States of Negative Parity in ^{7}Li

N_{max} = 5, f = [43], [421]

2J 2T = 11, 31, 51, 71, 13, 33, 53, 73

Table 10.12, figs. 10.18, 10.19

The interaction SOM clearly turns out to give the most satisfactory and consistent results. This holds true in particular for the relative position of supermultiplets, as could be seen already in ^{6}Li. The relative position of the two resonances J = $\frac{5}{2}^-$, which differ mainly in the partition, is well reproduced. In the energy region E = 9 ... 11 MeV we get six predicted levels of partition f = [421] which should be observable. Among them is the first state with T = $\frac{3}{2}$ which apparently corresponds to the computed state JT = $\frac{3}{2}\frac{3}{2}$. To discuss the other states we compare also fig. 10.19. This figure shows that the relative positions of the levels decrease with extension of the model space. The J = $\frac{1}{2}$ state moves down to an energy near E = 10 MeV where Harrison [HA 67] finds evidence for a resonance J = $\frac{1}{2}$. The two J = $\frac{3}{2}$ states could be correlated with resonances proposed by Lejeune and Sator [LE 74] at E = 9 MeV and by Presser et al. [PR 69] at about E = 11 MeV. The only computed state not identified has then J = $\frac{5}{2}\frac{1}{2}$. There are two computed higher states with T = $\frac{3}{2}$. They could be related to states proposed by Mani and Dix [MA 68] in ^{7}Li at E = 12.5 and 13.6 MeV or by Battey et al. [BA 68] in ^{7}Be at E = 11.7 and 12.8 MeV since these states are characterized by a comparatively small width (Γ < 1 MeV).

The shell model computation by Cooper et al. [CO 71] is comparable to our calculations for N_{max} = 3, at least with respect to the position of the first state with T = $\frac{3}{2}$. The computation by Kumar [KU 74] for ^{7}Li agrees much better with our results than for ^{6}Li. The modifications of the relative positions under extension of the model state are found to be less pronounced for ^{7}Li than for ^{6}Li, compare fig. 10.19.

Table 10.12 Calculated contributions of central, spin-orbit and tensor interactions (κ = 0, 1, 2) for the lowest states of negative parity in ^{7}Li

J T	SOM			SWTH			EJMSS		
	$\kappa = 0$	$\kappa = 1$	$\kappa = 2$	$\kappa = 0$	$\kappa = 1$	$\kappa = 2$	$\kappa = 0$	$\kappa = 1$	$\kappa = 2$
$\frac{3}{2}\frac{1}{2}$	− 14.3	− 1.8	0.12	− 2.92	− 1.4	− 3.8	− 7.23	− 1.6	− 2.3
$\frac{1}{2}\frac{1}{2}$	− 14.25	− 0.7	− 0.2	− 2.7	− 0.6	− 4.6	− 7.01	− 0.6	− 3.0
$\frac{7}{2}\frac{1}{2}$	− 8.71	− 2.9	0.2	1.98	− 2.6	− 0.17	− 1.47	− 2.7	− 0.04
$\frac{5}{2}\frac{5}{2}$	− 7.99	− 0.7	− 0.5	3.57	− 0.06	− 3.7	− 0.15	− 0.21	− 2.9
$\frac{5}{2}\frac{5}{2}$ *	− 5.6	− 2.7	− 0.14	6.65	− 3.01	− 1.61	3.43	− 3.4	− 1.11

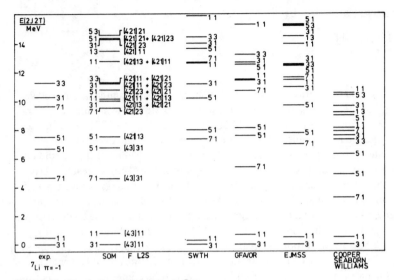

Fig. 10.18 States of negative parity in ⁷Li

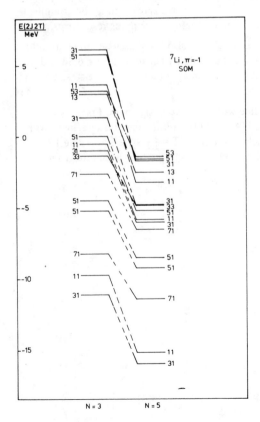

Fig. 10.19

States of negative parity in ⁷Li under extension of the model space

States of Positive Parity in ^{7}Li

N_{max} = 6, f = [43], [421]

2J 2T = 11, 31, 51, 71, 13, 33, 53, 73

Table 10.13, fig. 10.20

From the general comparison of the calculations with photodisintegration data we assign the energy of the lowest state as E $(\frac{1}{2}\frac{1}{2}$ [43] 01) = 9.5 MeV. The calculated spectra show states with partitions f = [43] and f = [421]. The states with f = [331] are expected at E = 18 MeV and are not included in the present computation. The experimental evidence for resonances comes from the reactions ^{7}Li(γ, n), ^{7}Li(γ, p) and ^{7}Li(γ, t) studied by Allum et al. [AL 64], Manucio et al. [MA 66] and others. The ^{6}Li(γ, t) reaction cross section shows a number of maxima between E = 9 ... 17 MeV, a decrease above E = 17.5 E = 17.5 MeV and a new rise at higher energies [MA 66]. Most of these maxima appear also in the ^{7}Li(γ, n) reaction [AL 64]. We apply again the rules given in the analysis of the states of ^{6}Li, π = – 1. Only the supermultiplet f = [43] should contribute to the ^{7}Li(γ, t) reaction via two-body disintegration whereas (γ, p) and (γ, n) are allowed for both f = [43] and f = [421]. The rise in the (γ, t) cross section above E = 17.5 MeV could be associated with states of the partition f = [331]. In Table 10.13 we list the computed levels according to their energy, indicate the possibility of triton decay and give from [AL 64] and [MA 66] the experimental energies and observed decays. A reasonable agreement in the grouping is observed, but the calculations imply the existence of many overlapping resonances.

States of positive parity with J = $\frac{3}{2}$, $\frac{1}{2}$ in ^{7}Li have also been discussed in relation to the ^{6}Li(n, α) ^{3}He reaction. Uttley et al. [UT 70] postulate such states at E = 6.56 and 10.5 MeV respectively. Fort and Maquette [FO 72] on the other hand place stese states at E = 9.8 and 11.7 MeV respectively, together with the J = $\frac{3}{2}^-$ resonance found at E = 9 MeV.

Our calculations would be more in line with the latter assignment. Finally we note that the shell model calculations by Aswad [AS 73] yield results in good agreement with the present ones. Note that we did not include the first JT = $\frac{3}{2}\frac{1}{2}$ state into Table 10.13 since E1 decay would not involve ΔS = 0. Correspondingly the transition rate given by Aswad is comparatively low.

Table 10.13 Calculated states of positive parity which should contribute to $^7Li(\gamma, {}^3H)$ and observed resonances according to [AL 64] and [MA 66]

E_{calc}	2J2T f L2S	decay	E_{exp}	decay
17.4	31 [43] 21	t	17.3	t
17.4	33 [43] 21	t		
16.7	31 [421] 21			
	+ 31 [43] 21	(t)		
16.4	53 [43] 21	t	16.2	t
15.4	51 [43] 21	t		
14.5	31 [43] 11	t		
14.4	11 [43] 01	t	14.2	t
	+ 11 [43] 11	t		
14.4	51 [421] 21			
	+ 51 [43] 21	(t)		
14.2	13 [421] 01	.		
13.8	51 [43] 21	t	13.5	t
13.1	31 [43] 21	t	12.5	t
13.1	11 [421] 01			
11.8	51 [43] 21	t	11.4	t
9.5	11 [43] 21	t	9.5	t

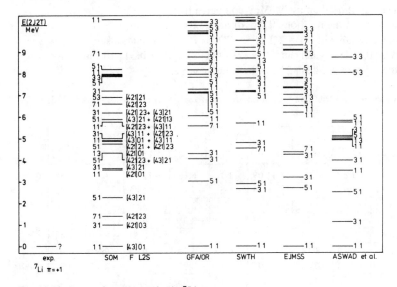

Fig. 10.20 States of positive parity in ^7Li

States of Positive Parity in ^{8}Be

$N_{max} = 8$, $f = [44], [431], [422]$
$JT = 00, 10, 20, 30, 40, 01, 11, 21, 31, 41$
Tables 10.4, 10.14, figs. 10.21–10.24

The first three calculated levels belong to the partition $f = [44]$. Only when the model space is extended to $N = 8$ we get the onset of the supermultiplet $f = [431]$ at about the right energy for the state $JT = 20$. We choose $E(20 [431] 11) = 16.6$ MeV. This level is used in fig. 10.23 for the comparison of calculated and experimentally known levels. The first six levels have $J = 2, 1, 3$ along with two values $T = 0, 1$ of the isospin. They correspond to well-known levels which show in part isospin mixing. The next level has $JT = 10$ and can be associated with a resonance at 19.9 MeV reported by Bevington, Rolland and Lewis [BE 61]. All other levels with $T = 0$ and $f = [431]$ can be identified with known levels up to $E = 26$ MeV. Of particular interest are the levels with partition $f = [422]$ which appear in the calculation at $E = 20$ MeV with $JT = 40$, at $E = 22$ MeV with $JT = 20$ and at $E = 25.5$ MeV with $JT = 00$. The experimentally known level with $JT = 40$ at $E = 20$ MeV is reported to have a very small proton width [KU 71]. This is most easily explained by noting that the partition $f = [422]$ cannot be decomposed into $[431] + [1]$ corresponding to the channel ^{7}Be + n. The calculated level with $JT = 20$ appears experimentally near the ^{6}Li + d threshold. Its computed structures $LS = 02$ (with an admixture of $LS = 21$) agrees with results of a phase-shift analysis due to Seiler [SE 75]. The situation is more involved for the $T = 1$ states. Comparing lower states one finds that in the computations these states appear at an energy shifted up by 0.5 MeV compared to the $T = 0$ states. Presser et al. [PR 72] propose from the reactions ^{7}Li(p, n) and ^{7}Li(n, n) a state with $JT = 1^+1$ at $E = 20$ MeV and a state with $JT = 2^+1$ at $E = 22$ MeV. The calculations, taking into account a shift by 0.5 MeV, yield candidates 21 [431] 21 and 11 [431] 10 for the lower energy and a candidate 21 [431] 20 for the higher energy.

Table 10.14 Calculated contributions of central, spin-orbit and tensor interactions ($\kappa = 0, 1, 2$) for the lowest states of positive parity in ^{8}Be

JT	SOM			SWTH			EJMSS		
	$\kappa = 0$	$\kappa = 1$	$\kappa = 2$	$\kappa = 0$	$\kappa = 1$	$\kappa = 2$	$\kappa = 0$	$\kappa = 1$	$\kappa = 2$
00	− 26.44	− 1.8	0.04	− 11.09	− 1.2	− 6.18	− 17.15	− 1.49	− 3.88
20	− 23.54	− 1.95	0.02	− 8.24	− 1.36	− 5.99	− 14.45	− 1.57	− 3.93
40	− 13.7	− 2.84	0.05	2.13	− 1.82	− 3.1	− 3.65	− 2.08	− 2.34
20	− 11.21	− 3.91	0.24	5.73	− 3.32	− 3.05	− 0.25	− 3.51	− 2.04
21	− 10.61	− 3.31	0.05	5.22	− 3.1	− 2.19	− 0.37	− 3.21	− 1.44
10	− 11.37	− 0.19	− 2.14	5.1	0.02	− 4.74	− 0.79	− 0.03	− 4.02
11	− 10.13	− 2.28	− 0.03	4.9	− 2.1	− 0.97	− 0.32	− 2.17	− 0.91
30	− 10.1	− 1.76	− 0.27	6.2	− 1.77	− 3.06	0.5	− 1.7	− 1.55
31	− 8.05	− 3.75	0.27	7.22	− 3.23	− 0.59	1.9	− 3.7	− 0.27
10	− 10.25	− 0.82	− 1.16	− 5.93	− 0.75	− 4.18	0.75	0.6	− 3.4
40	− 6.41	− 5.54	0.52	9.68	− 5.1	− 1.1	4.29	− 5.27	− 0.48
20	− 9.17	− 1.01	− 0.17	6.72	− 0.25	− 4.59	1.73	− 0.86	− 2.43

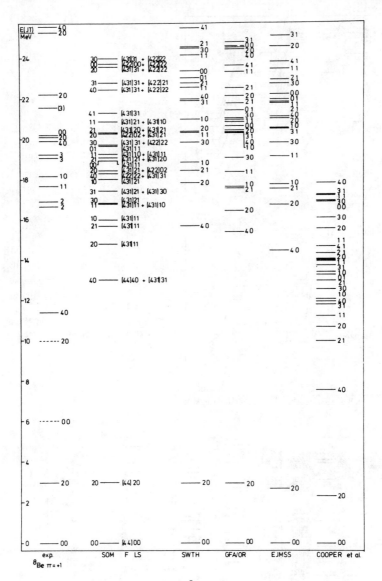

Fig. 10.21 States of positive parity in ^{8}Be

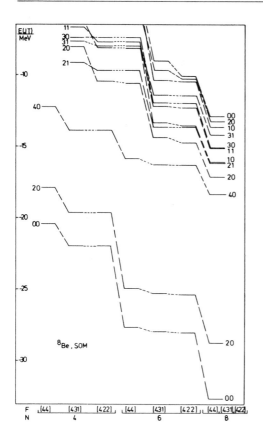

Fig. 10.22

States of positive parity in ^{8}Be under extension of the model space

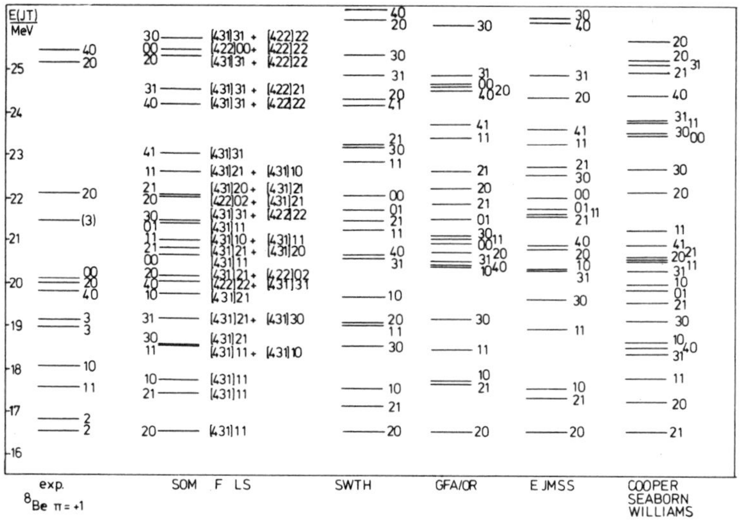

Fig. 10.23 States of positive parity in ^{8}Be

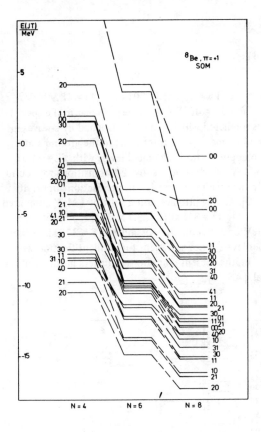

Fig. 10.24

States of positive parity in ^{8}Be under extension of the model space

States of Negative Parity in ^{8}Be

N_{max} = 7, f = [44], [431], [422]

JT = 00, 10, 20, 30, 40, 01, 11, 21, 31, 41

Fig. 10.25

The lowest calculated level has JT = 2 and we choose E(20[431]11) = 18.9 MeV. The known levels JT = 10, E = 19.5 MeV and JT = 40, E = 20.9 MeV appear in the spectrum. An additional level with JT = 00 is predicted which cannot be reached by s-waves in the ^{7}Li + p channel. The T = 1 levels should appear in E1 transitions to the ground state. If we assume the selection rule ΔS = 0 to apply we find calculated levels with JT = 11 at E = 23 MeV and with JT = 31 at E = 25 MeV which should show E1 transitions to ground and excited states in ^{8}Be. Experimentally the maxima in the ^{7}Li(p, γ) reaction appear at about E = 22 MeV and E = 24 MeV [FI 70]. Taking into account a shift of 1 MeV compared to the T = 0 states one could associate the state JT = 3^-1 at E = 23.1 MeV [PR 72] with the calculated level 31 [431] 31 at E = 24 MeV and exclude the possibility JT = 3^+1 since there is no candidate. The information on other levels is not sufficient for an identification with calculated levels. In contrast to the case ^{7}Li, the present computation differs in the position of the levels from the one by Aswad et al. [AS 73].

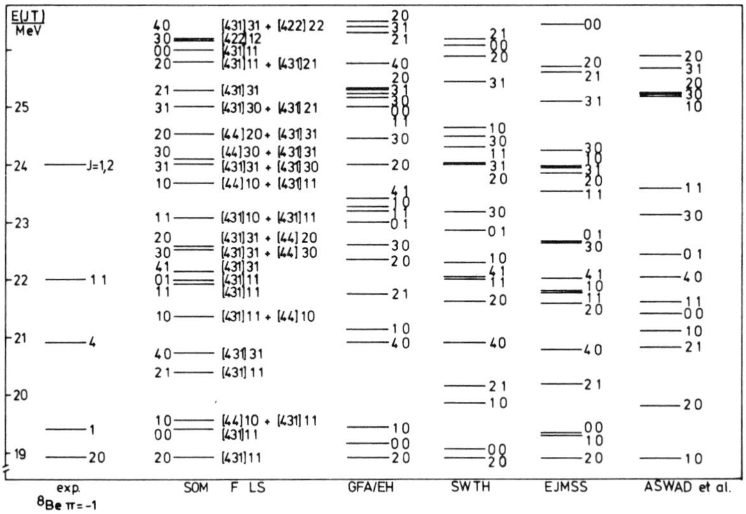

Fig. 10.25 States of negative parity in ^{8}Be

States of Negative Parity in ^{9}Be

$N_{max} = 7$, f = [441], [432]

2J2T = 11, 31, 51, 71, 13, 33, 53, 73

Table 10.15, figs. 10.26, 10.27

The lowest supermultiplet f = [441] and lowest excitation N = 5 allows for L = 1, 2, 3, 4 and hence gives rise to pairs of equal-J states which can be mixed by the spin-orbit interaction. Admixture of L = 2 in the calculated ground state is in line with the increased quadrupole moment, admixture of L = 3 in the first excited state is required by the neutron decay of this level, compare Bouten et al. [BO 68, BO 69]. The evidence for the next levels with f = [441] is not conclusive. While the existence of a level with $J = \frac{1}{2}^{-}$ is confirmed by now, other resonances in the region E 4 ... 5 MeV are under discussion, compare [Gu 70, KR 68 and ES 72]. At any rate these resonances are strongly coupled to the neutron or ^{4}He channels and should be broad. Note that the levels $J = \frac{7}{2}, \frac{9}{2}, LS = 4\frac{1}{2}$ were not computed but can be expected around E = 11 MeV. The experimentally kown levels at E = 11.28 and E = 11.81 MeV differ considerably in their coupling to reaction channels so that only one of them may be identified as an L = 4 level.

Turning now to the partition f = [432] we find a more definite situation than for f = [431] in ^{8}Be. Looking at fig. 10.27 it can be seen that the relative energies of these levels are stable when going from N = 5 to N = 7. Comparing with experimental data we find that the level $JT = \frac{3}{2} \frac{3}{2}$ is placed correctly at E = 14.4 MeV. Assuming that the relative spacing is correct we expect seven more resonances of f = [432] below this energy. Tentatively we assume that the level at E = 11.8 MeV corresponds to $JT = \frac{5}{2} \frac{1}{2}$. Then the only level between E = 11.8 MeV and E = 14.4 MeV must be assigned as $JT = \frac{3}{2} \frac{1}{2}$.

The predicted four levels below E = 11.8 MeV are not easily identified in particle reactions. The conclusion of Barker [BA 66] that there are no such levels was based on old β decay data [HA 65] and cannot be justified in view of more recent work [ES 72]. Electromagnetic transitions and electron scattering in this region is reported by Slight [SL 73], Vanpraet and Barber [VA 68], Hughes et al. [HU 75] and Thomas et al. [TH 72]. These data confirm the existence of several resonances at higher energy. The present calculation shows that there should exist a very complex set of states both of negative and positive parity belonging to the partitions f = [441] and f = [432]. For an attempt of of correlating predicted and observed resonances we refer to the discussion of positive parity states.

Cocke [CO 68] finds in the reaction ^{7}Li(^{3}He, p) ^{9}Be three resonances at E = 11.29; 11.81 and 13.78 MeV with $J = \frac{1}{2}$ and a width of the order 500 KeV. This suggests the assignment $J = \frac{5}{2}, \frac{5}{2}, \frac{3}{2}$ and f = [432] for such levels which should appear in addition to the doublet $J = \frac{9}{2}, \frac{7}{2}$, f = [441] mentioned above. The level just below E = 14.4 MeV mentioned by Thomas [TH 72] would then be identified as $JT = \frac{1}{2} \frac{1}{2}$, f = [432]. Between E = 15 and E = 16 MeV, two levels are reported by Hardy et al. [HA 71], Bergstrom et al. [BE 73] and by Glukhov et al. [GL 71] and Thomas et al. [TH 72] near the energies E = 15.1 MeV and E = 15.9 MeV respectively. The reported widths of these levels is compatible with the assignment $JT = \frac{5}{2} \frac{1}{2}$ and $JT = \frac{3}{2} \frac{1}{2}$ respectively.

Table 10.15 Calculated contributions of central, spin-orbit and tensor interactions ($\kappa = 0, 1, 2$) for the lowest states of negative parity in ^{9}Be

J T	SOM			SWTH			EJMSS		
	$\kappa = 0$	$\kappa = 1$	$\kappa = 2$	$\kappa = 0$	$\kappa = 1$	$\kappa = 2$	$\kappa = 0$	$\kappa = 1$	$\kappa = 2$
$\frac{3}{2}\frac{1}{2}$	-24.51	-3.71	-0.14	-5.58	-3.18	-0.67	-12.37	-3.5	-0.48
$\frac{5}{2}\frac{1}{2}$	-22.76	-3.25	0.05	-3.94	-2.9	-0.56	-11.05	-3.03	-0.38
$\frac{1}{2}\frac{1}{2}$	-24.56	-0.22	0.03	-5.18	0.46	-1.68	-12.02	0.13	-1.33
$\frac{3}{2}\frac{1}{2}*$	-23.14	0.55	-0.2	-4.15	1.05	-1.41	-11.33	0.92	-0.99
$\frac{5}{2}\frac{1}{2}*$	-20.15	-0.91	-0.15	-0.34	-0.46	-2.62	-7.74	-0.63	-1.84
$\frac{7}{2}\frac{1}{2}$	-19.39	$-1.$	0.09	-0.96	-0.09	-0.39	-8.11	-0.29	-0.18
$\frac{3}{2}\frac{1}{2}**$	-15.53	-1.61	-0.53	5.57	-1.44	-4.38	-1.77	-1.5	-2.64

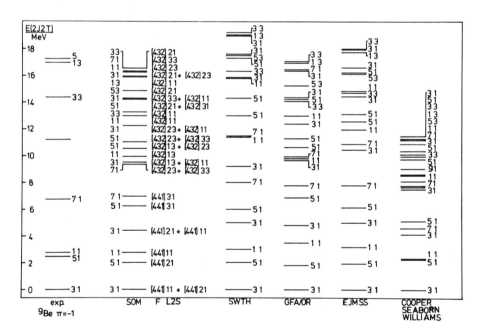

Fig. 10.26 States of negative parity in ^{9}Be

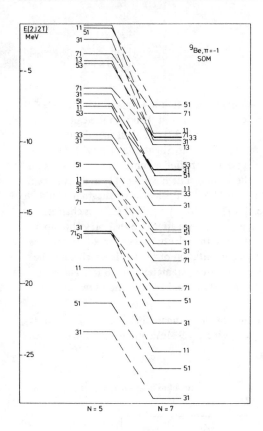

Fig. 10.27

States of negative parity in ^{9}Be under extension of the model space

In the literature, the second state with $T = \frac{3}{2}$ is always assumed to have $J = \frac{1}{2}$ which in the present calculation appears above a state $J\bar{T} = \frac{5}{2}\frac{3}{2}$. The only known resonance between $E = 16$ and 17 MeV is at $E = 16.67$ MeV and of width 41 KeV, compare Cocke [CO 68], Bergstrom et al. [BE 73] and Satchler [SA 67]. In particular, the data of [BE 73] do not contradict the assignment $J\bar{T} = \frac{5}{2}\frac{3}{2}$. There is another candidate $J\bar{T} = \frac{3}{2}\frac{1}{2}$ in this energy region which would explain the higher width. The levels which are strongly excited in the experiments of Bergstrom [BE 73] would then be characterized by $T = \frac{3}{2}$ below $E = 17$ MeV. This suggests that the calculated state $J\bar{T} = \frac{3}{2}\frac{3}{2}$ should be responsible for the resonance at $E = 17.3$ MeV. The last two levels with $T = \frac{3}{2}$ which we discussed have $L = 2$ according to the present computation. Other indications of resonances with $f = [432]$ are reported by Young and Stokes [YO 71] from the ^{7}Li(t, p) ^{9}Li reaction and by Strauss and Friedland [ST 72] above the ^{7}Li + d threshold. Above this energy region there should appear the supermultiplet $f = [4311]$. The state at $E = 6.41$ MeV in ^{9}Li corresponding to $E = 21$ MeV in ^{9}Be of width 100 keV may be an example of this partition.

States of Positive Parity in ^{9}Be

$N_{max} = 8$, $f = [441], [432]$

$2J\,2T = 11, 31, 51, 71, 13, 33, 53, 73$

Table 10.16, fig. 10.28

With $E(\frac{1}{2}\frac{1}{2}[411]\,01) = 1.68$ MeV we obtain the well-known states with $JT = \frac{5}{2}\frac{1}{2}$ and $JT = \frac{3}{2}\frac{1}{2}$ at low energy. There is a gap between $E = 5$ and 9 MeV in the calculations, followed by a number of states with $f = [441]$ and $f = [432]$. We shall first discuss the experimental evidence from the reaction ^{9}Be (γ, n) due to Slight et al. [SL 73], Thomas et al. [TH 72] and Hughes et al. [HU 75]. These authors find a number of resonances for E1 transitions. Now in terms of partitions the ground state has $f = [441]$ and could be excited into levels of the supermultiplets $f = [441]$ or $[432]$. The latter diagram would decompose under nucleon emission into $[431] \times [1]$ or $[422] \times [1]$. These exit channels are not available at energies below $E = 15$ MeV and hence we conclude that only the supermultiplet $f = [441]$ is excited. Moreover, we apply the selection rules for E1 transitions and assume $\Delta S = 0$. In Table 10.16 we give a computation of the levels which could be excited. In contrast to fig. 10.28 we used an oscillator parameter $b = 1.6$ fm. The comparison with the resonances reported in [TH 72, HU 75 and DO 69] shows reasonable agreement.

In contrast to the calculations by Grünbaum and Tomaselli [GR 71], our computation does not produce any states in the region $E = 5 \ldots 9$ MeV, and indeed the evidence for E1 excitations in this region is weak.

Table 10.16 Calculated states of positive parity which may contribute to the reaction ^{9}Be (γ, n) and resonances reported in [DO 69, TH 72] and [HU 75]

E_{calc}	$2J\,2T\,f\,L\,2S$	E_{exp} [DO 69]	[TH 72]	[HU 75]
18.3	11 [441] 11	(19.5)	18.1; 18.6	
17.0	11 [441] 01	(17.3)	16.5; 17.3	16.7
15.4	31 [441] 21		15.1; 15.9	
14.5	31 [432] 13 + 31 [441] 21 (23 %)	14.8	14.1	14.5
13.5	51 [432] 13 + 51 [441] 21 (11 %)	(13.5)	13.2	
12.3	11 [441] 11	11.8	12.2	12.6
10.7	31 [441] 21		11.2; 10.7	10.7
9.7	11 [441] 01		10.1	
9.2	51 [441] 21			
9.1	31 [441] 11		9.5	9.1
4.7	31 [441] 21			4.8
2.6	51 [441] 01			3.0
1.7	31 [441] 01			

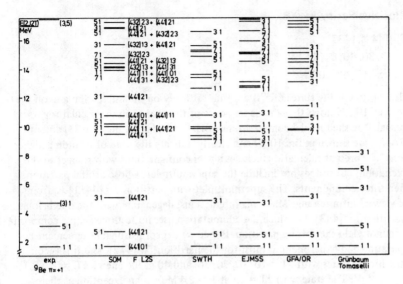

Fig. 10.28 States of positive parity in ⁹Be

States of Positive Parity in ^{10}B

$N_{max} = 8$, $f = [442], [433]$
$JT = 00, 10, 20, 30, 40, 01, 11, 21, 31, 41$
Table 10.17, figs. 10.29–10.31

The description of the states of ^{10}B depends critically on the interaction and on the model space. Fig. 10.31 shows that the dependence of the energy on the oscillator parameter is unusual. The shell model computations of Hauge and Maripuu [HA 73] and of Saayman [SA 73] are shown in fig. 10.29 and clearly indicate the need of including higher configurations. The present calculation includes higher configurations with respect to the oscillator excitation, but it does not include the supermultiplets whose orbital partition has more then three components. The supermultiplet with partition $f = [4411]$ is, from the point of view of infinite-range Majorana interactions, degenerate with the one belonging to the partition $f = [443]$, but since the computation uses up to three simple composite particles, it cannot yield the former partition. Hence we expect reasonable agreement between computation and experiment at most for the partition $f = [442]$, and this is confirmed for the lowest states with $JT = 10, 10, 20, 30$, and 40 at the energies $E = 0.7; 2.1; 3.6; 4.8$ and 6.0 MeV. The state with $JT = 20$ at $E = 2.4$ MeV is an exception as there seems to be no other computation that gives a low-lying state of this type. The experimental evidence for this state is controversial, a recent review is given by Karadeniz [KA 74] and by Shrivasta and Sah [SH 72].

The first two states with $T = 1$ and an admixture of $f = [433]$ to $f = [442]$ are computed at energies about 2 MeV above the experimental values. These states are lowered by about 2 MeV through the admixture of $f = [433]$, and if the missing supermultiplet $f = [4411]$ would have the same effect, it would bring these states down to the experimental values.

Around $E = 8$ MeV we expect the onset of states with partition $f = [4411]$. These states can be distinguished by specific reactions. For example the reaction ^{9}Be(p, γ) should excite states with $f = [442]$ or $f = [4411]$ stronger than those with $f = [433]$ since the ground state of ^{9}Be has $f = [441]$ and $[441] \times [1] \rightarrow [442] + [4411]$. The state with $J = 01$ at $E = 7.59$ MeV is excited in ^{9}Be(p, γ) and is likely to be the first state with $f = [4411]$.

The states with dominant partition $f = [433]$ are not likely to be seen in nuclear reactions. The appropriate channel ^{7}Li + ^{3}He with the partition $[43] \times [3] \rightarrow [442] + [433]$ opens only at $E = 17.8$ MeV.

Table 10.17 Calculated contributions of central, spin-orbit and tensor interactions ($\kappa = 0, 1, 2$) for the lowest states of positive parity in ^{10}Be

	SOM			SWTH			EJMSS		
JT	$\kappa = 0$	$\kappa = 1$	$\kappa = 2$	$\kappa = 0$	$\kappa = 1$	$\kappa = 2$	$\kappa = 0$	$\kappa = 1$	$\kappa = 2$
30	-28.86	-5.28	0.5	-3.92	-4.75	-0.06	-12.69	-6.29	-0.28
10	-31.63	-1.2	-0.02	-6.06	-0.91	-2.56	-13.94	-2.09	-1.14
10*	-29.15	-2.82	0.47	-4.37	-1.82	0.67	-13.05	-2.44	-0.36
20	-28.49	-2.54	-0.33	-3.87	-0.87	-3.35	-11.79	-2.83	-1.58
20*	-29.15	0.3	-1.24	-3.23	-1.04	-0.73	-12.72	0.19	-1.95
01	-27.84	-2.1	0.1	-2.76	-1.36	0.07	-12.07	-2.11	0.1
30*	-28.68	-0.33	-0.21	-3.75	0.02	-0.14	-12.32	-0.34	-0.71
40	-26.27	-1.35	-0.29	-1.16	-1.23	-0.39	-10.37	-1.63	-0.41

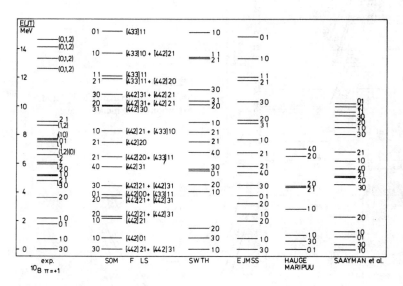

Fig. 10.29 States of positive parity in ^{10}B

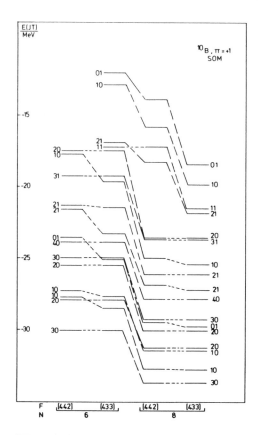

Fig. 10.30

States of positive parity in ^{10}B under extension of the model space

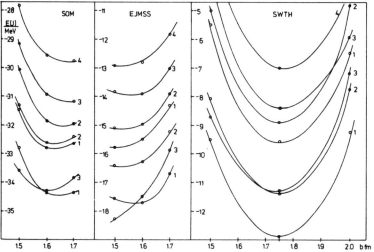

Fig. 10.31 States of positive parity in ^{10}B as a function of the oscillator parameter

States of Negative Parity in ^{10}B

$N_{max} = 9$, f = [442], [433]

JT = 00, 10, 20, 30, 40, 01, 11, 21, 31, 41

Table 10.18, fig. 10.32

Comparing the lowest calculated and the lowest experimentally known state we put E(20 [442] 11) = 5.11 MeV. Note that we cannot compute with the model states the super-multiplet f = [4411] which should yield states at low energy. The calculated states should be excited in ^{6}Li(α, γ) since the orbital partitions combine according to [42] × [4] → [442]. On this basis we identify the state at E = 6.13 MeV as 30 [442] 21 and the state at E = 7.84 MeV as 10 [442] 11.

Of particular interest are the states of partition f = [433]. These states should pre-ferably be excited in the ^{7}Li + ^{3}He reaction where the orbital partitions combine according to [43] × [3] → [442] + [433]. The computed states are listed in Table 10.18 along with some indications of γ transitions to the lowest six states in ^{10}B, $\pi = +1$ and of α transi-tions to the channel ^{6}Li + α. In the same table we list the known states from the reactions ^{7}Li(^{3}He, γ) ^{10}B and ^{7}Li(^{3}He, α) ^{6}Li according to work reported in [AJ 74]. The lowest calculated level has JT = 41 and L = 3, it cannot be reached by s-waves in the reaction. The next level state with JT = 21 can be reached by s-waves and may be associated with the known level at E = 18.4 MeV. The two next states JT = 21, JT = 31 very close to each other and have similar γ decay properties. They could be associated with the resonance at E = 19.3 MeV. There are two states JT = 11 which show strong supermultiplet mixing and

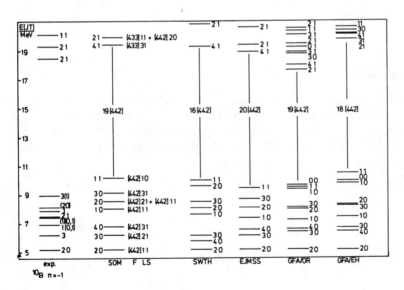

Fig. 10.32 States of negative parity in ^{10}B

appear at energies E = 20.7 MeV and E = 22.5 MeV for the EJMSS interaction. These states allow for $\gamma_1\gamma_4$ transitions from the partition f = [433] and α_2 transition from the partition f = [442]. On this basis we assign the lower one to the resonance JT = 1^-1 at E = 20.2 MeV. The calculated statetJT = 01 at E = 21.1 MeV could be associated with the observed resonance at E = 21.1 MeV. Thus it appears that most of the calculated states correspond to known resonances in this reaction and lead to predictions of the more detailed structure for the corresponding states. There are some problems like the appearance of a resonance JT = 2^+1 at E = 18.8 MeV which decays via γ_4 and α_2. The present computation does not yield a state of this type between E = 15 and E = 27 MeV. If this state would have negative parity, it would be similar to the state JT = 1^-1 in Table 10.18 and one would be tempted to associate these two states with the ones of mixed supermultiplets.

Table 10.18 Calculated states of negative parity in ^{10}B with dominant orbital partion f = [433], predicted decay, and observed resonances and decays in the reaction ^{7}Li + ^{3}He according to [AJ 74]

E_{calc}	JTfLS	decay	$E_{observed}$	JT	decay
21.5	11 [433] 11 + 11 [442] 11	$\gamma_1\gamma_4$ α_2	21.1		γ_1
20.3	01 [433] 11	γ_1	20.2	11	$\gamma_4\alpha_2$
20.0	21 [433] 21	$\gamma_0\gamma_4\gamma_5$			
19.9	31 [422] 21	$\gamma_0\gamma_4\gamma_5$	19.3	21	$\gamma_0\gamma_5$
19.7	11 [442] 10 + 11 [433] 11	α_2 $\gamma_1\gamma_4$			
18.4	21 [433] 11	$\gamma_0\gamma_1\gamma_4\gamma_5$	18.4	21	$\gamma_0\gamma_5$
18.2	41 [433] 31	$\gamma_0\gamma_5$			

10.9 Notes and References

Most of the material of section 10 is taken from the Dissertation of one of the authors [SC 74]. The computations and interpretations have been revised and extended. Particular attention is given to states of non-normal parity. Preliminary reports are given in [SC 75] and [KR 75]. The references of the present section 10 have been separated in order to simplify reading.

References for Sections 1—9

[AK 69]   *Akiyama, Y., A. Arima, and T. Sebe*, Nucl. Phys. **A138** (1969) 273

[BA 61]   *Bargmann, V.*, Comm. Pure and Appl. Math. **14** (1961) 187

[BA 62]   *Bargmann, V.*, Rev. Mod. Phys. **34** (1962) 829

[BA 64]   *Baird, G. E.* and *L. C. Biedenharn*, J. Math. Phys. **5** (1964) 1723

[BA 67]   *Bargmann, V.*, Comm. Pure and Appl. Math. **20** (1967) 1

[BA 68]   *Bargmann, V.*, Group representations in Hilbert spaces of analytic functions, in: Analytic methods in mathematical physics, ed. by *R. P. Gilbert* and *R. G. Newton*, New York 1968

[BA 75]   *Bacry, H., A. Grossmann* and *J. Zak*, Geometry of generalized coherent states, in: Proc. IV. Int. Colloquium on Group Theoretical Methods in Physics, Nijmegen 1975, Springer Lectures Notes in Physics, Vol. 50, ed. by *A. Janner, T. Janssen* and *M. Boon*, Springer, Berlin, Heidelberg, New York, 1976

[BA 77]   *Bacry, H.*, Lectures on group theory and particle theory, Gordon and Breach, New York 1977

[BA 77a]   *Barut, A. O.* and *R. Raczka*, Theory of group representations and applications, Polish Scientific Publishers, Warsaw 1977

[BI 72]   *Biedenharn, L. C., J. D. Louck, E. Chacon*, and *M. Ciftan*, J. Math. Phys. **13** (1972) 1957

[BI 72a]   *Biedenharn, L. C.* and *J. D. Louck*, J. Math. Phys. **13** (1972) 1985

[BR 60]   *Brody, T. A.* and *M. Moshinsky*, Rev. Mex. Fis. 9 (1960) 181

[BR 68]   *Brink, D. M.* and *A. Weiguny*, Nucl. Phys. **A120** (1968) 59

[BR 75]   *Brunet, M.* and *P. Kramer*, Complex extension of the representation of the symplectic group associated with the canonical commutation relations, in: Proc. IV. Int. Colloquium on Group Theoretical Methods in Physics, Nijmegen 1975, Springer Lecture Notes in Physics, vol. 50, ed. by *A. Janner, T. Janssen*, and *M. Boon*, Springer, Berlin, Heidelberg, New York, 1976

[BR 78]   *Brunet, M.* and *P. Kramer*, Semigroups of length increasing transformations, Rep. Math. Phys. 15 (1979) 287

[BR 78a]   *Brunet, M.* and *P. Kramer*, Complex extension of the representation of the symplectic group associated with the canonical commutation relations, Rep. Math. Phys., to be published

[BU 69]   *Burdet, C. M. N., C. Maguin*, and *A. Partensky*, in: Clustering Phenomena in Nuclei, IAEA, Vienna 1969

[CO 65]   *Cohen, S.* and *D. Kurath*, Nucl. Phys. **73** (1965) 1

[CO 68]   *Coleman, A. J.*, The symmetric group made easy, in: Advances in Quantum Chemistry, ed. by *P.-O. Löwdin*, vol. 4, Academic Press, New York 1968

[ED 57]   *Edmonds, A. R.*, Angular Momentum in Quantum Mechanics, Princeton University Press, Princeton 1957

[EL 53]   *Elliott, J. P., J. Hope*, and *H. A. Jahn*, Proc. Roy. Soc. **A218** (1953) 345

[EL 58]   *Elliott, J. P.*, Proc. Roy. Soc. **A245** (1958) 128

[EL 58a]   *Elliott, J. P.*, Proc. Roy. Soc. **A245** (1958) 562

[FR 63]   *Franzini, P.* and *L. A. Radicati*, Phys. Lett. **6** (1963) 322

[GE 50]   *Gelfand, I. M.* and *M. L. Zetlin*, Dokl. Akad. Nauk SSSR **71** (1950) 8, 825

[GL 63]   *Glauber, R. J.*, Phys. Rev. 131 (1963) 2766

[GO 75]   *Goldberg, D. A., J. B. Marion,* and *S. J. Wallace* (Eds.), Proc. Int. Conf. on Clustering
          Phenomena in Nuclei II, College Park 1975, United States Energy Research and Develop-
          ment Administration ORO-4856-26

[GR 57]   *Griffin, J. J.* and *J. A. Wheeler,* Phys. Rev. **108** (1957) 311

[GR 78]   *Grossmann, A.,* Geometry of real and complex canonical transformations in quantum
          mechanics, in: Proc. VI. Int. Colloquium on Group Theoretical Methods in Physics,
          Tübingen 1977, Springer Lecture Notes in Physics, vol. 79, ed. by *P. Kramer* and *A.
          Rieckers,* Springer, Berlin, Heidelberg, New York 1978

[HA 59]   *Hall, M.,* The theory of groups, MacMillan, New York 1959

[HA 62]   *Hamermesh, M.,* Group theory and its application to physical problems, Addison-Wesley,
          Reading 1962

[HE 69]   *Hecht, K. T.* and *S. Ch. Pang,* J. Math. Phys. **10** (1969) 1571

[HE 78]   *Hecht, K. T.* and *W. Zahn,* in: Proc. Int. Conf. on Clustering Aspects of Nuclear Structure
          and Nuclear Reactions, Winnipeg 1978, AIP Conf. Proc., New York 1978

[HI 53]   *Hill, D. L.* and *J. A. Wheeler,* Phys. Rev. **89** (1953) 1102

[HO 64]   *Horie, H.,* J. Phys. Soc. Japan **19** (1964) 1783

[HO 71]   *Holman, W. J.* and *L. C. Biedenharn,* in: Group Theory and its applications, vol. 2, ed. by
          E. M. Loebl, Academic Press, New York 1971

[HO 77]   *Horiuchi, H.,* Progr. Theor. Phys. **62** (1977) 90

[IA 69]   IAEA, Proc. Int. Conf. on Clustering Phenomena in Nuclei, Bochum 1969, IAEA, Vienna
          1969

[IT 67]   *Itzykson, C.,* Commun. Math. Phys. **4** (1967) 92

[JA 51]   *Jahn, H. A.* and *H. van Wieringen,* Proc. Roy. Soc. **A209** (1951) 50

[JA 80]   *Jansen, L.* and *R. W. J. Roël,* Pauli principle and indirect exchange phenomena in mole-
          cules and solids, in: Groups, Systems, and Many-Body Physics, ed. by *P. Kramer* and
          M. Dal Cin, Vieweg, Braunschweig 1980

[JO 73]   *John, G.* and *P. Kramer,* Nucl. Phys. **A204** (1973) 203

[JO 74]   *John, G.* and *T. H. Seligman,* Nucl. Phys. **A236** (1974) 397

[KA 61]   *Kaplan, I. G.,* JETP (USSR) **41** (1961) 560, Soviet Phys. JETP **14** (1962) 401

[KA 61a] *Kaplan, I. G.,* JETP (USSR) **41** (1961) 790, Soviet Phys. JETP **14** (1961) 568

[KL 75]   *Klein, D. J.,* Finite groups and semisimple algebras in quantum mechanics, in: Group
          theory and its applications, vol. 3, ed. by *E. M. Loebl,* Academic Press, New York 1975

[KR 66]   *Kramer, P.,* Z. Naturforschg. **21a** (1966) 657

[KR 67]   *Kramer, P.,* Z. Phys. **205** (1967) 181

[KR 68]   *Kramer, P.,* Z. Phys. **216** (1968) 68

[KR 68a] *Kramer, P.,* J. Math. Phys. **9** (1968) 639

[KR 68b] *Kramer, P.* and *M. Moshinsky,* Group theory of harmonic oscillators and nuclear struc-
          ture, in: Group theory and its applications, ed. by *E. M. Loebl,* vol. 1, Academic Press,
          New York 1968

[KR 69]   *Kramer, P.* and *T. H. Seligman,* Nucl. Phys. **A123** (1969) 161

[KR 69a] *Kramer, P.* and *T. H. Seligman,* Nucl. Phys. **A136** (1969) 545

[KR 69b] *Kramer, P.* and *T. H. Seligman,* Z. Physik **219** (1969) 105

[KR 69c] *Kramer, P.,* Group theory and the supermultiplet scheme, in: Clustering Phenomena in
          Nuclei, IAEA, Vienna 1969

[KR 70]   *Kramer, P.,* Rev. Mex. Fis. **19** (1970) 241

[KR 72]   *Kramer, P.* and *T. H. Seligman,* Nucl. Phys. **A186** (1972) 49

[KR 73]   *Kramer, P.* and *D. Schenzle,* Nucl. Phys. **A204** (1973) 593

[KR 73a] *Kramer, P.* and *D. Schenzle,* Rev. Mex. Fis. **22** (1973) 25

[KR 74] *Kramer, P.,* Permutation group in light nuclei, in: Symmetry properties of nuclei, Proc. of the 15th Solvay Conference on Physics, Gordon and Breach, London 1974

[KR 75] *Kramer, P., M. Moshinsky,* and *T. H. Seligman,* Complex extensions of canonical transformations and quantum mechanics, in: Group theory and its applications, vol. 3, ed. by *E. M. Loebl,* Academic Press, New York 1975

[KR 77] *Kramer, P.,* Finite representations of the unitary group and their applications in many-body physics, in: Group Theoretical Methods in Physics, ed. by *R. T. Sharp* and *B. Kolman,* Academic Press, New York 1977

[KR 80] *Kramer, P.* and *M. Dal Cin* (Eds.), Groups, Systems, and Many-Body Physics, Vieweg, Braunschweig 1980

[LA 66] *Lauritsen, T.* and *F. A. Ajzenberg-Selove,* Nucl. Phys. **A79** (1966) 1

[LO 70] *Louck, J.,* Amer. J. Phys. **38** (1970) 3

[LO 73] *Louck, J. D.* and *L. C. Biedenharn,* J. Math. Phys. **14** (1973) 1336

[LO 78] *Louck, J. D.,* Applications of the boson polynomials of U(n) to physical problems, in: Proc. VII. Int. Colloquium on Group Theoretical Methods in Physics, Austin 1978, ed. by *W. Beiglböck,* Lecture Notes in Physics, vol. 94 Springer, Berlin 1979

[MA 63] *Mackey, G. F.,* Mathematical foundations of quantum mechanics, Benjamin, New York 1963

[MA 64] *Mahmoud, H.* and *R. K. Cooper,* Annals of Physics **26** (1964) 222

[MO 63] *Moshinsky, M.,* J. Math. Phys. **4** (1963) 1128

[MO 68] *Moshinsky, M.,* Group theory and the many-body problem. Gordon and Breach, New York 1968

[MO 71] *Moshinsky, M.* and *T. H. Seligman,* Ann. Phys. **66** (1971) 311

[MO 71a] *Moshinsky, M.* and *C. Quesne,* J. Math. Phys. **12** (1971) 1772

[MO 74] *Moshinsky, M.* and *C. Quesne,* Oscillator systems, in: Proc. 15th Solvay Conf. on Physics, Gordon and Breach, London 1974

[NA 65] *Nagel, J. G.* and *M. Moshinsky,* J. Math. Phys. **6** (1965) 682

[NE 31] *Neumann, J. von,* Math. Ann. **104** (1931) 570

[NE 64] *Neudatchin, V. G., V. G. Shevchenko,* and *N. P. Yudin,* Physics Letters **10** (1964) 180

[NE 65] *Neudatchin, V. G.* and *Yu. F. Smirnov,* Atomic Energy Review **3** (1965) 157

[NE 69] *Neudatchin, V. G.* and *Yu. F. Smirnov,* Nuclear Associations in Light Nuclei, Moscow 1969

[OE 78] *Oers, W. T. H. van, J. P. Svenne, J. S. C. McKee,* and *W. R. Falk* (Eds.), Proc. Int. Conf. on Clustering Aspects of Nuclear Structure and Nuclear Reactions, Winnipeg 1978, AIP Conf. Proc., New York 1978

[RO 61] *Robinson, G. de B.,* Representation theory of the symmetric group, University of Toronto Press, Toronto 1961

[RO 75] *Roman, P.,* Some modern mathematics for physicists and other outsiders, Pergamon, New York 1975

[RO 76] *Roël, R. W. J.,* On the many-body formalism: Perturbation theory for interacting systems, the quantum mechanical eigenvalue problem and double coset decomposition of the symmetric group, Doctoral Thesis, University of Amsterdam 1976

[SE 63] *Segal, I. E.,* Mathematical problems of relativistic physics, Proc. Summer Seminar on Appl. Math., Boulder Colorado, 1960, Amer. Math. Soc., Providence, Rhode Island, 1963

[SE 74] *Seligman, T. H.,* Double coset decompositions of finite groups and the many-body problem, Habilitationsschrift, Universität Tübingen 1974

[SE 76] *Seligman, T. H. and W. Zahn*, J. Phys. **G2** (1976) 79

[SO 70] *Souriau, J.-M.*, Structure des systèmes dynamiques, Dunod, Paris 1970

[SO 76] *Souriau, J. M.*, Construction explicite de l'indice de Maslov. Applications, in: Proc. IV. Int. Colloquium on Group Theoretical Methods in Physics, Nijmegen 1975, Springer Lecture Notes in Physics, vol. 50, ed. by *A. Janner, T. Janssen,* and *M. Boon,* Springer, Berlin 1976

[SM 69] *Smirnov, Yu. F.*, Translationally invariant shell model, in: Proc. Int. Conf. on Clustering Phenomena in Nuclei, Bochum 1969, IAEA, Vienna 1969

[ST 78] *Sternberg, S.*, Some recent results on the metaplectic representation, in: Proc. VI. Int. Colloquium on Group Theoretical Methods in Physics, Tübingen 1977, Springer Lecture Notes in Physics, vol. 79, ed. by *P. Kramer* and *A. Rieckers,* Springer, Berlin, Heidelberg New York 1978

[SU 72] *Sünkel, W. and K. Wildermuth,* Phys. Lett. **41B** (1972) 439

[SU 73] *Sullivan, J. J.,* J. Math. Phys. (N. Y.) **14** (1973) 387

[SU 76] *Sünkel, W.,* Phys. Lett. **65B** (1976) 419

[VA 67] *Vanagas, V. V. and A. K. Petrauskas,* Yad. Fiz. **5** (1967) 555; Sov. J. Nucl. Phys. **5** (1967) 393

[VA 71] *Vanagas, V.,* Algebraic Methods in Nuclear Theory, Vilnius 1971

[WE 31] *Weyl, H.,* The theory of groups and quantum mechanics, Princeton University Press, Princeton 1931

[WE 46] *Weyl, H.,* The classical groups, Princeton University Press, Princeton 1946

[WH 37] *Wheeler, J. A.,* Phys. Rev. **52** (1937) 1083

[WH 37a] *Wheeler, J. A.,* Phys. Rev. **52** (1937) 1107

[WI 37] *Wigner, E. P.,* Phys. Rev. **51** (1937) 51

[WI 77] *Wildermuth, K. and Y. C. Tang,* A unified theory of the nucleus, Clustering Phenomena in Nuclei, vol. 1, ed. by *K. Wildermuth* and *P. Kramer,* Vieweg, Braunschweig 1977

[WO 75] *Wolf, K. B.,* The Heisenberg-Weyl Ring in Quantum Mechanichs, in: Group theory and its applications, vol. 3, ed. by *E. M. Loebl,* Academic Press, New York 1975

References for Section 10

[AJ 74] *Ajzenberg-Selove, F. and T. Lauritsen,* Nucl. Phys. **A227** (1974) 1

[AL 64] *Allum, F. R., C. R. Crawley,* and *B. M. Spicer,* Nucl. Phys. **51** (1964) 177

[AS 73] *Aswad, A., H. R. Kissener, H. U. Jäger,* and *R. A. Eramzhian,* Nucl. Phys. **A208** (1973) 61

[BA 66] *Barker, F.,* Nucl. Phys. **83** (1966) 481

[BA 68] *Batty, C. J., B. E. Bonner, E. Friedman, C. Tschalär, L. E. Williams, A. S. Clough,* and *J. B. Hunt,* Nucl. Phys. **A120** (1968) 297

[BE 61] *Bevington, P. R., W. W. Rolland,* and *H. W. Lewis,* Phys. Rev. **121** (1961) 871

[BE 73] *Bergstrom, J. C., I. P. Auer, M. Ahmad, F. J. Kline, J. H. Hough, H. S. Caplan,* and *H. S. J. L. Groh,* Phys. Rev. **C7** (1973) 2228

[BO 68] *Bouten, M., M. C. Bouten, H. Depuydt,* and *L. Schotsmans,* Phys. Lett. **27B** (1968) 61

[BO 69] *Bouten, M., M. C. Bouten, H. Depuydt,* and *L. Schotsmans,* Nucl. Phys. **A127** (1969) 177

[CO 68] *Cocke, C. L.,* Nucl. Phys. **A110** (1968) 321; *Cocke, C. L.* and *P. R. Christensen,* Nucl. Phys. **A111** (1968) 623

[CO 68a] *Cooper, B. S.* and *J. M. Eisenberg*, Nucl. Phys. **A114** (1968) 184

[CO 71] *Cooper, B. S., J. B. Seaborn,* and *S. A. Williams*, Phys. Rev. **C4** (1971) 1997

[DO 69] *Dolbilkin, B. S., A. I. Isakov, V. I. Korin, L. E. Lazareva, N. V. Linkova,* and *F. A. Niko-laev*, Sov. J. Nucl. Phys. 8 (1969) 534

[EL 68] *Elliott, J. P., A. D. Jackson, H. A. Mavromatis, E. A. Sanderson,* and *B. Singh*, Nucl. Phys. **A121** (1968) 241

[ES 72] *Esterl, J. E., D. Allred, J. C. Hardy, R. G. Sextro,* and *J. Cerny*, Phys. Rev. **C6** (1972) 373

[FE 75] *Fetisov, V. N.* and *Y. S. Kopysov*, Nucl. Phys. **A239** (1975) 511

[FI 70] *Fisher*, Thesis, Standford U. (1970), ref. FI 70 F in AJ 74

[FI 73] *Fiarman, S.* and *W. E. Meyerhof*, Nucl. Phys. **A206** (1973) 1

[FO 72] *Fort, E.* and *J. P. Maquette*, European-American Nuclear Data Committee Report, EANDC (E) 148 U (1972)

[GA 70] *Galonska, J. E.* and *A. Faessler*, Nucl. Phys. **A155** (1970) 465

[GL 71] *Glukhov, Y. A.*, Sov. J. Nucl. Phys. 13 (1971) 134

[GO 69] *Gogsadze, G. S.* and *T. I. Kopaleishvili*, Sov. J. Nucl. Phys. 8 (1969) 509

[GR 70] *Gruebler, W., V. König, P. A. Schmelzbach,* and *P. Marmier*, Nucl. Phys. **A148** (1970) 391

[GR 71] *Grünbaum, L.* and *M. Tomaselli*, Nucl. Phys. **A160** (1971) 437

[GU 69] *Gunye, M. R., J. Law,* and *R. K. Bhaduri*, Nucl. Phys. **A132** (1969) 225

[GU 70] *Gul, K., B. H. Armitage,* and *B. W. Hooton*, Nucl. Phys. **A153** (1970) 390

[GU 74] *Gückel, F. A.* and *D. Fick*, Z. Phys. **271** (1974) 39

[HA 65] *Hardy, J. C., V. I. Verrall, R. Barton,* and *R. E. Bell*, Phys. Rev. Lett. **14** (1965) 376

[HA 65a] *Hayward, E.* and *T. Stovall*, Nucl. Phys. 69 (1965) 241

[HA 67] *Harrison, W. P.*, Nucl. Phys. **A92** (1967) 260

[HA 71] *Hardy, J. C., J. M. Loiseaux, J. Cerny,* and *G. T. Garvey*, Nucl. Phys. **A162** (1971) 552

[HA 73] *Hauge, P. S.* and *S. Maripuu*, Phys. Rev. **C8** (1973) 1609

[HU 75] *Hughes, R. J., R. H. Sambell, E. G. Muirhead,* and *B. M. Spicer*, Nucl. Phys. **A238** (1975) 189

[IR 73] *Irvine, J. M.*, et al., Int. Symp. on Correlations in Nuclei, Balatonfüred 1973

[JO 74] *John, G.* and *T. H. Seligman*, Nucl. Phys. **A236** (1974) 397

[KA 74] *Karadeniz, M. C.*, J. Phys. **A7** (1974) 2284

[KR 68] *Kroepfl, J. J.* and *C. P. Browne*, Nucl. Phys. **A108** (1968) 289

[KR 75] *Kramer, P.*, in: Proc. Int. Conf. on Clustering Phenomena in Nuclei II, College Park (1975), ed. by *D. A. Goldberg, J. B. Marion, S. J. Wallace*, United States Energy Research and Development Administration ORO-4856-26

[KU 71] *Kumar, N.* and *F. C. Barker*, Nucl. Phys. **A167** (1971) 434

[KU 74] *Kumar, N.*, Nucl. Phys. **A225** (1974) 221

[LE 74] *Lejeune, A.* and *R. Sartor*, J. Physique **35** (1974) 895

[LI 72] *Lin, E. K., R. Hagelberg,* and *E. L. Haase*, Nucl. Phys. **A179** (1972) 65

[MA 66] *Manuzio, G. E., G. Ricco,* and *M. Sanzone*, Nuovo Cim. **40B** (1966) 348

[MA 68] *Mani, G. S.* and *A. Dix*, Nucl. Phys. **A106** (1968) 251

[MU 70] *Murakami, A.*, J. Phys. Soc. Japan **28** (1970) 1

[NO 73] *Nocken, U., U. Quast, A. Richter,* and *G. Schrieder*, Nucl. Phys. **A213** (1973) 97

[PR 69] *Presser, G., R. Bass,* and *K. Krüger*, Nucl. Phys. **A131** (1969) 679

[PR 72]   *Presser, G. and R. Bass,* Nucl. Phys. **A182** (1972) 321

[RA 70]   *Ramavataram, K. and S. Ramavataram,* Nucl. Phys. **A147** (1970) 293

[RI 71]   *Ripa, P. and E. Maqueda,* Nucl. Phys. **A166** (1971) 534

[RO 67]   *Roynette, J. C., M. Arditi, J. C. Jacmart, F. Mazloum, M. Riou,* and *C. Ruhla,* Nucl.
           Phys. **A95** (1967) 545

[SA 67]   *Satchler, G. R.,* Nucl. Phys. **A100** (1967) 497

[SA 73]   *Saayman, R.,* Z. Physik **265** (1973) 69

[SC 74]   *Schröder, H., K. K. Kern,* and *D. Fick,* Physics Lett. **48B** (1974) 206

[SC 74]   *Schenzle, D.,* Supermultipletts, Dreiclusterkonfigurationen und Struktur der Atomkerne
           A = 4 – 10, Dissertation, Universität Tübingen (1974)

[SC 75]   *Schenzle, D.,* in: Proc. Int. Conf. on Clustering Phenomena in Nuclei II, College Park
           (1975), ed. by *D. A. Goldberg, J. B. Marion, S. J. Wallace,* United States Energy Research
           and Development Administration ORO-4856-26

[SE 64]   *Senhouse, L. S.* and *T. A. Tombrello,* Nucl. Phys. **57** (1964) 624

[SE 75]   *Seiler, F.,* Nucl. Phys. **A244** (1975) 236

[SH 67]   *Shakin, C. M., Y. R. Waghmare, M. Tomaselli,* and *M. H. Hull,* Phys. Rev. **161** (1967)
           1015

[SH 72]   *Shrivastava, M. L.* and *J. P. Sah,* Indian J. of Pure and Appl. Physics **10** (1972) 200

[SL 73]   *Slight, A. G., T. E. Drake,* and *G. R. Bishop,* Nucl. Phys. **A208** (1973) 157

[SO 73]   *Sommer, B.,* Bericht Jül-924-KP, Kernforschungsanlage Jülich 1973

[ST 72]   *Strauss, L.* and *E. Friedland,* Z. Physik **250** (1972) 370

[SZ 72]   *Syzdlik, P. P., J. R. Borysowicz,* and *R. F. Wagner,* Phys. Rev. **C6** (1972) 1902

[TA 64]   *Tabakin, F.,* Ann. of Phys. **30** (1964) 51

[TH 68]   *Thompson, D. R.* and *Y. C. Tang,* Nucl. Phys. **A106** (1968) 591

[TH 72]   *Thomas, B. W., D. M. Crawford,* and *H. H. Thies,* Nucl. Phys. **A196** (1972) 89

[UT 70]   *Uttley, C. A.,* Proc. European – American Nuclear Data Committee, Argonne 1970

[VA 68]   *Vanpraet, G. J.* and *W. C. Barber,* Z. Phys. **211** (1968) 213

[VE 71]   *Ventura, E., C. C. Chang,* and *W. E. Meyerhof,* Nucl. Phys. **A173** (1971) 1

[VE 73]   *Ventura, E., J. R. Calarco, W. E. Meyerhof,* and *A. M. Young,* Phys. Lett. **46B** (1973)
           364

[VL 77]   *Vlastou, R., J. B. A. England, O. Karban,* and *S. Baird,* Nucl. Phys. **A292** (1977) 29

[WA 71]   *Wagner, R. F.* and *C. Werntz,* Phys. Rev. **C4** (1971) 1

[WE 68]   *Werntz, C.* and *W. E. Meyerhof,* Nucl. Phys. **A121** (1968)

[WI 66]   *Wilkinson, D. H.* and *M. E. Mafethe,* Nucl. Phys. **85** (1966) 97

[YI 73]   *Ying, N., B. B. Cox, B. K. Barnes,* and *A. W. Barrows,* Nucl. Phys. **A206** (1973) 481

[YO 71]   *Young, P. G.* and *R. H. Stokes,* Phys. Rev. **C4** (1971) 1597

Subject Index